ETHICAL BOUNDARIES OF CAPITALISM

Corporate Social Responsibility Series

Series Editor:
Professor David Crowther, London Metropolitan University, UK

This series aims to provide high quality research books on all aspects of corporate social responsibility including: business ethics, corporate governance and accountability, globalization, civil protests, regulation, responsible marketing and social reporting.

The series is interdisciplinary in scope and global in application and is an essential forum for everyone with an interest in this area.

Also in the series

Ethical Boundaries of Capitalism

Edited by

DANIEL DAIANU
National School of Political and Administrative Studies (SNSPA)
Bucharest, Romania

RADU VRANCEANU
Ecole Supérieure des Sciences Economiques et Commerciale (ESSEC)
Cergy-Pontoise, France

ASHGATE

Published by
Ashgate Publishing Limited
Gower House
Croft Road
Aldershot
Hants GU11 3HR
England

Ashgate Publishing Company
Suite 420
101 Cherry Street
Burlington, VT 05401-4405
USA

Ashgate website: http://www.ashgate.com

British Library Cataloguing in Publication Data
Ethical boundaries of capitalism. - (Corporate social
    responsibility series)
    1. Capitalism - Moral and ethical aspects 2. Social
    responsibility of business
    I. Daianu, Daniel II. Vranceanu, Radu, 1964-
    174.4

Library of Congress Control Number: 2005925669

ISBN 0 7546 4395 6

Printed and bound in Great Britain by MPG Books Ltd, Bodmin, Cornwall

Contents

List of Contributors   *vii*
Foreword   *ix*

PART ONE: ETHICS FROM WITHOUT

1   The Ethics of Capitalism   3
     Laurent Bibard

2   Capitalism as an Ethical System: The Ideal and its Feasibility   25
     Michael Keren

3   How Capitalism Lost its Soul: From Protestant Ethics to Robber Barons   43
     Marie-Laure Djelic

4   Ethical Lapses of Capitalism: How Serious Are They?   65
     Daniel Daianu

5   Moral Divide in International Business: A Descriptive Framework   85
     Nicoletta Ferro

PART TWO: ETHICS FROM WITHIN

6   Capitalism: Foundations of Ethical Behavior   105
     Mircea Boari

7   The Ethical Environment of the Free Market   127
     Sorin Cucerai

8   The Spirit of Free Enterprise: Ethics and Responsibility   145
     Arnaud Pellissier-Tanon

9   On Ethical, Social and Environmental Management Systems   157
     Antonio Argandoña

PART THREE: ETHICAL ISSUES IN PRACTICE

10   Is Ethical Marketing a Myth?   175
     René Y. Darmon

11   Firms and the Environment: Ethics or Incentives?   199
      André Fourçans

12   Deregulating Dishonesty: Lessons from the US Corporate Scandals   219
      Radu Vranceanu

13   An Exchange of Values: The NYSE's Governance Crisis   239
      Andrei Postelnicu

14   A Concluding Comment   255
      Daniel Daianu and Radu Vranceanu

Index   *257*

List of Contributors

Antonio Argandoña, Professor, Chair of Economics and Ethics, IESE Business School, University of Navarra, Barcelona, Spain.

Laurent Bibard, Professor, Department of Management and Human Resources, ESSEC Business School, Cergy, France.

Mircea Boari, Professor, Department of Political Science and Public Administration, University of Bucharest, Bucharest, Romania.

Sorin Cucerai, Researcher, Ludwig von Mises Institute-Romania, Bucharest, Romania.

Daniel Daianu, Professor of Economics, The National School of Political and Administrative Studies (SNSPA), Bucharest, Romania.

René Y. Darmon, Emeritus Professor of Marketing, Department of Marketing, ESSEC Business School, Cergy, France and Affiliate Professor of Marketing, at HEC-Montreal, Canada.

Marie-Laure Djelic, Professor, Department of Management and Human Resources, ESSEC Business School, Cergy, France.

Nicoletta Ferro, Researcher, Corporate Social Responsibility and Sustainable Management Research Area, Fondazione Eni Enrico Mattei, Milano, Italy.

André Fourçans, Distinguished Professor, Department of Economics, ESSEC Business School, Cergy, France.

Michael Keren, Emeritus Professor, Department of Economics, Hebrew University, Jerusalem, Israel.

Arnaud Pellissier-Tanon, Senior Lecturer, Faculty of Management, Paris 1 Panthéon Sorbonne University, Paris, France.

Andrei Postelnicu, Reporter Financial Markets, The Financial Times, New York, United States of America.

Radu Vranceanu, Professor, Department of Economics, ESSEC Business School, Cergy, France.

Foreword

Daniel Daianu and Radu Vranceanu

After the fall of the Iron Curtain in the late eighties, the capitalist system, based on private ownership and voluntary exchange, became the dominant model in both the developed and the developing world. Its strengths should not be underestimated: high productivity, efficient allocation of resources, healthy transmission of information, dynamism and growth. However, in recent years, the issues of the ethics of managerial behavior and corporate social responsibility have been thrust to the forefront of public debate. The spate of corporate scandals across the Atlantic, and similar cases in the European Union in the early 2000s, illustrate a complex reality, casting new doubts on the ability of capitalist societies to spontaneously impose natural limits on greed, selfishness and aggressive rivalry between economic actors. Today's capitalist economies also face major difficulties in coping with worldwide issues such as global warming, persistent poverty in many areas of the globe, episodes of financial and political instability, etc.

No suitable social response to such drawbacks in the capitalist system can ignore the ethical dimension. In particular, social scientists must address the question of whether capitalism provides fertile ground for the development of ethical behavior, spontaneous emergence of valuable social norms and self-regulation; or whether, on the contrary, an incompressible dose of unethical behavior is an inherent feature of capitalist systems. If so, what role can the government play in containing this deviant behavior?

This book aims at providing some answers to these questions by bringing together the views of several experts in various fields of the social sciences: philosophers, sociologists, economists, and management researchers, from both developed and developing countries. This editorial strategy of diversity reflects the multiple facets of ethical issues, which require a pluridisciplinary approach to supply the full picture. It is only in comparing and contrasting a range of possibly conflicting perspectives that the reader may develop his/her own critical perspective on a given ethical dilemma.

In the first part of the book, several authors argue that capitalist societies are not in fact able to bring about first-best solutions to ethical issues, and discuss whether regulation and governance may help achieve a better outcome. The chapters contained in the second part analyze the ethical virtues of capitalist systems, and draw favorable conclusions, in particular with respect to the ability of free markets to support universal human values. The arguments put forward in these two lines of reasoning are not necessarily contradictory, if real-life open societies are seen as imperfect forms of free-market systems. The big question, therefore, appears to be in what proportions self-regulation and 'top-down' regulation (imposed by the

State) should combine in order to provide the optimal environment. The third and final part of the book presents several case studies, analyzing ethical issues within applied contexts: corporate governance in the light of recent corporate scandals, aggressive vs. efficient marketing and environmental protection.

This thesis-antithesis approach to the ethical challenges of capitalism will be of interest not only to students of business, economics, social sciences and philosophy, but also for practitioners seeking to broaden their understanding of modern societies and improve the quality of their decisions.

Going into more detail, in Chapter 1, Laurent Bibard introduces the basic ethical dilemma embedded in capitalist systems, and points out the risks that may come with what he identifies as a major capitalist value, the individual's faith in his ability to control his environment. In Chapter 2, Michael Keren argues that if the State does not ensure the ethical dimension is internalized, capitalism may fail in supporting long-term progress, although it has come out on top in the competition with socialism. In Chapter 3, Marie-Laure Djelic paints a lively landscape of the main ethical perspectives pertaining to the capitalist system. She argues that the founding moral principles have gradually faded, to the point where the Robber Baron lifestyle has become representative of today's capitalist economies. In Chapter 4, Daniel Daianu draws up a list of significant ethical lapses by contemporary capitalism, and investigates the role of reputation in the genesis of individual and organizational capital. In the last chapter of the first part of the book, Nicoletta Ferro introduces the moral divide issue as a strategic tool for business, and provides a critical analysis of the strengths and weaknesses of both ethical relativism and universalism in a comparative cultural perspective.

The second part of the book begins with a chapter by Mircea Boari. He argues that capitalism consists of a structured and intricate system of rewards expressed as profit, which creates an ethics of positive incentives, mutual gain and regard for the other with no precedent in human history. In Chapter 7, Sorin Cucerai analyses the ethical virtues of a free market society, and presents the potential ethical risks connected to finite social orders such as government intervention or the hierarchy within the firm. In Chapter 8, Arnaud Pellissier-Tanon expands on the corporate ethical dilemmas pertaining essentially to the French business context, within a general perspective that emphasizes the role of individual responsibility. In Chapter 9, Antonio Argandoña argues that self-imposed ethical norms may be an essential component of better management systems. His general perspective on the relationship between corporate ethics and the organization of the firm provides a natural transition to the third part of the book, which contains several applied studies.

Marketing activities in general, and advertising in particular, are essential to the capitalist economic model where goods and services are produced to be sold. Starting from a definition and analysis of some basic principles for ethical behavior by marketers, in Chapter 10, René Darmon emphasizes that the ethical issues raised by the practice of marketing are often more complex than first impressions suggest. Chapter 11 is devoted to the topical environmental issue. André Fourçans argues that effective environment-friendly measures will come about only if the appropriate incentives are at work, although ethical considerations may help in devising these incentives. In Chapter 12, Radu Vranceanu studies the economic and institutional factors that paved the way for the proliferation of unethical managerial behavior during the US Internet bubble of the nineties. In Chapter 13, Andrei Postelnicu draws a picture of the managerial abuses that were reported at the New York Stock Exchange in the early 2000s, building on his own experience as a financial reporter with the *Financial Times*.

It is generally agreed that within the realm of philosophy, ethical issues are the most controversial. While the analyses presented in this book do not disprove this assertion, there are important points on which all the experts agree. All in all, ethical problems can and must be anticipated. If the ethical dimension is incorporated into all social analyses, policy recommendations can only improve. If social actors in capitalist societies become more aware of ethical issues, capitalism can only become a better system. The task is difficult, but not impossible.

Acknowledgements

The idea of putting this book together first emerged during the *Workshop on Ethics and the Economy*, organized in Bucharest, 12-13 December 2003 by the *New Europe College*, the *Romanian Economic Society* and the *Konrad Adenauer Foundation*. Professor Andrei Pleşu and Anca Oroveanu, director of research at NEC, were instrumental in having this workshop happen. The support from the *ESSEC Research Center* is also gratefully acknowledged, as is the advice of Professor David Crowther, which helped us significantly improve the structure of the book.

PART ONE

ETHICS FROM WITHOUT

Chapter 1

The Ethics of Capitalism

Laurent Bibard

1 Introduction

To present a sufficiently thorough, evocative picture of the ethics of capitalism as the first chapter of a book discussing those ethics, an overview of the history of the concepts involved is required. The full meaning taken on by any historical outline will depend on the underlying choices, the decisions over whether to say one thing or another, to the detriment of something else. Anyone attempting to trace the history of an idea immediately finds herself accountable for the choice or choices made; thoughtfully undertaken, the task confers great responsibility. The aim here is to present the ethics of capitalism, acknowledged to be primarily a specifically 'Western' object or historical event (Weber, 1978), even though eventually it spontaneously develops a tendency to spread worldwide (Marx, 1887; Weber, 2001). To encompass the ethical issues characteristic of capitalism in a generally coherent and comprehensible approach, our brief tour can usefully begin by presenting the concept of 'the West' and its genesis. Contemporary developments in human and non-human sciences and techniques are closely related to the advent of the concept of 'the West' (Kojève, 1964). The way we imagine scientific knowledge, particularly historical knowledge, is to a great extent directly shaped by the triumph of 'Western' thinking over other ways of thinking (Weber, 1978; Weber, 2004). If our aim is to provide a relevant presentation of how the ethics of capitalism have evolved, we need to take a standpoint external to its foundations, and more precisely external to contemporary notions of scientificity and historicity. In other words, to open out the forum for discussion provided by this book, we must problematize this presentation of the ethics of capitalism from a standpoint that is neither historical nor scientific in the contemporary sense of the words.

This decision is supported by reasons more pressing than mere reasons of method. The etymology of the term 'ethics' relates to 'behavior', hence the term ethology – the contemporary science of animal behavior. Going beyond the restrictive statement that ethics is the behavior of an animal, it can reasonably be decided that in discussing the ethics of capitalism we are discussing fair and unfair human behavior. Coupled with the notion of unfairness, the concept of fairness relates in one way or another to the concepts of good and evil, and thus to ethics' close relative, morals. Of course, there is no 'science' of morals or ethics in the general sense of the term; if there were, ethics and morals would be based on knowledge of an objective, neutral or even incontestable nature, or knowledge that is scientifically (i.e. experimentally, then theoretically) falsifiable (Popper, 1977) – and this is not the case. Ethics engages men's responsible behavior according to their opinion of fairness or justice, not an objective description of a 'nature', human or otherwise (Aristotle, 1985). Any attempt to develop a 'science' of ethics is by construction absurd (Weber, 2004). This, in addition to the method-related reason discussed earlier, is the reason *par excellence* that this presentation cannot claim to be scientific, in the contemporary sense of the term. However, given our earlier methodological comment about the historical outline of the ethics of capitalism which concerns us here, we must ensure this presentation is fundamentally ethical by taking full responsibility for the choices made in sketching out the 'ethical' landscape of contemporary capitalism. In its earliest sense, taking 'responsibility' for a choice meant 'responding', or answering for it. This chapter is thus just as much a presentation of the ethics of capitalism as we understand them, as a presentation of the reasons leading us to that understanding. This dual presentation makes up the 'problematization' of the concept of the ethics of capitalism just encountered.

If ethics is not a science, lying instead in the art of making the soundest decision for each case (Aristotle, 1985; Aristotle, 1998), it cannot be described theoretically like any object of scientific theory. Ethics, rather, is the art of asking the right questions, so as to correctly identify the real problems involved in action. Sooner or later, the difficulty with action will be that it contains blind spots: when we are acting, we can never see everything we are doing (Weil, 1974; Nelson and Winter, 1982). In other words, because we are acting, it will somehow eventually become impossible for us to correctly identify the true problems inherent to the action we are taking (March and Simon, 1958). One of the constituent difficulties in the action of 'Western'-born capitalism is the attempted complete control by its action over human and non-human nature. To use terms now considered old-fashioned but which no doubt still contain some truth, the desire to accumulate capital in order to maximize the profit derived from private enjoyment of production and consumption resources tendentially limitlessly available cannot see that it relies on the impossibility of ever being fully satisfied in a coherent, complete manner. Sooner or later, from the very heart of the dynamic system of modern sciences, techniques, and economics, or from the boundaries of this system, emerge non-control, impossibility, need, pain, suffering, insufficiency, unhappiness and failure. The emergence of ethics as a field of questions without any immediately clear answers is one example of 'non-control' intruding into the very heart of control and mastery. This chapter's next section shows how control issues affect the capitalist world, especially enterprises. We then examine how the 'history' of 'the West' allowed the advent of a world specifically shaped by the theory that total control by man over his action was both desirable and possible (Section 3), before concluding with an examination of some of the consequences of the advent of this world for significant categories in ethics such as generosity, selfishness, attention to others, etc (Section 4).

2 Capitalism and Ethics

2.1 Capitalism and the Implicit Assumption of Perfect Rationality

Since the Cold War ended, the US has represented and claimed to represent the world's greatest political, economic and military power. The US also represents the largest cultural power to favor the capitalist system (Strauss, 1964). Whether or not this is true, the positions taken by other nations and political entities in relation to the US are representative of the stances adopted in relation to capitalism's contemporary symbol *par excellence*. Whatever their real motives, the attacks of September 11 must be understood in this context. Even the investigators appointed to determine the conditions that made such an event possible admitted that the competent American authorities underestimated a risk signaled by several forewarning factors (Clarke, 2004). In other words, in evaluating the risk of terrorist action of the type that took place on September 11, the assumption that American skies were impregnable outweighed any assumption to the contrary. This type of assumption is part and parcel of the dominant decision-making system within the capitalist system. Capitalism consists not only of the private appropriation of consumption and production resources, but also, if not more fundamentally, of the assumption that complete control over the conditions of any action is both desirable and possible. This relates to the classic economic assumption that decision-making by actors is governed by perfect rationality. The perfect nature of this rationality is typically indicated by the fact that actors have access to full information on the conditions of a transaction, will necessarily choose the solution that maximizes their satisfaction, and that there is no need to verify the effect of a decision, as it is by construction guaranteed (Cyert and March, 1963). Perfection of rationality implies that the time of any decision is reversible, such that actors can always come back to the initial conditions of the decision-making system. The type of rationality involved in decisions in a capitalist system is always ultimately the perfect rationality described by general equilibrium theorists.

Empirical evidence of a reality contrary to this assumption became increasingly widespread in the human and social sciences during the 20th century. The first theorists to draw attention to the discrepancy between the assumption of perfect rationality in economic and organizational decisions and the empirical reality of the decisions proposed the 'bounded rationality' concept (March and Simon, 1958). Since then, there have been many attempts to move closer to theories of empirically observable reality. This has not prevented managers from believing in the perfection of rationality, quite simply because the assumption of total control over the everyday decisions made in organizations is directly, not to say exclusively, in step with the purpose of capitalism, i.e. the maximization of profit. For several decades now, the human sciences, including management science, have been fine-tuning their initial assumptions in order to bring these theories closer to the reality of concrete observations. Meanwhile, most actors remain consciously or unconsciously convinced that the perfect rationality assumption is valid.

This gap between the advances in theory and the real-life situations within organizations has been exemplified in two events seventeen years apart at NASA: the decisions to launch the space shuttle *Challenger* in January 1986, and bring the shuttle *Columbia* back into the earth's atmosphere in February 2003. In both these cases, an unacceptable risk of accident was identified by a single person or teams of engineers, but they were unable to make themselves heard by the organization they belong or belonged to. In both these cases the problems concerned technical issues specific to the equipment used (the quality of the rubber seals designed to avoid gas leaks from the boosters for *Challenger*; damage caused by a stray block of foam to the left wing's leading edge for *Columbia*), but also to the particular circumstances of the decision, and NASA's internal organizational dynamics as shaped by its culture (NASA, 2003). It is well known that NASA's organizational culture includes the 'taken-for-grantedness' of its technical and management competence. This is accepted by the individual and collective actors involved, and up to a point quite rightly, but only up to a point. In other words, the capitalist system implies the existence of institutions organized rationally or 'bureaucratically' as Weber puts it (Weber, 1978), in order to maximize production or profit, and has a spontaneous tendency to assume it has no boundaries and no limits. Seen from this angle, the problem of the ethics of capitalism is as follows.

Organizational theory grew up against a backdrop of questioning regarding the way enterprises functioned (Taylor, 1947). Capitalist enterprises are the ultimate object of organizational science, which is in the end a science, or an attempt at the science of management or entrepreneurial action. Consideration of the ethics of capitalism requires investigation into those ethics as they are experienced in practice within organizations. From an ethical point of view (as opposed to legal, for instance), the level at which this investigation should take place is that of everyday management operations. High-profile media coverage of fraud cases always provides an opportunity to point out the possibility of ethical problems, but the problems are not solved at that level; it is simply the level on which indignation can be spontaneously expressed. Proven identification of corruption on that level means a case can be taken before the judges, who must decide on the penalty to be applied for various actions. But the 'ethical' extent of a behavior is not always so clear when the actors concerned are convinced that they were doing the right thing: in fact, ambiguous organizational situations are the most likely sources for revelation of the true issues inherent to the ethics of capitalism. The decision-making dynamics that came into play in 1986 and then 2003 at NASA, which were almost identical from start to finish and led both times to the death of seven people, including on *Challenger* a civilian woman who had been supposed to teach lessons from aboard the shuttle as part of the 'Teacher in Space' program, are particularly good examples of decisions made entirely in good faith from the collective point of view. Entirely in good faith, that is, without the visibility necessary for the right decision to be made – a decision which would in both cases have avoided deaths. This raises a deeply serious issue of an ethical nature, since also in both cases, the organization concerned (NASA) had had timely warning from one or more members or partners of the risk involved in its operations and decisions.

The ethical problem specific to capitalism is therefore as follows. The assumption of perfect rationality is at least implicitly active in the practices engendered by the system at all levels, although it does not conform to the organizational, institutional and political reality revealed by empirical studies. Even though the theories are advancing towards systematic incorporation of the true circumstances of any decision, the actors in the field spontaneously persist in their assumption, at least implicit, that the rationality of decisions conforms to the perfect rationality model. In other words, far from sinning by excessive cynicism as is often claimed, the capitalist system, if indeed it sins at all, sins by excessive naivety regarding its own resources and skills. Before looking into the whys and wherefores of this situation, it will be useful to present a model of the way all real management decisions are made: empirically.

2.2 Limits of Perfect Rationality: Individuals, Organizations and Temporality

Organizational theory identifies three main decision-making models: the perfect rationality or 'economic' model, the organizational model as such, and the political model. These three models respectively apply to the case of a single actor with access to full information on the conditions of the decision to be made, and who necessarily makes the best decision (Walras, 1954; Pareto, 1971), the organizational case of a decision conditioned by the past (Cyert and March, 1963), and the negotiations and arbitration needed between actors for the collective to make the least bad decision possible in view of the strategies involved in the choice process (Crozier and Friedberg, 1980). The first case is the one already mentioned above: the assumption of complete control by the actors over the conditions of the decisions they make. This means that whatever the actual number of actors or agents concerned, the process takes place as if there was a single decider, as all information is supposed to be fully available and totally transparent, such that all possible decision options can be envisaged and simultaneously classified in an instant, leading necessarily to the best choice. Intuitively it goes without saying, and theory has demonstrated it for several decades, that this decision-making model is not a descriptive model, but a normative model, describing what should be. The decision-making model based on the assumption of pure, perfect rationality is the normative model *par excellence* for all decisions presumed to be 'right' decisions. It is the ideal model of an exclusively rational, coherent actor. It describes the agent or actor that all practical-minded people consciously or unconsciously aspire to be. It describes an agent or actor who is omnipotent (i.e. necessarily choosing the best possible option, or the option that maximizes his satisfaction) because omniscient (i.e. having access to all information on the state of the decision-making system he must follow). It describes the all-powerful 'god' of the monotheisms derived from the Jewish religion.

The second case is diametrically opposed to this model, as it describes empirical situations where due to their past, organizations and individuals can only solve problems they are already familiar with. Because of their know-how, being used to recognizing certain characteristics in the environment, and only those characteristics, individuals and organizations become tendentially incapable of identifying problems or questions never before encountered in their practices (Nelson and Winter, 1982; Argyris and Schön, 1996). The process by which an organization or individual gradually becomes blind to the scope of its or his competence can be described as follows. The more effective a know-how, and the more its holder is consciously or unconsciously convinced of its efficiency, the more he/it relies on that efficiency to carry out the operations that fall to him. Meanwhile, the more the know-how confirms its appropriateness through repeated implementation, the more it specializes the (individual or collective) actor using it by shrinking his scope of rationality, i.e. of possible questioning or problematization. The more the local rationality of know-how is appropriate, the more the actors' scope for rational questioning shrinks, depending on what skills they have already acquired. The controversy that arose in France in 1986 following a series of deadly train accidents illustrates this difficulty. After three fatal accidents during the summer, the management of the French national railway company SNCF publicly accused its drivers of not knowing the train driving code properly. Led by the autonomous drivers' union, the train drivers retorted that they knew it all too well, and that the code was badly designed. The argument was based on the observation that ever since trains had had only one driver on board, those drivers had been subjected to a technical system designed to ensure that they obeyed all signals on the network: every ten seconds or so, they had to push or release a handle in an action intended to confirm their state of vigilance. They claimed that the formal demands of this system, as it was applied, led to automatic internalization and reflex responses to signals from the network. Far from maintaining vigilance levels, the required movements dulled their responses because they were too frequent and repetitive. The drivers maintained that the most serious accident of 1986 had resulted from this type of response, which had become automatic. A signal ordering trains to slow down crossing a works site at Argenton-sur-Creuse station had been emitted: the driver had seen that he should slow down, and indicated to the network that he had seen the signal, but did not in fact execute the order and continued at the speed used for normal conditions. Weick's proposed interpretation of the Tenerife air crash in 1977 follows the same pattern: when, in response to an emergency, an organization's decision-making collective – even a temporary one, consisting for instance of a control tower and two aeroplane cockpits – no longer fulfills its role as a drainer of information and maintainer of vigilance, the actors' individual reactions regress to a reflex level corresponding to the most routine, internalized, simple operations, which thus depend on the agents' past rather than the decision currently being made (Weick, 1990; Bibard and Jenkins, 1999).

Contrary to what might initially be supposed, the concern for 'in the field' reality in this decision-making model, and all models taking on board the empirical reality of practical decision-making dynamics, does not make them any truer than the models developed based on an assumption of pure, perfect rationality as discussed earlier. They tend to be built exclusively on the actors' or organizations' past, making them just as unilateral, and therefore false, as the first group. Being exclusively normative, thus developed on the basis of an ideal operating consciously or unconsciously, decision-making models based on the notion of tendentially pure, perfect rationality are exclusively, although sometimes implicitly, developed with reference to the future only. A norm prescribes what should exist in order for the present and past to change favorably: if anything new needs to happen, or a good decision needs to be made, then that is because it does not yet exist or has not yet existed, and what the norm prescribes is for application 'in the future', i.e. from now on, or in a near future, so that the future will be better than the present and the past.

Organizational models developed based on individual or collective cultures on one hand, and 'rational' or single-actor models on the other, are respectively and exclusively past-oriented and future-oriented. Neither takes into consideration the whole time made up of the three instants which energize the present, which brings together past and future at every moment. Only the 'political' models, which incorporate analysis of the constantly ongoing confrontations between bounded rationalities resulting from the actors' past, according to their personal or collective aims, which themselves depend on the future they desire and are prepared to envisage, truly take into consideration the dynamic totality breathing life into any organization or individual. In themselves, the models developed on the assumption of perfect rationality and the models developed on the assumption of bounded rationality are equally incomplete. The incompleteness of the first group has been sufficiently highlighted. That of the second group is reflected in the fact that fortunately it is empirically false that an individual or organization only solves problems he/it is already familiar with. If that were so, no new learning would be possible and the notion of innovation or even straightforward survival would be meaningless. The only models that are 'true' or appropriately describe the individual and collective operation of people and organizations, are those that seek to describe the tense, dynamic confrontation between the tendentially pure rationalities of the norms, and the bounded rationalities always related to the individual or collective past.

In asserting that due to these constant confrontations, decision-making processes are continuous (Crozier and Friedberg, 1980) and concern the everyday life of institutions, the 'political' decision-making models assert, even if only implicitly, that organizations actually consist of the series of decisions made within them. In other words, any organization, institution or enterprise consists of the dynamic, ongoing event of decision-making in the present, depending on its past(s) and future(s).[1] Two series of comments are now called for to conclude this first section, before explaining the reasons why it is specific to capitalism, or specifically 'Western', that the problems of ethics relate to the assumption that complete control of action by man, both individually and collectively, is possible and

---

[1] The cases of decision catastrophes or failures are cases where the whole of time is not factored into the decision. The train accidents of 1986 and the 1977 air crash referred to earlier are noteworthy illustrations. In both situations, the actors made their decisions based on rules that were supposed to ensure future safety for all, but were sufficiently internalized to become reflexes and as such a threat to proper current operation: skills were then applied inappropriately because they were not adapted to the circumstances.

necessary. These comments will concern first ethics, then the notion of individuality.

2.3 Towards the Specificities of Capitalism: Ethics, Perfection, Individuality

Ethics concerns what should be fair – it is always up for review. It is never definitive on the practical, non-scientific level of the action it concerns. Responsibility for doing what is fair is renewed in each case, at each moment, once a relatively unfamiliar action is engaged. Ethics, as an imperative of fairness (or justice), is conjugated in the future. It concerns the normative and on a decision-making level ideally concerns the perfection of a rationality that seeks to do everything according to the meaning it confers on fairness and unfairness. 'All we need to do is...', 'we have to...' are everyday-language references to the imperative that ethics concerns what must be better in the future. The expression of indignation is always an inverted indication of an imperative for action.

As noted earlier in relation to the media, immediate expression of indignation is never the level on which ethical problems are solved. At most, it is the level on which they become visible, or where symptoms are expressed. Organizational theory is full of examples of situations where the formal expression of an imperative – particularly an ambitious imperative – not only turns out to be powerless to solve the problem it claims to solve, but is actually an obstacle to implementation of a suitable solution. 'Suitable' means primarily taking into consideration the field in which the formally proposed solution will be applied. The vast majority of explicit managerial solutions proposed in response to problems encountered by organizations (whether national or international, public or private) end in failure if they do not take into consideration the specific conditions of the organization concerned, the state of the organization; or to put it another way the field of action, the existing situation, with the irreducible limits of its learned rationalities and its culture, according to its specific inertia.

In other words, the technical reliability of a new product or new process cannot be guaranteed without any pre-existing knowledge, economic performance cannot be guaranteed without actors and agents already involved somehow in the dynamics of production and consumption, the ethical correctness of a rule or behavior cannot be guaranteed without a minimum of values that were already active collectively or individually. There is no future without a past, no impetus without a stable base, no time to come that is not grounded in the past, understood as binding the decisions to be made to the present. Capitalism tends to forget this threefold observation, and be exclusively future-oriented. Ideally, time is reversible, i.e. the past is nothing to humans (whether grouped into collectives or not) and everything is indefinitely malleable. This is the ethics of capitalism, dreaming (mostly unconsciously) of the absolutely unbroken possibility of always starting over again. Always starting over is always being young, being only young, and never being at fault or having to forgive. In a sense, it is being totally unbound by any relationship to any kind of otherness, particularly human of course, or any responsibility. This second point now requires further development.

The broad-stroked description of the 'rational' decision-making models earlier pointed out that these are so-called 'single-actor' models. This is mainly because the actor deciding is supposed to be capable of doing anything, since he knows everything, given the perfect rationality which in principle comes into play. The ultimate model for the actor in these models is the Jewish, then Christian and Muslim, 'god', who is omnipotent because omniscient. Any individual or collective entity can take on the appearance of the Jewish-origin divinity, if that divinity is understood as the guiding totality of things (Hegel, 1998; Hegel, 1991). In other words, even if the 'single actor' is one in his acts and decisions, he may be made up of several elements, as long as the orientation of those elements depends on the single decision made by the agent or actor concerned. Conversely, although so far in a less systematically univocal way, the decision-making actors of the organizational decision-making models, which were developed based on know-how acquired through the past within the organizations, have been considered to refer to collectives. The fact remains that in the end any human individual is, via his innate and acquired memories, made up of collectives, being of necessity heir to his two biological parents and their respective ancestries, together with the socio-cultural complexes encountered since birth (Eyssalet, 1990). In other words, the future-oriented decision-making models always concern individuated projects, even if they are empirically speaking the effects of collective entities, just as the organizational models always describe the present effects of multiple bounded rationalities, even if those rationalities are interacting at the core of a single individual and in the same way as that individual, with his ideal plans and actual contradictions. This implies that the continuous decision-making tensions referred to by the political decision-making models making up organizations equally well define the tensions that constitute every human individual. In other words, in its own present, any entity is tension between an irreducibly collective past, which both defines its foundations and restricts its rationality, and an idealized future taking the form of a perfected rationality capable of knowing and deciding on its future in all sovereignty, without in the present considering the past which has made it possible just as much as it holds it back. The tension between past, bounded rationalities, collectives and know-how internalized through learning, both innate and acquired, and a future chosen perfectly rationally on the basis of plans developed in all sovereignty, is characteristic of the true present of every organization, and every individual.

If such is the case, the difference between capitalism and non-capitalism grows uncertain. It is now necessary to show how the past-present tension identified, although universally active, is particularly characteristic of contemporary capitalism, and the ethical issues it raises. Further light is thus required on the reasons why the ethical issues raised by capitalism focus on the notion of 'control' by men of the circumstances of their actions.

3 Control and Lack of Control: A Heritage for the Future

The intrinsic reason for ethical failures, or poor decisions by organizations and individuals, appears to be a highly damaging lack of vigilance in the present of the decision-making situations. A decision-making process takes place as if the 'political' model – at best the only one capable of accountability for effective decisions – is inappropriate, thus leaving room only for the 'rational' and 'organizational' model, without any continuity between the two. Torn between the requirement to do the right thing in a future-oriented way, and the practical 'in the field' individual or collective reality resulting from the past, the actors' presence in the situations they are experiencing, and in which they must make a decision, is constitutively obliterated. Past and future are juxtaposed with no link between the desire or plan for the necessary action and the operational competence. The argument in this section is the following. This two-way struggle with no continuity between the past and the future is tendentially an underlying feature of all human action, and is exacerbated in the case of 'Western' culture to the extent of entirely defining it, according to the 'Western' understanding of time. The objective now is to show why this is the case. Below is a brief presentation of how the notion of 'the West' came into being, followed by some of the consequences of its definition, and a description of certain consequences of its advent, considered in relation to the Christian notion of 'perfection.'

3.1 'The West': Between Paganism and Judaism

It can safely be asserted at no great risk of historical infidelity that 'the West' consists of an encounter between two cultures which had initially developed independently, Judaism and Greek paganism (Strauss, 1953). These two cultures are fundamental opposites, starting with Judaism's claims of god's unicity, meaning it is not only constructed in opposition, but becomes the opposition itself to polytheisms, while Greek paganism is fundamentally polytheistic. Underpinning a considerable portion of Western ethics, Judaism by its own definition consists of a new, exclusive declaration of its god's unicity (*Exodus* 20:3-4, *Deuteronomy* 5:6-7). The unicity of the Jewish god is the direct expression of his power: if he is one, it is because it is unimaginable that he might share his kingdom with other gods or any other powers, and if that is the case, it is because he is the power of all powers, at the origin of everything. This idea is illustrated and asserted by the Jewish concept of creation. This assertion, the cornerstone of Western theology, has decisive consequences for ethics. Since 'god' is the power of all powers, even if man is created in his own image (*Genesis* 1: 27), his access to god is seriously problematic: his god moves in mysterious ways (ref), and only if He wishes can a man, chosen as prophet, come to know Him or know something of His plans. Otherwise, in man's ordinary life it is totally impossible to have any knowledge of his god at all, and yet man is commanded to believe in and revere only Him, to seal the covenant and love Him. This is the original spirit of Judaism: man must believe in the unverifiable, be guided by the unknown, and accept as valid a law whose origin will forever remain obscure, since it is humanly unverifiable whether Moses is a true prophet or a usurper. Built on a doubt that can never be removed, Judaism consists of the decision to believe *nevertheless*. In fact it *is* this very decision, and paradoxically the more events may foster doubt, the more reasons there are to decide to believe nevertheless, or simply to believe. In the original sense of the three Western monotheisms, believing is believing despite the odds, or even against the odds. It is up to the individual to take responsibility for sealing the covenant, loving and obeying the incomprehensible, and in god's image, acting according to the law dictated by god, or on the contrary transgressing that law and suffering the consequences for all eternity. The notions of decision-making and free, responsible action in a situation of essential uncertainty are systematically taken up as themes in the West through the *Torah*.

The situation is very different over in Greece, which for the West represents a symbol of all the paganisms Judaism sought to combat. Greek polytheism, and pagan polytheism in general, implies that regardless of his power, the god of all gods (Zeus in ancient Greece, after Chronos) is not the ultimate power behind matter. This is clearly stated in Plato's dialogue *Timaeus*, which declares that there was no creation of the universe out of nothing by a god, as in the Jewish view, but a simple 'ordering' of the world by a demiurge (Plato, 2000). Before or beyond the gods, something else spontaneously exists, 'nature.' For the paganisms, particularly Greek paganisms, nature (*physis* in Greek) is the ultimate reference. The Greeks declare that neither gods nor men can change anything in nature. As the saying goes, 'A leopard cannot change its spots.' In contrast to the Jews, who declared that through language, man would have dominion over the plants and the beasts (*Genesis* 1:26-28), the Greeks invented the notion of excessive pride (*hubris*). This excessive pride is an attempt to surpass nature and its laws; such an attempt is bound to fail. Since nature cannot be changed in any way, and there is no point in acting on nature (human or otherwise) in the sense of transforming it to improve it and improve men's lives, the best attitude to adopt towards nature is to conform. And the best way to conform is, as far as possible, to know nature. Not all of nature is knowable: nature likes to hide. But knowing is part of human nature or destiny. In fact, that is the highest definition of man: first a political animal, then a reasonable animal or animal who knows and conforms to his destiny, or his nature (Aristotle, 1998, 1991). Knowing nature is knowing *physis* or turning it into the science of physics, in order to best conform to man's place in the world and live wisely in it. Stoic wisdom later confirmed that an accomplished man loves to conform to what he is and live in harmony with the laws of nature. He loves the wisdom of which he is potentially capable, and is in the strict sense of the word a 'philosopher.'[2] Being a 'philosopher' means being open to what nature tells man about human and non-human nature, and living according to this teaching. The notions of listening, and therefore dialogue, are to be found at the heart of Greek ethics.

Obviously, it is largely artificial to contrast the notions of free, responsible actions and decisions, and the notions of dialogue and listening. The Greeks, more than any other civilization, conceptualized decision-making, and Caesar's *alea jacta est* is a famous part of the resulting legacy; the Jews, more than any other world and sometimes dramatically, insisted on listening to the word of god, his laws and commandments, and the importance of interpretative dialogue with the

---

[2] In ancient Greek, 'loving wisdom' is expressed in the two words *philein* (to love) and *sophia* (wisdom), hence 'philo-sophy.'

law, to the extent of inserting the *Talmud* as a sacred text alongside the *Torah*. But the fact remains that 'the West' is constructed on a both dramatizing and fertile difference between paganism and Judaism, clearly caused by the latter, which was specifically and explicitly developed against polytheistic idolatries. And its difference from paganism, particularly in its Greek expression, lies in the difference between its god and 'nature.'[3] I take the ethical and methodological responsibility for underlining this difference, because it is determinant for what was to become of the concept of 'the West.' Not only did the West consist of the meeting of paganisms – particularly Greek paganism – and Judaism, and the respective ethics of those two worlds; subsequently it came to be determined as the deliberate intertwining of those two worlds, causing a third set of ethics to emerge: the ethics of Christianity.

The argument now turns as follows. Contrary to the claims sometimes made for good form's sake, the ethics of capitalism derives directly from the ethics of European humanism, which was contemporary with the Renaissance. Humanism's fundamental aim is to give man his place in this world, to the detriment of the divine or natural authority or conditions that precede him and constrain him. Humanism is constructed by appropriating Christianity's idea of man and ridding it of its purely theological content (Feuerbach, 1958; Marx and Engels, 1970). Below is a brief summary of the core content of Christian theology and anthropology, and the impact on contemporary ethics of their secularization by humanists.

3.2 Humanist Ethics, the Daughter of Christianity

In declaring that not only Jews, but also (or above all) pagans, can and must be converted, Christianity is making a conscious, deliberate decision to mix paganisms and Judaism, in the form of what for Christians is permanent subsumption of pagan idolatries to Jewish theology and faith. This subsumption is a direct effect of the specifically Christian dogma of incarnation (Kojève, 1964). In calling himself 'my father's son', Jesus Christ causes understandable scandal among the Jews by referring to himself as the 'natural' son of his father, yet this father is presumed to be the god of the Jews, who had been trying to separate themselves from nature for over a thousand years.[4] It is as if Jesus was telling his fathers and peers that by unilaterally denying the pagans, the Jews were keeping them in existence. The best way to deny paganism is to acknowledge what the pagans themselves acknowledge, the ultimate power of nature, whose ultimate law is death. Only once nature – or its ultimate law, the death of all things – has been acknowledged can man surpass it. In other words: it is only in first acknowledging death or the finiteness of human beings, in becoming incarnate, that Jesus Christ can then show anyone prepared to believe him that he is risen from the dead, infinitely surpassing the natural death of the living, or that his glorious

---

[3]   According to L. Strauss (1956).

[4]   The miraculous and eminently paradoxical virginity of Jesus' mother is the symbol *par excellence* for the contradiction, of which Jesus Christ is both aware and proud, between the pagans', 'nature' and the divinity he claims for himself.

resurrection, as revealed by the empty tomb after the three days of the Passover and at Pentecost, take away all the sins of the world. And he asks his followers to do the same as him: believe in what he is doing. This belief or faith *ipso facto* contains its own effects: in believing, the believer is saved. In believing in the son of man, a believer is infinitely detached from nature, or 'supernatures' the nature in himself and in the world towards a god who has not simply brushed aside 'nature', the ultimate reference of all paganisms, but subjected it to his own laws.

While it disagrees with the theological content of Christianity, Renaissance humanism does adopt the Christian idea of man: the idea of a tendentially all-powerful man, just like Genesis man, created in his god's image, but now unencumbered by a law defining how he should believe and live. Man created in the image of a god whose law is now his own will or his sovereign desire is himself god on earth, man with dominion over the plants and the beasts, and no faith or law other than his own will or desire, which is presumed to be infinite – infinite like the will of the Jewish, Christian and Moslem god. So says Descartes in calling man 'master and possessor of nature' in his famous *Discours de la méthode*.[5]

The tool *par excellence* available to humanist man's liberated desire is his intelligence, his 'reason', his capacity to know the nature he finds himself in. Starting from the Renaissance, the meaning attributed to 'nature' was to undergo a fundamental change. 'Nature' was no longer the unsurpassable sovereign authority, to which it was ethical or wise to conform in order to live a good life; it now became a set of raw materials and potential riches freely provided (by god[6]) for man, or specifically the set of objects of his desire and knowledge (Kant, 1999; Heidegger, 1992); to shape it as he wished, all man had to do was labor it (Locke, 1690).

Control and transparency, or active or practical control over nature (human or otherwise) *by virtue of* its cognitive transparency to man: these were the key words of humanist anthropology, which sought to make a place for man to the detriment of the religious authorities and the natural conditions which had hitherto pre-existed him. Before examining some of the determinant consequences of the advent of contemporary secular anthropology for the ethics of capitalism, all ethical teaching drawing on humanists' appropriation of Christian anthropology and theology must be put into perspective.

3.3 Perfection, Globalization and Christianity

It was noted earlier that the core ethical weakness of individuals and organizations lies in an artificial juxtaposition of past and future in decision-making situations where attention to the present is in fact vital for good decisions – 'fair' decisions from an ethical point of view. Although tendentially universal, this weakness is exacerbated in contemporary capitalism, particularly due to the ethical legacy received from humanism as encountered and broadly described above. The final

---

[5] Descartes (1956), Part six.
[6] See Locke (1690), V, 'Of Property'.

section of this article takes a last look at the reasons why the ethics of capitalism are directly and specifically concerned by the humanist heritage, with reference to the modern concept of individualism, and the related concept of free enterprise. But first, we turn explicitly to the link between the Western concept of time and the concept of perfection.

In exhorting those who believe in him to imitate him, Jesus Christ places in the hearts of men the desire to perfect 'nature' in themselves as he himself did. In other words, he exhorts them first to acknowledge in themselves, for example in the act of contrition, or in the pains taken in their labors, all limitations, all sins and all death, and to infinitely surpass that death initially acknowledged through forgiveness, which depends both on infinite divine mercy and faith in God. Christian anthropology and theology specifically and exclusively encompass the concept of perfection, or 'supernaturation' of nature. Perfection and supernaturation of nature are always in the future, since their grace is weighed down by the things of this world: according to the great believers, the great mystics, the search for salvation must be constantly renewed. Every moment of time is thus understood as the dynamic event enabling man, god's heir and imitator, to accept and acknowledge the nature he is already, or his past, with a view to the perfect future he is striving to reach and which saves him. Man's true present is ceaselessly acknowledging his condition as a sinner, or death which has irredeemably threatened him since his past, so he can be saved paradoxically by his decision to believe in future salvation. The Christian notion of perfection, supposed to remove the finiteness that comes from his past, fundamentally forces man towards the future: the modern, or 'Western' concept of time is directly conditioned by the assertion of man's infinite perfectibility. It is exclusively, unilaterally future-oriented, to the detriment of what has already been. For humanists and their heirs (ourselves), the Christian acknowledgement of nature so as to surpass it infinitely towards god has become an exclusively for-the-future orientation, acknowledging anything which within and without us is from the past only as a raw material for our desires and intentions. As seen earlier, acting *as if* the past had never existed is by construction harmful, as the past always catches up with men, individually or collectively, whose task it is to decide on their future freely and single-handedly.

Consciously or unconsciously sweeping aside the past is not the sole prerogative of capitalism; everything that can be considered as man's 'modernity' is marked by the same feature. Against the backdrop of the cultural heritage brought out thus far, we now need to identify what relates specifically to capitalism, and define the specific ethical issues.

4 Capitalism, Ethics and Politics

Ethics, or the fairness of an individual or collective behavior, eventually requires a connection with the individual or collective behavior of others; there can be no feeling of fairness or unfairness, i.e. of the appropriateness of a decision or behavior, without reference to the viewpoint of the object of that decision or behavior, and possibly a third party (Smith, 1869). In other words, being fair 'on one's own' is meaningless. This is what Kant has in mind when he describes the content of the categorical moral imperative as the necessarily universalizable nature of the maxim of any action (Kant, 1996; Kant, 1965). However, the currently dominant decision-making model, at least unconsciously, is the rational, single-actor model: whether the actor is a collective or an individual, he is supposed to be able to decide alone on the best option in a decision-making situation, whatever its content, especially on an explicitly ethical question. Not only is he supposed to be capable of deciding alone, but the best way to decide is deemed to be individual: the collective ultimately comes to represent the cumbersome inertia ultimately specific to acquired rationalities that are always to some degree habit, etc. As far as possible, people are supposed to make their judgments alone, as sole, exclusive leader.[7] As seen and illustrated above, this specifically modern option is always ultimately counterproductive. It is valid for a while, or in particular circumstances, but sooner or later becomes hemmed in by its insufficiency, and by the occasionally catastrophic consequences of being considered as the best and only way to reach decisions. This can be expressed by asserting that to be approached appropriately, ethics is better understood from the political decision-making standpoint, which orients understanding of ethics according to the question of the actors' present vigilance, to the detriment of the rational decision-making model. Or to put it another way, good understanding of what is at stake in ethics in general, and the ethical stakes in a decision, requires a political or deliberative understanding of ethics rather than a normative or moral understanding alone (Bibard, 2003). The humanist legacy energizes and at least unconsciously structures decision-making according to the ideal of a perfect future, presumed to be perceived individually. The links between perfection and the expected future have been identified above; it remains to be seen how liberal individualism, or individualistic liberalism, is the third basic foundation of the capitalist decision-making attitude. This requires a brief presentation of the history of Western political thought.

The major legacy inherited by Western political thought is Greek thought: the first known democracy, intended as such, was in the Athens of the fourth century B.C. The most comprehensive political thought of the time was that of Plato and Aristotle. The basis of 'classical' Greek political philosophy can reasonably be described in the terms of Aristotle, that man is naturally or spontaneously political (Aristotle, 1998). Rightly or wrongly, until transformed into modern political science, political thought asserted that collective life was, despite the obvious diversity of private interests (Cropsey and Strauss, 1987), natural to man. In sociological terms, this comes down to granting holism priority compared to methodological individualism.[8] Classical political 'holism' is associated with the following additional features. All collectives are spontaneously hierarchically

---

[7] On the authority of the leader with regard to other possibilities, see Kojève (2004), *La notion de l'autorité*, Gallimard, Paris.

[8] This is the debate underpinning sociology, originally represented by the tension between the followers of Durkheim and Weber.

organized (Aristotle, 1998), defining the relationship between governors and governed on one hand (Plato, 1968), and friends and enemies on the other hand (Aristotle, 1998). This structure of relationships between men conditions all their relationships, including those between individuals: a pre-political man is infrahuman or simply animal, while a post-political man is supposed to be suprahuman or divine (Aristotle, 1998). In other words, the notion of individuality has no meaning for classical thinkers, i.e. in the West, the Greeks, until Hobbes in the seventeenth century.

The situation is also the same in the strict old testament tradition, which can be said to convey political thought that is determinant for the Jewish people, organized as a people or a political entity *par excellence*, by Moses (Cropsey and Strauss, 1987). With the exception of personal commitments arising from each individual's faith in god (Buber, 1980), Judaism contains and conveys a political thought that was to pass to Islam: the structuring fundamental revelation, for both Jews and Moslems, is that of the law prescribing how life should be lived (Strauss, 1935). Christianity is the only one of the three monotheisms ever to have declared the individual's priority over the collective, or personal choice over the political. This option is clear in the gospels, which state that the greatest commandment is to love one's neighbor as one's god and oneself (*Mark* 12:28-33, *Matthew* 22:34-40, *Luke* 10:25-28). In declaring that love is the fundamental commandment, Jesus Christ states he has come not to abolish but to fulfill the law (*Matthew* 5:17), thus underlining the law's need for fulfillment. The danger in any law is that it may become lost in formal obligations with no meaning relevant to real life, or become a dead letter for people even though they may scrupulously respect it in their everyday actions. Respecting the letter of the law rather than its spirit is precisely the accusation Jesus levels at the Pharisees (*Matthew* 15:1-20, 23:27). Arguing that what is Caesar's should be rendered unto Caesar (*Matthew* 22:21), or the symbol of the political in the gospel era, Jesus Christ is pleading for the Jews to rediscover individual faith on the basis of the law that structures them as a people. He exhorts each Jew to stop being content with formal observation of the law's prescriptions, and authentically or 'in his heart' recommit himself to his god: the parable of the adulteress says the same in indirectly, revealing that the very people who respect merely the letter of the law silently sin against it (*John* 8:1-11). Every individual must do as Jesus does, believe as he does in his own resurrection. In absolute terms, every believing Christian recommences what the individual *par excellence*, his god made incarnate and risen from the dead, has done, said and shown to anyone willing to listen and see.

Christianity has no equivalent to Jewish or Islamic law. Despite the constant historical entanglements of church and States, the Vatican is the only authentic Christian State, and if there are any 'Christian' laws, they are the monastic rules followed by the men and women who decide to devote their lives to god outside the arena of any worldly political life. Christianity thus tendentially frees the political space from any obligation of a theological nature. No matter how late they may come about, church-state separations are a necessary consequence of Christian theology and the concept of man it involves. Just as the ideas of perfection and future salvation were secularized by Renaissance humanism, the classical political thought inherited from the Greeks and monotheisms was to be radically transformed under the influence of this Christian heritage, becoming atheist. The first author to spark off a revolution in Western political thought was Hobbes. A brief look at the main features of his political thought is sufficient to evoke the ethical issues specific to contemporary capitalism.

Following the path first traced by Machiavello (1981), Hobbes was the first political thinker to explicitly go against Aristotle in stating that human life is not spontaneously collective, structured, hierarchically organized and, despite the diversity of individual and collective interests, ordered.[9] For Hobbes, humans are always first and foremost free, rational individuals, by nature equal, with a right to life and a duty to make every endeavor to respect that right (Hobbes, 1982). From this natural state of humans, Hobbes has no difficulty in deducing a state of war of all men against all men (the famous 'struggle for life'). In order to live, each individual must obtain the necessary resources, which are always rare; the rarity of resources means that sooner or later the same object will be desired by several individuals, who will fight to win it (Kojève, 1980). The natural state of humans is chaotic, unstructured, non-hierarchic and potentially violent. Since its initial development by Hobbes, modern political theory has been enriched by a number of theoretical variations, but the theory of the State has remained substantially the same throughout, based on the notion of the social contract. Conscious of the violence of their initial situation, individuals make a conscious, deliberate decision to attribute to a single third party the right to use violence in settling the conflicts which are bound to arise from interaction between individuals.[10] The 'social contract' comes down to a decision to attribute to a single third party a monopolistic right to use violence to enforce structure, order and hierarchy, and restrict individual interactions to those allowed by the laws (Weber, 1978; Weber, 2001; Weber, 2004). This third party, called the Leviathan by Hobbes, is of course the State, in its many and variable institutional expressions: the police, the law, etc (Hobbes, 1982).

It is useful to stress that Hobbes' inauguration of political science consists of a secularized adoption of Jewish political theology: just as it can be claimed that it was the Jews who, in giving themselves or electing their god, set themselves up in return as the 'chosen people', here we have all individuals of a future society giving themselves their State, so as to guarantee each man and woman the possibility of living freely, or, as the American constitution supremely puts it, the right to 'life, liberty and the pursuit of happiness.' Whatever the subsequent variations in political thought, the collective or its sovereign representative, the State, was to be considered as being at the service of the society of individuals whose freedom is the ultimate goal of any organization, structure, or hierarchy. And whatever historical or empirical success may be achieved by the various forms of modern institutions, including of course communist institutions, their ultimate declared goal is to serve man, not any power, to further individual happiness, not the power of any collective (Marx, 1995; Friedman, 1962). From this standpoint,

---

[9]   See Hobbes (1982), Section I, Chapter 1.

[10]   According to the definition of 'right' proposed by Kojève (2000).

capitalism and communism have exactly the same aim, and only differ in the means employed. The risk of extremism is present in the very root of the modern notion of state sovereignty, since states are potentially endowed with absolute power (Hobbes, 1982). The explicitly capitalist option, however, is opened up by Hobbes' discerning successor, Locke, who was the first to consider the people's right to revolt against the legality of laws was legitimate if the state was deviating from its mission, which is to serve the enjoyment of private individual property based on the labor of each person (Locke, 1690).

The advent of modern political science tendentially marked the collapse of classical political thought, its ethics, and its dominant categories. Dominant contemporary thinking tendentially accepted as obvious the individual's priority over the collective, individual freedom over any kind of collective sovereignty, happiness as each man and woman understands it over a collective definition of what is a good life. In turn, the tendential consequences of these choices were the minimization of public powers' role by placing them at the service of private interests (arbitrations, social policies, miscellaneous regulations), and the right and duty of each man and woman to endeavor as far as possible to make their own happiness. Christian faith was replaced by sentiment (Smith, 1869), built on the sentiment that each was as worthwhile as anyone else (Tocqueville, 1961), in the sense of the specifically Cartesian proposition, 'good sense is the most evenly distributed thing in the world' (Descartes, 1956). Classical education, which trained individuals in collective and sooner or later religious values, providing guarantees on a political level, was gradually replaced by the transmission of technical resources for self-preservation, self-enrichment, self-empowerment, or self-instruction, without any prejudgment on what it is good or bad to desire or do. It is hardly an exaggeration to hold with Rousseau that we are potentially in the presence of an entirely democratic universe of gods, or chaos (Rousseau, 1970), where each has absolute sovereignty over his world, even though that would now mean more than six billion gods. This universe, which tends towards social homogeneity (Kojève, 2000) potentially concerns the whole world, affecting all local political traditions, whether Shintoist, Islamic, Buddhist, animist, Jewish, Christian (theist) etc, and the corresponding sovereign State is ideally the heir to the League of Nations, the United Nations of course being part of it: a 'suprastate' allowed to have a monopoly on the use of violence in order to defend the legitimate interests of each man and woman, including the fundamental right to enterprise, against the potential violence of those who would oppose it.

5 A Concluding Comment

To fully problematize the ethical issues now encountered and raised by capitalism, which is the only living alternative (apart from a few exceptions) to orthodox communism for sovereignty as Hobbes understood it, a look back over the ground covered is necessary, starting from the empirical observation that there is as yet no universal, homogeneous State corresponding to a universe that has apparently become entirely 'modern.'

Quite simply, there is no worldwide sovereign State reigning over each State, since each State declares itself and intends to be sovereignly sovereign at its own level, even when like the European Union, in order to guarantee its sovereignty by remaining on the level of high political, economic and military competition, it attempts to find allies, expand and organize itself accordingly. Currently, no political authority can legitimately declare itself sole defender of individual liberty worldwide. For example, when the USA justifies its war against Iraq by claiming that it is defending world democracy, there is room for legitimate doubt, and the appropriateness of those claims can easily be challenged without calling into question the good faith of the authorities concerned.

This can be expressed differently, by granting classical political thought and modern political science only the status of intellectual paradigms of an ethical nature *simultaneously active in the present*. While it can reasonably be presumed that the world State corresponding to a universe of rational, free and equal individuals, a State marking the end of the history that led up to it (Fukuyama, 1992; Kojève, 1980), will never happen as such, it must be acknowledged that the age of the collective taking priority over the individual is over in all the world's communities. That was an age when in one way or another, laws for civil life were considered to come from gods (Plato, 1968) and the past (Aristotle, 1998; Strauss, 1964). The contemporary age of sovereign, free, rational individuals equal at least in law is an age strongly oriented towards the future, as encountered at the start of this investigation. Each in their own way, classical and modern political thought respectively emphasize and defend one moment in time to the detriment of others, the past for the classical, the future for the modern. As was the case for organizational theory's decision-making models, none of these philosophies hold all the truth. Each is only true in confrontation with the other, in the present of the theoretical and practical arbitrations which depend on the political problems agitating the reality of the world we live in, and determine it. The 'clash of cultures' much discussed recently is the world's only true present. This observation calls for some final methodological, terminological and conceptual explanations.

The tension between the past and future, identified as a structurer of the ethical issues encountered by organizations, particularly enterprises, concerns all levels of contemporary existence, from the smallest (individual) to the vastest (the whole world).[11] Its fundamental form of expression is through the tension between the collective past of any individual and any collective, and the desired and supposedly perfect future of any individual and any collective. No psychological, political or organizational theory which sets out to describe only one of the aspects of this tension can hold all the truth exclusively: the only true theories or models are those capable of describing the encounter in the present between the past and future of humans, considered individually or collectively. On the contemporary political level, this encounter takes on the appearance of 'globalization', understood not exclusively on the basis of the future, or of extension to global level of Western

---

[11] For more on this correlation between the smallest and largest, and its difficulties, see Plato (1968) and Strauss (1964).

'rationality' derived from Christianity and secularized by humanism, but as the *tension* between this modern 'Western' rationality and logics primarily and forcibly oriented by the past, i.e. the religious logics of other cultures of the world, including those at the roots of the West, paganisms including of course Greek paganism, and to varying extents Judaism, Islam, etc. On this basis, the West must be understood no longer as a particular geographical and historical 'place', but as the advent of the rationalism specific to the single-actor decision-making model, and the corresponding ethical attitude. 'Western' ethics are ideally the ethics of complete control over all human action, based on total technical control of nature (human and otherwise) through its transparency or absolute accessibility to scientific knowledge, to serve on principle the desire of all individuals. Thus the 'West' becomes not only its own advent, but the corresponding attitude, tendentially universally active. All of humanity is currently both attracted by the desire for and the theoretical possibility of total control by man over the world he lives in, or ideally total control by each individual over the course of his life, and simultaneously reticent over those desires and theories. Many events and many decisions like those discussed earlier illustrate the limitations of such ethics. It can only be concluded that true ethics are ethics that are positioned *between* the 'modern' Western ethics of absolute human control over their worlds, and the ethics of ancient or traditional civilizations, which sometimes become violently withdrawn in reaction to those modern Western ethics. By construction, these intermediate ethics would require constant reinvention in the present, the arena for occurrence of unforeseeable events whose consequences are always uncertain and risky, between an imperfect, limited past which whether we like it or not eventually defines our foundations, and a future we attempt to direct towards the perfection we dream of. Between ethics conceived as a behavior learned according to individuals' or collectives' innate or acquired past, and ethics as an ideal norm tracing out our futures, we defend ethics as taking responsibility for risky decisions, in the uncertainty specific to the present, with if possible unfailing vigilance and attention. This is ethics as a dialogue, ethics as taking on board differences and different points of view, the ethics of this book which by virtue of its editors' intentions, makes room for discussion, disagreement and dialogue.

References

Aristotle (1991), *The Metaphysics*, Prometheus Books.
Aristotle (1998), *Politics*, Oxford University Press, New York.
Aristotle (1985), *Nicomachean Ethics*, Hackett (trad. Terence Irwin), Indianapolis.
Argyris, C. and Schön, D. (1996), *Organizational Learning: A Theory of Action Perspective*, Addison-Wesley Longman.
Bibard, L. and Jenkins, A. (1999), *Leadership, Uncertainty and Management Education*, Actes du 9th colloquium on Business and Economic Ethics, IESE, Barcelona.
Bibard L. (2003), *Entreprise, Ethique et Politique*, Vème Université de Printemps de l'Audit Social, Audit Social et Responsabilité Sociale de l'Entreprise, Corté.
Buber, M. (1980), *The Jew*, University of Alabama Press.
Clarke R. (2004), *Against All Enemies*, Free Press/Simon & Schuster.

Cropsey, J. and Strauss, L. (ed.) (1987), *History of Political Philosophy*, The University of Chicago Press, Chicago.

Crozier, M. and Friedberg, E. (1980), *Actors and Systems: The Politics of Collective Action*, University of Chicago Press.

Cyert, R. and March J. (1963), *A Behavioral Theory of the Firm*, Prentice Hall.

Descartes, R. (1956), *Discourse on Method*, Prentice Hall.

Eyssalet, J.-M. (1990), *Le secret de la maison des ancêtres*, Trédaniel, Paris.

Feuerbach, L. (1958), *Essence of Christianity*, Peter Smith Pub.

Friedman, M. (1962), *Capitalism and Freedom*, University of Chicago Press, Chicago.

Fukuyama, F. (1992), *The End of History and the Last Man*, Free Press.

Hegel, W. (1998), *Hegel's Science of Logic*, Prometheus Books.

Hegel, W. (1991), *Elements of the Philosophy of Right*, Cambridge University Press.

Heidegger, M. (1992), *The Principle of Reason*, Indiana University Press.

Hobbes, T. (1982), *De Cive: or The Citizen*, Greenwood Press Reprint.

Homer, (1975), *The Homeric Hymns*, W. W. Norton & Company.

Kant, E. (1999), *Critique of Pure Reason*, Cambridge University Press.

Kant, E. (1965), *Roundwork of the Metaphysics of Morals*, Perennial.

Kant, E. (1996), *Critique of Practical Reason*, Prometheus Books.

Kojève, A. (1980), *Introduction to the Reading of Hegel*, Cornell University Press.

Kojève, A. (2000), *Outline of a Phenomenology of Right*, Rowman & Littlefield Publishers.

Linhart, R. (1981), *The Assembly Line*, University of Massachusetts Press.

Locke, J. (1690), *Of Civil Government*, Ntc Contemporary Publishing Company.

Machiavel, N. (1981) *The Prince*, Penguin Books, New York.

March, J. & Simon, H. (1958), *Organizations*, Wiley, New York.

Marx, K. (1887), *Capital*, Progress Publishers, Moscow.

Marx, K. (1995), *The Poverty of Philosophy*, Prometheus Books.

Marx, K. and Engels, F. (1970), *The German Ideology*, Lawrence & Wishart.

NASA (2003), *Report of Columbia Accident Investigation Board.*

Nelson, R. and Winter, S. (1982), *An Evolutionary Theory of Economic Change*, Harvard University Press.

Pareto, W. (1971), *Manual of Political Economy* (trad. A. Schwier), A. M. Kelley, New York.

Plato (1968), *Republic* (trad. Allan Bloom), Basic Books.

Plato (2000), *Timaeus*, Hackett Publishing Company.

Popper, K. (1977), *The Logic of Scientific Discovery*, Hutchinson, London.

Rousseau, J. J. (1970), *Social Contract*, Free Press.

Smith, A. (1869), *Theory of Moral Sentiments*, A. Murray, London.

Solzhenitsyn, A. (2000), *One Day in the Life of Ivan Denisovich*, Penguin Books.

Strauss, L. (1964), *The City and Man*, The University Press of Virginia.

Strauss, L. (1953), *Natural Right and History*, The University of Chicago Press, Chicago.

Strauss, L. (1935), *Philosophy and Law*, The Jewish Publication Society of America.

Taylor, J. (1947), *Scientific Management*, Harper & Row.

Tocqueville, de, A. (1961), *Democracy in America*, Oxford University Press, London.

Holy Bible (1990), Riverside World Pub Co.

Walras, L. (1954), *Elements of Pure Economics*, Harvard University Press.

Weber, M. (1978), *Economy and Society*, University of California Press.

Weber, M. (2004), *The Vocation Lectures: Science as a Vocation, Politics as a Vocation*, Hackett Publishing Company.

Weber, M. (2001), *The Protestant Ethic and the Spirit of Capitalism*, Routledge.

Weick, K. (1990), The Vulnerable System: An Analysis of the Tenerife Air Disaster, *Journal of Management*, 16, pp 571-593.

Weil E. (1974), *Logique de la philosophie*, Vrin, Paris.

Chapter 2

Capitalism as an Ethical System: The Ideal and its Feasibility

Michael Keren

1 Introduction[1]

It is not fashionable to consider capitalism as an ethical system, as a creed that bears a moral message. But every beginning economics student is made aware of the fact that the creed ascribed by Marx to socialism is in fact the organizing principle of the general equilibrium of a competitive market economy, the model that aspires to explain the functioning of the capitalist economy. To each according to his contribution is Marx's distributive principle of the socialist phase of transition to communism. Competitive equilibrium rewards each factor by its marginal product, i.e., its contribution. This differs from Marx's socialism only in the recognition that labor is not the only factor of production, and that non-labor factors such as capital and land are also productive and are entitled to some income, which is given to, or diverted by, their owners. Indeed, an efficient resource allocation requires that the wages of non-labor factors be equal to their contribution.

The claim of this chapter is that the ethical problem with capitalism lies not with its theoretical underpinnings but with the latter's translation into reality. Theory assumes that the model functions of its own, unassisted by any institutional framework. A 'government' is introduced only where markets fail and the basic assumptions of competitive equilibrium do not hold, i.e., where there are increasing returns to scale, externalities, public goods and the like. Even then this institution, The Government, is left as a black box that by some magic wand fulfills the tasks expected of it. But the problems with the translation of the model into reality arise even when these market failures are absent, and can be summarized under the three 'C's: crime, corruption and capture. They arise because the role of government is much more basic than the provision of a cure when markets fail: the market system depends on the security of property and contract in the presence of actors who, if given the opportunity, would take possession of others' goods without compensation to their owners. Hence a provision of law and order, a basic set of public goods, is required, as Hobbes has already claimed some 400 years ago. But criminals continue to exist even where a State and institutions for keeping

[1] This paper was presented at the international seminar on 'Economy and Ethics', organized by NEC and SOREC in Bucharest, 12–13 December 2003.

the peace exist, the struggle of the enforcers of law against criminals is never-ending, and the latter try to corrupt the keepers of the law. Even the law itself is often subverted: law makers are captured by interested parties, with the result that the actual rules of the games often do not tend to apply the distribution advocated by the principles of capitalism. And where they do, the governing bodies that run the economic organizations often fail. The outcome of this interplay between the State and the criminal sector, the illegals as I shall refer to them, given governance failures, shapes the economic game: it endows decision makers in firms with their incentives, and may lead to behavior that is at variance with that assumed by theory. It is the real economic system, expressed in this game, and on some of its ethical implications, on which I focus below.

In what follows I explore in brief the economic system and outline those parts of it that lead to divergence between the theory and the outcome of capitalist markets. The model focuses on the interrelations between three types of organization: firms, organizations that produce goods and services, governmental organizations that are to lay down and to enforce the rules of the economic game, and criminal organizations, or the illegals, that flout these rules. The structure of incentives that the firms face determines the efficiency of the system, and the incentives depend on the rules that emerge as a result of the struggle between the government and the illegals.

Section 2 outlines in brief the ethics of capitalism. Section 3 presents the model of the economic system, and Section 4 shows how problems of economic malfeasance and governance arise as we move from the simple firm assumed by textbook models to more realistic models of firms. Section 5 looks at possible remedies to these problems, and 6 concludes on a somewhat pessimistic note.

2 The Ethics of the Capitalist Model

The outcome of the economic game, given conditions that I shall specify below and that never apply in practice, is an income distribution that equates labor wages and asset rents to their marginal product, i.e., to their economic contribution. The conditions are familiar: no increasing returns, no public goods and no externalities. Since these conditions never apply, we have the first divergence, amply discussed, between the model and reality. Since it is well-known I shall not further expand upon it, except to say that it is a basis of much of governmental economic intervention, from environmental legislation and the provision of services in general to anti-monopolistic policies. I suspect that, once this intervention is in place, the effects of this divergence on income distribution need not be large. In other words, the fact that the above conditions do not apply cannot be the basis of the glaring injustices of the capitalist economic system that we are witnessing.

I venture to claim that people do in general accept that income inequalities that result from unequal contributions are fair, even just and desirable. People do not usually begrudge successful artists and sportsmen their enormous incomes. When they disagree with a large income, they usually dispute the contribution, not the principle. This is despite the fact that the outcome of the economic game depends on the distribution of assets – human capital as well as land and physical capital –

and that this distribution is in general very unequal. Much of it is the outcome of accumulation over many generations, and can therefore not be described as fair, if we consider fairness to include the equality of opportunities. In other words, if we divide income in two constituents, labor income and income from capital and land, to use the conventional classification, there would be little argument about the fairness of rewarding labor income in accordance with its contribution. Even Marx referred positively to such a distribution, calling it a socialist principle of distribution.

Matters are more complex when it comes to the income of such assets as capital and land. Here too one part is unobjectionable: people accumulate assets by investing their savings over their lifetime, and it is only fair that such savings should be rewarded. The problem lies in the substantial part of assets that is inherited and not due the efforts of their owner. Incomes originating from these assets are much more difficult to justify as 'fair'. Furthermore, the value of assets, be it human capital or physical assets, is highly uncertain. People who invest in specific skills or machines make a gamble that may either succeed or fail, and the resulting income distribution is therefore quite random. In spite of this, I submit that people in general accept the resulting distribution, as long as they believe that it expresses returns to contributions. They accept it subject to some redistribution of income, known to be costly and associated with some output loss, to which modern capitalism does not object.

There is however another perspective of capitalist ethics: it looks at the assumed motivation of Man (and Woman), at his (and her) selfish acquisitiveness which is blamed on capitalism. The model, perhaps even more than reality, assumes that people are selfish, out to maximize their own well-being with utter disregard for their human environment. But Man is a social animal, and healthy people are usually concerned with the welfare of their relevant reference group, be it their family, clan or wider society. This limits selfishness. But this is not the whole story. A selfishness promoting factor is inherent in the very principle of distribution: if it is true that income and wealth mirror people's social contribution, then they are also a visible sign of individuals' worth. Therefore the desire for riches is driven not only by the needs of consumption but also by the desire to display this success, to demonstrate to all one's economic success and one's presumed social contribution.

But is the striving for self-enrichment limited to capitalist societies? It is a delusion to believe that Individuals in socialist societies were free from greed. The difference was only that they often tried to hide their riches, lest they draw the attention of the authorities or the illegal *vory*, thieves, who would blackmail them by threatening to expose them to the authorities (Volkov, 2002). Thus the difference boils down to one of flaunting one's wealth: is it really better to live in a world of concealment, of lies?

My claim is that the serious problems arise not because of the working of the model, but because it does not function as it should, because of system failures. No system works as its theoretical blueprints would make it, but to understand why the capitalist system or its possible substitutes fail, we have to look at the way economic systems function.

3 The Economic System

It is convenient to think of the actors who make up the economic system as arrayed in two planes, a primary and a secondary one. Primary actors are the individuals. But individuals almost never act as islands on their own. They act economically through organizations, the second level of agents. I focus on the latter level in this chapter, but individuals too will have a role to play later on.

Three sets of secondary actors play the economic game. The organizations that create all wealth, that produce all that we covet, are the firms. Their efficiency depends on their objectives, and these are provided by the rules of the economic game. The latter are enacted by the organizations that compose the government, a set of interconnected but only partially coordinated organizations. These organizations are also entrusted with the enforcement of these rules. There is however also a third set of actors, the illegals, who flout the rules. The actual rules of the game are the outcome of the game between the organizations of the government and the illegals, and they are what shapes the incentives that drive the firms.

3.1 Firms

Firms are the only organizations that produce all that creates welfare, and the scale of their operations and the efficiency at which they function determines the economic potential of any society. Clearly, the fewer the resources, labor and cooperating factors, that are diverted to other tasks, the better. But in a modern economy only a shrinking proportion of the labor force is employed in production proper. Of the remainder many are employed in governmental organizations and others in administrative capacities inside the firms themselves. We have to assume that at least some of these 'non-productive' workers are in some manner productive, and they can be productive by affecting the productivity of the directly productive workers, possibly indirectly. But how?

The task of the non-productive workers that are employed in firms is to manage production in the widest sense. They coordinate the work of the teams that make up the firm, monitor them, and coordinate exchange with other firms. In a modern interrelated economy their functions are clearly indispensable. The contribution of top managers, those who select the firm's strategy and chart its development course, can be paramount in determining its success or failure. But their contribution to the product and profits of the firm is much more difficult to ascertain than that of directly productive workers, and there is no intra-firm market that determines it. Their rewards are therefore determined by the firm's owners or their representatives. Here the incentive structure of the firm and problems of governance come in – will the incentives really make managers' interests conform with those of the owners?

It is usually assumed that firms seek profits or, in a dynamic framework, value. We should however remember that universities and hospitals too are firms, firms that we would not usually wish to maximize profits. Organizations do what their decision makers, i.e., their managers, deem best for themselves, for the managers, that is, what their incentives encourage their managers to do. The incentives that firm managers face depend on the economic system. Profit seeking has much to commend it: an economy whose firms seek profit can be run by decentralized markets. When decentralization breaks down, as it must in any socialist economy, then the economy has to be run in a centralized manner (Keren, 1993; 2002). A centralized bureaucratic environment endows its firms with bureaucratic incentives whose deficiencies are well known to students of socialist economies. This is the basis of the superior efficiency of the capitalist system – its ability to solve in a decentralized way the allocation problem in an economy composed of a myriad of interlocking units.

But profits have another advantage: they present a straightforward and objective success indicator that is measurable, albeit with some difficulty. It therefore provides an objective criterion by which the manager's contribution can be assessed and thereby constrain the arbitrariness of managerial compensation. This is not the case with alternative objectives which are all but impossible to quantify and lead to an arbitrary assessment of the justified reward, assessed by bureaucrats for bureaucrats. This problem is even more intractable when we come to the government sector.

In conclusion, although the success indicator of capitalism is both better for decentralization and as an objective criterion, the problem of an objective measurement of higher ups' contributions remains unsolvable, and regardless of system their remuneration cannot be but subjective.

3.2 Governmental Organizations

The State, the set of organizations that make up the executive, legislative, and judicial branches of government, consists of a multitude of distinct and often ill-coordinated bureaus. Their primary task is to set and enforce the rules of the game; those that concern the economic game are our concern.

The most basic rules are those that determine the ownership and transfer of assets. These rules define, to a large extent, the economic system. As I said above, an efficient productive sector needs a decentralized and competitive market system to function, and this cannot exist without the maintenance of an effective mechanism of law and order which protects property rights and sees to it that no party is coerced into any transactions. This cannot be provided except by a State that maintains an effective monopoly over the use of force.[2] This is the basic requirement of the market system, and it cannot be taken for granted, certainly not in transition countries, but not only in them. When individuals are not permitted to own property, and the rule of law is limited to the exclusion of individuals from State property, the economy becomes a centralized socialist one. When all

---

[2] Volkov (2002) shows that organized criminal groups can also provide protection for property and contract, but the price they exact is high and can be prohibitive. Furthermore, they would also, as part of their services, exclude competitive entry – not a desideratum of an efficient market.

individuals are permitted to own property and all are granted legal protection, we have one of the necessary conditions for a capitalist market economy.

The extent of State involvement in economic life is another variable. Sometimes the choice of the rules of ownership restricts the State's involvement: once individuals have been excluded from the ownership of productive assets, markets become impossible and the State is forced into resource allocation (Keren, 1993, 2002). But even the most limited State, the State that aims at the least involvement in economic life, is forced into the provision of some basic services, namely those that enforce the law and protect the realm. Most States extend the range of the services they provide over a wider gamut of markets and very often prohibit the supply of certain goods and services, e.g., drugs, gambling and prostitution. As we shall see below, these markets are thus singled out to become the preserve of the illegals, and the breeding ground of organized crime.

It should be remembered that State organizations are staffed by individuals who have their own interests. It cannot be assumed that they are always permeated with the aims of the State, whatever these may be. It is the incentive mechanism of these organizations that determines the actual decisions of the individuals who run the bureaus and the latter's actions.

The contribution of the State, the maintenance of law and order, although essential for the economy and society, is next to impossible to gauge. It is therefore all but impossible to determine salary scale that will at one and the same time be incentive compatible and just – i.e., equate payment to indirect productivity, and also be generally agreed to be anything but arbitrary. Salaries are determined bureaucratically, often result from a power struggle, and are usually perceived not to correspond to productivity. And there is another dilemma: there is always the tension between the need to enlist able civil servants, and this popular perception that they do not deserve whatever they get.

3.3 The Illegals

In any society, any economy, there are those who do not obey the rules of the game and try to live off goods and services produced by others. They are an inseparable part of the economic system, although most descriptions and analyses disregard them. One of the primary lessons of transition has been that their role has been critical: where the Mafyia (Handelman, 1995), the Russian-type mafia, became too strong, the path of transition became very bumpy.

The illegal sector is composed of a multitude of single operators as well as larger groups of organized crime. Criminals as such do not produce anything. They divert to themselves some of the output produced by others. They may also own productive establishment, which thus belong to both the productive and the illegal sector. These productive firms may be of two types: they may supply goods or services prohibited by law, but they may also be perfectly legal establishments. In the former type they take advantage of the markets set aside by the government to become the mafia's monopolies, whose profits are often invested in the legal, second type business (Fiorentini and Peltzman, 1995; Volkov, 2002).

Illegals often infiltrate the other sectors, in particular government organizations. In this manner they may manage to influence legislation in ways that benefit them, or may protect themselves against the hands of the law. Infiltration of productive firms may enable them to divert resources. Both of these methods proved to be significant in Russian transition.

Since they only damage the economy and their contribution is negative, illegals do not deserve any positive income. What they do in fact receive should be regarded as a random tax. Its relevance in the present context lies beyond the obvious wounds inflicted on any conceivable ethical principles. It does also damage the system in general by affecting firms' incentives. When the mafia becomes very strong and takes over the provision of law and order, firms' chances of survival, let alone success, often depend on their relations with the underworld, not on any productive effort. It strengthens the criminal instincts in the business community and selects against honest business in favor of the venal and dishonest.

4 Where Do the Ethics Go Wrong? Crime, Corruption and Capture

The capitalist model has recently failed on two grounds: in some transition countries it failed because the State failed in its most basic task of property protection. In the established markets of the west it failed because of serious problems of governance. The former problems are in principle solvable. Elsewhere, in OECD countries, they have been solved and although cases of fraud and theft do occur there, they are the exception. In Eastern Europe they can arguably be blamed on the previous socialist regime which destroyed property relations and left behind devastation that requires a speedy formation of institutions that have elsewhere taken centuries to build. This is not an easy or simple task. It involves the establishment of a state of law of a type that has not existed before. Although it cannot be solved from one day to the next, given time, it will be solved, even though its ill effects, such as the initial distribution of assets and riches that has been created in the absence of State-supplied law and order, are likely to persist. Problems of governance, on the other hand, are perhaps insolvable in principle. At the very least, so far they have nowhere been solved, and they are therefore by far a more serious challenge.

Subsection 4.1 argues that the simple textbook case assumes settled and secure property relations and simple exchange, and therefore raises no governance issues. The latter arise when we come to terms with the fact that most firms are managed by hired managers (subsection 4.2). Subsection 4.3 examines the effects of transition with its insecure property relations. Subsection 4.4 discusses the tendency of the business sector to capture the government agencies that are entrusted with the control of business and markets.

4.1 The Textbook Case

In the simple textbook capitalist market there are only owner operated firms, no government and no illegals. The qualities of all goods are transparent, all exchanges are immediate and synchronous, and no complex contracts are required. There are no disputes regarding ownership or contract enforcement – there is no need for any dispute settling and violence wielding authority, no government. No effort is required to operate firms, and effort as such is not a productive input. Hence the identity of the manager is of no import and there is therefore no place for a market for managerial services. And since all owners wish to maximize their consumption, for which they have to exert no effort, profit maximization follows, and the competitive equilibrium results, provided of course that the necessary conditions hold. It should be noted that this simple strong outcome depends on the strong simplifying assumptions listed above, that in reality never hold.

4.2 Berle and Means, and the Governance of the Firm

Berle and Means' *Modern Corporation and Private Property*, published in 1932, highlighted the fact that the simple model of Subsection 4.1 rarely applies in reality. Hired managers are the rule, and they require proper incentives if their interests are to mesh with those of the owners. Incentives have to answer two criteria: they have to drive the manager to seek profits and they have to make him exert the proper amount of effort on his job. Since managers may differ in their aptitudes, this also opens up a market for managerial services. Thus a simple tie of income to profits will not do the trick, since each firm has to assure its manager the minimum alternative income available in alternative jobs, given her managerial aptitude.

These desiderata open up the field of firm governance. The basic difficulty is that the manager's contribution is hard to calculate even in a capitalist profit-based production sector. Current profits are an important measure, but they owe to past investments and to general market conditions as much as to the current manager's efforts. And the most important part of the manager's current effort may relate to his investment decisions, whose fruits may be harvested by her successors. Hence there is no simple gauge to assess a manager's contribution. The organizational response is double pronged:

- Bonuses or options – an explicit or implicit contract with the manager which ties her salary to the owners' goals, e.g., by awarding bonuses that are related to some measurable index of success, e.g., to the value of the firm's shares, and
- Oversight – a board representing the owners is appointed to evaluate the manager's performance and determine her reward, given the contract.

Both parts of the response are open to abuse and explain much of the failures of capitalist distribution to conform to the model and the consequent malaise of capitalism. Let me take them up in sequence.

Bonuses. These can take various forms, from a simple function of profits or share price, a change in either of these, to options which may be exercised at given dates. The advantage of the latter is their high leverage: the marginal increase in share price is what provides a large rise in income, thus presumably providing a serious incentive for the exertion of intensive managerial effort. The disadvantage of all these methods is that they tie rewards to momentary indicators, which, at the best of times, have a large random element in them.[3] What is even worse – and was not sufficiently realized before the scandals of the last couple of years – is that over the short run indicators can be manipulated by managers. The selective release of information, e.g., through doctored accounts, can fool investors and help raise share prices for a while, permitting managers to cash in on their bonuses and options. This was done by hiding costs in off-balance-sheet entities (*Enron* and *Parmalat*), advancing future sales to the present (*Xerox*) or registering current costs as investment (*WorldCom*).[4] Can this be remedied?

Boards of directors and the market for managerial talent. The primary task of the owners' committee that selects and oversees the manager is doubtlessly the choice of the CEO. This single decision may make or break a firm: a Jack Welch or a Bill Gates can raise the value of a firm by billions of dollar, while a failing CEO may lead it to bankruptcy. Executive pay also plays the role of a signal: its cost is less important than its message, 'we have found a promising CEO – look at what we are ready to pay him.' Hence the board has an incentive to raise top managerial rewards.

A ratchet principle is involved here: the base line from which remuneration committees start is the average reward paid to other CEOs at similar firms. Hence any contract that specifies an income that lies below this average is a signal that a sub-average manager has been selected, not a choice in which the committee will be proud. This in itself is one of the causes for the inexorable rise in executive salaries (Economist, 2003b).

But there is also a more sinister reason for high managerial incomes: those who sit on boards of directors are themselves present or aspiring CEOs, and as such they have an interest in a high level of CEO rewards. One remedy might seem to be the addition of directors who are not themselves managers. But these, unless they are themselves past managers, have no experience running firms and less likely to be effective monitors.[5]

It hardly deserves an explanation why the most blatant cases of misgovernance in the West appeared when the dotcom cycle was at its crest. As well as an opportunity, a high enough return is needed before acts which border on the illegal are undertaken. Potentially huge returns were available when the stock market was climbing very fast, when gullible punters were eager to discover shares that may help them make a killing. Under these circumstances it was relatively easy to influence share movements over the short period by manipulating information regarding, say, profits. Overstated profits could lead to a sharp rise in share prices that could be used to cash in options. The important point however is that these events point toward loopholes in the system of governance that have yet to be plugged.

---

[3] For novel incentive instruments, see Economist (2004d).
[4] See Economist, 2001, 2003a, 2004a, 2004e.
[5] Bebchuk and Fried (2004) raise the critical issue of directors' incentives – another unsolved problem.

4.3 Criminals

Some of the misdeeds of western managers in the late 1990s are in the nature of punishable crimes, and their perpetrators have been or may be punished. But the main problems with illegals have appeared in transition countries and were best publicized in the Russian Republic, and not in the developed west where the protection of property and contract is relatively satisfactory. Corruption and criminality in transition countries can be blamed on two causes, the inheritance of a criminal sector from the communist past and the lack of essential market institutions. These two causes affected different countries to a very different degree. Russia and the other new states which inherited the old Soviet Union suffered most; Poland and Hungary least.

It is important to remember that the Russian Federation is a new state. It did inherit many of the apparatuses of power from the SU, but in a radically altered context. In particular, in a state whose center is weakened and whose periphery, the provinces and republics, which have always been more corrupt than the central authorities in Moscow, strengthened.[6] The weak State was quite unable to provide the protection of property and contract that the nascent market required, and its leaders possibly did not see the establishment of law and order as an essential priority (Volkov, 2002). In the days of communism the forces of law were used to protect State property from potential marauders. This is what these forces inherited from the previous regime, and the new leadership did not invest any priority in their reorientation. What was even more serious – these forces were not even able to protect as yet unprivatized State property from being grabbed by private individuals. This was the stage on which the privatization drama was to unfold.

We have ample information regarding the illegals in the Soviet Union: Handelman (1995), who coined the term Mafiya, provides a colorful picture of its inception in the communist system and its growth in transition Russia. Volkov (2002) provides a full up-to-date history as well as a fascinating analysis of the processes that have transformed a previous purely criminal sector into a provider of services which are usually the preserve of the state. Even the coercive communist state was unable to subdue violent criminals, and corruption was encouraged by the extensive arbitrary powers and latitude granted to the bureaucracy by the economic system. With its disintegration and the weakened control over the law enforcers – whose domains have suddenly changed – additional forces joined in to try to get control over the State's property. The result was the kleptocracy that led to the concentration of much of the nation's property in the hands of a handful of oligarchs.

It is customary to blame this outcome on shock therapy, on the transition to capitalism that progressed too rapidly. This is plainly wrong. The real problem was that transition was too *slow* because the essentials of capitalism, clear boundaries of ownership and a hard budget constraint, have started to appear only after the crisis of 1998. Until then the corrupt State continued to support private firms that had a hold on it, and the remnants of State property were being taken over by

---

[6]   See Keren (2000), Mohacsi Nagy (2000), Volkov (2002).

oligarchs with inside connections. There were three villains in the play: enterprising individuals, the illegals of the budding Mafiya, and their corrupt allies in governmental bureaus. The result was a rapid transfer to favored private individuals of the jewels of State property at a tiny fraction of their value. This was crowned by the 'shares for loans' scandal. As a result Russia became a State with extreme inequalities of property ownership. Even now the machinery of law and order is not functioning, and the illegals of the Mafiya, or, with the passage of time, private protection agencies, have become the main protectors of property and contract.[7] The strongest evidence to this fact is the stark difference between the process of transition in the Visegrad countries of Eastern Europe, where the state never collapsed and where there was no mass takeover of industry by either oligarchs or organized crime. These countries have gone much farther on the road to a viable capitalist market, even though privatization in them – the Czech Republic is an exception – was much slower.

The State started its slow reemergence as the pretender to the position of the monopolist wielder of violence fairly late, after the economic collapse of 1998, and with it began the taming of the illegal forces of order. By now the State monitors private providers of protection to property, and a fairly satisfactory security is bought at a higher price than would be possible if the State would have provided it as a monopoly.

It may now seem that Putin has found the way to establish the rule of law in Russia. The fight against the oligarchs who have amassed their fortunes illegally may seem to be just such an example. The problem is that he seems to be using the powers of the law as a whip against his enemies, as an example of what can be done to anybody, be it an oligarch, who may cross him. Thus it is *his* law and *his* order that he imposes, and not the letter of an impersonal law that rules by the book. Law has again become a weapon in the ruler's hands, as it was under communism. It would be quite different if Putin would have announced openly that all the thefts of public property in the early 1990s are to be prosecuted, i.e., that all privatization outcomes will be reopened. But that would imperil the economic upsurge that has started in Russia and may plunge it back into a long period of decline.

The serious problem is that the ill-effects of the last decade of the 20th Century are not easy to correct. The Putin-Khodorkovsky drama which is unfolding before our eyes provides a timely warning (Economist, 2003c). It is therefore likely that the highly skewed distribution of wealth that has been established in the period of kleptocracy will be in place for decades to come, and that the establishment of a rule of law and order in the manner known in the West will take some time. The eradication of the injustices of the past is too costly.

4.4 Regulation and Capture

Faced with market failure, governments often resort to regulation or nationalization

---

[7] See Volkov (2002) for a fascinating description of the transition of illegal wielders of violence into law abiding capitalist protection agencies.

of the offending sectors. These remedies are problematic: not only do state-ownership and regulation often lead to waste – and this has been the focus of extensive literature, but regulators (and this term will subsume bureaus that oversee state enterprises) are often captured by the industries they are supposed to control. The likelihood of capture is even greater when the government does nationalize. The reason is simple: the regulator, or the government bureau that monitors and is to control the State-owned firm, needs information. The experts in the field are mostly involved with the regulated firms. Often the staff of the regulating agency is recruited from these very same industries. As a result the regulator often becomes regulated by his wards, and the industries manage to soften their budget constraint, enabling their stakeholders to raise their incomes. When the service in question is a monopoly, strikes and threats of strikes may also serve to raise the rents of employees above their contribution. It is interesting that these sins against the income distribution principles of capitalism are not usually mentioned when the iniquities of the system are catalogued.

5 Are There Remedies?

Can capitalism remedy its injustices within the capitalist system? Or is an outsider, the State, required to set capitalism right? Is there an alternative, e.g., socialism, that can create a more just society, even at a price? Subsection 5.1 opens with an attempt to answer the last question, and subsection 5.2 argues that transition countries will eventually end up as working market economies, but subsection 5.3 argues the system cannot of itself and within itself remedy its defects and that government assistance is necessary. Section 5.4 argues that, to be effective, government has to be small, not to extend itself into every nook and cranny where its help may be desired.

5.1 Is Socialism a Remedy?

What exactly is socialism? Some may call a western welfare state a social democratic economy. This, in the present framework, would be a misnomer, because such a state is really a capitalist market with extensive redistribution and public services. It would be subject to all the ills of capitalism, possibly ameliorated by regulation – as is suggested below.

The definition of socialism that I use below is Marxian, i.e., a system in which all productive assets are State-owned. I have argued elsewhere (Keren, 1993; 2002) why such a system cannot operate in a decentralized manner as a socialist market, and space does not permit me to repeat the arguments here. Thus socialism must per force run a centralized economy whose dysfunctions have been known for a long time. In particular, it cannot provide its members with a standard of life that is close to that provided by a decentralized market economy. But is it any more just than a capitalist system?

Income distribution in a centralized economy is concentrated in the hands of a small number of people, whose decisions are then 'corrected' by the intervention of the illegals inside and outside the governmental structure. It is well-known that large income differentials emerged in the Soviet empire, interregionally and intra-regionally. The basic structure of wages was arbitrary, and sectors that seemed worthy received high incomes. The main difference may have been that income differentials were not publicized and remained hidden, partly because they were not converted immediately into consumption differences. In particular, high incomes were not flaunted, lest they attract undesirable attention from the internal intelligence services or from illegals, who used blackmail to convince their prey to part with their riches.

In other words, the main difference does not lie in the principle, but in its execution in an atmosphere of fear and lawlessness. Those in power had as much ability and opportunities to obtain undeserved incomes, but the general atmosphere of suspicion restrained them from overdoing their self-enrichment. Will the same constraint necessarily exist in any future socialist system? This is by no means sure, since with economic concentration comes political power, and socialism can possibly degenerate into a pure autocracy, with no limits on the powers of the ruler, as it seems to have happened in North Korea. In that case we can easily arrive at extreme income inequalities and injustices. Furthermore, the vast power which the ruler and his henchmen possess in a centralized economy, by itself creates enormous political and social inequalities which are at least as unjust as income inequalities.

5.2 The Rule of Law

The rule of law took centuries to set up in the West, and it will take decades to establish in Russia. Present event are a timely reminder to the complexity of the situation. Today's distribution of riches resulted from the kleptocratic anarchy of the early 1990s, and not a single oligarch earned his possessions lawfully and justly. Up to the Khodorkovsky case it was widely agreed that the deals by which State property was transferred to the private sector should not be re-examined and annulled. It was felt that this risks returning the economy into renewed anarchy and a serious plunge in the level of output and standard of living, which has at long last started to rise. It was generally agreed that bygones should be bygones, and that the rule of law should be enforced into the future but not into the past.[8]

This general agreement may have been shaken by the audacity of Putin. His decision to single out one of the oligarchs, be he the richest of the lot, for special treatment, strengthens the arbitrariness of the ruler and the ability of every bureaucrat to act arbitrarily. This ability, which has been used extensively by the mafia – e.g., the threat of using sanitary and fire inspections in order to extract protection – weakens the state of law that the market requires. Markets need impersonal rules, rules that do not depend on the identities of the parties to any dispute. This is not the message of the present battle against Khodorkovsky (FT, 2003).

---

[8] E.g., Economist (2003b). Even Volkov (2002) is of this opinion.

To underscore this point: the powers of the State to impose law and order have to be strengthened, but its meddling in economic affairs has to be vastly reduced. The authority of bureaucrats to grant or refuse permits and licenses, their ability to harass business, provides them with the power to extract bribes. This authority must therefore be drastically curtailed until a new generation of honest bureaucrats is bred.

But this does not mean that the rule of law and capitalist justice will not arrive. It only means that it may take longer than the optimists have believed. Economic and social pressures will eventually make property and contract as secure in the advanced economies of the former Soviet Bloc as they are in the West.

5.3 Why Regulation is Necessary

The governance failures which we see in the West are much more serious for the capitalist system. These are defects which cannot be blamed on another system, a predecessor. They are symptoms of unworkability of the basic safeguards of the system. They are fundamental system failures, and like market failures can only be treated from outside the system, i.e., by the government. Consider just two issues, the position of the external accountant and that of top management.

Accountants are supposed to be the agents of the owners, the watchdogs for the shareholders, whose task is to report on the true financial state of the firm. They are supposed to check the activities of the firm and to make sure that funds are not diverted to the personal use of the staff, and that information provided to the owners and the markets regarding the firm's profitability does correspond with the accountants' best judgment. But what are the accountants' own interests? Do the owners get from the accountants all that they are paying for? Herein lies a basic failure of the system which is not simple to remedy.

The first question, that of incentives: He who pays the piper calls the tune, and it is the managers who choose the piper and pay him. Can this be changed? Can the shareholders choose the accountant? Obviously not, because they are, in all interesting cases, splintered among groups of conflicting aims and interests, and to let a single group of shareholders call the tune may be a cure that is worse than the original disease.[9]

Attempts have been made to limit the services provided by the accountants to 'bean counting' as the *Economist* likes to call their basic task, and to rotate them frequently, in order to avoid collusion between them and managers. But accountants gain specific human capital and insight into the firm's operations when they go through the firm's books, and frequent changes would waste these assets. Furthermore, since they also have information on the markets which they gain through the inspection of other firms' accounts, it would be a waste to deprive the firm's management of their advice. Hence the attempt to create Chinese Walls between the basic task of the accountant and his role as an advisor is doomed to fail.

---

[9] A new experiment lets the audit committee select the auditor, but this may create dysfunctional tensions with the directors (Economist, 2004c).

The problems with control over managerial behavior and compensation are similar, and have been discussed above (subsection 4.2). The outside directors who are to evaluate the CEO are usually picked by him and are therefore indebted to him. And when there are strong groups of shareholders who can impose their own directors, we are back to the incentives of the directors themselves (subsection 4.2).

It is clear that firms cannot be left alone to take care of these governance failures. Does the system, the competitive capitalist market help them? Clearly not, as the above discussion shows. The question is whether the external guardian of the system, the government, can help by proper regulation. There is little doubt that outside bodies like the SEC can help police firms. The question is whether the checking of managers' remuneration can be thrust upon government agencies, and whether the behavior of accountants can be policed by outside bodies. The serious problem is that such policing is very hard to institute without a clear code of behavior, and that such a code invites attempts of evasion by stepping on the border of the permitted or just beyond it.

Furthermore, it is widely agreed that a radical reduction of average managerial compensation is urgently required. But this has to be done without giving up the incentives embodied in managerial rewards, i.e., the fruits of success of a successful manager. This can surely not be done by the heavy hand of a regulator. Thus it is by no means clear how the ills of the system can be remedied.[10]

5.4 Limits to Government?

The previous section has suggested the addition of another task to the government, a set of organizations that is already overburdened with duties that it finds very hard to fulfill. Since the safeguarding of the economic system should be seen as one of fundamental duties of any government, it should surely receive a high priority in the long list of its obligations.

But the government should be thought of as a huge administrative system which cannot easily tie the rewards of its members to their contribution. It therefore has to police itself to make sure that all its parts are on their job and that no collusion with the illegals is taking place. Each bureau needs to be kept attuned to changing circumstances. This is an enormous task. In the business sector this is accomplished through competition, which weeds out those organizations that do not manage to keep up with the changing environment. In the public sector this has to be done bureaucratically. But there is a limit to the span of control of the controller, a limit to the number of functions that a bureau can oversee effectively. This limit means that each additional task that is undertaken by the government reduces the mean efficiency with which all other services are being provided. Hence, to be effective, the government has to limit itself to those tasks that have the highest priority. If it is a priority that the economy run efficiently and fairly,

---

[10] But see the latest suggestion by *The Economist*: force CEOs to announce their intention to sell shares in the companies they manage a week ahead of the sale, to permit the market to gauge their hidden private information (Economist, 2004b).

those tasks that are essential for this aim need to receive priority and others have to be given up. Such a self-abnegation is not easy to find among politicians, who are incessantly called upon to correct all conceivable and inconceivable ills that members of the public meet. In other words, to be able to avoid the most damaging cases of injustice, the State may have to forgo the desire to undo all injustices.

6 Conclusions: We Know Too Little

The experiences of the last dozen years have highlighted some of the ethical flaws of capitalism, some of those aspects of the system that make it diverge from its principles of distribution. Those who sit near the levers of economic power have found ways to enrich themselves far beyond their deserts, while at the same time depriving others of their hard-won savings (Economist, 2001). We have seen the diversion of State property in the transition countries of Eastern Europe, and we have seen unfair stock exchange practices and the dereliction of duty by accountants in the US and Western Europe. The former are really the fault of the socialist system, which destroyed the definition of property, and allowed those who knew, with the help of the Mafiya, to pull the strings of power, to take hold of the best parts of the riches of Russia, and impoverish the great majority. The system there will surely be set right in due course, but the initial highly skewed distribution of assets is likely to entrench poverty for years to come.

The problems with the West are more serious, and show basic faults with the capitalist system. Our ethical model was built on the assumption of owner-managers and not on huge firms, managed by hired CEOs, who may be tempted to use any kind of subterfuge to increase their own wealth while destroying that of the owners. These problems, we saw, cannot be remedied within the capitalist system, and have to be tackled from the outside by the chief guardian of the system, the State. Regulation is required to control the operations of managers and accountants.

Here our ignorance comes in: we do not yet have the proper tools to deal with the problems which the economic system is facing. The problems have been with us since the beginning of capitalism, but the long years of triumphal prosperity of the 1990s, the belief in the New Economy, the very realization that the fate of mammoth firms depends on the wisdom and intuition of a single CEO, have assured a privileged group of individuals that they deserve untold riches, and opened the dam to a flood of gargantuan incomes even as a payment for failure. They have pointed out loopholes in the system, but nobody yet knows how to plug them.

References

Bebchuk, L. and Fried J. (2004), Pay without Performance: The Unfulfilled Promise of Executive Compensation, http://ssrn.com/abstract=537783.

Berle A. and Means G. (1932), *The Modern Corporation and Private Property*, Macmillan, New York.

Economist (2001), Enron: The Twister Hits, *The Economist*, 17 January 2002.

Economist (2003a), Corporate Culture: When Something Is Rotten, *The Economist*, 25 July 2002.

Economist, (2003b), Executive Pay: Fat Cats Feeding, *The Economist*, 9 October 2003.

Economist (2003c), Russia: Vlad the Impaler, *The Economist*, 30 October 2003.

Economist (2004a), Skimming off the Cream, *The Economist*, 22 January 2004.

Economist (2004b), Corporate Crime: Lead Bosses not into Temptation, *The Economist*, 26 February 2004.

Economist (2004c), Non-executive Directors: Where's All the Fun Gone? *The Economist*, 18 March 2004.

Economist (2004d), Executive Compensation: A Better Option, *The Economist*, 15 April 2004.

Economist (2004e), Pay for Performance: Running Out of Options, *The Economist*, 9 December.

Fiorentini G. and Peltzman S. (1995), Introduction, in: Fiorentini G. and Peltzman S. (eds) (1995) *The Economics of Organized Crime*, Cambridge University Press, Cambridge, UK.

FT (2003), Wagstyl S., Jack A. and Ostrovsky A. (2003), A Creeping Bureaucratic Coup, *Financial Times*, 3 November 2003.

Handelman S. (1995), *Comrade Criminal. Russia's New Mafiya*, Yale University Press, New Haven.

Keren M. (1993), On the (Im)Possibility of Market Socialism, *Eastern Economic Journal*, 19, 3, pp. 333-344. An earlier version appears in Kennett D. and Lieberman M. (eds) (1993), *The Road to Capitalism: Economic Transformation in Eastern Europe and the Former Soviet Union*, The Dryden Press, Harcourt Brace Jovanovich, New York, pp. 45-52.

Keren M. (2000), An Essay on the Political Economy of Transition: How the Collapse of the Russian State Led to Russian Non-Transition, *The Soviet and Post-Soviet Review*, 27,1 (2000), pp. 7-16.

Keren M. (2002), Socialism and Stalinism: Never the Twain Shall Part?, or Why Can't We, the Public, Choose Liberal Socialism?, paper presented at the meeting of the *European Public Choice Society* in Belgrad, 4-7th April, 2002.

Mohacsi Nagy P. (2000), *The Meltdown of the Russian State: The Deformation and Collapse of the State in Russia*, Edward Elgar, Cheltenham, UK.

Volkov V. (2002), *Violent Entrepreneurs: The Use of Force in the Making of Russian Capitalism*, Cornell University Press, Ithaca and London.

Chapter 3

How Capitalism Lost its Soul:
From Protestant Ethics to Robber Barons

Marie-Laure Djelic

1 Introduction

A serious discussion of capitalism and its development cannot avoid the confrontation, at one moment or another, with ethical issues. Historically, there have been quite a number of different positions in the debate – giving us a sense that the confrontation is, indeed, a complex one. When it comes to the connection between ethics and capitalism, we can differentiate between at least four different ideal typical perspectives.

First, we find what we call the missionary perspective. 'Missionaries' are in general associated with the liberal tradition. They picture capitalism as a deeply and naturally ethical system and as, in fact, a structural condition for the development and stabilization of ethical behavior. Discussions in the 1990s around the corruption and dysfunctions associated with the Communist heritage fit in there. The idea was that unethical behavior on a large-scale was a systemic heritage from the Communist times and that the move towards a capitalist logic was the necessary precondition to ethics and ethical behavior in the economy. Missionaries tend to believe, and argue, that the capitalist market necessarily goes together with political freedom and democracy, and together with social but also moral progress (Knight, 1982; Knight and Merriam, 1979; Hayeck, 1962).

A second perspective can be termed here 'Nietzschean' in that it positions capitalism beyond – or before – ethics. Here again, the intellectual inspiration can be traced back to classical liberalism but the focus has been the 'natural', i.e. pre-historical, pre-social and hence pre-ethical character of the capitalist logic. There is a double consequence here. On the one hand, capitalism as a natural order is ultimately inescapable and unavoidable. On the other hand, the boundaries between ethics and capitalism are and should be watertight. The business of business is to make profits and create wealth. Ethical preoccupations should remain absent from both the capitalist logic and the economic realm so as not to muddy and tamper with natural forces and dynamics (Friedman, 1962; Brennan and Hamlin, 1995). Within this second perspective, capitalism is an a-moral economic order that can readily articulate with different types of social, political and ethical systems. It can, in particular, accommodate itself of political dictatorship as the cohabitation in

Chile between the 'Chicago Boys' and the Pinochet regime has for example historically shown (Valdès, 1995; Fourcade-Gourinchas and Babb, 2002).

The third perspective is a critical one and the argument here is that capitalism is a profoundly and essentially unethical system. Critical perspectives have different intellectual roots but they are in particular associated with certain strands of Christian thought and with the Marxist tradition broadly understood (Leo XIII, 1891; Pius XI, 1931; Belloc, 1977; Marx and Engels, 1998; Wallerstein, 2000). Individual greed and power are the motors of the capitalist logic and the consequence, from that perspective, is exploitation. Exploitation in turn can manifest itself in many different forms – between individuals, across classes, gender, ethnic or religious groups or across nations for example. Here, the logical consequence is that overcoming the capitalist logic is a necessary precondition to an ethical world – likely to be reached only through a revolutionary platform. Such a perspective had been considerably weakened during the 1990s with the demise of Communism. However, the consequences of globalization for certain groups and countries associated with the multiplication of corporate scandals, at the heart of the capitalist system, have recently revived that perspective, at least within parts of the anti-globalization movement.

We label the fourth ideal-typical perspective the 'regulatory one.' The argument here is that capitalism is not a naturally ethical or self-regulating system. The idea, though, is that it can be – and needs to be – combined with regulatory efforts to create the conditions for ethical behaviors and interactions (Dunning, 2001; 2003). Ethics can be defined, from that perspective, either as locally and generally nationally grounded codes of conduct or else as a set of universally applicable norms (Küng, 2003). With the first definition, the regulatory effort will likely be driven by the national state or national political institutions (Clegg, Ibarra-Colado and Bueno-Rodriques, 1998). The second definition implies a quite different regulatory frame, where states play a role but are not the only actors. Transnational organizations and bodies, of a semi-public and even sometimes of a private nature, will also be involved in this case in the regulatory effort (Djelic and Quack, 2003, Drori et al., 2003, Djelic and Sahlin-Andersson, 2005). This is the Menchevik tradition that has inspired many reformist programs. The Keynesian New Deal also fits here and so does a fair share of the contemporary debates on the limits and dangers potentially associated with globalization.

In most historical periods, those four perspectives have co-existed, representing different intellectual and practical positions on the connection between ethics and capitalism. Interestingly, empirical evidence can be found to ground all four of those perspectives – although the bodies of data and the methods for data collection will naturally vary. The objective of this chapter is to overcome the dichotomy and the opposition between those four perspectives. We engage in a genealogical journey and we show that the story is not one of all or nothing. Capitalism, we argue has gone historically from being a system with a strong ethical foundation to, in a sense, 'losing its soul' under a combination of different kinds of pressures. The contemporary consequence is that capitalism is indeed today a-moral or a-ethical (rather than immoral or unethical). As a consequence, in the present context, we argue that combining capitalism with an ethical agenda will call for regulatory intervention. The decision to do so is ultimately political, in the deepest sense of the term (Weber, 1959). Such a decision should reflect the priorities of given human and social collectives (as expressed in national states or wider transnational entities such as the European Union for example). But this chapter clearly claims, in the end, that the 'iron cage' of capitalism cannot be assumed today to be a spontaneous ethical order and to self-regulate as such.

The chapter starts by unearthing the missing ethical link in the liberal tradition. The idea is to show that Adam Smith, the father of liberalism, did not in fact argue that capitalism was a spontaneous and natural ethical order. Rather, a full reading of Smith shows that the ethical character of capitalism depended upon the existence of a code of morality deeply inscribed in individual actors. We show the similarities between this perspective and that developed by Max Weber to explain the structuration of modern rational capitalism. Here again, a profound ethical structure was shown to underpin and foster the development of capitalism. Then, we turn to the next stages – when this deep structure progressively faded away and capitalism 'lost its soul.' A marking moment, there, is the period of 'Robber Barons' capitalism in the United States (Josephson, 1932). We show the combined impact, then, of ideological shifts and profound structural transformations. Ultimately, this leads us to argue, in the conclusion, that contemporary capitalism is a-ethical and that regulatory intervention is necessary if we want capitalism to combine with a particular ethical agenda.

2 Adam Smith and the Missing Ethical Link

Let us start from the widely shared assumption that Adam Smith's *An Inquiry into the Nature and Causes of the Wealth of Nations*, first published in 1776, was a defining work that played a key role in the emergence of the modern field and science of economics (Smith, 1999). As such, this particular book has significantly contributed to the ideological and institutional structuring of modern capitalism (Blaug, 1986; Manent, 1987; Fourcade-Gourinchas, 2001). Going back to the text and to the context of its production is illuminating. It shows, in particular, that Adam Smith had deep ethical preoccupations but that the latter did not find their way into *The Wealth of Nations*. Smith's ethics are to be found in his first book, *The Theory of Moral Sentiments*, originally published in 1759 – a work that has been on the whole ignored (Smith, 1982; but see Coase, 1976). Such 'division of thought' would prove to be extremely consequential and the 'bible' of modern capitalism is, in a sense, missing one leg – the ethical one.

2.1 Smith and the Liberal Inspiration

In his economic thinking, Adam Smith was building and expanding upon the contributions of the great founders of political liberalism – John Locke in particular. For John Locke, a state of nature predated the social contract. In contrast to Hobbes, however, Locke's picture of the state of nature was not one of essentially chaotic and destructive anarchy. Instead, this state of nature was stabilized by natural law – the right to private property based on the work of the individual. In the state of nature, each individual was facing nature and interactions between these individuals turned around, precisely, that interface. These interactions had to do with work, the products of work, property and ownership. Pre-political man – 'natural' man – was clearly in that context an economic man before anything else (Manent, 1986; Locke, 1997). The social and political contract came only after, as a reaction to potential and real threats to the natural order. And the role of this social and political contract was merely to create a collective responsibility for the respect of natural law – hence for the protection of private property.

Building upon the idea of 'natural man' as economic man, Adam Smith re-affirmed strongly both the autonomy of the economic sphere and its moral and historical precedence over all other spheres of human life (Smith, 1999). The systematic disembeddedness and self-contained character of economic activity so characteristic of most orthodox economic thinking in the 19th and 20th centuries follow directly upon that. Adam Smith then also took over the idea that this preeminent and autonomous economic sphere was by nature a stable state, structured as it was by 'natural laws' – in this case division of labor, invisible hand and competition. Economic or natural man had, according to Adam Smith, a natural propensity to 'truck, barter and exchange one thing for another', to exchange the fruits of individual labor (Smith, 1999, p. 117). The market was in fact a natural, emergent and essential reality of human and social life stemming from this very propensity. The propensity to exchange had for direct consequence that each individual did not have to rely only on herself to provide for the whole range of her needs. She could find answers to parts of those needs on the market and obtain them in exchange for the things she produced. The extent and complexity of the division of labor depended upon, in each historical period, the spread and density of the market. The latter was itself in direct correlation with the demographic context and with the development of infrastructural conditions allowing exchange and the transportation of goods (Smith, 1999, I, iii). Adam Smith went even further. He argued that the historically progressive extension and expansion of markets and the associated advance of the division of labor meant, ultimately, greater individual and collective well being as well as, in fact, moral, social and political progress away from feudalism and towards yeomanry, away from tyranny and towards democracy (Smith, 1999, III).

Another 'natural law', according to Adam Smith, was that markets were orderly. The miracle of that order was that it did not stem from an all-knowing, all-powerful regulator or planner. Rather, it emerged from a multiplicity of transactions and their combination. The collective good was achieved not by planning it but by leaving free rein to the natural propensity of market players to maximize their individual welfare and personal gains. The image used by Adam Smith to illustrate the idea of the Invisible Hand has become quite famous.

> It is not from the benevolence of the butcher, the brewer or the baker that we expect our dinner, but from their regard to their own interest. We address ourselves not to their

humanity but to their self-love and never talk to them of our own necessities but of their advantage (Smith, 1999, p. 119).

Ultimately, however, the multiplicity of such acts motivated by individual selfishness led to a collective good. The greediness of individuals turned, through combination in the market, into a morally satisfying and welfare maximizing collective order. This was the miracle of the invisible hand, which required however specific conditions.

In particular, the invisible hand would not come to play lest free rein was left to the competitive mechanism. Competition emerged, in the work of Adam Smith, as a basic, natural and structuring principle of the market. In a market where competition was left free rein, the scarcity of a particular good should naturally lead to the emergence of new providers and over supply should in turn discourage some of the producers. In both cases, this would mean that the balance between demand and offer could be reestablished. However, this could happen only if the market was left to function freely. Smith mentioned the large number of players, the free flow of goods, resources and information, as key conditions for the free play of the competitive mechanism (Smith, 1999, I, vii). At the same time, Smith pointed to different forms of tampering with the market mechanism that he argued should be avoided or at least limited as much as possible. One was about individual market players themselves and 'people of the same trade' who 'seldom meet together, even for merriment and diversion, but the conversation ends in a conspiracy against the public, or in some contrivance to raise prices' (Smith, 1999, I, x, 232). This part of Adam Smith's work has generally been neglected but it is clear that Adam Smith was conscious that competitive markets – where the miracle of the invisible hand can play its part – were not automatically self-sustaining. He was conscious furthermore that the threats could come from individual players and private interests themselves. The other, more obvious form of tampering, which has been so symbolically associated with economic liberalism – in the European sense of the term – since Adam Smith, is that to be attributed to the state and political authorities. Adam Smith systematically and regularly denounced this form of tampering with 'naturally self-regulating markets'.

> No regulation of commerce can increase the quantity of industry in any society beyond what its capital can maintain. It can only divert a part of it into a direction into which it might not otherwise have gone: and it is by no means certain that this artificial direction is likely to be more advantageous to the society than that into which it would have gone of its own accord (Smith, 1999, IV, ii, 3).

2.2 The Forgotten Ethics of Adam Smith

Reading Adam Smith only through *The Wealth of Nations* gives a peculiar picture of the ethical dimensions of capitalism. The moral imperative, in Smithian capitalism, seems to be that individuals should maximize their self-interest – hence be selfish and greedy. This is a world beyond – or rather before – good and evil. 'Economic man' is 'natural man' – hence pre-dating in his behavior social, political or moral codes of conduct. A miracle, though, happens through the assumed but mysterious alchemy of the market and its 'invisible hand'. The aggregation of multiple a- and un-ethical individual actions turns into a morally and ethically satisfying collective good. In *The Wealth of Nations*, individuals are a-moral; the market though is inherently albeit mysteriously producing a moral order. In that book, the moral or ethical nature and power of the market has the characteristics of a constitutive assumption, a 'foundation myth' more than it is scientifically demonstrated (Nelson, 2001).

The idea that the market is a moral structure – beyond the dimension of efficiency – is still with us today. It is present in all variants of neo-classical economic theory, as 'natural law' – hence unchallenged, unquestioned and not to be scientifically demonstrated (Nelson 2001). Arguably, this is one of the most striking – and consequential – legacies of *The Wealth of Nations*. If the market is indeed a moral and ethical structure, then a direct consequence should be that there is no need to bring in ethical considerations at the level of individual behaviors. Furthermore, the reasoning could well be that if we attempted to do that, we would only distort and disturb the natural regulative mechanisms of the market (Friedman 1962). Hence, we could be tampering with and destroying the capacity of the market to produce a morally satisfying collective good. A correlate conclusion could then well be that capitalism will be working at its best when individual behaviors are left unfettered and free to explore all the paths leading to a maximization of self-interest, including when those paths could be judged to be a- or un-ethical.

This rendering or interpretation of Adam Smith's thought becomes more problematic when we consider not only *The Wealth of Nations* but also the *Theory of Moral Sentiments*. In *The Wealth of Nations*, economic man is pre-social – in the sense that the natural propensity to trade and barter precedes the social contract. But trading and bartering imply contacts and interdependence and in that sense human nature is profoundly social – individuals are not and cannot be self-sufficient monads. This becomes all the clearer when we read *The Theory of Moral Sentiments*. The market and its invisible hand reveal a Rational (i.e. Divine) plan and order and individuals are linked to each other in and through that plan (Nelson, 1991). The theological dimension of economics has been neutralized today to a great extent (albeit not fully, i.e. Nelson, 2001). It is relatively absent from *The Wealth of Nations* but highly visible in the *Theory of Moral Sentiments*. The individuals placed in this Rational/Divine scheme are endowed – presumably by the Author of Nature – with certain faculties (such as reason or imagination) and particular propensities (Smith, 1982).

There are two such propensities – self-love that expresses itself in particular in the maximization of self-interest but also 'fellow feeling' as the first sentence of the *Theory of Moral Sentiments* shows:

> How selfish soever man may be supposed, there are evidently some principles in his nature, which interest him in the fortune of others, and render their happiness necessary to him, though he derives nothing from it except the pleasure of seeing it (Smith, 1982, I.i.1.1).

Fellow feeling, as much as self-love, is a survival kit and a condition of man's fitness for that social state and interdependence in which he finds himself by divine design. Fellow feeling implies sympathy and empathy. It means a disposition to seek the approval of his fellows and also to be worthy of approval:

> Nature, when she formed man for society, endowed him with an original desire to please, and an original aversion to offend his brethren... The desire of approbation, and this aversion to the disapprobation of his brethren, would not alone have rendered him fit for that society for which he was made. Nature, accordingly, has endowed him not only with a desire of being approved of, but with a desire of being what ought to be approved of; or of being what he himself approves in other men (Smith, 1982, III.2.6-7).

2.3 The Missing Link – The Structuring Ethics of the Wealth of Nations

The search for approval and worthiness points to the ideas of 'propriety' and 'restraints' (including self-imposed ones) and hence to an ethical project. The individual has a natural disposition to form judgments (applied both to herself and others) concerning what is fit and proper to be done or to be avoided. But since this natural disposition may conflict with self-love, it is probably not enough, Smith tells us, as a source of control. It should be strengthened and reinforced by the setting up of socially defined 'general rules concerning what is fit and proper' – the latter resulting from an inductive generalization of continual observations upon the conduct of human beings and ultimately revealing the commands and laws of the Deity (Smith, 1982, III.4.8).

This code of morality – this ethical project – may be the missing link in *The Wealth of Nations*; the one that could explain that the aggregation of self-interested actions turns ultimately into a morally satisfying collective good. A code of morality that would be deeply inscribed in the individuals themselves – although it may sometimes conflict with and contradict self-love – could create the basis for collective self-restraint and relative harmony. It appears, in fact, when we read *The Wealth of Nations* and the *Theory of Moral Sentiments* together, that the proper workings of the market and its ethical character were deeply conditioned for Adam Smith by the presence of what could be called an ethical foundation infusing through all individual actors – even if that ethical foundation could conflict on a case-by-case basis with the pressures of self-interest.

3 Protestant Ethics and the Spirit of Capitalism

Once we stand there in our reading of Adam Smith, we are not too far in fact from Max Weber and from his account of the dynamics and balance of early modern capitalism. Max Weber pointed to the profound ethical structure underpinning modern capitalism and sustaining its early development and expansion. This silent structure acted through socialization and deep personal appropriation by individual actors. Hence in a sense, just like 'fellow-feeling' and its associated code of morality, this deep and silent structure was mostly invisible. Nevertheless, it was highly real and consequential in Weber's account. It was an important mechanism of both movement and stability, of both the dynamics of capitalism and its sustainability.

3.1 Calvinism and its Invisible Hand

In the *Protestant Ethics and the Spirit of Capitalism*, Max Weber explored the fit and the elective affinities existing between the Calvinist creed and a particular form of rationality or 'spirit' associated with modern capitalism (Weber, 1958; Giddens, 1971). Max Weber differentiated between several ideal types of capitalism that had marked history in varying ways. Leaving aside predatory, trade or warfare capitalism, Max Weber was mostly fascinated by the emergence in early modern Europe and in Puritan North America of what he termed 'rational capitalism'. He saw that form as more than just an impulse for acquisition and in fact he defined it as being 'identical with the restraint, or at least a rational tempering, of this irrational impulse' (Weber, 1958, p. 17). Capitalism, he argued, 'is identical with the pursuit of profit, and forever renewed profit, by means of continuous, rational, capitalistic enterprise' (Weber, 1958, p. 17).

The first signs of emergence of that form of rational and systematic capitalistic accumulation were found, Max Weber tells us, in a modernizing European continent. The birth of rational capitalism depended upon and was associated with free labor, the development of the Western city, the structuring of the nation state, the progressive separation of the productive enterprise from the household and accounting innovations such as double entry bookkeeping. The argument of Max Weber, however, is that those structural and material conditions were necessary but not sufficient to account for the development and expansion of rational capitalism. The key there, for him, was the existence of a propensity in human beings to behave in such a rational, accumulative but also restrained manner (Weber, 1958: 20). According to Max Weber, such a propensity was not linked in any way to 'human nature.' Rather, it was highly conditioned by the spiritual and religious context in which individual and collective actions were embedded. And in contrast, when this propensity has 'been obstructed by spiritual obstacles, the development of rational economic conduct has also met serious inner resistance' (Weber, 1958, pp. 26-27).

The next stage in Max Weber's demonstration was to show that some forms of Protestant denominations – particularly those associated with the teachings of Jean Calvin – were indeed quite conducive to the emergence and stabilization of such a propensity in given populations. Hence, the main explanation for the rapid expansion of rational capitalism in early modern Europe and Puritan America was, according to Max Weber, the encounter, the fit and the affinity between the material conditions identified above and the spiritual tenets of Calvinist Puritanism. The ethics associated with that type of religious denominations were a deep structure fuelling and fostering the propensity towards rational capitalist accumulation. Calvinist ethics were in other words in very close elective affinity with the spirit that was necessary for that type of capitalism to develop and expand. That type of normative structure worked through collective socialization and deep individual appropriation and in a sense acculturation. To that extent, it was indeed 'invisible' and nevertheless highly powerful – framing behaviors, interactions and mindsets a priori and hence reducing the need for external constraints, controls and expressions of power.

Jean Calvin was a Franco-Swiss preacher. Together with Martin Luther, he was a key actor of the Protestant Reformation movement in Europe during the 16th century. An important element of Calvinist teachings was the doctrine of predestination. The original version of that doctrine was extremely rigid. The Calvinist God was a stern and all-powerful master planner that had divided humanity from immemorial times between a few that were elect and would be saved and the rest who would be damned. The Universe was created to further the glory of God and the motives of that almighty God were beyond human understanding. The division between those bound for damnation and those who would be saved was fully pre-determined. When born, a particular individual was already assigned to one of those two categories without having any means to know which – and even less power to change his or her fate. Good deeds, human merits or repentance could have no impact whatsoever on whether one was part of the elects or not. In this rigid version, the doctrine of predestination was a source of deep existential anguish and pessimistic disillusion. It produced an 'unprecedented inner loneliness of the single individual' (Weber, 1958, p. 104).

3.2 From Calvinist Doctrine to Practical Ethics

In such a rigid form, this doctrine was too harsh and unbearable. Practical takes on the doctrine of predestination hence soon emerged. It was a duty to consider oneself one of the chosen. And it was possible to look for the signs of salvation in a positive contribution to the glorification of God's Kingdom on earth and in 'intense worldly activity' (Weber, 1958: 111-12). This could be done through an absolute focus on one's 'calling'. The idea of the calling – or 'Beruf' – was that each single one of us was put on this planet by the Great Master Planner into a particular position and with a particular duty. Signs of our election could be found in the successful accomplishment of our 'Beruf.' In contrast, the refusal to do one's calling, the refusal to work so as to help fructify God's pre-ordained world turned into a sign of damnation. Quite unlike what was the case in Catholicism, where the highest form of religious sentiment was otherworldly contemplation and the denial of the self and of the world as symbolized by the monk, in Calvinism the fulfillment of one's duty in worldly affairs was the highest form that the moral and religious activity of individuals could take (Weber, 1958, pp. 108-10).

In that context, the creation of wealth became a clear sign of divine election. But in Calvinism, existential anguish was a permanent state – and the search for signs of election also was and should be permanent. And in fact, 'the God of Calvinism demanded of his believers not single good works but a life of good works combined in a unified system' (Weber, 1958, p. 117). The wealth that was being created was not created for enjoyment and it should not be used towards self-aggrandizement. Wealth should not lead to personal pride; it should not on the other hand be used as a tool to diminish, harm or exploit others. Nobody, after all, was responsible for his or her own salvation or damnation; nobody 'deserved' one or the other – we are all just being confronted to a mysterious divine scheme. And all of us have our place and our position – necessary and predefined – in the earthly expression of that divine scheme. Acquisition should not be pursued to satisfy material needs and allow pleasure. In fact, straying away from an ascetic work ethic – through enjoyment, pleasures, unnecessary spending, pride, spite or the use of wealth to exert power – may be interpreted as signs of damnation. Wealth should be created and immediately and forever reinvested to fructify further God's Kingdom on earth. And the greater the possessions, 'the heavier, if the ascetic attitude toward life stands the test, the feeling of responsibility for them, for holding them undiminished for the glory of God and increasing them by restless effort' (Weber, 1958, p. 170).

3.3 The Prophecy of Max Weber

Such combination of a rational and perpetual search for accumulation and wealth creation with an ascetic lifestyle proved to be a perfect spiritual ground for the development of modern rational capitalism. And for Max Weber, the encounter between the early material conditions for rational capitalist accumulation and the Calvinist ethos turned out to represent one of those moments when history accelerated. The Calvinist ethos was the spiritual fuel that structured and stabilized at its beginnings the emerging capitalist order. Hence, from that perspective, modern rational capitalism was indeed a deeply moral and ethical order. But it was so historically and not essentially or naturally and, as Max Weber showed, this difference was highly consequential.

The prophecy of Max Weber, at the dawn of the twentieth century, was that modern capitalism was already in the process of 'losing its soul' and its moral and ethical backbone. And in fact, the Calvinist revolution in itself had been an important step towards a disenchantment of the world.

> The rationalization of the world, the elimination of magic as a means to salvation, the Catholics had not carried nearly so far as the Puritans had done. To the Catholic…the priest was a magician who performed the miracle of transubstantiation and who held the key to eternal life in his hand (Weber, 1958, p. 117).

The practical ethics of Calvinism generated their own internal contradictions. In time, the latter were coming to weaken the invisible spiritual structure of developing capitalism. Calvinism, in its doctrinal form, denied individuals the very possibility of contact with a jealous, all powerful and sternly hidden Deity. The only approximation to such an interaction was in fact indirect, through intense activity in this world – leading to the production of riches and hence to a furthering of God's Kingdom on earth. The rationalization of economic life was therefore initially tightly connected to an ethical and religious project that required and implied its own material and this worldly translation. Such materialization of a spiritual project, though, inherently generated tensions. Wealth and the materialism associated with its production were seen by Max Weber to have a deeply secularizing influence (Weber 1958, p. 174). As a consequence, they were bound, he argued, to weaken the spiritual structure that originally sustained them. Max Weber found the best descriptive expression of that process in a text written by John Wesley already at the end of the 18th century. Founder of the Methodist movement, John Wesley feared that:

> ...wherever riches have increased, the essence of religion has decreased in the same proportion. Therefore, I do not see how it is possible, in the nature of things, for any revival of true religion to continue long. For religion must necessarily produce both industry and frugality, and these cannot but produce riches. But as riches increase, so will pride, anger and love of the world in all its branches...So, although the form of religion remains, the spirit is swiftly vanishing away (Wesley as quoted in Southey, 1855, p. 308).

4 Towards The 'Iron Cage' – The Disenchantment of Capitalism in the United States

The prophecy of Max Weber was in process already in the United States during the last decades of the nineteenth century. American capitalism was on its way to 'losing its soul', becoming 'disenchanted' and hence turning into an 'iron cage.'

> The Puritan wanted to work in a calling; we are forced to do so. For when asceticism was carried out of monastic cells into everyday life, and began to dominate worldly morality, it did its part in building the tremendous cosmos of the modern economic order. This order is now bound to the technical and economic conditions of machine production which today determine the lives of all individuals who are born into this mechanism, not only those directly concerned with economic acquisition, with irresistible force. Perhaps it will so determine them until the last ton of fossilized coal is burnt....In the field of its highest development, in the United States, the pursuit of wealth, stripped of its religious and ethical meaning, tends to become associated with purely mundane passions...(Weber, 1958, p. 181-82).

There were essentially two sources of pressure, we argue, driving the process of disenchantment in the United States. On the one hand, the rapidly increasing clout of social Darwinism undeniably played a role. On the other hand, the deep institutional transformations that were profoundly reshaping American capitalism also pushed in that same direction.

4.1 Social Darwinism...

In his *Origins of Species* (1859), Darwin outlined one general law that 'led to the advancement of all organic beings – namely multiply, vary, let the strongest live and the weakest die.' The argument was that minor transformations or variations in living organisms resulted either from the chance process of reproduction or from the use or lack of use of certain organs in the context of a changing environment. These transformations or variations were 'selected' and stabilized in a particular species if they gave an adaptative advantage to those organisms which had developed them first – advantage measured by survival and reproductive success. 'Selection', in other words, happened through the 'struggle for life'. And this 'struggle for life' took place at different levels – between individuals from the same species, across species or directly between individuals and the environment or physical conditions of life.

Very rapidly, the evolutionary argument proposed by Charles Darwin was adapted and transferred to social sciences. The idea was that what applied to man as an animal or as an organism could also work for the study of man as a social, cultural or political being. Charles Darwin himself turned out to play a key role in that transfer and he undeniably was one of the first 'Social Darwinists' (Hawkins, 1997, Jones, 1978). As such, he believed that most features of social and human life – ethics, religion, political institutions, the rise and fall of nations and civilizations as well as psychological or behavioral characteristics – followed the general law of evolution. Variation was triggered through confrontation with the environment, other practices or chance encounters. Selection followed through 'struggle for life' and 'survival of the fittest', leading to the disappearance of those features and practices that 'failed', appearing less 'fit' or inadequatly adapted. From there, it was relatively easy to associate evolutionary change with social, human, or even moral progress. And this indeed has often been a feature of social Darwinian arguments. Charles Darwin himself did not shy away from deducing the superiority of civilized anglo-saxon nations over other countries from his general law of evolution (Hawkins, 1997).

To this day, evolutionary theory has been quite directly and obviously related to the work of Charles Darwin. One should not forget, however, the role of Herbert Spencer in shaping evolutionary theories in the social sciences. And, in particular, Spencer's 'theory of inevitable progress' had quite a significant impact in the United States. It was instrumental in shaping the local versions and readings of the evolutionary argument. From 1848 to 1853, Spencer was editor at *The Economist*, the key British financial weekly that was then already a mouthpiece of liberal economic thinking in its purest form. One rapid and somewhat schematic way to describe Herbert Spencer and place his contribution to the evolutionary argument relative to that of Charles Darwin is to say that Spencer was somewhat of an extremist and definitely a determinist. In his first book, *Social Statics* (1851), he claimed that:

> Progress, therefore, is not an accident but a necessity.... The modifications mankind has undergone and is still undergoing result from a law underlying the whole organic creation. And provided the human race continues and the constitution of things remains the same, those modifications must end in completeness and progress.

4.2 ...And its Transfer to the United States

For the most part, the evolutionary argument was transferred to the United States in its Spencerian rather than Darwinian version. From the beginning, evolutionary theory and liberal economic thinking were highly intermixed and intertwined in that country (Hawkins, 1997). There were clear elective affinities, in any case, between both ideologies and they combined on American soil, strengthening each other in the process. The Spencerian variant of the evolutionary argument was positive and quite optimistic. Progress was the necessary outcome of evolution, as long however as the natural process of evolution was left full and free rein. Spencer identified the struggle for survival as the main mechanism around which this natural process was articulated. And this struggle for survival was often associated, combined and conflated in his writings and those of his followers with the liberal economists' understanding of competition. Free and unhampered competition emerged as the principal mechanism of the evolutionary process – a mechanism bringing about both variation and selection.

Such a Panglossian view of evolution and a deterministic sense of inescapable progress meant that Spencer believed in and championed strict *laissez faire*. Any kind of interference could only be detrimental to the longer term and natural evolutionary process. There was no need whatsoever, in the Spencerian world, for politics, collective bargainings or welfare initiatives. Furthermore even, not only was there no need for those but they could be highly destructive. They were bound to disrupt the natural process that should lead to the 'survival of the fittest' and to the shouldering aside of the weak. Herbert Spencer was the real author of that phrase which became such an icon in American evolutionary theory as well as, episodically but regularly, in American economic practice.

Progress was an end that justified the means. And progress was endogenous to the system. It could only be defined in a circular way and it was measured in fact by survival. It did not have any more the spiritual dimension that had been associated with Calvinist Capitalism. Capitalism was clearly losing its 'soul' there and turning into a self-reinforcing 'iron cage.' To play itself out, 'survival of the fittest' – i.e. progress – required an entirely unfettered and free field for individual action. Gone was the fellow feeling of Adam Smith as a necessary foundation of market interactions. Gone also were the self-control of the Calvinist and his inscription within a higher order project – that of ensuring his own spiritual salvation through serving God in his earthly Kingdom.

The transfer of social darwinism in its Spencerian variants from the old to the new continent took place in the few years before and after 1870. The Spencerian argument did resonate particularly well with the conditions that characterized the United States after the Civil War. Hence, it spread fast and was eagerly appropriated. This was a time of upheaval, turbulence, transformations and unpredictable developments where the old rules were inadequate and the new ones still to be invented (Kolko, 1963; Chernow, 1990). In that context, Spencer's ideas became the intellectual foundation for the social Darwinism that came to characterize the 'Robber Barons.' The 'Robber Barons' were that generation of businessmen that thrived initially on the chaotic conditions associated with the American Civil War and then established firmly their power and legitimacy during the period of corporate reinvention of American capitalism, at the end of the 19th century (Sklar, 1988; Zunz, 1990; Roy, 1997; Djelic, 1998). The 'muckracker' journalists, and in particular Matthew Josephson were the first to use the label 'Robber Barons' to refer to the capitalist captains in that period of American history (Josephson, 1932). Spencer's ideas also spread within American intellectual circles, with significant impact in particular in American universities. Amongst the most famous and influential American champions of Spencerian evolutionism were John Fiske (philosopher and historian), William Graham Sumner (professor of political economy at Yale) or William James (Harvard) (Hawkins, 1997).

When Herbert Spencer went to the United States in 1882, he was received with the highest honors. Andrew Carnegie or John D. Rockefeller revered him (Chernow, 1998). Spencerian evolutionism could, in and of itself, justify – including in a moral sense – the brutal tactics that were then characteristic of American capitalism. Violent and rapacious behavior, in the context of 'free', in the sense of wild competition, were identified as necessary means leading to progress through struggle. The 'elimination' of the weak and the institutionalization of a hierarchical and unequal division of labor were also given legitimacy in this way. The Robber Barons were unsurprisingly the first to seize upon an ideology that turned in this way struggle, violence and brutal use of power into necessary steps towards progress (Hawkins, 1997).

The spread, in the United States, of social Darwinism in its Spencerian form proved to be, in retrospect, an important factor contributing to and hastening the secularization of capitalism in that country. The idea of an emergent natural order was a common dimension of economic liberalism in its Smithian variant, of Calvinism and of social Darwinism in the Spencerian version. In all three bodies of thought, that natural order was considered to be beyond human intervention. In fact, in all three cases, that order could only be revealed if natural laws were left free play. Natural laws had a divine dimension both in Calvinism and in a complete reading of Adam Smith. In the version of economic liberalism that forgot the *Theory of Moral Sentiments*, though, as well as in Spencerian social Darwinism, natural laws were essentially mechanistic. They had no 'deeper meaning', no ethical foundation – they just were there to be reckoned with.

Like Calvinism, economic liberalism and Spencerian social Darwinism were highly conservative ideologies but they were so in a different sense. Calvinism justified the status quo and the position that all occupied in the divine scheme of things was reflected in the social hierarchies of this world. There was, however, room for all in this world – the weak and the strong, those who would be damned and those who would be saved. Economic liberalism in its mechanistic variant and Spencerian social Darwinism justified instead the logics of evolutionary dynamics – and the survival of only the fittest and most competitive, which implied as correlate the disappearance, death or disintegration of the weak and the least competitive. Those logics were not (and should not be) mitigated by any form of self-restraint or 'fellow feeling' – as had been the case both in a full reading of Smithian liberalism or in Calvinist capitalism. Instead, the fight of all against all should be given absolutely free play even if it expressed itself in the most violent and brutal manner. In that context, ethics were reconstructed as mere obstacles – just like laws, regulation and state intervention – to the free play of natural, mechanistic, forces. Ethics, as a consequence, did not belong with economic logics and were in fact bound to disturb those logics.

4.3 The Corporate Reconstruction of American Capitalism

In spite of an apparent intellectual affinity between economic liberalism, Calvinism and Spencerian social Darwinism, the argument here is therefore that the deep ideological structure sustaining capitalism changed significantly in the United States towards the end of the 19th century. The secularization of capitalism happened through the progressive marginalization of spiritual motives for economic action – as predicted both by John Wesley and Max Weber. Calvinism gave way and a combination of mechanistic liberalism and Spencerian social Darwinism progressively took over and imposed itself as the intellectual structuring frame for capitalist dynamics.

This subtle but nevertheless highly significant intellectual evolution correlated in the United States, reinforced and was being reinforced by profound structural transformations that were in fact redefining the meaning of capitalism in that country. Fathers of the American Constitution, and Thomas Jefferson in particular, had identified freedom as a constitutive element of the future American social and economic space (McCoy, 1996). In sparsely populated and essentially rural territories, the ideal typical situation of many individual and independent entrepreneurs, competing healthily in a mostly unregulated environment, seemed a legitimate ambition. Such a 'proprietary-competitive' – one could say classical liberal – type of capitalism appeared to embody freedom, the very spirit of the new Nation (Sklar, 1988). The small firm was an economic but also a moral entity. The individual acquired through it not only the means of his physical survival but also the means of his freedom – essentially independence, wealth and social status. Like motherhood and apple pie, the small firm was the stuff of the American dream.

In a short period of time, though, during those years bridging the 19th and 20th centuries, the economic component of the American dream would come to be radically redefined. By the 1920s, 'big' was undeniably becoming 'efficient', if not always 'beautiful' in the American economy (Sklar, 1988; McCraw, 1984; Adams and Brock, 2004). A corporate version of capitalism, increasingly regulated at the federal level, was pushing the small producer republic to the periphery of the national economy. Emerging within the context of significant economic and technological disruptions, corporate capitalism had also been shaped within particular historical and institutional conditions. The reconstruction of American capitalism, or the invention of corporate capitalism, was in fact a fairly messy process, revealing social and political confrontations as much as it was reflecting economic and technological evolution. The institutional environment, particularly in its political and legislative dimensions, set significant constraints. Still, the multiplicity of actors, characterized by bounded rationalities as well as divergent and complex motives, meant that unintended and contingent developments played a part.

The American Civil War and its associated disruptions set the stage to the structural revolution that characterized American capitalism. In a mostly unregulated and fairly turbulent environment such as had been the case during that period of war, business arrangements and agreements had multiplied – mostly in the form of loose cartels or trusts. This generated a public concern with the 'trust question' – reflecting the growing power of those large business aggregates and their use of ruthless practices in what came to resemble economic warfare (Lloyd, 1894; Josephson, 1932; Chernow, 1998). The growing uproar and discontent amidst, in particular, small independent business owners and western or southern farmers indicated that the 'trust question' could indeed have destabilizing effects on the American social and political scene. The pressure was such that the American Congress did enact first a legislation regulating railroads – the *Interstate Commerce Act* in 1887 – and, a few years later, a general antitrust act – the *Sherman Antitrust Act* in 1890.

The intent behind the *Sherman Act* was initially to curb the threat that aggregates of economic power were perceived to represent and to reestablish the conditions for free and fair competition. The unique set of conditions, however, in which this Act was enacted limited its domain of applicability and had unintended consequences of significance (Peritz, 1996). Early court cases showed that cartels and other 'restraints of trade or commerce' across the states of the Union would be prohibited *per se*. As a Federal legislation, however, the Sherman Act did not apply within states. Tight combinations or mergers within the legal frame of particular states that made them possible (such as New Jersey) seemed to fall outside its reach (Roy, 1997). And corporate lawyers were soon identifying mergers as an alternative to cartelization, legal under Sherman Act (Sklar,1988). The passing of the Sherman Act was thus indirectly a triggering force in the first American merger wave (1895-1904). In an irony of history, the fight for competition in the United States led to the emergence of large, integrated firms and contributed to the oligopolistic reorganization of American industries. The Sherman Act was read as *per se* outlawing cartels and loose forms of agreements. With respect to size, however, and hence mergers, the interpretation that ultimately came to dominate in the Supreme Court was that illegality stemmed not from size *per se* but from 'unreasonableness' – as revealed by the proven intent and purpose to exclude others and stifle competition (Peritz, 1996). By the 1920s, both the *per se* prohibition of cartels and the 'rule of reason' with respect to mergers had become trademarks and defining features of the American antitrust tradition. In the United States, collusion and cooperation between independent firms became legally and morally impossible. Instead, competition was valued – but in practice the American antitrust tradition was fostering oligopolistic competition and not the type of classical competition championed by Adam Smith and other liberal economists (Djelic, 2002). Those highly significant early first steps triggered in turn other consequential transformations, leading ultimately to a profound reinvention of capitalism in the United States. We identify here six pillars or dimensions that define the form of capitalism emerging in the process. The latter is quite different indeed from the Smithian (or Jeffersonian) ideal of classical liberalism.

Those six dimensions have emerged in the United States in quite unique historical and institutional conditions and sometimes even in quite unexpected ways (Fligstein, 1990; Roy, 1997; Djelic, 1998; Lipartito and Sicilia, 2004). First, as we have seen, the very meaning of competition came to differ significantly. In the emerging corporate capitalism, the competitive logic was that of oligopolistic markets policed by antitrust (Djelic, 2002). Second, the large-scale merger wave associated with the oligopolistic reorganization of industries led to the dominance of large and capital intensive firms (Chandler, 1962; 1990). Third, the constitution of large firms often through mergers and acquisitions at the end of the 19th century was made possible by and required a change in legal status. The joint stock corporation with dispersed ownership became quite common as a legal structure in American capitalism (Roy, 1997; Lipartito and Sicilia, 2004). Four, those joint stock corporations were listed on stock exchanges where they found a large share of the vast capital they required (Navin and Sears, 1955). Five, those corporations also soon came to be ruled by professional managers, whose legitimacy did not reside in ownership rights (Berle and Means, 1932). Six, the separation between ownership and the everyday handling of company affairs turned out to be a major revolution. It triggered the emergence of a profession – management – and the structuring of an organizational field around that profession (Sutton et al., 1956; Zunz, 1990).

The structural transformation of capitalism could only reinforce the process of disenchantment that was already at work. The separation of ownership and control, in particular, had consequences of significance. An important consequence was that the link between work and wealth creation was severed – turning a class of formerly hard working and ascetic business owners into a leisure class living to spend what their money (and not their work) had earned (Veblen, 1924). A second consequence was the professionalization of management that ensued from the transformed meaning of ownership (Berle and Means, 1932). When ownership means holding a few shares in a large corporation, it does not grant the right to manage or decide. The void is then filled by the professionalization of the management activity and by the rapid development of a new class – that of professional managers. The professionalization of management has meant one further step towards a rationalization of the economic sphere. The pervading influence of science, associated with such professionalization, could only render more anachronistic references to and reliance upon spiritual motives in that sphere. Finally, the corporate revolution in the United States has vastly expanded in time the scope of the 'iron cage' while tightening the latter further. The corporate revolution has transformed large numbers of petty owners, farmers or entrepreneurs into the salaried servants – whether as operatives or managers – of the new corporations. Progressively, but ever so rapidly, the possibilities to escape the corporate and organizational cage have become increasingly rare (Perrow, 2001). This has been true both in the private and in the public sectors, in law, medicine or education. The cage, indeed, has become all but inescapable at the same time that it was losing its soul or 'spirit' (Weber, 1958, p. 181).

5 Conclusion: Beyond Robber Baron Capitalism?

Originally, modern capitalism reflected a spiritual and ethical project. One can agree or disagree with the ethical agenda that underpinned the development of modern capitalism. Nevertheless, it is probably fair to argue that this partly invisible but quite strong ethical and spiritual structure was a powerful fuel, initially, of the rapid development of rational capitalism. Internal contradictions in a system that turned spirituality into materialism combined with ideological shifts and structural pressures to weaken, in time, the spiritual and ethical superstructure of modern capitalism. Although the process has naturally been much more multi-faceted, it makes some sense, symbolically, to associate this progressive disenchantment with the triumph, in the United States, of Robber Baron capitalism.

5.1 Robber Barons and the Search for Redemption

Interestingly, Robber Barons as a group had many characteristics of a transitional force. They led the way from one world to another with brutal energy and nevertheless unconscious regrets and nostalgia. Seizing upon the ideological combination of mechanistic liberalism and social Darwinism, they launched into a raw 'struggle for life'. They justified and legitimated their individual thirst for ever greater personal wealth and power as being part of a progressive collective scheme – where survival indicated superiority ('fit') and superiority ('fit') was measured by survival (Josephson, 1932; Dolson, 1959; Gordon, 1988, Chandler, 1986). The social world was a raw evolutionary scene where an unhampered struggle of all against all would lead to progress and collective good.

In their private lives, many of those Robber Barons were of protestant lineage and quite attuned in fact, through their parents, grand parents and families to the ethical and spiritual dimension of capitalism (Josephson, 1932; Winkelman, 1937; Chernow, 1990; 1998; Stasz 1995). In their daily actions as businessmen, they evacuated and rejected the spiritual dimension and the ethical restraints that had underpinned the economic behavior of their parents or grand parents. They only played by the rule of self-interest and its maximization (Schreiner, 1995). Fellow-feeling was left on the wayside not only of economic action but also quite often of their lives. The biographies of many of those men show a dire lack of fellow-feeling and in some cases even heartless violence in their closest personal relationships – with their wives and children in particular (Josephson, 1932; Wall, 1970; Chernow, 1990). At least, this was generally the case during the longest part of their lives – the part when they were in full activity.

But then, another pattern emerged towards the end of their lives. As if in a search for redemption, when the day of reckoning was getting near, Robber Barons turned philanthropists (Josephson, 1932; Winkelman, 1937; Flynn, 1941; Nevins, 1953). This happened to a whole generation from the 1910s to the 1930s – and most of the big private American Foundations were created then. The wealth that had been accumulated through sometimes violent maximization of self-interest suddenly seemed to burn their fingers. The last years of many Robber Barons were busily spent redistributing some of that wealth through good deeds. Fellow-feeling finally expressed itself and sometimes on a big scale. Money was spent on education, health, social and cultural projects. Motives, as they can be reconstructed, were mixed. Naturally, part of that can be explained by the search for social legitimacy in a period when muckrackers were violently denouncing, in the United States, the ways in which many Robber Barons had accumulated wealth (Sinclair, 1988; Tarbell, 1905; 1924; Brady, 1984). But buying back one's reputation in this world was probably not enough to explain the scale and scope of the philanthropist involvement. Undeniably, existential fears also played a role. The need to feel chosen and hence saved was getting more urgent and the Puritan God required a life of 'good works.' Because wealth had often been created in such a ruthless manner, its redemptive power was probably not so obvious, including to the Robber Barons themselves. The consequence was that they fell back on what can be called a 'catholic pattern' – trying to make up for past behaviors through alms and good deeds:

> The giving and receiving of heart offerings without price, deeds that win crowns and scepters in Heaven (Mrs Jane Leland Stanford, Inscriptions, Memorial Church at Stanford University).

5.2 Capitalism as an a-*Ethical System*

This generation brutally accelerated the transformation of capitalism into an a-ethical system, simply preoccupied with the creation of wealth as an end in itself. However, this generation was also a transitory one that still inscribed itself in the spiritual heritage that had marked the development of early modern capitalism. The turn to philanthropy in the later part of their lives showed that. In most cases, their lifestyles also showed that. Many of those Robber Barons were highly ascetic men and imposed an ascetic lifestyle on their families, in spite of their incalculable wealth (Chernow, 1990; 1998, Stasz, 1995).

By the end of the Robber Barons period, however, and of its associated ideological and structural transformations, the spirit had all but left the cage. Ethical and spiritual preoccupations were clearly becoming separated from daily economic practice (and theory). In a sense, the strict separation between wealth creation and philanthropic redistribution, as pioneered by the Robber Barons, would come to characterize the world of the twentieth century. The economic logic, the logic of wealth creation differed significantly and should be unrelated to ethical projects and behaviors – and vice-versa. This has undeniably left us with a profoundly a-ethical system of economic production. Contemporary capitalism is a system beyond good and evil – and the aggregation of self-interest maximizing behaviors does not spontaneously lead to an ethical and moral collective good, far from it. If it is to exist, this ethical and moral collective good has to be defined as a political project. It can only articulate with the contemporary capitalist architecture through a regulatory agenda that could be proposed and championed at the national and/or at the transnational level (Djelic and Quack, 2003; Dunning, 2003; Djelic and Sahlin-Andersson, 2005).

References

Adams, W. and Brock J. (2004), *The Bigness Complex*, Stanford University Press, Stanford, USA.

Belloc, H. (1977 [1912]), *The Servile State*, Liberty Fund, Indianapolis, USA.

Berle, A. and Means G. (1932), *Modern Corporation and Private Property*, Macmillan, New York.

Blaug, M. (1986), *Great Economists Before Keynes*, Cambridge University Press, Cambridge UK and New York.

Brady, K. (1984), *Ida Tarbell*, Seaview/Putnam, New York.

Brennan, G. and Hamlin A. (1995), Economizing on Virtue, *Constitutional Political Economy*, 6, pp. 35-56.

Chandler, A. (1962), *Strategy and Structure*, MIT Press, Cambridge, USA.

Chandler, A. (1990), *Scale and Scope*, Harvard University Press, Cambridge, USA.

Chandler, D. (1986), *Henry Flagler*, Macmillan, New York.

Chernow, R. (1990), *The House of Morgan*, Atlantic Monthly Press, New York.

Chernow, R. (1998), *Titan*, Random House, New York, USA.

Clegg, S., Ibarra-Colado E. and Bueno-Rodriques L. (1998), *Global Management: Universal Theories and Local Realities*, London and Thousands Oaks: Sage.

Coase, R. (1976), Adam Smith's View of Man, *Journal of Law and Economics*, 19, pp. 529-546.

Darwin, C. (1999[1859]), *The Origins of Species*, Bantam Classics, New York, USA

Djelic, M. L. (1998), *Exporting the American Model*, Oxford University Press, Oxford, UK.

Djelic, M. L. (2002), Does Europe Mean Americanization? The Case of Competition, *Competition and Change*, 6 (3), pp. 233-250.

Djelic, M. L. and Quack S. (eds) (2003), *Globalization and Institutions*, Edward Elgar, Cheltenham, UK.

Djelic, M. L. and Sahlin-Andersson K. (eds) (2005), *Transnational Regulation in the Making*, Cambridge University Press, Cambridge, UK and New York.

Dolson, H. (1959), The Great Oildorado: The Gaudy and Turbulent Years of the First Oil Rush: Pennsylvania, 1859-1880, Random House, New York.

Drori, G., Meyer J., Ramirez F. and Schofer E. (2003) *Science in the Modern World Polity*. Stanford University Press, Stanford, USA.

Dunning, J. (2001), *Global Capitalism at Bay*, Routledge, London and New York.

Dunning, J. (ed.) (2003), *Making Globalization Good*, Oxford University Press, Oxford, UK and New York.

Flynn, J. (1941), *Men of Wealth*, Simon and Schuster, New York, USA.

Fourcade-Gourinchas, M. (2001), Politics, institutional structures and the rise of economics: A comparative study, *Theory and Society*, 30, pp. 397-447.

Fourcade-Gourinchas, M. and Babb S. (2002), The rebirth of the liberal creed: paths to neoliberalism in four countries, *American Journal of Sociology*, 108(3), pp. 533-579.

Friedman, M. (1962), *Capitalism and Freedom*, Chicago University Press, Chicago.

Giddens, A. (1971), *Capitalism and Modern Social Theory*, Cambridge University Press, Cambridge, UK.

Gordon, J. S. (1988), *The Scarlet Woman of Wall Street*, Weidenfeld and Nicholson, New York.

Hawkins, M. (1997), *Social Darwinism in American and European Thought, 1860-1945*, Cambridge University Press, Cambridge, UK and New York.

Hayeck, F. (1994[1944]), *The Road to Serfdom*, University of Chicago Press, Chicago, USA.

Josephson, M. (1932), *The Robber Barons*, Harcourt, Brace and World, New York.

Kolko, G. (1963), *The Triumph of Conservatism*, Free Press, New York.

Knight, F. (1982), *Freedom and Reform*, Liberty Press, Indianapolis, USA.

Knight, F. and T. Merriam (1979), *The Economic Order and Religion*, Greenwood Press, Westport, USA.

Küng, H. (2003), An ethical Framework for the Global Market Economy, in Dunning, J. (ed.), *Making Globalization Good*, Oxford University Press, Oxford, UK and New York.

Leo XIII (1891), Rerum Novarum, reprinted in Treacy, G. (ed.) (1939), *Five Great Encyclicals*, The Paulist Press, New York.

Lipartito and Sicilia (eds) (2004), *Constructing Corporate America*, Oxford University Press, Oxford and New York.

Lloyd, H. (1894), *Wealth against Commonwealth*, Harper & Brothers, New York.

Locke, J. (1997), *Locke: Political Essays*, Cambridge University Press, Cambridge, UK and New York.

Manent, P. (1987), *Histoire intellectuelle du libéralisme*, Calmann-Lévy, Paris.

Marx, K. and Engels F. (1998[1848]), *The Communist Manifesto*, Signet Classics, New York.

McCoy, D. (1996), *The Elusive Republic:Political Economy in Jeffersonian America*, University of North Carolina Press, Chapel Hill, NC, USA.

Navin, T. and Sears M. (1955), The Rise of a Market for Industrial Securities, 1887-1902, *Business History Review* 29, pp. 105-138.

Nelson, R. (1991), *Reaching for Heaven on Earth*, Rowman and Littlefield, Lanham, USA.

Nelson, R. (2001), *Economics as Religion*, The Pennsylvania State University Press, University Park, Pennsylvania, USA.

Nevins, A. (1953), *Study in Power*, Charles Scribner's Sons, New York.

Peritz, R. (1996), *Competition Policy in America*, Oxford University Press, Oxford and New York.

Pius XI (1931), Quadragesimo Anno, reprinted in Treacy, G. (ed.) (1939), *Five Great Encyclicals*, The Paulist Press, New York.

Roy, W. (1997), *Socializing Capital*, Princeton University Press, Princeton, USA.

Schreiner, S. Jr (1995), *Henry Clay Frick*, St Martin's Press, New York.

Sinclair, U. (1988[1906]), *The Jungle*, University of Illinois Press, Urbana and Chicago, USA.

Sklar, M. (1988), *Corporate Reconstruction of American Capitalism, 1890-1916*, Cambridge University Press, Cambridge, UK, and New York.

Smith, A. (1982[1759]), The *Theory of Moral Sentiments*, Liberty Press, Indianapolis, USA.

Smith, A. (1999[1776]), The Wealth of Nations – Books I-III (editor Skinner, A.), Penguin Books, London and New York.

Southey, R. (1855), *The Life of Wesley, Volume II*, Second American Edition, Harper, New York.

Spencer, H. (1970[1851]), *Social Statics*, Augustus M. Kelley Pubs, New York.

Stasz, C. (1995), *The Rockefeller Women: A Dynasty of Piety, Privacy and Service*, St Martin's Press, New York.

Sutton, F., Harris, S., Kaysen C. and Tobin J. (1956), *The American Business Creed*, Harvard University Press, Cambridge, USA.

Tarbell, I. (1905), John D. Rockefeller: A Character Study, *McLure's Magazine*, July and August.

Tarbell, I. (1924), The Oil Age, *McLure's Magazine*, November.

Valdès, J. (1995), *Pinochet's Economists: The Chicago School in Chile*, Cambridge University Press, Cambridge, UK and New York.

Veblen, T. (1924[1899]), *The Theory of the Leisure Class*, George Allen and Unwin, New York.

Wall, J. (1970), *Andrew Carnegie*, Oxford University Press, Oxford and New York.

Wallerstein, I. (2000), *The Essential Wallerstein*, New Press, New York.

Weber, M. (1958), *The Protestant Ethic and the Spirit of Capitalism*, C. Scribner's Sons, New York, USA.

Weber, M. (1959), *Le Savant et le Politique*, Plon, Paris, France.

Winkelman, B. F. (1937), *John D. Rockefeller: The Authentic and Dramatic Story of the World's Greatest Money Maker and Money Giver*, Universal Book and Bible House, Philadelphia, USA.

Zunz, O. (1990), *Making America Corporate*, University of Chicago Press, Chicago, USA.

Chapter 4

Ethical Lapses of Capitalism: How Serious Are They?

Daniel Daianu

> Trust and similar values, loyalty and truth-telling…have real, practical, economic value; they increase the efficiency of the system, enable you to produce more goods or more of whatever values you hold in high esteem. But they are not commodities for which trade on the open market is technically possible or even meaningful (Arrow, 1974, p. 23).

1 Introduction[1]

Adam Smith is seen by many as the father of economics for his book *The Wealth of Nations* (1776). But he also wrote *The Theory of Moral Sentiments* (1759), which underlines moral underpinnings of a vibrant and socially cohesive society. As the Nobel prize winner Amartya Sen points out 'not only was Adam Smith a professor of moral philosophy at the University of Glasgow, but the subject of economics was for a long time seen as a branch of ethics' (Sen, 1987, p. 2). Arguably, if a market-based society is to function properly, its members have to behave decently toward one another, according to socially accepted seals of approval; the latter would explain why individuals care about how they relate to each other. These seals form a code of morality.[2] Some may be tempted to discard ethical boundaries in social and economic life in the name of ethical relativism; an analogy could be used, in this respect, with Arrow's impossibility theorem of constructing social preferences (Arrow, 1951). But, as in the case of revealed comparative advantages revealed social preferences, that rely on ethical motives, operate in society.

One can link Adam Smith's vision to Max Weber's famous work on *Protestant Ethics and Capitalism* in order to strengthen the link between values, institutions

---

[1] This chapter builds on a presentation made at the international seminar on 'Economy and Ethics' organized by the New Europe College, the Romanian Economic Society and the Konrad Adenauer Foundation, Bucharest, 12-13 December, 2003. I thank participants to this seminar, Rachel Epstein, Laurian Lungu and Michael Keren for their suggestions and remarks on an early draft.

[2] As mentioned by Shearmur and Klein (1997, p. 36), 'Morality, its maintenance, and its effective internalization as our conscience all depend upon the monitoring of our conduct by others.'

and economic performance (Weber, 1958). A more recent book, by a leading development economist, Deepak Lal, highlights the cultural dimension of economic development; in an insightful observation he connects the social cement of a society – which is needed for better economic performance – with the existence of the socializing emotions of *guilt* and *shame* (Lal, 1999). I would submit that, where shame and guilt are missing, or declining on a large scale, cynicism, unethical behavior and social irresponsibility get the upper-hand and aggregate economic performance can hardly escape worsening over the long run.[3]

Lately, the issues of ethical behavior and social responsibility of firms and individuals have come prominently to the forefront of public debate. Some find roots of unethical behavior in the logic of market competition (Shleifer, 2004). At the same time, widespread corruption and unethical behavior are primarily seen as features of institutional fragility and lack of democratic credentials, which are to be found in the developing world, in particular. Most transition (post-communist) countries have been, by definition, placed in this category. And not a few in the Western world were quick to attribute the financial crises in Southeast Asia, in the late 1990s, to wide-ranging corruption and cronyism and institutional fragility. Nonetheless, the vigorous economic recovery in the Asian economies, of recent years, illustrates a more complex reality. Likewise the spate of corporate scandals across the Atlantic, in recent years, and similar cases in rich parts of Europe points in the same direction. One should remember that a similar wave of scandals gripped the US in the 1980s.

If institutional fragility in the developing world seems to have relevant explanatory power regarding behavioral patterns the situation in advanced economies is begging for clearer answers. Is there a cyclical pattern in advanced economies, linked with unavoidable behavioral excesses during periods of economic exuberance, which would subside over time following policy and institutional adjustments? Or, one can establish institutional circumstances and peculiar policies which enhance unethical behavior, and which do not trigger adequate/counter-acting responses automatically. Can social and economic dynamics of capitalism be linked to apparent shifts in some of the values which drive entrepreneurs' behavior? Is the profit motive similar to greed, or to use Alan Greenspan's famous words, when does it turn into 'infectious greed' and 'irrational exuberance?' What is the role of norms (formal and informal), or standards of conduct, in constraining socially irresponsible behavior?

Questions like those mentioned above prompted the writing of this chapter. Against this background ethical lapses in economic behavior are considered by using the concept of reputation as an *asset* of individuals and firms; the build up of reputation capital would enter the utility function of an individual, or firm. Why bad equilibria persist and the macroeconomic context are also examined through this interpretation of reputation. Likewise, self-regulation and the regulatory functions of the state are judged from this perspective. The chapter broadens the analysis to the international framework.

---

[3] Ethics assumes a socially accepted (codified) judgment of what is right and wrong in society.

2 Ethics and Economy

The early 1990s were accompanied by great euphoria following the collapse of communism; this euphoria seemed to engulf Western intellectual and political circles. Fukuyama encapsulated this outburst of optimism in his *End of History* (Fukuyama, 1990), which extolled the virtues of liberal democracy and talked about the end of ideology. It was like human society was on the brink of entering a golden age, unconstrained by social and political inhibitions. The only concern would have been the pace of technological advance and its economic reverberations. In a sense Fukuyama was right; communism was coming to an end as an economic and political system. But his optimism was less warranted in terms of the vistas for rapid economic development, as these were deemed to open to the rest of the world; similarly, his vision of the demise of conflicting ideas/paradigms was less convincing.

A fallacy, or *naiveté*, of those years was an apparent underlying belief that capitalism, as a the big victor of a century long ideological war, was liable to shed its own weaknesses and become a perfect society. Not a few seemed to forget Winston Churchill's famous aphorism. Interestingly enough, Fukuyama himself became much more subdued in a subsequent work (Fukuyama, 1999). Nowadays, social scientists are more sober in their analysis of social and economic dynamics. As Shearmur and Klein (1997, p. 29) mention: 'Market-based societies are living upon moral capital – capital that they cannot themselves replenish. This moral capital is eroded by some of the very factors that seem to make such societies so attractive.'

Post-communist transition has offered an immense social laboratory for those immersed in the study of social and economic behavior. Transformation of former command systems was based, in Europe, on fast privatization, liberalization, and trade opening. This policy thrust was strongly imbued with the *neo-liberal zeitgeist* of the past decade. In this context corruption and deviant behavior, in general, were put under scrutiny, as post-communist transition has been replete with unethical attitudes.

Two trains of reasoning can be detected with respect to explaining behavioral patterns during transition, which can be extrapolated to developing economies in general. A handy answer would be the very institutional weakness of post-communist societies, a precarious functioning of checks and balances and a corrupted judiciary together with very feeble law enforcement capacity. In an optimistic vein, this reasoning highlights the advance of structural and institutional reforms, which would allow transition societies to diminish malign (unethical) behavior considerably over time and reduce what Blanchard (1997) called 'disorganization.' Gradually, both micro-inefficiencies and resource misallocation would diminish. This approach seems to rely and favor an organic institutional development – very much in the Hayekian mold.

Joining the European Union can be seen through the lenses of this upbeat logic as the EU would, arguably, provide an extraordinary anchor for systemic transformation. As a matter of fact, the entry of eight transition countries in the EU on May 1st, 2004, seems to substantiate this line of reasoning. On the other hand, one could say that these new member countries are in the proximity of the EU and have benefited on more lenient communist legacies. It should be said, however, that these countries still evince substantial institutional fragility; this should provide a stimulus to examine the linkage between regulations (*alias* public policy) and economic performance, on one hand, and values/norms and economic behavior, on the other.

A pessimistic answer on explaining behavioral patterns would stress a bad 'path dependency' and point at the persistence of widespread corruption, precarious institutions and malfunctioning markets in large parts of the world. Latin America offers a glaring example in this regard. *Mutatis mutandis*, one can say that Latin American countries have been in transition for more than a century and that this undermines ground for robust optimism. Thence a question arises: what explains the persistence of bad social equilibria and poor economic performance over long stretches of time? The plight of Argentina, in the last decade, is the most recent and vivid case of overblown expectations of economic reforms and durability of substantially improved economic performance. Why is it that vicious circles, traps of underdevelopment, are so hard to break away from?[4] The media in and outside these countries constantly reveal instances of corruption that involve top politicians and business people.

It appears that the experience of Latin America is a very bad omen for less advanced transition countries – for Balkan countries and former Soviet republics. In South East Europe, for instance, the weak state syndrome and the fragility of institutions, in general, as well as the large criminality in economic life should be a cause of deep concern regarding the ways and means for reversing an unfavorable path dependency. The counter-argument would be that the European Union can provide an extremely powerful anchor and transformation tool for this region as well, as it did for central Europe. But, there is little doubt that the process will be more time consuming and painful in view of specific local conditions, including political and inter-ethnic conflicts.

The rich, advanced countries have not been immune to big scandals in the business world. The turn of the century will, probably, go down in economic history books through a series of big corporate scandals in the USA, in particular, and Europe. The burst of the Internet bubble, the demise of the 'new economy' and the 'new paradigm', the disgrace which accompanied the fall of *Enron, WorldCom, Tyco*, etc., the involvement of illustrious Wall Street institutional names in a series of financial scandals with multifarious ramifications, the collapse of LTCM, the ignominious disappearance of *Arthur Andersen*, the *Parmalat* case, widely rigged financial and energy markets, etc., tell a lengthy and significant story. It is increasingly clear that the years of intense deregulation favored not only more aggressive and innovative business behavior, but they also entailed a wide array of

---

[4]   Albert Hirschman, Gunar Myrdal, Ragnar Nurkse Paul Rosenstein-Rodan, who are famous names in the panoply of development economists, wrote extensively about the resilience of these traps decades ago.

breach of trust, of decent relationships between agents and principals. The recent years have revealed egregious and wide ranging situations of conflict of interests and irresponsible damage done to shareholders' interests by unchecked (greedy) managers and defective principal-agent arrangements. The last two decades can be judged, in advanced economies, via a combination of excessive deregulation and erosion of moral values as well as weaknesses in the corporate structures of governance.[5]

The alternative lines of reasoning which were mentioned for developing economies can be used for interpreting behavioral patterns and excesses in advanced economies, too. Thus, an optimistic interpretation would look into history and observe recurrent cycles of manias, panics and crashes, albeit these evolved in mitigated forms after the Great Depression (Kindleberger, 1989). Michael Milken and Ivan Boeski's names as individuals and Drexel Lambert as a corporate entity, in the financial world, remind us of excesses perpetrated two decades ago, which culminated with the crash at the New York Stock Exchange in 1987 (the Black Friday). A pessimistic reading of events would look at what may perpetuate bad equilibria and cause big damage in an increasingly interconnected world economy (Eatwell and Taylor, 2000).[6] It is not accidental that Larry Summers insightfully, remarked that 'Central to global integration is financial integration...as the events of the late 1920s and early 1930s remind us, central to global disintegration can be international financial breakdowns' (Summers, 2000, p. 1). He rightly highlights the international dimension of public governance. And Stanley Fischer, a leading macro-economist and former deputy managing director of the IMF says that 'the overall challenge to economic globalization is to make the global system deliver economic growth more consistently and equitably' (Fischer, 2003, p. 23).

Economic and social dynamics reveal a constant play between forces which ask for liberalization and those that deem regulations as useful public goods. Individual and collective agents (entrepreneurs), who pursue their interests under various constraints operate in specific institutional contexts that influence behavioral patterns. These contexts include formal and informal codes of conduct and explain economic performance over the long haul. Arguably, national economies compete in the global space in terms of institutional contexts, though actual drivers of competition are firms (Krugman, 1994). This is why national policy-makers are concerned about the quality of local business environments. Liberalization may be pursued in order to invigorate sclerotic, rigid structures (Olson, 1982), and this may lead to positive outcomes. But there is also a dark side of the story, amply illustrated by cases of fraud and wide ranging unethical behavior. From here arises the importance of striking a right balance between the private and the public sector and the need for an optimal degree of regulation.[7]

---

[5] Among business circles this loss of moral ground has raised serious concerns and triggered a process of soul-searching (see Bebear, 2003).

[6] See Stiglitz (2003) as well.

[7] There is need for an optimal combination of self-regulation by industries (which rely on market incentives), state regulation and internal regulations by firms (Argandoña, 2004).

The public outrage in the USA and Europe at the cases of misbehavior in the corporate world and the perceived insufficiency of regulation of certain markets has prodded governments to react. It appears that society does not accept complacency in this regard and is not likely to bet recklessly on the optimistic line of reasoning – which assumes the organic capacity of institutional regeneration. Likewise, it appears that Western societies have judged the social costs of waiting for such regeneration to take place as too large. Hence the policy response of introducing new regulations and new auditing and accounting rules at the start of this decade. Obviously, pragmatic motives have been asking for a policy response. But, it can be argued that 'virtue ethics'[8] has also played a role.

3 Understanding Micro and Macro Behaviors

3.1 The Distinction between Ethics and Legality

Unethical behavior can be met in both advanced and underdeveloped societies; it can be met in both the official economy and the informal sector. The official economy reveals unethical behavior as the outcome of breaking laws, regulations and codes of conduct. In advanced economies unethical behavior has more scope for operation in times of liberalization and institutional innovation like financial innovation, which can lead to under-regulation.

There is a need to make a distinction between ethics and legality. Some business operations may be legal, but unethical. Whenever conflicts of interest are poorly regulated, or legal frameworks present major loopholes, some individuals leave aside ethical considerations for the sake of making big gains. It is of high notoriety Arthur Levitt's endeavor to introduce more severe regulations in the securities industry in the USA in the early years of the last decade. Though as powerful he was as Chairman of the *Securities and Exchange Commission*, his attempts proved futile when confronted with the formidable lobbying power of vested interests. As some would argue; morality has no place in business. Only the crisis that burst out at the end of the decade compelled many interested parties to revisit this issue, which led to the *Sarbanes-Oxley Act* to be enacted. But some people are regrouping and fighting bitterly back – claiming that 'over-regulation' hurts business. One can see that this is an ongoing battle.

Monopoly power can be blatantly abused and ethically misused. *Microsoft* got into trouble because of its endeavors to keep a market captive and abuse its power. Even more questionable ethically are operations of the big pharmaceutical companies, which have used R&D related expenditure as an argument for

---

[8] Virtue ethics focuses on the conformity between right thinking and desire (Koehn, 1995, p. 536). In this respect it differs from a deontological ethic which 'always runs the risk of developing schizophrenic agents who are compelled to do what duty dictates irrespective of whether they want to perform that act.' Virtue ethics can be linked to altruistic behavior. For an analysis of altruism, morality and economics see the volume edited by Phelps (1975).

justifying the high prices they charge for their products in poor countries. In this case ethics is clearly divorced from business, although practices may be perfectly legal.

The underground sector is made up of legal and illegal operations. For instance, subsistence agriculture is legal and pretty extensive in many poor countries. Some activities in the informal sector may be illegal from a narrowly defined perspective; I am referring to very small manufacturing and repair activities, which do not pay taxes, but do not bring damage to the public at large. Are such activities unethical? In one way they are, for the individuals who undertake them may use public goods in the course of their work. On the other hand, these activities are useful and provide jobs and incomes to people who, otherwise, may be unemployed and would strain the public budget when safety nets operate and individuals are entitled to them. It is also true that, in developing economies, the underground sector reflects also the attempt by individuals (firms) to go around red-tape and survive under very adverse circumstances. These attempts frequently mirror inadequate incentives. Therefore, the picture is pretty clouded in this respect.

The underground sector hosts criminal activities, which, ipso facto, involve unethical behavior. This situation is encountered on a large scale in developing economies, where institutions to fight organized crime are quite weak.

An interesting case is offered by post-communist countries (transition economies), which have experienced a period of institutional interregnum (vacuum) in the aftermath of the collapse of the command systems. This state of affairs has allowed many individuals and firms to operate unethically without fear of penalties. A distinction should be made, in this respect, between questionable practices, which are the result of missing institutions (regulations), and unethical behavior, which may become deeply entrenched and damage economic performance through time. Developing economies, in general, provide ample leeway to ethically 'fuzzy' behavior because of precarious institutional contexts. This state of affairs has prompted De Soto (2000) to emphasize that large efficiency gains, and overall development could be achieved in poor countries, by defining and enforcing property rights adequately and by empowering citizens.

3.2 Over-regulation and Under-regulation

Regulations impact aggregate economic performance. Arguably, the more regulated (and taxed) is an economy the more induced are agents to operate in the underground sector. It can be submitted that there is an optimal *structure* and *level* of regulation of the economy which maximizes societal welfare; the optimal structure and level of regulation depend on social norms, values and principles which validate what people at large appreciate as being positive and negative externalities.

This optimality can be illustrated graphically by dividing the economy into two sectors: the official and unofficial sectors which, both, consume factors of production – labor and capital (Daianu, 1997). Both over-regulation and under-regulation lead to inferior compositions of the economy in terms of societal welfare. Thus, over-regulation means an expansion of the underground economy against the background of reduced overall efficiency. Likewise, an under-regulated system (as in the case of environmental protection, or securities legislation) can bring about an 'official' expansion of socially pernicious activities, which also reduces societal welfare. The shape of the combination curve indicates that both hyper-regulation (as in a command system) and the lack of regulation (no rules) can lead to a worse economic performance.

When regulations (or taxes) rise there is a shift of the price line in favor of the unofficial sector in the sense of stimulating its expansion – this happens because the goods produced in the official sector become more expensive. Another effect is an increase of the nominal prices of the goods and services in the underground economy – although they become relatively cheaper – which can only partially be mitigated by its expansion (which puts downward pressure on prices in the unofficial economy).

In a simplified way agents' behaviors can be understood by comparing the benefits and costs of operating in the underground sector. The benefits are: the avoidance of the tax rate and the cost of regulations compliance. The cost of non-compliance includes, *inter alia*, the penalty fee, which can be adjusted by the probability of being caught. A variable whose size is most critical is the cost of non-compliance. A main thesis of this chapter is that when standards of reputation are low the cost of non-compliance is diminished, which enhances the functioning of the unofficial sector. This issue is revisited when the emphasis will be put on explaining reputation as an asset.

The minimum price acceptable in the unofficial sector can be defined as the official ruling market price from which the tax rate and the cost of regulations compliance are deduced, and the penalty fee adjusted by the probability of being caught is added. Clearly, the price mentioned above is the minimum for not incurring losses. The equilibrium price in the underground sector depends on the intensity of competition, which further depends on the cost of non-compliance. Thus, when the modified cost of non-compliance goes up, the underground economy shrinks and vice-versa; likewise, the equilibrium price, rises; when the cost of non-compliance goes down the underground economy expands but, eventually the equilibrium price goes down since competition intensifies.

More intense competition in the official economy and a rise of the cost of non-compliance would tend to bring closer the values of the minimum price and the equilibrium price. As it was emphasized the cost of non-compliance depends essentially on the entrenched rules of the game in the local environment. To be more specific, the size of the probability of being caught depends on rule enforcements, social norms, and the local standards of reputation. It can also be assumed that the rules of the game depend on how agents (companies) view their reputation as an asset to be built up.

3.3 Variety of Institutional Contexts and of Economic Performance

The variety of institutional circumstances, with their correspondence in regulatory frameworks and economic performance, is studied by comparative economics. This field of economics is staging a comeback lately, but under a new guise:

instead of examining market based systems as against communist (command) systems (as until 1989) the focus now is on examining the variety of capitalism, various brands of market economy.

Djankow et al. (2004) show that specific institutional contexts can be conceptualized through an IPC (institutional possibilities curve); this curve illustrates various combinations of private orderings, independent judges, state regulations and state ownership; an optimal state of affairs would be when social losses are at a minimum. This analysis can explain both the pressure for deregulation in the last couple of decades, against the backdrop of intense technological change and financial innovation, and consequences of excessive deregulation.[9] While EU member countries seems to be over-regulated in certain regards (the Lisbon Agenda tries to address this situation) the USA economy appears to have accumulated increasing social losses in the late 1990s because of too much deregulation (or the lack of proper regulations). For, it is fair to say, technological advance and financial innovation created major new opportunities, which were not envisaged by those who had conceived regulatory frameworks. But these new opportunities contained seeds of evil as well. Thus, referring to the cynicism of energy and financial companies during the boom of the last decade an *International Herald Tribune* editorial notes that 'One energy trader gloats about cheating "poor grandmothers". Another suggests shutting down a power plant in order to drive up electricity prices...*Enron* and other major energy companies manipulated California's energy markets in 2000 and 2001 in ways that cost the state billions.' The same editorial observes that '...Wall Street analysts acknowledged that the stocks they were peddling were mostly dogs...' (8 June 2004).

The IPC framework suggests that too much regulation, as well as too little regulation, are not good for the economy, or society as a whole. But the optimal combination changes over time, in view of evolving institutions and technology. Individuals' behaviors can be included in this picture. In general, developing economies are less adept at identifying optimal institutional combinations.

Informal sectors tell much about institutional contexts, for such portions of economy are the cover for illegal, criminal activities. By definition, criminal behavior is unethical. Nonetheless it is notable that some people may enter the underground sector because of an improper structure of incentives – as these are constructed by public policy. In this case, analysis has to use analytical nuances; what is qualified as unethical behavior (because it is in the informal economy) can easily come into the open, and be positively judged provided the set of incentives changes in the right direction. An example is the huge social security contributions which are practiced in not so few European countries, which induce many entrepreneurs to use black market labor. The bottom line is that a large informal

---

[9] The IPC framework, as an illustration of the so-called 'new' New Comparative Economics, is regarded with some skepticism by the proponents of the 'old' New Comparative Economics (see Dallago, 2004). In my opinion, the IPC framework, in spite of its limitations, provides an interesting way of examining institutional settings and can be much fruitful for analysis.

sector is more likely to present unethical behavior as against the formal economy. Both over-regulation and under-regulation can favor illegal activities and unethical behavior.

A big question is why socially precarious equilibria are resilient, albeit most of the players would be better off by changing their behaviors. This looks like an obvious coordination problem, which this chapter tries to answer by examining the concept of reputation.

3.4 Explaining Low Equilibria: Reputation as an Asset

I would submit that *reputation* is the source of all positive social externalities, be they *trust, trustworthiness, truth-telling, loyalty*, etc. By accumulating reputation individuals and communities increase the amount of individual[10] and social capital. Likewise, the quest for better reputation necessarily contains unethical behavior and implies less illegal acts.[11]

One can think about the accumulation of reputation in both static and dynamic terms, as stock and flow. Thus, it should be quite appealing to common sense to view higher reputation (and, consequently, trust and loyalty) as a means to reduce X-inefficiency (at micro-level) and allocative inefficiency, as an addition to the stock of overall capital. Higher stocks of reputation can be captured analytically in two ways: either by increasing the stock of overall capital (capital augmenting) and, therefore, output; or by enhancing efficiency and, concomitantly, output. In the latter case one can easily resort to the concept of transaction costs (Williamson, 1985) and conclude that higher reputation as an average trait of a system reduces transaction and information costs. Reputation can be viewed as a means to reduce the trade-off between specialization of work and trust under conditions of anonymity of participants to exchange. This would be the static portion of analysis. On a diagram this can be shown by an outward shift of the production possibilities curve.

In the dynamic case one can think analogously of the role of human capital build-up, and particularly of education, in economic growth.[12] Higher *reputation* has several implications. By making agents more efficient this likely raises their propensity to accumulate and invest over time. In addition, higher reputation raises overall efficiency (including allocative efficiency) within the national environment and, thereby, it creates higher rates of return, which further may stimulate saving and investment. Krugman (1994) argues that nations do not compete. However, when economies are seen as 'clusters of activities', which create synergies, they do compete. Summing up, one can dray an inference: higher reputation, seen as asset accumulation, is liable to make both individual agents and a national environment more efficient and competitive; this would enhance R&D, growth prospects – like in endogenous growth model stories. On one hand, this shifts the production

---

[10] A company's reputation for ethical behavior is part of its brand-name capital (Brickley et al., 2002).

[11] For various ways of dealing with reputation in formal models, see Klein (1997).

[12] See Becker (1964) and Schultz (1961).

possibilities curve of economy outwards; on the other hand, it does raise the growth path of the economy.

3.5 Reputation in Transition Economies

Intangible goods (which are positive social externalities) like *trust, truth-telling, loyalty* were scarce commodities in the command economies. This legacy cannot be overcome instantaneously during transition. The explanation for this state of affairs is essentially twofold: institutional change, and social relations in general, are time-consuming – *natura non facit saltus*; society and the structure of property rights are still too fuzzy in order to shape behaviors clearly and penalize misconduct. One can talk in this respect about a certain ethos, a business culture which reflects the nature of institutions; this business culture does not encourage better economic performance.

Unethical behavior is a facet of the lack, or neglect of reputation. In a society where clear rules of behavior and codes of ethical conduct (as 'seals of approval') are the norm, reputation is highly valued; reputation can be built up, or destroyed, and this affects the evolution of individuals in society as well as their expected income streams in economic life. This logic would apply to enterprise life as well. An individual, who optimizes for the long run, would be much concerned about his or her reputation and would not undertake actions inimical to it. Why isn't this type of optimization the rule of the social game during transition? There can be several explanations in this respect. One, which was already alluded to, is linked with the fuzzy state of property rights. Another explanation can be connected with uncertainty, which reduces the time horizon used by individuals and organizations. These are, certainly, valid arguments. But what frequently motivates people is the appeal of easy to obtain gains by speculating legal loopholes and by overlooking social consequences of their acts.

Neglect of reputation can be met in politics, too. Usually, a politician should be much concerned about deeds which can harm his or her reputation. Frequently, one sees politicians' behavior much focused on the short term, which can hardly be rationalized by the pressure of current events. This attitude seems to be related more to an optimization that involves the public position as a purveyor of *rents*. The public function is conceived as a good business, but not for a long time, and a *big discount is applied to reputation.* One could argue that this type of behavior fits those who enter politics for extra-political (economics) reasons. On the other hand, since this behavior is quite pervasive the resultant 'competition' leads to increasingly bigger discounts. In this way society as a whole is a loser and the 'rule of law' becomes a long distanced image.[13] This social low equilibrium can persist for a long time.

How could this biased behavior be captured at a micro-level? A possible way is to use a utility function which includes *reputation* as a variable. The optimizing (satisfying) behavior implies the maximization of a function, namely a utility

---

[13] A fallacy of composition is involved here; what seems to be rational for individuals becomes detrimental for society. A negative externality thus emerges.

stream. The utility stream depends on the stock of reputation at the present time t, a time horizon used by agents (which cannot exceed the potential active life), and a discount factor applied to future utility flows. Obviously, the assumption is that higher reputation implies higher utility. The dynamic of the stock of *reputation* can be illustrated by its own function. In a normal environment, an agent would be interested in accumulating reputation and maximizing the utility function in the long run.

The analysis can incorporate the degree of *fuzziness* (including property rights) in the system. A relationship can be established *between fuzziness* and the time frame used by economic and political agents. It thus makes sense to assume that the higher is the degree of fuzziness, ceteris paribus, the bigger is the propensity to work with a reduced time horizon.

3.6 Why do Low Equilibria Persist?

An interesting aspect can be brought into the analysis at this point, which may shed light on and explain why relatively low standards of reputation and high corruption are resilient in many areas of the world. This would also illuminate why people seem to accommodate their habits and condone what some may consider to be unacceptable patterns of behaviors and which, should presumably, change over time. It can be submitted that, when it is seen in relative terms, *reputation* depends on local standards of ethics and morality (corruption), on local seals of approval. This is a different sort of ethical relativism than the one that basically dismisses ethical considerations. The existence of local yardsticks of ethical behavior is more realistic when globalization of economic life, and of universally held standards of business ethics, have less of an impact. Therefore, a revised form of a reputation function, takes into account what is perceived as 'normal' by the local environment. The above formulation says that the degree of corruption, or the moral (ethical) laxity in the system regarding the observance of normal (not local) standards of reputation affects the perception of one agent's reputation. When corruption is widespread and the interpretation of laws is highly arbitrary agents become almost indifferent to *reputation* as an asset.[14] Under such circumstances

---

[14] One can imagine situations of multiple equilibria – good or bad – related to individuals' behaviors. An example is when people pay their due taxes, or they evade it. There are models which try to portray such situations. Thus, it is assumed that the production of an individual firm (index i) is an increasing function of a public good provided by the state. It is assumed now that the level of public good $g=nt$, where t indicates the degree of fiscality, and n denotes the number of firms that pay taxes. The individual production function can be written as $q_i=q+ag$, with $a>0$. In the case of tax evasion, $q_i=q$. Different equilibria appear. Let us assume that $a<1<N$. The firm income after tax is $(q+ag-t)$ if all firms pay taxes and (q) if no firm pays taxes. It seems that the decision is clear for the firm; it tries to avoid taxes as long as $t<ag=ant$, or $n<1/a$. If $n=1$ (which means that all firms practice tax evasion) the firm N is also stimulated to get into tax evasion since $n<1/a$ (according to the assumption made). If $n=N$, then the firm is interested in paying taxes since $n>1$ (see also Sachs, 1994, p. 48). This reasoning can be applied to any kind of criminal or illegal act.

concern about reputation, namely its consolidation becomes insignificant, or even negative. It is a case of sacrificing any trace of reputation for the sake of realizing exceptionally high material gains in the short run. In this case the trade-off between *reputation* and other factors that enter into the utility function do not favor the build up of reputation.

When short-term materials gains get the upper-hand *vis-a-vis* the accumulation of reputation the optimization process gets more complicated. Thus, the optimal stock of reputation can be seen as being dependent on the local rules of the game, and the specific 'weight' of the agent. In this case the utility function is revised by making a distinction between reputation as a goal in itself, and the marginal utility derived from being concerned about reputation; this latter utility denotes potential material gains to be made by using the 'rules of the game' and the knowledge of the local environment (including inside information and the use of networks).

Under sufficiently constraining conditions of the local 'rules of the game', or by very small incremental gains which induce agents not to care about reputation, a situation can be imagined when higher reputation is not accompanied by higher utility; it is like a point from which the marginal cost of 'puritanical' behavior exceeds its marginal benefit. This means that material gains, however these are acquired, prevail over the accumulation of reputation. In such a context feelings of guilt and shame of bad deeds do not constrain behavior meaningfully.

The discount rate (applied to future streams of utility) depends also on the degree of uncertainty regarding the evolution of the legal environment. The less clear and more uncertain is an environment compared to an ideal framework, the lower is the discount rate. Why the specific 'weight' of actors is mentioned? For there are people, who, through their critical mass (which includes reputation) can influence the rules of the game and the environment. For such individuals, whose dimension goes beyond the frontiers of the local environment, *reputation* acquires different parameters of definition and possible compromises they may get into have a different nature and other implications. Such individuals may develop the ability to stand up morally and not be forced to 'howl with wolves.'[15] Virtue ethics, as against narrowly defined deontological ethics, play a high profile in their behavior. There are cases when highly respected individuals, once they take over public positions, can improve the image of the public entity (the or country) they represent. This can be the situation of a minister of finance, or of a governor of a central bank. Obviously, this reasoning can be extrapolated to a whole government. For such circumstances a collective utility function includes as a variable the reputation of key public servants (ministers).[16]

---

[15] Once, a commercial banker confessed to me that the world of business 'does not like those who are more catholic than the Pope.' This prodding meant that that one needs to be particularly heavyweight in order to be successful as a businessman while being 'excessively puritanical' in behavior.

[16] One factor that might help explain the persistence of bad equilibria is the annihilation (or even the physical elimination) of individuals that attempt to build a stock of reputation – either for themselves or for an institution/group they represent. Examples could relate to situations existent in Italy, decades ago, or, nowadays, in countries in South America.

When new norms are not rooted socially well enough and since a new moral order cannot emerge instantaneously the role of 'moral models' acquires exceptional importance. Leaders of great charisma and moral probity, with vision and determination are essential in making change for the better possible. But such leaders are not easy to find. *Leadership* is an issue that underlines the moral dimension of a society's transformation. Ultimately, however, repaired or solid institutions have to come into being in order to make societies perform better.

4 Institutional Responses to Ethical Lapses

Institutional responses follow various tracks. One involves public policy as when governments react by adopting new regulations. Another track is a response by organizations which represent producers and consumers, which leads to new regulations and modifications of codes of conduct; this is change from below. The changes under way in accounting and auditing rules reflect both policy tracks. Likewise, modifications in best practices are a venue for improving (constraining) harmful behavior by individuals and firms. The battle for improving governance in public and private sectors, around the world, is driven by culture, ethical considerations as well. Not least education gets into the picture. The revival of business ethics courses in business schools curricula and the efforts to enlist major corporations under the banner of promoting corporate social responsibility is part of the same process.

Institutional responses, of whatever sort, are influenced by major social and ideological cycles. As a matter of fact, the events of recent years have triggered a lot of soul-searching in western societies and people talk more profoundly about the next stage in the evolution of capitalism. On the other hand, the very social and economic dynamics of global capitalism force policy-makers to reexamine the regulatory frameworks under which economies operate.

Ethics can be examined in the international economy as well. The dispute over free trade vs. fair trade revolves also around the perception that rich countries preach what they do not practice; their hypocrisy is amply indicated by agricultural subsidies while poor countries' main exports are made of farm products. The issue of ethical attitudes concerns financial relations as well; the pressure put on emerging economies to open their capital account in the 1990s was the outcome of powerful lobbies exerted by financial industries in the wealthy economies. Therefore, the crises which erupted in a series of South East Asian countries in the late 1990s have an obvious moral dimension as well. The list of global issues with ethical implications includes poverty, fighting diseases, environmental protection, etc.

The past decade has been suffused with claims that economic policy, in the advanced countries, is being driven by an emerging new consensus on principles and practice. The ideological fallout was pretty obvious in Anthony Giddens' expression 'The Third Way', which connotes neither traditional social-democracy, nor blatant liberalism – in the European sense (Giddens, 1998); this formula was adopted by the 'new' Labor Party in the UK as its quasi-philosophical mantra and other social democrats have tried to foray deeply into it. Highly glamorous seminars featuring Bill Clinton, Tony Blair, Gerhard Schroeder, Lionel Jospin, and others were quite en vogue in the late 90s. In the United States, George W. Bush used 'compassionate conservatism' as an ideological means to enhance his presidential message. It appeared as social-democrats (in Europe) and democrats (in the USA), on one hand, and center-right parties (in Europe) and republicans (in the USA) were coming closer, in terms of both principles and practice of economic policy.

The sources of this apparent 'new' consensus are, arguably, several. One origin could be traced to the ever longing desire of Man to control his environment (nature) and to be more efficient. Thus, in the first quarter of the past century Max Weber's 'rationalization of life' referred to rational accounting, rational law, rational technology, which by extrapolation, can be extended to 'rational economics', as a form of *hard science* (as *Newtonian economics*). Later on (in the seventies), another famous sociologist, Daniel Bell, upheld the primacy of knowledge and theory-related activities in ordering our life, man's technological and economic ascendancy – which would imply that economic wizards can secure a fool-proof policy (Bell, 1973). Quantitative methods may have also entrenched this intellectual propensity. Even the clash between Keynesism and monetarism, as the two main competing macro-economic paradigms, could be seen in the vein of searching for the ultimate piece of wisdom. Another origin of policy amalgamation comes out of the death of communism. Fukuyama's *End of History* was seen by many as an embodiment of the, presumably, single ideology (liberal democracy) which was meant to rule the world. Last, but not least, globalization – as an incarnation of unfettered markets and downsizing of government, operating worldwide – also provided an impetus to the vision of the 'ideal' type of economic policy.

At the start of the new century facts are disavowing over-simplifications. There are numerous examples which prove that conflicting ideas are with us, that reality cannot be encapsulated into a Procustian ideological bed; that economics continues to be softer than some of us try to make people believe. Let's be more specific. Policy-wise, it is increasingly clear that trimming the welfare state and the public sector is not enough in order to achieve the expected efficiency gains; this endeavor needs to be accompanied by effective regulations of various markets (financial and energy, in particular), which, otherwise, can easily be rigged; 'the new economy', the 'new paradigm' (which claimed to combine high growth rates with very low unemployment), proved to be, simply put, a mirage of the 1990s. Recent developments in the US and elsewhere offer ample proofs in this regard; these events motivated public authorities to intervene. Likewise, as against the prevailing tenets of not many years ago, economic policy, as it is currently undertaken in the US and Europe, does not preclude running larger budget deficits during a downswing of the cycle; this is the explanation for some basic Keynesian recipes returning to the limelight.

How does globalization fit into this picture? The pressure of more intense competition forces governments to streamline their public sectors, which does frustrate trade-unions and many citizens, at large. But rich countries, in the West, remain welfare states, *par excellence*, albeit in an evolving manner. One can detect here a rising/returning Keynesianism in macroeconomic policy-making with a retreat when it comes to social policy; there is an apparent policy contradiction herein. Another consequence of globalization is the creation of an international policy agenda. By omission and commission, some of the wealthy countries' less inspired policies have given renewed high profile to issues such as: fair vs. free trade; dealing with abject poverty in the world; protecting the environment as a public good for mankind; the code of conduct for international corporations, how to manage contagion effects in the world economy; policy coordination among the leading economies of the world, etc. There is an obvious ethical dimension assigned to this international agenda.

As a matter of fact, the traditional ongoing battle between left and right – within the framework of democratic politics – is being shifted, partially, into the international arena. The debate on global governance reflects a growing awareness that there are issues that need to be addressed internationally, in a multilateral context and using collaborative approaches. Arguably, the choice between globalization and 'managed globalization' is between accepting the effects of completely free markets, with policy disregard for market failures and their social consequences, and trying to construct an international policy, which should address/prevent massive coordination failures. The controversies surrounding globalization touch upon ethical considerations as well. Concomitantly, the debate over which form of capitalism, and what type of state intervention in the economy, turns, partially, into a debate on which form of 'global capitalism.'

A second policy route, namely the setting of an international policy agenda, does make sense in a global economy in which there is acceptance of the need for international public goods.[17] Otherwise, under increasing pressure from foreign markets and other threats (including terrorism, illegal immigration, spreading diseases, etc), governments would resort to national means of protection – such as trade protectionism and trade clashes, competitive devaluations, etc.

Ideology is not dead, and it does shape social and economic policies – although in subtler forms and following cyclical patterns. It may be less felt nationally to the extent the battlefield of ideas expands increasingly beyond national borders. In any case, globalization is likely to reflect ever more the battle of ideas, including the ethical dimension, with traditional politics delving increasingly into the international domain. How would policy-makers address the hot issues in the international economy would provide clues regarding its dynamics, to what extent ethical considerations come to the fore.

---

[17] The ecological concerns would pay attention also to the fact that future generations cannot voice their concerns on how current generations deplete the Earth's resources; this is a major flaw of revealed 'rational calculation' as it is provided by completely free markets and an argument in favor of public intervention. See Boulding (1978) for a wide ranging plea in this respect as well as in addressing the issue of complexity of economic processes.

5 Conclusion: Whither Capitalism?

It is hard not to share Sen's thought that 'it is precisely the narrowing of the broad Smithian view of human beings, in modern economies, that can be seen as one of the major deficiencies of contemporary economic theory. This impoverishment is closely related to the distancing of economics from ethics' (1987, p. 28). Arguably, this distancing has an impact on real life (economies), on how people live, on how they relate to each other. When people lose the moral compass and virtue ethics fades away they become oblivious to the Socratic question regarding the purpose of one's life. Sooner or later this brings misery and disappointment in individual lives and causes social pain on a massive scale.

Society reacts one way or another. For instance, the years which followed the Great Depression brought about new regulations that aimed at restraining excesses and unethical behavior stemming from the free-market social organization of society. An example was the *Glass-Steagall Act* in the US, which split investment banking from commercial banking. Institutional adjustments followed the end of the Second World War as well. And the big failures in financial and energy markets, in the past decade, have ushered in a new period of market regulation, which reshapes public policy accordingly. The *Sarbanes-Oxley Act* of 2002 in the US is a clear example of such new activism. Firms, too, are reexamining their internal regulation systems in order to cope with unethical behavior. And new accounting and auditing rules are being put in place. Such policy responses, at macro and micro levels, are meant to make capitalism function better.[18]

Policy pragmatism is in higher demand than policy fundamentalism nowadays, although hard-nosed 'ideologues' are present in the corridors of power. Nevertheless, public policy is forced to reconsider older themes (e.g. the State needs to provide public goods) in order to regain the moral ground, which was partially lost owing to major scandals in the corporate world. The moral ground relates to domestic as well as international politics.

In European transition economies the prospects of joining the EU have operated as a catalyst for reforms and a strong support for dealing with the pains and frustrations of societal change. But not a few citizens are disappointed by the results of reforms, and the widespread corruption and unethical behavior incense most of the population; some citizens relate these phenomena to market reforms, and this perception does show up unabashedly in the polls. Once the first wave of EU eastern enlargement would be well underway benefits would accrue to many citizens, but disappointments, too, are likely to become more intense. Such likely outcomes beg a candid discussion on the linkage between values, morality and the dynamics of capitalism and what it takes to make it more fulfilling for most of the population. This is why the public debate on effective regulations and institutions which should strengthen the ability of markets to deliver for the satisfaction of most citizens (consumers) and avoid massive social exclusion has not lost any relevance. The scope of the state in providing public goods should be judged in the same vein, albeit this role should be judged in conjunction with the need for a

---

[18] Greider would call it 'reinventing capitalism' (Greider, 2003).

streamlined and more efficient public sector, which should not crowd out (undermine) the proficiency of the private sector.

The public debate on ethics and economy acquires new overtones when looking at the world under the impact of globalization and other forces at work. Aside from international terrorism, one can point at the dark side of globalization: inability to cope with global issues (such as global warming), massive illegal immigration, increasing poverty in many areas of the world, poor functioning of international financial markets, trade disputes, etc. In this context, the issues of governance, both in the public and private spheres, get more salience. And governance cannot be dissociated from the moral values, the mindsets of those who make decisions.

To sum up: history indicates cycles of policies and institutional adjustments following large economic dynamics. It may be, that after a deregulation euphoria which featured so highly on the agenda of governments, especially, in the Anglo-Saxon world, during the last couple of decades, a new phase is about to set in; this phase would underline the need for effective market regulations and a more enlightened working together between the public and the private sphere. This logic would have to apply to the international economy as well, which needs public goods so badly, which further demand reshaped international institutions – capable of ensuring global governance. The latter, clearly, asks for more international cooperation and a common vision on how to tackle the major challenges confronting mankind. These challenges cannot be dealt with unless economic rationality blends with social and moral values, unless *shame* and *guilt* maintain the cement of societies.

References

Argandoña, A. (2004), On Ethical, Social and Environmental Management Systems, *Journal of Business Ethics*, 51, 1, pp. 41-52. Also available as a chapter of this book.

Arrow, K. J. (1951), *Social Choice and Individual Value*, New York, Wiley.

Arrow, K. J. (1974), *The Limits of Organization*, New York, Norton.

Bebear, C. and Manière, P. (2003), *Ils Vont Tuer le Capitalisme*, Paris, Plon.

Becker, G. (1964), *Human Capital*, New York, Columbia University Press.

Bell, D. (1973), *The Coming of Post-industrial Society*, New York, Basic Books.

Boulding, K. (1978), *Ecodynamics. A New Theory of Societal Evolution*, Beverly Hills, Sage Publications.

Brickley, J. A., Smith, C. F and Zimmerman, J. L. (2002), Business Ethics and Organizational Architecture, *Journal of Banking and Finance*, 26, pp. 1821-1835.

Daianu, D. (1997), Reputation as an Asset, paper presented at a *Workshop of the European Association of Comparative Economics* in Budapest, 1997. See Institutions, Strain and the Underground Economy, *The William Davidson Institute Working Paper*, 98.

Dallago, B. (2004), The 'Old' and the 'New' CES: A Synthesis, paper presented at the VIIIth *Bi-annual Conference of the Association of Comparative Economic Studies*, Belgrade, 23-25 September, manuscript.

De Soto, H. (2000), The Mystery of Capital. Why Capitalism Triumphs in The West and Fails Everywhere Else, New York, Basic Books.

Djankov, S., Shleifer, A., Glaser, A. L., La Porta, R., De Silanes, F. L. (2004), *The New Comparative Economics*, mimeo.

Eatwell, J. and Taylor, L (2000), Global Finance At Risk. The Case For International Regulation, New York, The New Press.

Fischer, S. (2003), Globalization and its Challenges, *American Economic Review, AEA Papers and Proceedings*, 93, 2, pp. 1-30.

Fukuyama, F. (1990), *The End of History*, New York, The Free Press.

Fukuyama, F. (1999), *The Great Disruption*, New York, The Free Press.

Giddens, A. (1998), *The Third Way. The Renewal of Social Democracy*, Oxford, Basil Blackwell.

Greider, C. (2003), The Soul of Capitalism. Opening Paths to a Moral Economy, New York, Simon and Schuster.

Kindleberger, C. (1989), Manias, Panics, and Crashes. A History of Financial Crises, New York, Basic Books.

Klein B. D. (ed.) (1997), Reputation. Studies in the Voluntary Elicitation of Good Conduct, Ann Arbor, University of Michigan.

Koehn, D. (1995), A Role for Virtue Ethics in the Analysis of Business Practice, *Business Ethics Quarterly*, 5, 3, pp. 533-539.

Krugman, P. (1994), Competitiveness: A Dangerous Obsession, *Foreign Affairs*, March-April, 73, 2.

Lal, D. (1999), Unintended Consequences. The Impact of Factor Endowments, Culture, and Politics on Long-Run Economic Performance, Cambridge (MA), MIT Press.

Phelps, E. S. (1975), *Altruism, Morality and Economic Theory*, New York, Russell Sage Foundation.

Sachs, J. (1994), Russia's Struggle with Stabilisation. Conceptual Issues and Evidence, paper prepared for the *World Bank's Annual Conference on Development Economics*.

Schultz, T. (1961), Investment in Human Capital, *American Economic Review*, 51, 1, pp. 1-17.

Sen, A. (1987), *On Ethics and Economics*, London, Basil Blackwell.

Shearmur, J. and Klein, D. B. (1997), Good conduct in the Great Society: Adam Smith and the Role of Reputation, In: Daniel B. Klein (ed.), *Studies in the Voluntary Elicitation of Good Conduct*, Ann Arbor, University of Michigan Press, pp. 29-46.

Shleifer, A. (2004), Does Competition Destroy Ethical Behavior?, *American Economic Review*, 94, 2, pp. 414-418.

Stiglitz, J. E. (2003), *The Roaring Nineties*, New York, W.W. Norton.

Summers, L. (2000), International Financial Crises: Causes, Prevention, and Cures, *American Economic Review, AEA Papers and Proceedings*, 90, 2, pp. 1-16.

Weber, M. (1958), The Protestant Ethic and The Spirit of Capitalism, New York, Scribners.

Williamson, O. (1985), *The Economic Institutions of Capitalism*, New York, Free Press.

Chapter 5

Moral Divide in International Business: A Descriptive Framework

Nicoletta Ferro

Chacun appelle barbarie ce qui n'est pas son usage (Montaigne, *Essais*, 1580).

1 Introduction

Globalization is the buzzword of the moment, internationally demonized as the source of all ills or uncritically proclaimed as the solution to the world's pains. If considered from an economic perspective, globalization means the growing integration of world markets and economies. Whether this integration should include any sort of ethical integration is a question of heated debate. This chapter advances the thesis of the existence of a moral divide within corporations and beyond them, and related to differences in ethical standards and norms across cultures. From this point of view, globalization seems to create favorable conditions for all sorts of forms of particularization, including ethical particularization, to emerge (Van Londen and De Ruijter, 2003). From an international business perspective, moral divide issues pose new and urgent challenges corporations seem quite unprepared to face.

Since transnational corporations emerged as new actors on the global scene, they came to fill the gap created by the progressive weakening of the links between territorial states and corresponding national production. Acting this way, corporations have become the most significant part of the world economic bloodstream (Chandler, 2001). While presenting similarities with multinational enterprises – the typical organizational structure of the 1980s – transnational corporations hold some distinguishing features. Firstly, if decentralization of industrial production is common to both multinational and transnational corporations, the way this global flexibility has been achieved is quite different. While multinationals' main feature is dislocation of production processes through subsidiaries and affiliates in target countries controlled by the home industry, transnational corporations' production and sales are 'distributed' (and not only dislocated) within independent and specialized units crossing national boundaries (Williams, 2000). This new kind of multilayered economic entity provides business transactions with flexibility within policy guidelines established by corporate headquarters, which are predominantly based in Western Europe, North America and Japan. Further differences lie in the fact that while on the one hand, multinational enterprises generally choose to expatriate their national staff (managers and technicians) to coordinate local branches while holding home based managers with responsibilities for foreign operations, on the other hand, transnational corporations create intercultural teams employing local staff as well as expatriate officers. Last but not least important, economic and political power achieved by some transnational corporations is unknown to multinationals. A study realized in 2000 and focusing on transnational corporations concluded that the top 200 transnational corporations' combined sales are bigger than the combined economies of all countries minus the biggest nine; that is to say their sales surpass the combined economies of 182 countries thus having almost twice the economic clout of the poorest four-fifths of humanity (Anderson and Cavanagh, 2000). Therefore a key concern regarding both transnational and multinational corporations operating in the global scenario is represented by the direction taken by foreign investments. Transnational corporations tend to establish subsidiaries in countries where conditions are most favorable to their business operations, specifically developing countries and countries in transition from socialism to capitalism. Moreover they take advantage of governments of less industrialized countries which are burdened by debts, low commodity prices, and high levels of unemployment and which are consequently more willing to attract corporations through liberalization of investment restrictions, privatization of public sector industries in addition to maintaining lower wages and fewer environmental regulations in comparison with developed countries (The Economist, 1993).

Furthermore less developed countries take advantage of the fact that dislocation processes typical of recent multinational and transnational companies are not limited to labor-intensive production processes, but to functions of labor-intensive service industries such as information technology, financial functions, customer services and managing human resources which started to be outsourced thanks to improvements in international communications and related reduction in costs. Therefore it is now increasingly common to find transnational companies headquartered in Europe, but with research, design, and production facilities spread over Asia and North America, additional production facilities in Latin America, marketing and distribution centers on every continent, and lenders and investors in Taiwan and Japan.

The aim of this chapter is to provide an insight on the moral divide issues affecting transnational corporations. Starting from organizational culture, Section 2 examines transnational corporations through the lenses of moral divide, shedding light on the challenges it poses to international business as well as to corporate social responsibility policies and philanthropic interventions. Section 3 analyses several relevant case studies. Section 4 discusses *universalism* and *relativism* as the traditional approaches used by corporations in dealing with moral divide issues and weighs the pros and cons of both. Section 5 investigates the relationship between moral divide and law with particular attention to international standards and corporate codes of conduct. The last section presents a set of general conclusions for the management of moral divide issues in corporate social responsibility areas in particular.

2 Transnational Corporation: the Moral Divide Issue

2.1 The Origin of the Problem: Organizational Culture

Culture is a fundamental part of our existence. In every particular society, at every moment in history, shared values exist. They are a part of a wider collective conscience framing desires and needs (Durkheim, 1893). Anthropologists call this common conscience culture. A concept that can still be defined through the definition provided by B. P. Tylor and considering culture as the complex whole that includes knowledge, belief, art, morals, law, custom and any other capabilities and habits acquired by man as a member of a society (Tylor, 1994).

It should be noted that, not only societies, but every form of organization, holds its own unique culture even though it may not have consciously tried to create it. Most of the times organizational culture is rather the unconscious result of the values imposed by the founders of the organization and of the leading example of the executives who run it. These elements are combined in a corporate culture that is partly codified and partly implicit (De George et al., 1998). Even if organizational culture should be distinguished from national cultures, several studies such as those by Hofstede (1980) and Trompenaars (1997), support the idea that corporate culture is partly influenced by national characters, and that despite the global ramification system created by transnational corporations, the cultural make-up of some companies known world-wide hardly lose their national character (Bollinger and Hofstede, 1989). Despite the possible links between corporate culture and national features, the importance of culture for organizations is undeniable. Organizational culture cannot be regarded as an accessory but it becomes the foundation on which the organization will exist in the world (Trompennars, 2001) as well as the key to organizational excellence, the function of leadership being limited to the creation and management of this culture (Schein, 1992). The distinguishing elements of organizational culture are to be found in the system of shared meanings, values, perceptions, behaviors, symbols and rituals, framing the company distinctiveness and uniqueness in the business world.

2.2 Moral Divide: Framing the Concept

As already pointed out, organizations are as diversified as society and several forms of subculture can coexist within an organization. The conglomerate of individuals forming an organization is, beyond an apparent uniformity, different in several ways and especially in the moral attitude towards life.

As Durkheim (1893) argued:

If there is one fact that history has irrefutably demonstrated it is that the morality of each people is directly related to the social structure of the people practicing it. The connection is so intimate that, given the general character of the morality observed in a given society and barring abnormal and pathological cases, one can infer the nature of that society, the elements of its structure and the way it is organized. Tell me the marriage patterns, the morals dominating family life, and I will tell you the principal characteristics of its organization (Durkheim, 1961, p. 87).

Moral, according to the Kantian perspective, is the self-managed collocation of a person in the world and revolves around home culture and the personal background. The coexistence of people with different sexual preferences or religious beliefs, for instance, vividly illustrates the point and provides a proof of the existence of a divide, namely a moral divide, acting within and beyond organizations, and crossing cultural and national boundaries. It should be noted that the moral divide is but another divide within divides (Sapelli, 2002). It follows the digital divide, namely the gap existing between those who can effectively use new information and communication tools and those who cannot, while having nothing to do with it. Moreover moral divide is similar to the ethnic divide while being more related to the ethical frame of reference of an individual. To sum up, what is referred to as moral divide is but the gap existing within different moral orientations and values and acting both within organizations and across them as a prevalent feature of organizational culture.

In order to better frame the issue, three different dimensions affected by the moral divide have been identified:

- Micro-dimension: consisting in the gap between personal moral orientations, such as those expressing religious or sexual preferences, within the organization.
- Meso-dimension: consisting in the gap between personal moral values and orientations and those values and orientations framing the overall corporate culture of the organization a person works for.
- Macro-dimension: consisting in the gap between home values and host country moral values experience by transnational corporations in their doing business abroad.

The feeling that very few companies can be defined as truly global in their approach seems quite widespread among experts and refers to transnational companies as well as to multinational companies. Moving to foreign countries to relocate subsidiary production means, for most multinational and transnational corporations, transplanting their own western corporate culture and mind set together with staff and production, no matter where the corporation's branches, affiliates or subcontractors are located (Dunfee and Fort, 2003). As a consequence, western corporations appear like seeds sown on hostile ground, and find it increasingly difficult to face the cultural shock caused by otherness and related to differences in the following areas:

- Cognitive frameworks (reasoning processes, space and time perception and use);
- Behavioral codes (manners and customs, food preferences, hygienic habits, attitude towards safety and environmental measures);

- Shared meanings perceptions (languages and body languages such as facial expressions, eye contact, gestures, posture);
- Symbols and rituals (religion and symbolic meanings given to colors or acts);
- Distinctive set of ethical values and standards giving conscious or unconscious directions on how to behave.

Within the context of economic organizations, the moral divide is related to differences in the way a wide range of issues are perceived by one culture or another as having moral import (Hendry, 1999). When two or more values-related issues conflict in the perception of the decision-maker and no clear right or wrong seems to dominate a plausible solution, that is the moment when cross-cultural ethical dilemmas become conflicts. To go deeper into the matter, conflicts and dilemmas due to moral divide are categorized into three main spheres. The first sphere is the meaning sphere, including practices considered morally acceptable in some settings but condemned in others. The second is the attribution sphere and it is about practices categorized as meaningful in one culture while losing any apparent meaning and importance in another. The last sphere (the relative development sphere) consists of a wide range of practices accepted by a particular society and depending on the level of relative development achieved by this society. Several cases relating to companies working in foreign settings, provide enough evidence of the corporation departments most affected by moral divide issues (note that this list should not be considered exhaustive).

- human resources management and supply chain management,
- production processes planning,
- cross border acquisitions, mergers and alliances,
- the whole area of communication including international marketing, advertisement, public relations, international negotiation and training and teamwork building,
- health and safety policies,
- risk assessment and crisis management,
- banking and finance,
- corporate social responsibility (CSR) policies, charity and stakeholder engagement.

2.3 Corporate Social Responsibility and Moral Divide

Society's expectations over the responsibilities of corporations in areas previously seen as the domain of the State have recently expanded. Corporations have for too long been given environmental and social carte blanche and a wide range of stakeholders such as citizens, anti-multinational activists, consumers, regulators, investors and non-governmental organizations began to demand that corporations assume broader responsibilities than the traditional Friedmanian profitability goals and achieve tency in their operations together with accountability for the social and environmental impacts of their actions. This new trend forced business organizations to assume wider responsibilities in order to play a pivotal role to make business a 'force for good', whilst remaining competitive and profitable (Davies and Nelson, 2003). As a result, transnational corporations started adopting proactive stances in addressing social responsibility issues in their operation management. However doing business in general and managing corporate social responsibility in foreign settings is not an easy task for the unprepared as it poses several threats.

Linkages between moral divide and corporate social responsibility policies appear evident as argued by Litvin (2004):

> I think the management techniques have often been rather simplistic and this I think even applies to some of the corporate social responsibility effort of modern companies. CSR often doesn't get to the heart of development problems (Litvin, 2004, p. 2).

In other words problems arise when policies for setting global corporate social and environmental initiatives take western culture as their only frame of reference. Consequently on the pretence of doing good and acting as good corporate citizens, corporations misunderstand local needs by focusing on what is internationally advocated (by Western activists for example) but which may not always be what is locally acceptable and desired. Therefore the unintended consequences of western CSR policies often lead to what are described as 'irresponsible business practices' rather than responsible (The Economist, 2002). This is not a new phenomenon since corporations time and time again, in a pattern that is too pronounced to be coincidental, have exercised their power in unplanned, unsophisticated or self-defeating ways, harming local communities (Litivin, 2003). The perverse outcomes of western corporations' efforts to behave well, proved to be effective over the following situations directly related to CSR policies and charity initiatives:

- Social connections: Bribery, corruption, nepotism, gift giving;
- Human Rights: Sweatshop conditions, gender and racial discrimination, exploitation of child and women labor, labor wages;
- Perceptions: Insider trading, software piracy, performance bonuses, remunerative standards, contractual obligations, employee theft;
- Relative Development: Untested or harmful product selling, harm to natural resources, consequences of temporary large-scale investments on local communities.

3 Moral Divide Case Studies

This section provides a categorization of conflicts generating from moral divide issues and relying on the distinction between conflicts of relative development and conflicts of cultural tradition, provided by Donaldson and Dunfee (1996).

Conflict of Relative Development are, from a business-oriented perspective, conflicts dealing with differences between host countries' legal standards and standards imposed by corporations and reflecting western tradition.

On the one hand differences in the level of economic development acquired by a nation state can be due to lower development of public institutions or legal frameworks. On the other hand it also possible that some less developed countries' governments, in order to attract foreign investments and capital, voluntarily keep wage rates, working hours and health standards low and not in conformity with major international regulations such as *ILO Conventions* and *OECD Guidelines for Multinational Enterprises*.

A typical example of a conflict of relative development is provided by the case of a drug for the treatment of serious viral infections, including measles, which had been rejected by the US market on the basis of a very sensitive new test for endotoxins[1] required by the US Food & Drug Administration (FDA), the American health agency. It is proper to note that the new test had been added to a previous test that has been the FDA standard for many years and showed a very low level of endotoxins in the drug. Since endotoxins can cause a high fever when injected into patients, but possibly no other problems, a double standard exists between the US, where the drug was not admitted for sale and many developing countries, where more sensitive tests were not compulsory. The dilemma arising in this situation is whether the selling of the drug should be allowed in those countries where more sensitive tests were not compulsory or whether the more advanced American standard should prevail? As this drug can potentially save thousands of lives especially among children, and given the low risks of side effects, the decision maker found enough room for a flexible solution of the dilemma and a limited sale of the drug to developing countries was allowed saving thousands of people.

Conflicts of Cultural Tradition is the shock provoked by otherness and occurs when business-making processes within western corporations are confronted with well-established norms and behaviors strictly linked to local settings and most of the time unfamiliar to the western mind-set. As a result norms and behaviors acceptable and considered normal in one setting, are unacceptable in another and cause conflict.

An example will clarify the situation. Let us take for instance a country such as Saudi Arabia where women, in the name of strongly held religious and cultural beliefs, are not allowed to serve as corporate managers, their role being strictly limited to education and health care positions. It is clear that this is not a conflict falling under the umbrella of relative development, as any increase in the country's level of economic development, which is already quite high compared to other Muslim countries, will not change the norms as they are generated by different cultural and religious beliefs from ours (Donaldson and Dunfee, 1999). The misunderstanding of cultural and religious beliefs proved to be fatal in the case of

---

[1] Endotoxins, which occur in the outer membrane of certain gram-negative bacteria, are not secreted but are released only when the cells are disrupted or destroyed. They are complex polysaccharide molecules that elicit an antigenic response resulting in fever and altered resistance to bacterial infections.

some consultants of a large US computer-products company who insisted on using exactly the same training regarding sexual harassment with Muslim managers, as that used with American employees in the United States. The short sightedness of this approach caused many problems because Muslim managers felt offended by that kind of unequivocal and direct training and the message about avoiding coercion and sexual discrimination was lost.

Further examples of conflicts of cultural tradition are evident when marketing and selling strategies fail to take into consideration the complexity of local cultural issues such as when McDonald's decided to enter the complex Indian business environment, counting only on its fast food global formula. Things became complicated when rumors about McDonald's cooking French fries in beef fat quickly spread throughout the country. As almost one billion of the Indian Hindu population worship cows as holy creatures, the problem was not an easy one to handle for the American Corporation. History tells more than we can learn as a similar situation in 1857 led to the revolt of Sepoys (the native Indian soldiers serving in the army of the East India Company under the British in northern and central India), as a result of the British using cow and pig fat in rifle cartridges. In the case of McDonald's, executives denied any wrongdoing and replied to allegations, arguing that they never meant to market themselves as vegetarian. Their restaurants incurred the wrath of locals, windows were smashed and statues of Ronald McDonald smeared with cow dung (Goodtsein, 2001). The Indian affair risked undermining the company's activity over an enormous market. As a result McDonald's started to slowly shift its approach from universalism to a self-conscious adaptation to local habits resulting in a pure vegetarian menu (vegeburgers made of soybeans) and lamb hamburgers sold throughout the Indian subcontinent. This gave McDonald's the chance to discover that the popularity of its product was increasingly qualified by exceptions (Trompennars and Humpden-Turner, 2001).

The case of the athletic footwear company, Nike, gives another example of the consequences deriving from ignoring religious beliefs and symbols belonging to cultures. In summer 1997, Nike created a new line of shoes carrying a logo which was meant to look like flames which were called Air Bakin', AirMelt, AirGrilland and Air B-que (Associated Press, 1997). The Council on American-Islamic relations (CAIR), a Washington-based Islamic advocacy group, felt deeply offended as, they argued, the design resembled the word 'Allah' in the Arabic script. The furious reaction of the Muslim world forced Nike to recall shoes from sensitive markets such as Saudi Arabia, Kuwait, Indonesia and Turkey and to rework them with the logo obliterated. Moreover, Nike agreed to sign an agreement with CAIR apologizing to Muslims, obtaining in exchange declarations urging Muslims not to boycott Nike products worldwide (Harrington, 1997).

A further level consistent with conflicts of cultural traditions is that involving practices categorized as ethical, or at least acceptable in one setting but unethical in another as in the case of nepotism in Indian firms or Guanxi in South East Asia. It is a common practice, within successful Indian companies, to offer their employees' children the chance to join the company once they have completed school. The habit is so deeply rooted in the Indian cultural context that companies tend to honor this commitment even when other applicants are more qualified than employees' children. It is evident that in Western countries this form of institutionalized nepotism would be branded as unacceptable. The Indian cultural context, on the contrary, with its catastrophic levels of unemployment and strong family linkages privileging clan and family relationships, consider nepotism a legitimate practice.

In addition the concept of business relations known as Guanxi is a prevalent social custom in collectivist cultures like China and East Asian countries where lack of governmental control and of coherent business law is remarkable. According to literature, the term Guanxi refers to tight, close knit networks (Yeung and Tung, 1996) and interpersonal connections (Xin and Pearce, 1996) and to the networks of informal relationships and exchanges of favors that dominate business activity in such contexts. In practical terms, in China 'Guanxi base' entails either an ascribed blood relationship or social interconnections achieved through going to the same school or living in the same neighborhood. As Guanxi base is insufficient to establish strong links, individuals must work over time to maintain relationships through invitations to visit one's home, place of business or entertainment or through gifts. No surprise then if many foreigners find themselves trapped with this ancient and unknown practice and often makes the easy identification of gifts with bribes and see Guanxi as the Chinese word for corruption. The practice is not limited to China as the words *blat* (Puffer and McCarthy, 1997) and *bakshish* (Izraeli, 1997) identify more or less the same thing in certain countries or areas of the world, posing challenges to western companies contemplating doing business there.

4 Organizations and Moral Divide

The competitive approaches traditionally adopted by business people in dealing with moral divide's dilemmas vary among the spectrum of 'Relativism' and 'Universalism.'

Relativism is based on the assumption that cultural pluralism is an undeniable fact, especially in a globalized world where moral rules and social institutions evidence an astonishing cultural and historical variability. The doctrine of cultural relativism holds that no culture is better than any other; therefore there are no rights and wrongs but only relative opinions (Rosen, 1980; Skinner, 1971). According to this formula, relativism developed into two different paradigms. In the most extreme form of 'Radical Cultural Relativism', culture is considered as the principal source of the validity of a moral right or rule inextricably linked to local settings and situations (Wilson, 1997). In this perspective only a few basic rights with virtually universal application are accepted, and a wide range of variations for most rights are justified. The true relativist must accept slavery, female mutilation, death penalty or any other practice that represents a genuine norm within a social group. However it is proper to note that very few modern philosophers support the strongest form of relativism. An alternative version of relativism is known as 'Weak Cultural Relativism', holding that culture may be an important source of the validity of a moral right or rule, but not the only one. In this case universality is initially presumed, but the relativity of human nature, communities, and rights serves as a check on potential excesses of universalism. Documents such as the Bangkok Declaration on human rights as well as the Asian Human Rights Charter, drafted in commemoration of the 50th anniversary of the Universal Declaration on Human Rights, by more than 200 non governmental organizations, support this view. Finally, at its furthest extreme, weak cultural relativism would recognize a comprehensive set of prima facie universal human rights, but allows occasional and strictly limited local variations and exceptions to them.

Universalism stands as the counterpoint to relativism and consists of simply ignoring differences, while maintaining one's own norms in different settings. According to universalism, people should behave everywhere exactly as they do at home in the name of a Golden Rule claiming to: 'do unto others as you would have them do unto you' (Bennet, 2002). This idea is based on the belief that some universal principles such as life, liberty, and physical well being transcend local customs and practices. Under this approach there is only one list of truths and they can be expressed only in one acceptable and right way. Obviously the right way is a synonym for the Western way and cultures and related practices can be considered immoral, if their generally accepted approaches violate universal norms. Therefore peculiarities exist even within the universalistic framework, as universal norms can be identified with national values, thus hiding seeds of nationalism or adopt corporate oriented approaches typical of imperialistic model of enterprises applying their own internal corporate ethical values. Lying between the two sides is the compromise model in which enterprises sometimes do it their own way adopting one-fits-for-all approach, while some other times choosing to accommodate differences (Donaldson and Dunfee, 1996).

If the pros and cons of these approaches are carefully weighed, neither of the two solutions seem acceptable because the danger lies in unintended consequences spreading from both approaches. Problems related to the relativistic approach are evident when dealing with the current debate about the propriety of paying bribes in foreign markets, the evidence of existing lower standards for plant safety overseas or the opportunistic use of child labor in developing economies. Relativists who defend such actions argue that local customs consider it mandatory that international enterprises follow local rules and habits. This assertion appears to be so tempting for enterprises that everything seems to be acceptable in the name of an imaginary self-adaptation to differences. Moreover when failing to do as the locals would do means forfeiting business opportunities and losing important networks, evidence is given for a pro-active relativistic choice with a hidden economic purpose. Such a view is ultimately based on what had happened when the practices in question were more damaging than petty bribery or insider trading.

The Bhopal tragedy, apart from being rightly considered the greatest industrial disaster in history, vividly illustrates the point, showing what happens when the life of thousands of people is put at risk in countries where local governments offer lower safety standards and regulations as a way to attract foreign investments and western investors simply adapt to the situation. Union Carbide, an American owned corporation, was licensed to manufacture a pesticide called Sevin in an overcrowded working class neighborhood in Bhopal, Madhya Pradesh, India between 1977 and 1984. In December 1984, during the early hours of the morning, a poisonous gas used in producing the pesticide, leaked from one of the plants into the surrounding areas. At least 3000 people died as a result of the accident, while figures of people injured currently range from 200,000 to 600,000 (Fortun, 2001). The official inquiry revealed that the plant had been built with inferior controls for avoiding accidental chemical releases than those required by Indian legal standards. Further inquiries revealed that safety standards and maintenance procedures at the plant had been deteriorating and ignored for months by the Indian staff who were far less experienced and trained than would have been expected and required in the US. American supervision did not compensate for Indian inexperience and negligence and it resulted in a lack of enforcement of safety measures. A complete absence of community information and emergency procedures (the emergency sirens had been switched off) did the rest. From a strictly ethical point of view, Bophal is a case in which the blindness of the relativistic approach appears clearly, in terms of silent acceptance of local standards as the right one only in the name of mere profit. Bophal is a well-known tragedy but not the only one as other less famous episodes attest to the negative effects of double standards accepted by western corporations in less developed countries as the case of German TNC Bayer's Chromate production factory in South Africa shows. In 1976, a South African government report noted health problems in nearly half the plant employees, which indicated a lack of concern regarding the physical welfare of workers. As chromate is a corrosive compound causing respiratory illness and in the long run lung cancer, its production should follow strict health and safety provisions. Things continued without any external regulatory intervention and in the 1990s South African trade unions learned that several workers had developed lung cancer and had not been informed that their disease might have been related to their employment. However, Chrome Chemicals management refused to review the plant's industrial hygiene record and in 1991 the firm was forced to shut down, dismissing most of its workers although lung cancer was not added to the list of compensable occupational diseases.

A further element of disbelief with regards to relativistic approach is that embracing such a position without any previous training, results in acting out an unfamiliar role, which will be easily perceived by the adversary resulting in mistrust and harming business interests in the end.

Universalistic approach on the other hand consists of an absolutist denial of national and sub-national ethical autonomy and self-determination that is neither acceptable nor realistic. As a matter of fact failing to take sufficient account of the complexity of the local context results in enterprises imposing a simplistic approach. This 'doing harm by doing good' paradigm reveals itself to be of questionable value and feasibility and most of the time paves the way to the socially irresponsible practices previously mentioned.

The Reebok case is just one of several examples showing that what is internationally advocated according to a universalistic approach is not always what is locally desired. The famous sportswear supplier, fearing the loss of western markets due to anti-sweatshop protesters, recently started a good corporate governance campaign. The aim of the campaign was the withdrawal of business from subcontracted factories accused of making employees work more than International standards allowed. Previous inquiries had revealed that workers in a factory in Thailand were accustomed to working more than 72 hours a week (The Economist, 2002). Protesters appeared to be winning the battle of public opinion and the factory was closed. As a result thousands of people lost their well-paid jobs and were forced into less paid and more hazardous activities. The unintended consequences of western compassion harmed more local communities than the existing situation did. While transnational companies may have deeper pockets and larger political clout vis-à-vis the poor unskilled laborers of a country, there is little evidence that the latter get lower wages and fewer jobs in the presence of those companies, compared to what they will get in their absence (Bardhan, 2003). Contrary to the impression created by the campaign in affluent countries against sweatshops run by transnational companies in poor countries, it can be pointed out that poor people are often banging at the gates of these sweatshops for a chance of entry, since their current alternative is much worse in inferior occupations or work conditions or unemployment. In the Thailand case, sweatshop protesters and Reebok decision-makers failed to consider that salaries in Reebok subcontracted factories were well above the average wage compared to the prevailing market conditions for similar jobs in Thailand. Moreover, the conditions offered by the factory were no worse than the general alternatives existing in Thailand and represented the only chance poor people had to achieve better conditions of life and to escape domestic violence (for women) or hazardous works for young people. In this case a lack of understanding of the Southeast Asian social structure was evident. In countries where governments do not provide social security, life is structured essentially around the building block of the family (Wikan, 1995). Extended families are made up of many people and build a sort of social safety net around their working members, allowing a longer workday which violates international norms.

5 Law and Moral Divide

5.1 International Standards and Moral Divide

International standards and norms are non-binding initiatives enhanced by international organizations for fostering responsible business conduct among multinational enterprises operating abroad. Despite the importance of these initiatives, their value is only nominal as they are based on a voluntary approach. Moreover the ratification of international standards on behalf of governments does not necessarily mean that the implementation phase will be reached. Although it is undeniable that compliance with the law should be regarded as a moral minimum in terms of providing guidance to international business, the law alone may not provide enough answers, especially when dealing with grey areas of ethical conflicts. Moreover it might be argued that, since most of the existing standards reflect a western perspective (this is partially balanced by ILO Conventions developed on a multilateral basis), they pursue a quest for universality, not globally shared.

An in-depth analysis of the OECD Guidelines for Multinational Enterprises[2] reveals a general lack of awareness concerning moral divide issues. To be more precise, the case for moral divide is briefly mentioned in some parts of the Guidelines while being neither clearly defined nor described in detail. In the first chapter, Concepts and Principles, it is argued that:

> Governments adhering to the Guidelines encourage the enterprises operating on their territories to observe the Guidelines wherever they operate, while taking into account the particular circumstances of each host country (OECD Guidelines, p. 18).

However the particular circumstances cited are not described in detail, leaving room for multifold interpretations. Paragraph seven adds that:

> Governments have the right to prescribe the conditions under which multinational enterprises operate within their jurisdictions, subject to international law. The entities of a multinational enterprise located in various countries are subject to the laws applicable in these countries.
> When multinational enterprises are subject to conflicting requirements by adhering countries, the governments concerned will co-operate in good faith with a view to resolving problems that may arise (OECD Guidelines, p. 18).

Chapter two, General Policies, provides an insight on the steps enterprises should take in the countries in which they operate, including:

> ...considering the views of other stakeholders through: respecting the human rights of those affected by their activities consistent with the host government's international obligations and commitments and encourage local capacity building through close co-operation with the local community (OECD Guidelines, p. 19).

5.2 Corporate Codes of Conduct and Moral Divide

Corporate codes of conduct are currently the vogue for major companies. The drive to adopt corporate and ethics codes started in response to the quest for transparency and accountability and was encouraged by ad hoc laws (such as the Federal Sentencing Guidelines for the US or legislative decree 231/2001, for Italy), making compliance programs, including corporate codes of conduct putting forth standards and principles for the conduct of business activities in the marketplace a legal requirement for companies in search of a social license to operate (OECD, 2001). Corporate codes address specific issues such as fair employment, labor rights, conflicts of interest, safety and environmental issues and are generally intended to

---

[2] A complete version of the *OECD Guidelines for Multinational Enterprises* is available at: http://www.oecd.org/document/28/0,2340,en_2649_34889_2397532_1_1_1_1,00.html.

cover both national and global operations. Indeed, the biggest hurdles to enforcing global compliance of ethics program and corporate codes of conduct are often rooted in cultural differences, preventing a code to establish global ethical business practices (Maher, 2004). Therefore the fact that these codes are of a voluntary and internal nature has important implications when considering moral divide issues. Evidence shows that self-regulatory tools such as corporate codes, encompasses voluntary standards and norms in dealing with moral divide issues, generally falling under the rubric of diversity issues. It might be argued that corporate codes of conduct can better address cross-cultural ethical questions and dilemmas through a negotiated approach adopted in drafting the code and valuable for comprehensively capturing the complexities inherent in host cultures. Texas Instruments, for instance, established a Global Business Practices Council of local committees made up of managers from all countries where the company operated to set up its corporate code (Donaldson, 1996). In addition local versions of corporate codes or insight on particular themes,[3] available in different languages are created by a minority of organizations.

6 Conclusions

As an upshot of these, the existence of an issue falling under the rubric of moral divide should become a matter of managerial concern, recognized within economic organizations. From a pure theoretical point of view, as the law alone (whether in the shape of international standards or corporate codes of conduct) fails to provide valuable solutions to cross-cultural ethical dilemmas and conflicts, a trip beyond law can be a thoughtful experience. The world beyond law is not the uncharted territory imagined by early jurists (Rouland, 1992). It responds to moral obligations everybody is expected to embrace, rather than to legal regulations. For what concerns organizations, going beyond law means taking the inner moral obligations they embody and bringing them to the surface as an active framework of action. In this sense, ethics, seen as the joining of moral values commonly shared in the aim of attaining mutual goals (Sapelli, 2002), extends far beyond legality (De George et al., 1998) and can be considered a valuable alternative in order to bridge moral divide successfully. Additionally, evidence suggests that not only the highest managerial levels conform to cross-cultural ethical conflicts, since the majority of ethically-charged situations are experienced at all levels and are everyday issues rather than the more dramatic and redundant episodes found in much of the literature. The task is complex for everybody because cross-cultural skills are rarely held by executives to be a part of their core business competencies.

Indeed moral divide issues assume a twofold perspective: the international version previously described and a domestic one, due to the increasing number of immigrants employed in national firms.

---

[3] See: Shell's 'Human Rights dilemmas a training supplement' and 'Diversity and Inclusiveness at Shell.'

To conclude, it is evident that business people, at all levels, should acquire competencies for approaching moral divide issues systematically through the creativity of a new managerial thinking consisting in a basic degree of context awareness, curiosity, inclusiveness and which is likely to become a part of core business competencies while being no longer separated from the more general considerations of good management. The final goal is to acquire, albeit temporarily, a mind-set consonant with the local scenario, allowing the successful maneuvering of the disturbing trends that lie at the intersections of different cultures (Donaldson and Dunfee, 1999).

Learning to manage ethical diversity means turning differences into strengths with important achievements for both corporations and local communities. In this perspective ethical diversity is assumed as a resource for fostering business rather than an obstacle to it. A resource for obtaining win/win solutions (if possible) and, in any case, avoiding lose/lose solutions.

Moreover if the goal for multinational and transnational is to act ethically as socially responsible organizations, a manager's knowledge of cross-country ethical issues is necessary, but far from being sufficient. A whole new paradigm of corporate social responsibility has to be developed within corporations. Under this new view, CSR should lose its monolithic appearance. Only through flexibility in both theoretical approach and practice, will CSR be able to penetrate and adapt to the cultural, religious and political issues the global scenario poses.

References

Anderson, S. and Cavanagh, J. (2000), *Top 200: The Rise of Global Corporate Power*, Institute for Policy Studies, Washington DC.

Associated Press, (1997), Islamic Ire over 'Air' on Logos of Nike Shoes, *The Indian Express*, April 11, p. 9.

Bardhan, P. (2003), *Globalization and the Limits to Poverty Alleviation*, Berkeley, University of California Press.

Bennet, M. J. (2002), *Principi di Comunicazione Interculturale*, Franco Angeli, Milano.

Bollinger, D. and Hofstede, G. (1989), *Internazionalità, le Differenze Culturali nel Management*, Guerini e Associati.

Chandler, G. (2001), Speech given at the Environment Foundation's Windsor Consultation on St. George's House, December 12, Windsor Castle.

Davies, R. and Nelson, J. (2003), *The Buck Stops Where? Managing the Boundaries of Business Engagement in Global Development Challenges*, International Business Leaders Forum, http://www.pwblf.org.

De George, et al. (1998), *Uncompromising Integrity: Motorola's Global Challenges*, Motorola University Press.

Donaldson, T. and Dunfee, T. W. (1996), Values in Tension, Ethics Away from Home, *Harvard Business Review*, 74, pp. 48-62.

Donaldson, T. and Dunfee, T. W. (1999a), *Ties that Bind: A Social Contracts Approach to Business Ethics*, Harvard Business School Press.

Donaldson, T. and Dunfee, W. T. (1999b), When Ethics Travel, the Promise and Peril of Global Business Ethics, *California Management Review*, 41, pp. 113-138.

Dunfee, T. W. and Fort, T. L (2003), Corporate Hypergoals, Sustainable Peace and the Adapted Firm, *Vanderbilt Journal of Transnational Law*, 2, 36, pp. 563-580.

Durkheim, E. (1893), *The Division of Labour in Society*, Translated by George Simpson (1960), New York, The Free Press.

Durkheim, E. (1961), *Moral Education: a Study in the Theory and Application of the Sociology of Education*, New York, The Free Press, pp. 206-207.

Economist (1993), Survey on Multinationals, Everybody's Favourite Monsters, *The Economist*, March 27, p. 29.

Economist (2002), Ethically Unemployed, *The Economist*, November 30, p. 59.

Fortun, Kim (2001), *Advocacy after Bhopal: Environmentalism, Disaster, New Global Orders*, University of Chicago Press.

Goodtsein, L. (2001), For Hindus and Vegetarians, Surprise in McDonald's Fries, *New York Times*, May 20, p. 7.

Hampden-Turner, C. and Trompenaars, F. (1997) *Riding the Waves of Culture: Understanding Diversity in Global Business*, McGraw-Hill.

Harrington, J. (1997), Nike Recalls Disputed Logo, *The Cincinnati Enquirer*, June 25, p. 3.

Hendry, J. (1999), Universalizability and Reciprocity in International Business Ethics, *Business Ethics Quarterly*, 9, pp. 405-420.

Hofstede, G. (1980), *Culture's Consequences: International Differences in Work-Related Values*, Newbury Park, CA, Sage.

Izraeli, D. (1997), Business Ethics in the Middle East, *Journal of Business Ethics*, 16, pp. 1555-1560.

Litivin, D. (2004), Ignoring Social and Political Reality Can Sink Global Companies, *Global Business and Global Poverty Conference*, Stanford Graduate School of Business, May 19.

Litvin, D. (2003), *Empires of profit, commerce conquest and corporate responsibility*, Texere.

Maher, K. (2004), Global Companies Face Reality of Instituting Ethics Program, *The Wall Street Journal*, November 9, p. 8.

OECD (2001), Codes of Corporate Conduct: Expanded Review of their Content in Corporate Responsibility: Private Initiatives and Public Goals, *Working Paper on International Investment*, 6, Paris.

Puffer, S. M. and McCarthy, D. J. (1997), Business Ethics in a Transforming Economy: Applying the ISCT to Russia, *University of Pennsylvania Journal of International Economy*, 18, pp. 1281-1304.

Rosen, H. (1980), *The Development of Socio-Moral Knowledge*, New York, Columbia University Press.

Rouland, N. (1992), *Antropologia Giuridica*, Giuffrè editore.

Sapelli, G. (2002), *Antropologia della Globalizzazione*, Bruno Mondadori, Milano.

Sapelli, G. (2002), Responsabilità Oltre la Legge, *Equilibri*, 2, pp. 83-123.

Schein, E. (1992), *Organizational Culture and Leadership*, Jossey-Bass.

Skinner, B. F. (1971), *Beyond Freedom and Dignity*, New York, Knopf.

Trompenaars, F. and Hampden-Turner, C. (2001), Transcultural Competence, the Key to Leadership in a Globalising World, *Financial Times*, January 15, p. 7.

Trompennars, F. (2001), Proceedings from the Seminar *The Cultural Factor in International Business*, presented at Oxford University.

Tylor, B. P. (1994), *Collected Works*, Routledge, London.

Van Londen, S. and de Ruijter, A. (2003), Managing Diversity in a Globalizing World, 18, *Nota di lavoro*, FEEM, pp. 2-12.

Wikan, U. (1995), Sustainable Development in the Mega-city: Can the Concept Be Made Applicable? *Current Anthropology*, 36, pp. 635-655.

Williams, O. F. (2000), *Global Codes of Conduct, an Idea Whose Time Has Come*, Notre Dame University Press.

Wilson, R. (1997), *Human Rights, Culture and Context: an Introduction*, London, Pluto Press.

Xin, K. R. and Pearce, J. L. (1996), Guanxi: Connections as Substitutes for Formal Institutional Support, *Academy of Management Journal*, 39, pp. 1641-1658.

Yeung I. Y. M. and Tung, R. L. (1996), Achieving Business Success in Confucian Societies: the Importance of Guanxi, *Organization Dynamics*, 25, pp. 54-66.

PART TWO

ETHICS FROM WITHIN

Chapter 6

Capitalism:
Foundations of Ethical Behavior

Mircea Boari

Nature is just toward men. She rewards them for their pains; she makes them hard workers because she attaches greater rewards to greater work. But if an arbitrary power removes nature's rewards, the distaste for work recurs and inaction appears to be the only good (Montesquieu, 1748/1989).

1 Introduction

The current understanding of the relation between ethics and capitalism comes in two forms. On the one hand, the type which can be termed 'the least of the possible evils.' It basically states that economic passions, such as greed, acquisitiveness and accumulation are preferable to other, more devastating passions, such as envy, pride, belligerence (thymotic passions). Both forms of passion have self-interest at their center. However, since economic passions depend to an extent of another human, the life of this other is sheltered from destruction. Besides, the coupling of numerous individual actions centered upon economic interest leads to beneficial results for all: the famous 'invisible hand' effect. From Adam Smith and Bernard Mandeville, through Benjamin Franklin's moral maxims in 'Poor Richard's Almanac' and Max Weber, to contemporary authors such as Friedrich Hayek, this minimalist view accepts capitalism not (necessarily) because of its intrinsic worth, but rather due to its desirable consequences of scale, and of its capacity of keeping at bay more devastating forms of conduct.

The synthesis of this view has been made in a small but influential work of Albert Hirschman, 'The Passions and the Interests' (Hirschman, 1977), and many contemporary authors get their view from it, whether knowingly or not. In brief, according to this view, capitalism is in its essence a phenomenon, to put it mildly, deprived of intrinsic moral worth, but one should accept it since its consequences are either good, or less bad than those of other forms of activity. What we are dealing here with, is a consequentialist moral justification of capitalism, but not a vindication of it. Let alone the hard-core Marxists and social-democrats, much of the politically minded economic thinking shares in this view.

The second view is based on the vindication of the intrinsic worth of acquisitiveness. It is generally credited to the Protestant ethics, eventually associated to the emergence of capitalist spirit (Weber, 1905/2001). Albeit, it is more likely that the political and the theoretical climate surrounding the English revolution, in particular the Levellers's ideology, was more instrumental (Macpherson, 1962). At any rate, in its lay format, this vindication of capitalism makes the core of a wide range of conservative views about capitalism. Two trends of such disseminated views are of particular significance. On the one hand, there are the ideas of various radical American thinkers of liberty from the XIXth century, such as Benjamin Tucker and Lysander Spooner. On the other hand, the Old World school of economics brought and continued in the United States under the name of 'Austrian School', and whose main representative is the economist Ludwig von Mises. These two trends have been captured during the last few decades in a theoretical attempt at advocating capitalism, generally labeled libertarianism. Major thinkers such as Robert Nozick, the Noble Prize laureates David Reismann and Milton Friedman, as well as remarkable ones such as David Friedman and Murray Rothbard are representatives of this theoretical trend. Various figures of interest, such as the novelist Ayn Rand and the politician Alan Greenspan, Governor of the US Federal Reserve, are associated with this philosophy. Reduced in a nutshell, and insofar as it pertains to our topic, capitalism is morally worthy because it gives best expression to the materiality and finiteness of human condition: human action is economic action, and the role of economic activity is to allow humans to survive and to pursue happiness and freedom in this life, since there exists no other.

Both antithetical views summarized above have their own merits and shortcomings. The definitive argument pro or against the intrinsic moral worth of a free market order has not yet been formulated – and, perhaps, it does not even exist. This being the case, the tendency of producing exaggerated claims is quite large. However, a further elucidation of causal links between economic action and the formation of the moral character is possible. Approaching the issue from several complementary angles, the present chapter aims at achieving such clarification. The argument is thus divided into the following parts: the provisioning of a working definition for moral behavior (Section 2); the examination of the relationship between reward and coercion in the production of moral behavior, and of the role of the profit motive as reward in the economy of moral behavior (Section 3, preamble); an analysis of two mechanisms by which profit acts as a regulator of behavior (Subsections 3.1 and 3.2); a discussion of the role played by calculative, profit driven intelligence in the creation of moral rules and the avoidance of conflict (Section 4); a brief appraisal of the ethical order generated by capitalism on the background of the evolved human nature (Section 5). From the numerous aspects which can be discussed, I believe these to be of a fundamental import. Some concluding remarks referring to the relationship between capitalism and morality will be given at the end of the chapter.

2 The Ethics of Reward

Definitions of morality vary along a large spectrum. At one end of this continuum, there are maximalist definitions, such as can be found in the ordinary, common or natural moral discourse, in religious discourse, such as the Christian dogmas, but also in systematic thought such as the doctrine of the categorical imperative (Kant, 1785/1996). Maximalist ethics have an appeal of their own, but there are three challenges which confront them and which, so far, have not been dealt with convincingly: the asymmetry between moral claim (injunction) and actual action; the asymmetry between the standard applied to other (in the form of moralistic injunctions) and the standard applied to self (in the form of rationalizations and justifications of action); a sacrificial dimension, blaming self-interested action and meant at extracting from another actions beneficial to oneself.

At the other end of the spectrum, there are minimalist definitions of morality which acknowledge that people are defective when it comes to the fulfillment of moral standards: even more so when it is expected that they give primacy to the interest of another, as opposed to self interest. As a consequence, the recommendation of such sober moral minimalism is merely to give due regard to the interest of another, and to determine one's course of action by taking it into consideration (Alexander, 1987). Although, at closer scrutiny, it is not at all obvious why the demands of such minimalist ethics could be easier to fulfill than the demands of the maximalist one.

What both approaches to morality seem to fail to acknowledge is the absolutely basic fact that *all ethical behavior is costly to the individual*. Consider a conventional example: jumping in the water to the rescue of a drowning person is more expensive a behavior than going about one's business. The equation becomes even more complex when one recognizes that it is a dynamic function: a contract agreed upon at moment t because deemed advantageous, could prove disadvantageous at time t_1, which means that its fulfillment at moment t_1 produces loses.

All forms of behavior recommended by the classic tables of virtue fall under the same observation: mercy is costly because one has no certainty that it will be answered to with gratitude (less likely) or revenge (very costly and more likely); gratitude itself is more costly than its denial and refusal; goodwill is costly because exposes one to harm which otherwise could be avoided by conservative strategies of vigilance and reserve; heroism and courage are definitely more costly than cowardice, since the price may well be life itself.

The obvious question which arises after such basic an observation is: why virtuous (moral, ethical) acts are performed at all?

At least since Jeremy Bentham's theory of morality it is accepted that the multitude of stimuli to which human behavior responds falls into two large categories: rewards and punishments (Bentham, 1781/1988). Apart from the psychological semantics suggested by these terms, therein lies the fact that reward and punishment are the *major modifiers of conduct*. And this capacity is due to the *modification of the relative cost of the actions performed*.

This modification takes place according to scripts (algorithms) which one easily recognizes as universal. When, according to one's view of the world, following an action considered 'virtuous' a reward is specified, the asset which the reward represents is subtracted from the present cost of the virtuous action, cost which thus falls bellow the cost of the behavior which is 'not virtuous.' By that, virtuous behavior becomes the reasonable thing to do. The more consistently the virtuous conduct is matched by the reward, the more consistent and systematic (permanent) virtuous behavior becomes.

A similar reasoning indicates why punishments/penalties lead to the same net result: the punishment, representing a net reduction of the fitness of the individual (imprisonment, fine, physical pain, death), is a cost added to the cost of 'non virtuous' behavior, making it more costly than the virtuous one and, thus, making it unreasonable.

Even though the net result may be the same, the *magnitude* and the *quality* of the result is different. Overall, rewards are better predictors of behavior consistent with moral norms than punishment. For illustration, the abolishment of slavery was as much due to moral campaigning as to efficiency calculations: the work under threat of penalty (the work of slaves) is much less productive than the work of free people.[1] Rewards lead to the betterment of one's condition, to an increase in the available resources, thereby to less fear of scarcity, exposure to randomness and hazard, to greater safety and satisfaction. None of this is brought about by punishment/penalty. Quite the contrary, punishments/penalties diminish the predictability of one's world; they achieve some result, but without bringing about an increase in the amount of satisfaction for the individuals; they add uncertainty and insecurity which both are negative predictors of productivity, efficiency, long term commitments. But the major difference between negative incentives (punishments/penalties) and positive incentives (rewards) is that the first reach quickly a saturation point beyond which the law of diminishing returns apply: so much can be extracted by force and no more. While positive incentives, linked as they are, to paraphrase Hobbes, to the infinity of human desires which cease only in death,[2] secure a way of avoiding the effects of this law (see next section). Therefore, while a variable geometry of positive incentives guarantees a continuous complexification of costly actions, the self-limiting geometry of negative incentives leads to de-complexification and the adoption of the least costly forms of behavior. Rewards stimulate risk taking, meliorism, striving for perfection, love of superbia; punishment stimulates conservative strategies, deception, evasion, baseness.

In brief: a world predominantly based on negative incentives, will be less rich, less complex and, insofar as morality is concerned, less virtuous, while insofar as sociability is concerned, less pleasurable to live in. Since ethical behavior

---

[1] Smith (1776/1981), I.viii.40-41, p. 98; III.ii.10-12, pp. 388-90.

[2] Desires according to Hobbes can be roughly classified as 'desire of power, of riches, of knowledge and of honour; all which may be reduced to the first, that is desire of power' (Hobbes, 165/1996, [53], p. 53). The normal human existence is thus a 'perpetual desire of power after power that ceaseth only in death' (op. cit., [47], p. 70).

presupposes added costs, only an efficient and systematic web of rewards will make it possible at any degree of consistency. A world based on rewards will be teeming with novelty and acts of apparent gratuity out of which, some at least, take the resemblance of generosity. In brief, a world of hope.

The above explanation, bordering on psychology, could be further extended to more complex considerations. There exists a relation between action in view of reward and the philosophical notion of free will. Whether free will exists, which is to say, the capacity to choose between good and evil, then reward is consistent with choice while punishment is not (since fear is no choice). Therefore, any philosophy which emphasizes the role of punishment implicitly ascertains that human beings are mere automata, which can be equally conditioned by punishment and reward. While any philosophy that emphasizes reward is more likely to acknowledge human beings free will, therefore choice and the corollary political freedom. It is perhaps no mere accident that the more apprehensive political philosophies and political regimes relied on both punishment and rejection of free will and choice and that these political philosophies were also anti-market and anti-capitalistic. This will make the object of further explanation bellow, while the development of the above line of argumentation must be relegated to a later time.

According to the definition hereby proposed, whether costly behavior, such as ethical behavior, is possible whenever a reward modifies the cost effectiveness of the action, the following basic ethical theorem can be formulated: *it is moral to expect a reward whenever a costly action, such as virtuous behavior, is required.* The corollary also holds true: *it is moral to offer a reward whenever a costly action, such as virtuous conduct, is expected from the individual.*

This definition responds quite accurately to our common sense and to our natural expectations, whenever they are stripped off of sophistry and the hypocrisy of excessive claims. It equally gives expression to our most cursory understanding of categories crucial for the organization of moral conduct, namely fairness and desert.

To affirm that virtuous behavior is costly does not mean that it will not happen; but that it will happen with higher probability under certain circumstances and with lower or next to zero probability in other circumstances. This allows us to move to the next paragraph.

3 Capitalist Profit as Reward

Social orders are schemes for the organization of human conduct via the administration of rewards and punishments. This is a synthetic formulation of consequences to be derived from the argument above. Meanwhile, it is a fact that, historically, most social orders have been built upon and maintained by punishment.[3]

---

[3]   The role of coercion and violence in the construction and maintenance of the social order in history hardly needs an illustration. However, for a systematic theory of the state based

Modern capitalist societies are the first social orders which are erected with the feature of reward central to them. The form in which reward becomes the structural scaffolding of these worlds is that which draws blame upon them, namely profit. While reward was not invented by capitalism, profit, in the complete sense of the term, as practice, discourse and criteria of excellence, was.

Not all economic activity is capitalistic.[4] Not any form of exchange or transaction is in view of profit (potlatch, gifts, services between friends; alms, charity, philanthropy). In order to qualify as capitalistic, besides being economic in nature, and besides presupposing an exchange, it must be performed in the clear view of a reward quintessentially sublimated in the form of profit. The purest form of profit, namely interest on borrowed money, and which gives the best expression to capitalist practices, was also that which supported, historically, the demonization of capitalism.[5]

In the light of the above, a thesis might thus be formulated. *Profit is that which makes it possible for forms of conduct which otherwise would simply not be performed, due to their cost* (the risk involved or the uncertainty of the enterprise being the most frequent type of cost). In different words, considering two different types of societal order, the world in which the profit motive operates on a systematic and structurally consistent manner would be essentially different from another world where this does not happen. In what morality is concerned, such a world would more virtuous, for essentially relying on reward as incentive for action.

The thesis is consistent with cursory political and social observation. Totalitarian orders were in strike contrast with whatever remained of the Modern liberal capitalism during the XXth century. The huge claims made upon the human individuals were virtually backed by the promise of a golden future, but factually by the reality of coercion and threat. Instead of the 'new man', they produced the specimen Homo Sovieticus (Zinoviev, 1985; Heller, 1988) whose major feature was an in-depth demoralization (Havel, 1975). Ultimately, and apart from it being a form of gratification, the reward is a recognition of one's worthiness, both generically, as a human being, and in particular, related to the specifics of the action performed. The reward is a confirmation that our actions are meaningful and truly useful to others. Far from separating and dividing individuals one from another (atomization), the reward is a form of reciprocal reassurance that they do

---

on such means, see Oppenheimer (1914/1997). For a history of oppression, see Turchetti, (2003).

[4] For a related distinction, Braudel (1985).

[5] Apart from some exotic persuasions, the modern intellectual critique of profit can be traced either to a Christian theological root, or to a materialistic, Marxist one. The epitome of profit maker, the usurer, was a particular, unredeemable type of sinner during Middle Ages (Le Goff, 1990). Consider also the list of illicit trades, in order to get an image of an almost complete ban on any profit making activities (Le Goff, 1977). The Marxist critique of profit is implicit in Marx's theory of surplus value, origin of both worker alienation and capitalist exploitation (Marx, 1867/1948; for a concise and visibly propagandistic explanation, never published during Marx's life but found in Engels's papers, see Marx 1898/1995).

good and a confirmation of the fact that one is in-dispensable and important. Totalitarian orders are 'anomic' and 'atomized' (Arendt, 1951/1979) precisely because such reassurance, objectified in the form of profit, is absent. And this is due to the fact that profit is not the result of some effective manipulation of the others, but of the satisfaction of real needs and wants. Otherwise, profit would actually be a penalty extracted from others by means of coercion.

If one reduces morality to the basic competence of differentiating between good and evil, rewards operate as unambiguous signals making the distinction possible. Much of human morality has a build in ambiguity (see last section) or, in technical jargon, noise. An operational system of rewards achieves two effects: on the one hand, it generates less redundancy (and, thus, loss by unneeded duplication) and more univocity; on the other hand, and this is crucial in any process of scale, it gradually eliminates noisy messages (ambiguous messages), making them less frequent. The desire of someone to generate rewards for another is a message which confirms that the action performed by the second receives the approval and endorsement of the former.

The subsequent question which spontaneously arises from the above is: in what does consist the efficacy of reward in determining behavior? Or, in different words, why does profit function at all, in general and, in particular, in an ethically desirable direction? The answer involves two mechanisms regulating behavior.

3.1 Desire

The first concerns the fundamental descriptor of human behavior called 'desire' and brings the present argument to the center of modern political theory via Hobbes, and in the vicinity of one of the grandest themes of philosophy, from Plato and Aristotle to Hegel and beyond, to contemporary postmodernism. Without getting into unnecessary technical explanations, human desires have, most often then not, been seen as detrimental. For Plato, desires belong to the appetitive and to the spirited (thymotic) parts of the soul, preventing it to elevate itself towards the world of ideas, towards knowledge (Plato, 1986; Lafontaine, 1902). Aristotle draws the distinction between desires which respond to necessities, and therefore legitimate, from desires which are superfluous and whimsical (Aristotle, 1921).[6] This distinction is made precisely in the context of a discussion about economy which, among other influences and insofar as our theme is concerned, had set down the basis of a critique of luxury, of superfluity of desire, which is still with us today in the form of the critique of consumerism, or of 'conspicuous consumption' (for influential illustrations, Baudrillard, 1970; Veblen, 1902). At his turn, Hobbes

---

[6] Aristotle's political economy is to be found almost entirely in Book I of the *Politica*. And it consists of a triple criticism: of trade (exchange other than barter) as form of rich-getting uncoupled from need and usage 1257a 15 – 1257b 40); of superfluity, luxury and license (1269b 12 – 1270a 15; 1295b 17, 1300a 7, 1310a 22), as opposed to necessaries of life, the only legitimate object of rich-getting (1253b 25; 1257a 6-34); of the insatiable character of human desires, which in fact is the origin of all the rest (1258a 1-13; 1263b 20-28; 1266b 25-30).

sees in desires, in their endless and insatiable character, the source of evil and destruction and thus, by ricochet, of the absolute power of the sovereign, meant to deflect them.[7]

All these authors glimpse, at the bottom of the human soul or of human nature, a deeply unsettling anthropological setup revolving around the problem of desires. Somehow, there appears a connection, a relation between desires and a tyrannical drive which makes desires altogether suspect. The problem is: are desires per se dangerous, or rather features pertaining to them, either necessarily or accidentally, make them so? What is the relation between something so innocuous and benign as the desire for a candy and the desire to owe control over others?

What disturbs classical authors about desires is their unruly character, the capacity of taking over the reins of personal conduct, of steering behavior we would say today, obsessionally, compulsively, towards their satisfaction: in disregard of prudence, calculative reason, moral judgment, in oblivion of the other. For, of course, one desires most often then not that which is another's good. The second character, shared by at least some desires (cravings, such as sex or particular substances, like alcohol), is their imperative, repetitive and insatiable character: their addictive capacity. The third upsetting aspect about desires is their multiplicity: at any one time, the soul is assaulted by concurrential and multifarious appetites.

Combining the three features, there emerges the pictures of a chaotic psyche, the human soul as the battle ground between *simultaneous*, *infinite* and equally *powerful* drives taking hold of the reins of action according to indiscernible, random shifts in the structure of the environment. The total capacity of satisfying any number of such drives at any one time expresses the common notion of power.

Now the link between desires and tyranny becomes transparent: tyranny is the capacity to maximize the effectiveness of such a mechanism, in terms of simultaneity, multiplicity and guaranteed iteration of one's desires. Since most of the desirable objects are either other persons or possessions of others (from traits to property), the said maximization amounts to the absolutization of power over other humans.

It can easily be understood why such a picture equals with hell for the purposeful, teleological, rational calculative action of the philosopher and of the theorist: *a maze of proximal causal mechanisms*, wherein inscrutable minute shifts in the balance of forces determines the momentary preeminence of one drive upon another.

Cast in this format, new vistas are opened for the classic theory of desire, since the network of proximal causes operational here are the drives biologically hardwired in the human brain, just as much as in any other species. But this will have to remain for a different study.

---

[7]   A rapport between desires and reason determines at Hobbes a certain configuration of the sovereign power: Hobbes's Leviathan is the Absolute State (Hobbes, op. cit., [62], p. 90 ff; [71], p. 100; [62], p. 88; [88], p. 121 ff). A different rapport, beneficial to rationality, has lead to the second great political theory of Modern times, namely the minimal state of Locke (Locke, 1690/1960).

In what the present argument is concerned, at this place, a cursory observation must be made. Even though capitalism is described overwhelmingly as an order aimed precisely at material gratification, which is to say, a world designed for the sole purpose of desire satisfaction, *capitalism does not manifest the chaotic character predicted upon the classic critique of desire*. At the height of its historical peak, during the XVIIIth century and the first half of the XIXth century, before the increase of political interference of the state, and in spite of the ebullience in innovation, change and growth, capitalism has shown a remarkable capacity of generating orderly, and at the same time highly dynamic, structures. This fact has not gone unnoticed by concerned theorists, and this capacity has been partially captured in the rather suggestive notions of 'invisible hand' (XVIIIth century, Adam Smith) or 'economic harmony' (XIXth century, Bastiat).[8] Capitalism, in truth, must introduce somewhere a new variable in the mechanism of desire, as described by the classic theory, modifying the equation of human action from modalities conducive to chaos to modalities conducive to an astonishing form of order. A turning of the tides, as it were, from chaos and tyranny to order and liberty.

It is hereby proposed that the variable which is capable of operating such a change is the universalization of the pursuit of profit. The action in view of reward achieves an ordering of the ebullience of desires, forcing upon them structure: hierarchy, which means sequence; prioritization, which means relations between them specifying the conditions according to which they become active or extinguished; compatibility, which aims at achieving non-contradiction between mutually exclusive desires and, if this is not possible, and according to established priority, decides their discarding. By such procedures, all set in motion and kept active by the wish to maximize one's rewards, there emerges an increasingly coherent structure which, via processes of maturation and growth, becomes indistinguishable from one's personality. People define themselves in varied ways: but the definition which takes as criteria one's dreams, aspirations, ambitions, no matter how trivial they may seem to an external observer, is a privileged self-definition. In the intricate structure of one's desires, in their arborescent structure, in the balance between probabilities of fulfillment, in the criticality of the expected rewards, people usually see the essence of their particularism, of that which differentiates them from numberless other individuals: all moved by similar desires, but each with a unique, personal equation resulting from their combination and modulation.

People are bundles of desires: and this is far from being a derogatory characterization, as much of the elitist or spiritualist tradition of thought maintains from Plato till today. The 'bundle of desires' is actually a synonym notion to 'subjective preference', central to the Austrian school of economics.[9] The market is

---

[8] See Smith (1776/1981), IV.ii.9, p. 457; Smith (1759/1984) IV.I.10, p. 184; Bastiat (1841).
[9] For Mises, the concept is coextensive with human action itself: 'the fundamental category of action [is] the act of preferring ad setting aside' (Mises, 1949/1966, p. 236). The present approach shares this comprehensivity. Subjective preferences are acts of *valuation* which involve, on the one hand, the particularity, the uniqueness of the individual; and,

driven by subjective preferences, which are the orders that consumers, inconspicuously and by aggregation, give to the producers and, thus, express their power. But, also, our subjective preferences, our desires, are the invisible glue of our social relations, especially those which matter most to us, those which are charged with intimacy, privacy, personalization. The bundle of subjective preferences is linked with the deepest chemistry which determine like and dislike, affiliation, group identity.

It is this complexity of the effects generated by desire which make it that the law of diminishing returns does not apply to rewards. The scaffolding of desires which make human subjectivity allows for, for all practical purposes, an infinity of permutations and combinations. This is why desires are an infinite motivational engine for self-exertion and achievement which can never be matched by punishment. Capitalism is the first human order which brought forth this latent potential, transforming it into a source of human satisfaction still challenging our understanding.

In conclusion, rewards, especially when captured in monetary form (money being the universal medium for the exchange of reward messages), give a quantitative measure to otherwise incommensurable desires; when they occur, they establish visible landmarks of one's achievement. In brief, profit gives an objective, measurable and by that finite expression to the otherwise bad infinity of human desires. By that, it tames them, making from agents of chaos, instruments of disciplined accumulation, progression, growth: both at the personal level, and at systemic level.

3.2 Teleonomy

As a separate effect, profit, reward, introduces a vector of sense in the maze of chaotic, multifarious and simultaneous desires; directness; orientation towards the future; it introduces *teleonomy* and purpose in a human activity, otherwise subjected to the randomness of contingent adaptive pressures. Another way of saying the same thing, is by making use of Aristotle's classification of causes: a network of proximal causal mechanisms, determined by instinct and natural drives, *profit introduces distal causal mechanisms*, or *final causes*. The expectation of profit is the normal outcome of actions which are *intentional* and result from explicit conscious design, by opposition to actions which spring from instinct and which are automatic and hardwired.

Insofar as teleonomy is seen as the essential feature of a species endowed with *cognizance of its ends* (teleology) (Aristotle, 1915;[10] Mises, 1949/1966;[11] Simon,

---

on the other hand, his/her will, his/her sovereignty. The rewards pursued by individuals are the corollary of his/her valuations. From a different angle, the concept of desire as used here describes the function of utility of mainstream economics.

[10] Aristotle's ethics is action based. And insofar as action is towards a goal, his ethics is a teleological ethics *par excellence*: 'man is a moving principle of actions' (1112b33). Within the context of teleology, reasonable desires are outlined as 'deliberate choice of things in our power' (1113a 11). This is a precondition for the achievement of the

1969), rewards are crucial for the accomplishment of the higher potential in man. By making possible costly forms of behavior (out of which ethical behavior is a class), reward distantiates man from his/her animal condition. Capitalism is a systematic, structured machinery for achieving that on a large scale, the scale of entire populations. This may be one of the reasons for which, in a phenomenological perspective, free market societies seem more accomplished, both at the individual and at the system level.

Teleonomy has one important characteristic, and this is what explains the capacity of profit pursuit in organizing behavior. Purposes do not refer to the present, but to future. The profit following economic activity is, unless the complete sequence of conditional actions is performed, *virtual reward*. The implications of this property are profound, touching on many of the classical observations related to 'the ethics of capitalism' and bringing them under a common explanatory umbrella. Some of these aspects, pertaining to our topic, will be more emphasized. Others, will just be briefly mentioned.

a. On the one hand, the reward, albeit future and virtual, bears causally upon the present: a temporal loop is thus closed between the desired future, and the current performance. The net result of this positive feedback loop between a possible future and a yet non-committed present, is the improvement of the present course of action. In order for the desired future to occur, obligatory moves ought to be made, such as the future which is merely *possible* to become *probable*. In pursuit of profit, the mind eagerly explores such nexuses, bypassing the most likely algorithms of action (the default settings of behavior, see next section), and considering costly courses of action, which are reasonable now, on the account of the anticipated reward.

This *exploration of possible, multiple futures* is part of the faculty which we call imagination. But what is specific to this form of imagination, as opposed to its aesthetic counterpart, is its binding to reality, its concrete character, and the fact that it calculates with possible ontologies, assigning degrees of probability. Herein lies a crucial difference between the effects of punishments and of rewards: punishment inhibits desire, and prevents active calculation of possible scenarios. Under threat, individuals fall upon the lowest but most desirable scenario, namely that in which the threat will not be applied. Rewards stimulate active exploration of alternatives and sharpens calculative competence: in brief, *intelligence, planning* and *forecasting*. Worlds based on reward are more productive, in the strict economic sense of the term, because they are based on a *productive calculative imaginary*. While worlds based on punishment are poor, both economically and aesthetically. Their output, both economic and artistic, are directed to the reinforcing of the punishing agency.

b. The fact that for a long time the reward pursued remains virtual gives capitalist economic action a peculiar pseudo-ascetic dimension. Virtual rewards tone down the expression of desires, giving prevalence to the cognitive dimension

---

supreme end, which is happiness (1097a 25 – 1097b 35). Both practical wisdom and virtue are 'calculation in view of the good end' (1140a 25-30).

[11] See in particular pp. 23, 25, 35, 107.

of the pursuit. One possible consequence is that, by habituation, the cognitive dimension of the pursuit of profit prevails over the achievement of profit itself.[12] The virtues formerly regarded as means for the achievement of profit, become more interesting than the profit itself and ends in their own. This peculiarity is that which gives birth to the cycles work-gratification specific for the so-called 'Protestant ethos' of capitalism.

    c. Virtual reward is the other side of the coin which is called delayed gratification. At its turn, delayed gratification has two important classes of effects. On the one hand, the habituation of postponing enjoyment strengthens the mind confronted with an assault of possible objects of desire. Thus, the resistance to thymotic passions and animal appetites advocated by most moralists is derived as a consequence of the economy of the apparatus of desire itself: a more correct epistemic procedure, since it satisfies the principle of Occam's Razor. Secondly, delayed gratification stays at the basis of two crucial economic behaviors: saving and investment. Saving is nothing else but the resistance to immediate gratification in view of future greater (or more comprehensive) satisfaction. At the scale of large population, generalized saving behavior is the crucial engine of growth, since resources are channeled in investment instead of being exhausted (Mises, 1979).

    d. Long-term reasoning is perhaps the most important implication of delayed reward.

    Each individual at any given moment is subjected to competing desires, as discussed earlier. The linking of profit to action oriented towards the future represents an added strength of a costly course of action which otherwise would succumb to short-term interests. Therefore, the profit motive is a reinforcer of a wider consideration of rationales, of a more comprehensive computing of conflicting claims upon oneself and, by that, a reinforcer of resoluteness, sobriety, consistency with one's promises, in brief, that which we call moral character.

    Without getting into details which would remove us from the topic of ethics proper, consequences *a* and *d* combined have a powerful implication for political science. Both Hobbes and a more liberal thinker like Hume located the origin of government into a natural insufficiency of reason expressed as a preeminence of short-term over long term thinking. The state, the government, supplants this deficiency by doing the thinking and then reinforcing it by laws upon the subjects (Hobbes, 1651/1996, cf. note 8 above; Hume, 1739/1992). The recasting of the problem of long-term rationality in a theory of profit makes it possible for the replacement of a voluntarist ethics justifying coercion with an ethics which respects and trusts individual will and freedom. In fact, the continuous decline of the state power and the increased reliance upon market mechanisms is an empirical observation consistent with the present theoretical predicament.

---

[12] An observation supporting this idea is mentioned in relation to George Soros: his collaborators are sometimes worried that he does not seem to pursue profit in his speculations, as they do, but rather he merely enjoys the game itself; Soros, G., Wien and Koenen, (1995). A similar observation in Nora (1987, p. 189): 'The M&A [Mergers and Acquisitions] is like a permanent chess tournament, an intellectual hocus-pocus but which effectively impacts the real.'

e. Future potential reward is a powerful modifier of the behavior oriented towards another (social behavior). The promise of profit has the crucial ethical capacity of curbing hostility, aggressiveness, and other similar innate responses. The virtual reward is an incentive for overcoming conflict and for the exploration of non-conflicting solutions. To this function we shall turn in the following section.

4 Ethical Creativity, Social Intelligence and Capitalism

One form of calculation in view of a future profit, and ethical in the narrow sense of ethics, presupposes other human beings. The calculation with another is, as a matter of fact, the cornerstone of any ethical system.

Formerly, it has been proposed that capitalism makes it possible on a large scale for types of behavior otherwise improbable/impossible. The essence of an ethics specific of capitalism, intrinsic to it, is the generalization of a certain type of calculation with another. This social calculative behavior is called in the literature 'cooperation', and its extensivity in free market systems is almost universally acknowledged. The term is more descriptive than explanatory. An explanation ought to clarify why cooperation works.

Cooperation is a form of costly behavior, as the classical paradigm of the 'prisoner dilemma' repeatedly demonstrated (Axelrod, 1984). In spite of its profitability, people systematically fall upon more basic forms of behavior, namely defection (cheating, betrayal, treason). In order for a cooperative setup to work, special arrangements are to be made: contracts and agencies for the reinforcement of contracts are part of these complex arrangements.

But, beside the skeptic's wisdom about the wickedness of human nature, the need to amply secure cooperation also demonstrates something else: that when appropriately motivated by the promise of future reward, humans are capable of organizing frameworks of interaction which are extremely complex, mutually advantageous and innovative in terms of adopted conditional behavior. The multiplicity of clauses, the anticipation of future contingencies, sometimes down to particulars, the drawing of courses of action pendant upon conditions forecast in a cluster of several possible futures, testify for the difficulty but, at the same time, for the astounding *ethical creativity* set in motion by profit.

The profit motive alters some of the most fundamental natural proclivities of human behavior. It is here that the utmost achievement of capitalism reveals itself. Profit can be achieved in a multitude of ways, most commonly, by infringing losses upon another in zero-sum games. Such games, when someone's gain is the loss of another, make the essence of political behavior, in the strict sense of games of power, and had given the substance of much of the known history until the advent of capitalism (Oppenheimer, 1914/1997; Nock, 1935). Systems based upon zero-sum games 'calculate with another' in the sense of infringing losses upon him/her, from the loss of goods (theft, robbery), down to the loss of freedom (servitude) and life (enslavement, murder in impunity). Capitalism is the first system whereby the calculation with another has in view his/her *gain*. The non-zero sum games, games whereby both parties gain, their generalization to a practically universal scale, are the singular most important ethical (and political) feature of capitalism. And it is the larger profit received by both parties, the larger future reward, that which allows for the imagining and the performance of sophisticated ethical puzzles.

The weakness of cooperation lies specifically with the request of iteration: apart from iteration, the best strategy to pursue remains defection and non-symmetrical distribution of profit. Cooperative strategies are effective when the game is repeated. But iteration does not necessarily mean 'between the same two partners.' Iteration refers to the prevalence of a given strategy in a population and its robustness to competition against of zero-sum strategies. Therefore, the intrinsic logic of non-zero sum games comes, apart from their productivity, with an added benefit: *inclusiveness*. By force of the requirement of iteration, more and more actors are required to enter the game. Capitalism generates, apart from material wealth, fairness, in the sense of equality of chances and openness. It is by virtue of this feature that contemporary democracies can safely call themselves *liberal* democracies.

There are three consequences which directly concerns our topic.

a. The pursuit of profit via cooperative games comes with the requirement of self-limitation. Which means that at any given moment, the participants ought to refrain from defecting, in the sense of switching to a win-loose strategy (which, in the liberal tradition, counts as a form of aggression). The important fact about this restraint in behavior is that it does not follow a normative injunction, as it is often the case with moral rules. Therefore, it does need little reinforcement in the form of a threat of punishment in case of defection: and, for well designed cooperative games, the only needed incentive is the sole rooting in the reward system, the expected profit. It is here that we find the explanation of the well known liberal notion of tolerance (Locke, 1689/1990; Mill, 1859/1999).

The second consequence is linked to the former.

b. Apart from the basic rule of transparency of the terms of cooperation, all the other rules are derivative. Therefore, an ethical system linked to the pursuit of reward has the advantage of deductibility, of obviousness, of reasonability. Herein lies the emphasis of the entire free-market tradition, liberal or conservative, on 'common-sense.'[13] In truth, capitalism is the only system which can dispense itself from an explicit, elaborate (and often counter-factual) ethics: and it is this weakness, derived from its main virtue, which has often been exploited by its detractors. Translated in juridical terms, this reasonableness peculiar to the liberal ethics makes the difference between legal systems based on natural right, such as the Anglo-Saxon law, versus those based on positive law conceptions, such as in most European Continental countries.

c. The third consequence concerns the mechanics of cooperation itself, and it provides and explanation which is more than intuitive. Every non-zero sum game can potentially pass through a stage when it becomes a game with sum zero: it is

---

[13] Occurrences are too many to quote, and sometimes it is rather a matter of style and attitude. For illustration, see Paine, (1776/1982); Burke, (1791/1999); Acton, (1906; Lecture XII, The Rise of the Whigs); Hayek (1994).

the moment when one of the partners defects. In the absence of a long-term vista, in the absence of the projected profit, this moment is critical for inter-human interaction, for it normally triggers a response of retaliation from the betrayed part. An arms race of punishments and counter-punishments, a 'doomsday machine' of sorts, is the standard ensuing outcome (Barkow, Cosmides, Tooby, 1992; Pinker, 1997).

During iterated cooperating games (tit-for-tat), the normal sequence of moves is different. The backbone of the strategy is a self-limited response: if the opponent defects, you should also defect. But if s/he resumes cooperation, you do the same, without retaliation. The question now arises why and how is this possible.

In a system based on the anticipation of a reward, the withdrawal of the promise of reward, the dramatic plunge of its probability brought about the act of defection *is itself a penalty*. And, in most of the situations, as the case of tit-for-tat demonstrates, it is sufficient a deterrent and cause for the resuming of cooperation. Which means that for a large number of potential conflicts, the only penalty needed is the withdrawal of the expected reward itself. The alteration of the cost-benefit equation for the defector leaves room for a swift correction, which otherwise would not be possible.

The corrective mechanism hereby described does not mean that confrontation will not arise. But the reward system underlying any form of cooperation functions as a buffer, as a first line of defense, in the absence of which 'doomsday machines' would trigger by default. And it is this self-limiting mechanism which makes of cooperation an evolutionary stable strategy, once it emerges (Maynard-Smith, 1982). This is also the reason for which, on the whole, worlds based on free markets, which is to say, on generalized systems of rewards are more peaceful.

5 Capitalist Ethics on the Background of Evolved Behavior

Cooperation brings about an increase of productivity as a consequence of people's compounded power. But in spite of this, cooperation is not at all an obvious thing to do. Cooperation means a lowering of the defenses, an increased amount of vigilance in regard of potential defection, a renunciation to playing power games. Above all else, iterated cooperation supposes commitment: which means a reduction of options and a channeling of resources in one direction, disregarding the normal oscillations when, temporarily, personal disadvantage overcomes advantages. The cooperator increases his/her exposure, his/her vulnerability and, thus, the cost of his/her survival. Besides all that, the high productivity of the cooperative nexus is easily recognized by third parties whom will want to share in the prize, without paying the cost: the fragility of the complicated ethical game established between the parties is easily undermined by free riders.[14] Any one of

---

[14] The problem has been addressed from both the evolutionary psychology perspective, and from the political economy perspective. It has special relevance in the discussion of public goods. For the former approach, Tooby, Cosmides and Price, (2002); for the second approach, Jasay, (1989).

the parties cooperating is thus exposed to manipulative or overt exploitation by deceptive partners.

Apart from all the above, most of the combinations of power, even if they remain genuine between the partners, are often directed towards other groups or sub-groups: which means that, even when it occurs, cooperation is aimed at aggression of others.

The sum of these observations aims at substantiating the notion that cooperation is erected upon ambiguous and shifting ground. This ground is the naturally evolved foundation of human behavior – and we are dealing with a bottom line that all moralistic and normative discourse must take into account if it wants to avoid mere interjection and, ultimately, the recourse to force in order to impose its normative content.

The available space and the genre of this anthology restraints an otherwise long and exciting detour, to few facts capable to directly enlighten our theme.[15] The general thesis is that there exists powerful natural factors limiting the potential for ethical intercourse, in general, and cooperation in particular. They are linked to the dynamics between competition and conditional cooperation at both the intra-group and inter-group levels.

a. The logic of altruism. The possibility of engaging in cooperative behavior is dependent upon, and restrained by, a biological apparatus whose main role is to secure the survival of the individual in a milieu where resources are limited and competition for them ubiquitous (from without as well as from without the species). Little room remains for behavior which benefits another and presupposes some cost to the benefactor: which is also a technical definition for altruism. Intuitively, altruism corresponds to that which was earlier in this chapter identified as a calculation with another aiming to produce a gain, and not a loss to this other.

On such a basis, the form of cooperation which is the most probable to occur between humans is *nepotistic* altruism.[16] Which means that costly acts, such as those presupposed by an ethical engagement of another (cooperation included), are likely to occur between genetic kin. The bias is determined by the algebra of costs-benefits, as modulated by genetic constraints: the higher cost is accepted because part of the potential profit of the costly action indirectly benefits the doer, due to the presence of his/her genes in the recipient. The likelihood of costly behavior in relation to another decreases inversely with the degree of kinship. The rule is known as Hamilton's Formula, and basically says that the benefit b of the recipient, multiplied by the degree of relatedness r, ought to be greater than the cost c of the altruist, or $br - c > o$ (Hamilton, 1963, 1964).

---

[15] For an extensive, systematic and inter-disciplinary presentation of the issues bellow (and others related), the following can be consulted: Wilson, (1978); Konner, (1982); Wright, (1994).

[16] For comprehensive discussions, see Alexander, (1987), pp. 63-73; Wilson, (1978), pp. 149-169. As for technicalities, the essential literature comprises (in chronological order): Hamilton, (1963), (1964); Axelrod and Hamilton (1981); Trivers, (1971); Maynard-Smith, (1998).

Occasionally strangers are co-opted in this system of biologically based cooperation, situation technically described as 'inclusive fitness.' There exists a wide variety of anthropological ritualized practices which enlarge the sphere of cooperation beyond kin, amounting in the end to the transformation of the stranger into kin. The taboo concerning strangers is, in all evidence, a universal feature of human sociality (Frazer, 1922/1980). In order to become recipient of altruism, the stranger must be integrated in the three major fluxes structuring the group: of females, of economic goods and of symbols (Levi-Strauss, 1978).

In what ethics is concerned, the above means that morality is biased: towards self, towards one's kin (family, extended family, tribe, nation) versus the stranger. This factual observation stays at the basis of a least one influential system of political philosophy, erected upon the distinction 'friend/foe' (Schmitt, 1932/1976). Any ethics aims at achieving universalization of its conclusions. In the basic biological fact mentioned above, which is perfectly consistent with cursory observation as well, we find the lowest level limiting factor of any such universality.

On the other hand, the moral bias on behalf of one's group does not necessarily imply a higher ethical standard operating within the group. To the contrary, groups where altruism is practiced by default (families), are also environments reputedly leading to large levels of violence (Daly and Wilson, 1988; Daly, Salmon and Wilson, 1997; Wilson, Daly and Daniele, 1995; Emlen, 1995). Violence is quite accurate an indicator of the capacity (or lack of capacity) of the individuals to arrange for remedies or solutions to their antagonistic interest. On this basis, a more general theorem can be attempted: the higher the level of indistinguishable individual interests, the larger the level of conflict. The more ambiguous are the conditional terms of the intercourse between individuals belonging to the same socializing unit, the more opportunity for conflict will arise.

b. The logic of intra-group homogenization. Humans' social reflexes are dependent on a long evolutionary history in small groups with a number of individuals in the order of tens. The social economy of such groups is characterized by a double scarcity: scarcity of resources, and scarcity of productive associations (Boari, 2000). Insofar as the double relative scarcity remains constant, social equilibria are preserved. Whenever scarcity becomes less stringent, the consecutive disruption of the equilibria awakes from latency complex social and political processes. Technological innovation, demographic growth, frequency of intercourse with other groups, are all factors threatening social stability. They stimulate desire, selectivity, differentiation and, at the limit, segregation, secession and dissolution of the group.

The production of a collective identity, process which involves a large part of that which is called 'culture', is the strategy *par excellence* to counter such centrifugal dynamics. A political discourse (ideology) of allegiance, loyalty and duty towards the group, on the one hand, versus a rhetoric of xenophobia towards other groups, are the byproduct of the homogenizing process. The corollary of the political ideology, is a morality of self-sacrifice, aimed at legitimizing the renunciation to the diversification of one's desires and choice of association. The working of these mechanisms is easily recognizable phenomenologically by cursory contemporary observation, whatever the organization level considered.

The result of these crossing processes is a social milieu where individual competitive interests are not given a transparent cognitive recognition and the discursive space in which to manifest themselves. This leads to a maximum difficulty in setting up cooperative frameworks, to a pervasiveness of moralistic aggressive discourse, and to an utter sensitivity of working cooperations to defection and/or invasion by predatory third parties.[17]

It is on this background, prepared by biology and reinforced by cultural and political practice that the ethical success of capitalism ought be measured. This success had been made possible by the acknowledgment of the fact that any cooperation, any form of ethical treatment of the other, takes place on the horizon of a fundamentally competitive game whose rules are hardwired, for biologically evolved. It is only subsequently that this biologically determined jungle can be transformed into a chessboard on which partners move according to agreed upon rules. And, as argued along the chapter, these rules exist and are performed because they are recognized as conducive to gain for both parties if adhered to.

It is this ethical substance of the capitalist game which brought about the more sophisticated awareness of the fact that, ultimately, competition is not problematic in itself, quite the contrary. Competition is a mechanism which opposes to any power a counter-power, only such an opposition being able to control its tyrannical drift. Market competition is, in fact, the equivalent of the mechanism of checks and balances which restraints political power.

The ethical merit of the capitalist order extends beyond its practical benefit. For it allows us to understand in a more sophisticated manner and in finer detail how the interference between the pieces of a machinery build by the blind process of an evolution 'red in teeth and claws' can generate the amazing filigree of cooperation, of a non-predatory engagement of the Other.

6 Conclusion

The background upon which the ethics of capitalism (or the lack of it) is to be grasped should be more complex and better informed in order to be evaluated. Philosophers, intellectuals, shapers of opinion, economists carrying interdisciplinary work, moralists, are often using maximalist definitions of ethics without due regard to the conditions of feasibility of the behavior thus expected. Maximalism may not be an issue, if the conditions of its realization are spelled clear. When this does not happen, maximalist ethics usually falls upon voluntarism and imposition, use of force and coercion. That the relationship between maximalist ethics and tyrannical power is not merely an arbitrary construction, there is ample theoretical and historical evidence (Strauss, 1954; Hollander, 1990).

There exists a multiplicity of directions from which the nexus between capitalism and ethics can be approached. Whichever this direction may be, whether

---

[17] For an extensive explanation of the mechanics summarized above, see Boari (2000).

prevalently philosophical, economical or sociological, an informed understanding of how humans function is indispensable. Otherwise, there is a great risk of claims without coverage and of recommendations which are missing their target. As argued above, ethical conduct imposes costs upon individuals. These costs can be compensated with due reward or, else, they can be pressed upon individuals by charisma, authority or, if anything fails, at the point of a gun. At the beginning of Modern times, Machiavelli made the distinction between unarmed and armed prophets, resolutely siding with the later group. If the analysis proposed in this chapter is not altogether wrong, capitalism, in the widest semantic coverage of the term, may well be the only form of moralism without weapons.

At the end of the day, any system of thought ought to confront the test of coherence and consistency. From this point of view, any maximalist, normative approach to ethics faces an arduous task. When all else fails, maximalist ethics must be able to exhibit morally consistent justifications of punishments, which is to say, of violence: this rather being an oxymoronic task. For, either an ethical system gives true recommendation as to how people should lead their lives which they could consent to, or imposes upon them that which they would not consent to. Ethical guidelines which people readily consent to hardly need a systematic exposition: just as, as mentioned above, liberal capitalism was in no need to produce. The larger the imposition upon individuals, the larger the need for justification. The larger the body of justification, the more it gets an arbitrary coherence: it is that which is commonly called an 'ideology.' But ultimately, that which needs to be justified, is why certain things should be imposed upon individuals. Ethics turns into politics, for there always must be an agency to decide the imposition and an apparatus to implement it.

Between ethical maximalism and arbitrary power there appears to exist a connection which cannot be easily canceled out. The utmost achievement of the capitalist order was to rephrase this link. Even while forms of arbitrary power may subsist under capitalism (which is reasonable to expect since free market liberalism is not an anthropogenetic project or an attempt at social engineering), the general rules of the game have been changed in such a way that its dominion had shrunk drastically, to the benefit of enormous numbers. To the extent that orders can exists without coercion, the epoch that we label as 'capitalism' is the first historical instance to make us ponder soberly upon their possible realization. To the extent that the optimism of the Enlightenment concerning *Bildung*, moral progress, ethical growth in individuals is possible, the ethics emerging from the capitalist system may well be an obligatory passage.

References

Acton, J. E. D. (1906), *Lectures on Modern History*, Macmillan, London.

Alexander, R. D. (1987), *The Biology of Moral Systems*, Aldine de Gruyter, New York.

Arendt, H. (1951/1979), *The Origins of Totalitarianism*, Harvest/Harcourt Brace Jovanovich, San Diego, New York, London.

Aristotle (1921), *Politica*, in: *The Works of Aristotle*, Volume X, Clarendon Press, Oxford.

Aristotle (1915), *Ethica Nicomachea*, in *The Works of Aristotle*, Volume IX, Oxford University Press, Oxford.

Axelrod, R. (1984), *The Evolution of Cooperation*, Basic Books, Inc., New York.

Axelrod, R., Hamilton, W. D. (1981), The Evolution of Cooperation, *Science*, 211, pp. 1390-1396.

Bastiat, F. (1841), *Harmonies Economiques*, Guillaumin & Cie, Paris.

Baudrillard, J. (1970), *La Société de Consommation*, Denoel, Paris.

Bentham, J. (1781/1988), *The Principles of Morals and Legislation*, Prometheus Books, Amherst, New York, esp. pp. 24-43, 178-204.

Boari, M. (2000), Ethnic Power, *Polis*, 1, pp. 114-154.

Braudel, F. (1985), *La Dynamique du Capitalisme*, Flammarion, Paris.

Burke, E. (1791/1999), An Appeal From the New to the Old Whigs, in: *The Portable Edmund Burke*, Penguin, London.

Cosmides, L., Tooby, J. (1992), Cognitive Adaptations for Social Exchange, in: Barkow, J., Cosmides, L., Tooby, J. (eds), *The Adapted Mind. Evolutionary Psychology and the Generation of Culture*, Oxford University Press, Oxford, New York, pp. 163-229.

Daly, M., Wilson, M. (1988), *Evolutionary Social Psychology and Family Homicide*, Science, 242, pp. 519-529.

Daly, M., Salmon, C., Wilson, M. (1997), Kinship: the Conceptual Hole in Psychological Studies of Social Cognition and Close Relationships, in: Simpson, J. A. and Kenrick, D. (eds), *Evolutionary Social Psychology*, Erlbaum, Mahwah NJ.

Emlen, S. T. (1995), An Evolutionary Theory of the Family, *Proceedings of the Natural Academy of Science*, USA, 92, pp. 8092-8099.

Frazer, J. G. (1922/1980), Creanga de Aur, Meridiane, Bucuresti, vol. II, pp. 127-137; translation of *The Golden Bough*, np, ny.

Hamilton, W. D. (1963), The Evolution of Altruistic Behavior, *The American Naturalist* 97, pp. 354-56.

Hamilton, W. D. (1964), The Genetical Evolution of Social Behavior I and II, *Journal of Theoretical Biology*, 7, pp. 1-16, 17-32.

Havel, V. (1975), Letter Dr. Gustav Husak, in Keane, J. (ed.) (1985), *The Power of the Powerless. Citizens Against the State in Central-Eastern Europe*, Hutchinson, London, Melbourne, Sydney, Auckland, Johannesburg, p. 35.

Hayek, F. von (1994), *Hayek on Hayek. An Autobiographical Dialogue*, University of Chicago Press, Chicago.

Heller, M. (1988), *Cogs in the Wheel. The Formation of Soviet Man*, Alfred A. Knopf Inc., New York.

Hirschman, A. O. (1977), *The Passions and the Interests. Political Arguments for Capitalism Before Its Triumph*, Princeton University Press, Princeton, New Jersey.

Hobbes, T. (1651/1996), Leviathan, Cambridge University Press.

Hollander, P. (1990), *Political Pilgrims. Travels of Western Intellectuals to Soviet Union, China, and Cuba*, University Press of America, Lanham.

Hume, D. (1739/1992), *Treatise on Human Nature*, Prometheus Books, Buffalo, New York; pp. 534 ff.

Jasay, A. (1989), *Social Contract, Free Ride*, Clarendon Press, Oxford.

Kant, I. (1785/1996), Groundwork for The Metaphysics of Morals, in *Practical Philosophy*, Cambridge University Press, Cambridge; pp. 73 ff.

Konner, M. (1982), *The Tangled Wing. Biological Constraints on the Human Spirit*, Henry Holt et Co, New York.

Lafontaine, A. (1902), *Le Plaisir d'après Platon et Aristote. Etude Psychologique, Métaphysique et Morale*, Alcan, Paris, pp. 42-84.

Le Goff, J. (1977), *Time, Work and Culture in the Middle Ages*, University of Chicago Press, Chicago, London, pp. 59-68.
Le Goff, J. (1990), *Your Money or Your Life. Economy and Religion in the Middle Ages*, Zone Books, New York.
Lévi-Strauss, C. (1978), Antropologie Structurala, Editura Politica, Bucuresti; translation of *Anthropologie Structurale* (1973), Plon, Paris, pp. 360-365.
Locke, J. (1690/1960), *Two Treatises of Government*, Cambridge University Press, Cambridge.
Locke, J. (1689/1990), A *Letter Concerning Toleration*, Prometheus Books, Buffalo, NY.
Macphearson, C. B., *The Political Theory of Possessive Individualism*, Oxford University Press, Oxford, New York, esp. pp. 137-154.
Marx, K. (1867/1948), Capitalul. Critica economiei politice, Editura Partidului Muncitoresc Roman, Bucuresti, esp. part 5, pp. 461-482; translation of *Das Kapital*, Verlag für Literatur un Politik, Wien-Berlin, 1932.
Marx, K. (1898/1995), Value, Price and Profit. *Speech at the First International Working Men's Association*, June 1865, html mark-up Mike Ballard, 1995, http://www.marxist.org/archive/marx/works/1865/value-price-profit/, accessed 2 November 2004.
Maynard-Smith, J. (1982), *Evolution and the Theory of Games*, Cambridge University Press, Cambridge, New York, Melbourne.
Maynard-Smith, J. (1998), The Origin of Altruism, *Nature*, 393, pp. 639-640.
Mill, J. S. (1859/1999), *On Liberty*, Broadview Press, Peterborough.
Mises, L. von (1949/1966), *Human Action. A Treatise on Economics*, Third Revised Edition, Contemporary Books & Yale University Press, Chicago.
Mises, L. von (1979), *Economic Policy: Thoughts for Today and Tomorrow*, Regnery/Gateway Inc. Chicago.
Montesquieu, J. de S. (1748/1989), *The Spirit of the Laws*, Cambridge University Press, Cambridge, p. 214.
Nock, A. J. (1935), *Our Enemy the State*, W. Morrow et Co, New York.
Nora, D. (1987), *Les Possédés de Wall Street*, Denoel, Paris.
Oppenheimer, F. (1914/1997), *The State*, Fox & Wilkes, San Francisco.
Paine, T. (1776, 1982), *Common-Sense*, Penguin, Hamondsworth.
Platon, *Republica* (1986), Editura Stiintifica si Enciclopedica Bucuresti, 439d.
Schmitt, C. (1932/1976), *The Concept of the Political*, Rutgers University Press, New Brunswick, New Jersey.
Sen, A. (1989), *On Ethics and Economics*, Blackwell Publishing.
Simon, H. A. (1969), *Sciences of the Artificial*, The Massachusetts Institute of Technology, Cambridge, Massachusetts.
Smith, A. (1776/1981), *An Inquiry Into the Nature and Causes of the Wealth of Nations*, Liberty Fund, Indianapolis.
Smith, A. (1759/1984), *The Theory of Moral Sentiments*, Liberty Fund, Indianapolis.
Soros, G., Wien, B. and Koenen, K. (1995), *Soros on Soros: Staying Ahead of the Curve*, Wiley, New York, Chicester.
Strauss, L. (1954), *De la Tyrannie*, précédé de *Hiéron* de Xenophon et suivi de *Tyrannie et Sagesse* par Alexandre Kojève, Gallimard, Paris.
Tooby, J., Cosmides, L. and Price, M. (2002), Punitive Sentiment as an Anti-Free Rider Psychological Device, *Evolution and Human Behavior*, 23, pp. 203-231.
Trivers, R. L. (1971), The Evolution of Reciprocal Altruism, *Quarterly Review of Biology* 46, pp. 35-57.
Turchetti, M. (2003), Tirania si Tiranicidul, Cartier, Bucuresti, Chisinau; translation of *Tyrannie et tyrannicide de l'Antiquité à nos Jours*, Presses Universitaires de France, 2001.

Veblen, T. (1902), *The Theory of the Leisure Class*, Macmillan, New York, pp. 68-101.
Weber, M. (1905/2001), *The Protestant Ethic and the Spirit of Capitalism*, Routledge, New York, London.
Wilson, E. O. (1978), *On Human Nature*, Harvard University Press, Cambridge, London.
Wilson, M., Daly, M., Daniele, A. (1995), Familicide: The Killing of Spouse and Children, *Aggressive Behavior*, 21, pp. 275-291.
Wright, R. (1994), *The Moral Animal*, Vintage Books, New York.
Zinoviev, A. (1985), *Homo Sovieticus*, Victor Gollancz Ltd., London.

Chapter 7

The Ethical Environment of the Free Market

Sorin Cucerai

1 Introduction: The Quest for Ethics

The main thesis of this chapter is that the free market generates an ethical environment based upon the decision by individuals to treat other individuals as fellow humans. Therefore, this chapter's fundamental task will be to provide an account of why and how this is so. This will be done by differentiating between a finite and a trans-finite order, both these types of order being analyzed according to the relation between each of them and aggression (Cucerai, 1999). The view taken here is that aggression is both the source and the outcome of disorder – the kind of disorder we usually describe as a 'jungle.'

For some people, 'the free market is a jungle.' This statement has two distinct meanings. One of them employs the word 'jungle' as a metaphor for disorder; the other one employs the same word as a metaphor for unethical behavior. When combined, the two offer us a vision of the free market as unethical disorder. The commonest way to understand such an unethical disorder is by regarding it as an expression of greed and selfishness, to which we usually oppose altruism.

For those who think this way, this suggests that altruism generates and promotes order, while selfishness is the ethical source of disorder.[1] Such an inference is blatantly false, and the failure to see its falsity has led some authors to praise the virtue of selfishness in order to find a way out from this moral trap.[2] A simpler and sounder way to avoid such apories is to notice that both altruism *and selfishness* make sense as ethical attributes only within a single kind of order – namely, a finite order (i.e. an end-state order). Only when goals and redistributive practices are predetermined within a world with clear limits does it make sense to qualify one's behavior as altruistic (if he or she behaves according to these goals and practices), or as selfish (if he or she doesn't). This clearly poses the problem of the

---

[1] This kind of reasoning is compatible with (if not derived from) the understanding of human vice as disobedience. The first philosopher to take this view was Augustine (354-430), most notably in *The City of God* (Augustine, 1995).

[2] This is what Ayn Rand does, for instance in Rand, (1964). Hayek adopts a different view, merely suggesting that altruism is not a virtue (Hayek, 2000).

intrinsically aggressive character of finite orders, and the second section of this chapter is dedicated to the exploration of this issue.

The chapter is organized as follows. In Section 2, State aggression is interpreted as an expression of a finite order. Section 3 provides an analysis of how trans-finite orders deal with the problem of aggression. Within a trans-finite order, one's behavior can be interpreted neither as altruistic, nor as selfish. But why, quite unlike their finite counterparts, are trans-finite orders successful in neutralizing aggression? One answer is provided within the first sub-section of Section 3. Simply put, this happens because, as I will try to prove, free exchange is based upon the ethical decision to consider the other individual involved in the exchange as a fellow human. In other words, *trans-finite orders have an intrinsic ethical quality*. However, this doesn't mean that aggression ceases to be a problem. If one (correctly) understands the free market (or modern capitalism) as the expression of a trans-finite order, one easily realizes that aggression (in the form of those hierarchies known as firms) is still likely to occur. The second sub-section of Section 3 will explore this issue. A second answer is provided in Section 4, which investigates the emergence and persistence of institutions within trans-finite orders. For the sake of parsimony, the analysis will focus on two institutions, seen as highly relevant: market-money and market-justice. It is important to notice that no such analysis can be done unless we keep in mind the distinction between finite and trans-finite orders, and unless we will be able to prove the very starting point of the argument: namely, that aggression is an intrinsic feature of finite orders. Section 5 concludes the chapter.

2 The State as Expression of Finite Order: A Critical View

By 'finite order' I understand an order which is conceived as having clearly defined behavioral boundaries that every human agent can see. Therefore, such an order is defined (and may be redefined) according to a goal (usually understood as the ordering expression of a will), in the same manner as we redecorate our houses. For the purposes of this chapter, it is irrelevant whether the State is the source or the outcome of a finite order. What is important is that the State is an expression – perhaps the most prominent one – of such an order.

If this is so, we cannot avoid the problem of aggression, and in the first sub-section I will deal with it extensively. But why does aggression become an unavoidable problem? Because, when living within a finite order, at least some individuals will necessarily treat others in the same manner as we treat our furniture when redecorating our houses – keeping this, disposing of that, entirely without consideration of any 'wishes' the furniture might have. In other words, the conflict between wills is an inescapable feature of this order.

It is tempting to use these findings to digress into the ethical and economic issue of redistribution.[3] However, I chose to take a different path. Therefore, I focused

---

[3]   This is done, for instance, by Nozick, (1997). However, for a refined analysis of redistributive justice as conceived by Aristotle, for instance, see MacIntyre (1988). One should keep in mind though that what Aristotle understood by *polis* is not similar to what

on a too-often-neglected question: Why do redistributive requests occur within finite orders? My answer is that within such an order we are bound to commit the logical fallacy known as 'the quantifier-shift fallacy.' It is precisely because of this fallacy that we are rather naturally compelled to think in conspiratorial terms, and therefore to conceive and justify redistributive patterns. The second sub-section is devoted to the analysis of this logical fallacy.

2.1 Aggression and Poverty

The State produces poverty by its simple existence, insofar as it is a producer of aggression.[4] There are at least two arguments to support this statement. The first one belongs to Milton and Rose Friedman (1980). According to them, there are four different ways of spending money:

I. spending your own money on yourself;
II. spending your own money on someone else;
III. spending someone else's money on yourself;
IV. spending someone else's money on still another person.

Category III refers to your spending someone else's money on yourself – lunching on an expense account, for instance. You have no strong incentive to keep down the cost of the lunch, but you do have a strong incentive to get your money's worth. Category IV refers to your spending someone else's money on still another person. You are paying for someone else's lunch out of an expense account. You have little incentive either to economize or to try to get your guest the lunch hat he will value most highly. However, if you are having lunch with him, so that the lunch is a mixture of Category III and Category IV, you do have a strong incentive to satisfy your own tastes at the sacrifice of his, if necessary (Friedman and Friedman, 1980, pp. 116-119).

Any governmental program falls both in Category III and Category IV. Such a program requires the existence of public officials. These officials spend other people's money for their own benefit, as salaries, and for acquisition of premises and other goods like travel, automobiles, education for their children and so on. On the other hand, the existence of governmental programs implies the existence of third parties: i.e., of those to whose benefit such programs are destined. Public officials have no special interest in offering to these third parties goods and services according to their (the third party's) preference.

Governmental programs are, therefore, self-contradictory. They necessarily produce waste and low quality goods. The obvious result of this production is

---

we understand by *State*. Therefore, to adopt Aristotle's view on distributive justice, and to apply it to modern States is often misleading.

[4] This doesn't suggest that statist orders are necessarily orders of (generalized) poverty, but rather that they are poorer than trans-finite orders. It also doesn't suggest that States don't provide for the wellbeing of some of their citizens (at the expense of others), but rather that, since they use aggression to provide it, the outcome will be not only debatable in ethical terms, but also less than what it is possible to achieve within a free market order.

poverty. Yet any State has public officials: a head of State, ministers, lawmakers, judges, soldiers and policemen. And all these public officials justify their existence by producing various sorts of programs. As a consequence, any State produces poverty by its very existence.

The second argument belongs to Hans-Hermann Hoppe, and consists in a critique of the public good theory (Hoppe, 1993). Public goods are usually defined as those goods which are not produced on the free market, but which, if produced, would be useful to consumers. Given the assumed 'limits' of the free market, the State takes upon itself the task of producing public goods. More precisely, the State compels its citizens to finance the production of the so-called public goods. It thus commits a paternalist aggression against non-aggressors, by proclaiming that it knows better than its citizens what goods and services these citizens really need.

What are the effects of this way of thinking? Before the State's intervention, non-aggressive individuals used their money to buy on the free market those goods and services they considered useful for them, according to their own subjective preferences. If one or more individuals thought that a certain good or service, now nonexistent, would be useful to him (or to them), sooner or later someone would produce that good or service. The fact that a certain good or service does not exist on the market at a certain time does not reflect the 'limits' of the free market, but the consumers' subjective preferences (or the temporary inability of potential suppliers to identify these preferences).

A good is a good only as long as it is valued as such, that is, only as long as there is someone who prefers it. In other words, there are no intrinsic goods. The subjective preferences of non-aggressive individuals are those that turn objects into goods (or into 'bads', for that matter). The intervention of the State as a supplier of so-called 'public' goods forces the individuals to use part of their money to pay for objects or services that *the State*, and not the individual, values as goods. By forgoing this amount of money, the individuals have access to fewer objects and services that they themselves value as goods.

As a consequence, the production of 'public' goods makes the individuals poorer. Any State produces at least four public goods: laws, trial procedures, military defense, and protection against domestic aggressors (against robbers, killers, and so on). Yet all these services could have been more effectively produced by private, for-profit vendors. As a consequence, the State fosters poverty simply by its existence.

How is this possible? One answer to this question is that within a finite order individuals are prone to a logical fallacy which has a quite unpleasant ethical consequence: it promotes reciprocal enmity. We will turn to this logical fallacy in the next sub-section.

2.2 Logic and Conspiracy

'Every human being has a backbone, and therefore there is a backbone belonging to all human beings.' This reasoning is obviously wrong. Logicians – people who, among other things, make an inventory of human mistakes – have adopted a name for such reasoning: 'the quantifier-shift fallacy.'

Now, of course, we don't have to be impressed by such a name. Logicians, like other researchers, have the right to create their own language. It is important for us to notice though that a logical error doesn't disappear by its merely having been identified and cataloged. There are research programs, and widely held opinions based on logical errors. Many destinies are blown to pieces because of opinions and behaviors based upon non-valid reasoning.

When the quantifier-shift fallacy occurs in political and ethical thinking, it becomes the very source of conspiracy theories. The logical structure of these theories is the following: every human action is determined by someone, and therefore there is someone who determines all human actions. The only feature by which conspiracy theories differ from one another is the identity of that 'someone' who is assumed to subjugate all the others.

One of the conspiracy theories that had a tremendous influence is Marxism (historical materialism). According to this theory, the ones who subjugate all the other people are, in the modern world, the bourgeois. As a consequence, we need a counter-conspiracy (i.e. the proletarian revolution) to annihilate the economic and political power of the bourgeoisie. Apart from Marxism, there are other conspiracy theories generating atrocities: anti-Semitism (especially its fascistic forms), xenophobic doctrines, Islamic fundamentalism, Argentinean anticommunism, or Milosevic's nationalism (claiming to protect the Serbs against the Albanians' conspiracy).

There are, of course, some milder conspiracy theories. In this category we may include feminism, for instance, (when stating that men rule the world), or contemporary social-democracy doctrines, promoting the welfare State. Social-democrat thinkers and politicians favor a fiscal control of wealth (through progressive taxes), so as to make it impossible for private wealth to exceed a certain limit. They thus imply a conspiracy of rich people against the other, less fortunate ones. The welfare State is thus conceived as an effective counter-conspiracy – a counter-conspiracy able to annihilate the eternal conspiracy of the rich (of the capitalist entrepreneurs always ready to manipulate the poor and honest people). Social democracy thus develops a temperate kind of conspiracy theory that doesn't have to actually commit much physical violence to neutralize the 'masters' of the world.

These few examples suggest that simple logical error can – and does – change our lives. Such an error generates political regimes, values and beliefs that affect each and every one of us.[5] It is, of course, frustrating to realize this. But, at the same time, there are grounds for hope.

Why so? Because we can remember that every conspiracy theory, be it temperate or not, is but a particular form of what logicians call the quantifier-shift fallacy. No conspiracy theory can invent its enemy without making this error. But,

---

[5] Popper (2001) suggests that an authoritarian frame of thought is primarily an individual choice: because one is authoritarian, one develops a certain epistemology and a subsequent ethic. The analysis presented in this sub-section takes the opposite view: because one inhabits a finite order, one is bound to commit the quantifier-shift fallacy, and therefore to adopt an authoritarian frame of thought.

since we know this, we can more easily fight against these theories; we can break the spell that, controlling our minds, controls the reality we generate. Since we are able now to understand the fallacy of all the conspiracy theories, we can, like Oedipus, answer the Sphinx's riddle and walk away safe.[6] For the time has come to explore the economics and ethics of the trans-finite order.

3 The Free Market as a Trans-finite Order: Presuppositions and Limits

Just as the State is the paramount expression of the finite order, the free market gives expression to the trans-finite order. Perhaps the best way to understand the difference between the two types of order is by comparing their ontological assumptions. The finite order seems to be grounded in ontological solipsism: every individual conceives himself or herself as the only living individual, while all the other individuals are interpreted as different (and usually lower) kinds of being. The trans-finite order displays, on the other hand, a version of what might be called ontological realism: the individual interprets the world as comprising *other individuals*. At closer scrutiny, this form of realism implies the ethical decision of considering other individuals as fellow-humans.[7] This ethical decision permeates both the trans-finite order and the processes of ordination, and to it we will turn our attention in the next sub-section.

However, the problem of aggression occurs not only within finite orders. More precisely, the trans-finite order of free exchange seems to produce of necessity entities like firms, and these firms seem to be in fact expressions of finite order. The second sub-section will address this topic.

3.1 Free Exchange as an Ethical Decision

The economic theory of interpersonal free exchange is beautifully simple. Given two individuals A and B, all we need for an exchange between them to take place

---

[6] The argument herein developed does not imply that conspiracies cannot occur. It states only that we are able to conspire, or to develop conspiracy theories, only if we interpret the world we live in as a finite order. And since the State is the expression of finite order, it is not surprising that within a statist order conspiracies and conspiracy theories flourish.

[7] It is important not to misinterpret the difference between a finite and a trans-finite order as the difference between a local and a universal order. A universal order may be conceived as the widest possible local order, where the *locus* of the order is the universe itself. The difference between finite and trans-finite orders is not one of degree, but of nature. A finite order is a given state, able to be clearly described in all its aspects, in the same manner we are able to describe our flat, for instance. A trans-finite order, on the other hand, is an emergent *and emerging* order; it is not given, but speculated, and developed simultaneously across different lines of actualization. This is why the attempt to understand the ethics of a trans-finite order in terms of an already existing ethical theory is misleading because, in my opinion, all the ethical theories available to us operate with the ontological presupposition of a finite order. Our task, therefore, is not to adopt one ethical standpoint or another, but to reinvent ethics.

is a double inequality. For example, suppose that A has an orange, and B has an apple. If A prefers B's apple more than his own orange, while B prefers A's orange more than his own apple, they will exchange.

This is simple, but it can also be misleading. Contemplating the theory, we might come to the conclusion that the double inequality is a *sufficient* condition for the interpersonal free exchange: whenever we have the double inequality, we also have the exchange. Or, to translate this in terms of demonstrated preference, whenever an exchange took place between two individuals, this happened because – and only because – a double inequality occurred and was observed by potential exchangers.

However, this conclusion doesn't hold. Suppose that we have the double inequality, but A doesn't consider B a human being. From A's point of view, B is nothing but an unusual apple tree. Consequently, he will try to appropriate B's apple in the same manner we usually pick apples from apple trees. However, unlike normal apple trees, B may fight to keep his apple.

A has two possibilities: pick an apple from an apple tree, or pick an apple from B. In both situations, A will engage in what economists call autarchic exchange. Apple picking is not costless, since one must give up something, such as physical energy and time, in order to pick an apple. If, on A's personal value scale, the goods he must give up in order to pick the apple are less valuable than the apple he desires, he will pick the apple.

Therefore, A faces a calculation problem. Which is the most cost effective way to have an apple: grab it from B, or pick it from a normal apple tree? The answer to this question depends upon many factors: how far is A from an unowned apple tree, how far is B from A, the intrinsic qualities of the different apples, A's physical strength, B's physical strength, A's ability to cheat B (in order to avoid a physical confrontation with B), B's ability to recognize A's cheating maneuvers, and so on.

In autarchic exchange, we deal with only one value scale: the one of the actor. Other value scales either don't exist or are irrelevant to the actor. In interpersonal free exchange, on the contrary, because we have two actors, we not only have two different value scales, we also have mutual recognition of the other person. In a free interpersonal exchange, both parties recognize themselves and the other party as actors, complete with (different) value scales.

In autarchic exchange, the problem of cost calculation looks like this: what must I give up in order to obtain something? In interpersonal exchange, the same problem looks like this: what must I give up in order to *get someone else* to (willingly) give something to me?

Therefore, the double inequality *is* not and *cannot* be a sufficient condition for the interpersonal free exchange to take place. For such an exchange to take place, we also have to meet another condition: the mutual recognition of both parties as fellow humans (or, in more general terms, as actors). In other words, the double inequality is but a *necessary* condition of interpersonal free exchange.

Recognizing the other as a fellow human, recognizing him or her as an actor, is an ethical decision – in fact, the most fundamental ethical decision. We engage in non-aggressive activities if and only if we decide that we deal with another actor. Whenever we don't make such a decision, we engage only in autarchic exchange.

One outgrowth of this argument is that autarchic exchange is the simplest explanation of aggression. If A treats B as an unusual apple tree, he will engage in predatory activities against B. This happens because, in autarchic exchange, the other is but a resource, while in free interpersonal exchange the other is *the owner* of the desired resource. Theft, rape, murder, enslavement, and so on proves that the victims' value scales were ignored by the agents who engaged in aggressive actions against them.

Since free interpersonal exchange presupposes not only a double inequality but also a mutual recognition of both parties as actors, the free market is an ethical environment. The expansion of the market means that more and more individuals are recognized as fellow humans, as actors with personal value scales. In other words, a free market is conducive to ethical behavior.

Conversely, criminal anarchy is possible only within non-market environments. The more restricted the market is, the more generalized autarchic exchanges become. Thomas Hobbes (1588-1679) described a hypothetical world where everyone is at war with everyone, and where life is short, brutish, and ugly (Hobbes, 1996).[8] It is important for us to understand that such a situation is possible only within a non-market environment. In other words, 'the law of the jungle' doesn't describe how individuals behave in a market, but how they behave *when there is no market.*

Within a non-market environment, an individual engages only in autarchic exchanges, like Robinson Crusoe on his desert island. From his point of view, the world comprises only unowned resources, and all the other individuals are treated as potentially dangerous resources – as tigers somehow carrying apples, for instance. When an individual doesn't recognize the humanness of the other, the only possible way of exchange left is aggression: the initiation or threat of physical force as a means to achieve goals.

This simply renders fabulous the myth of the good dictator or, in the case of welfare States, the myth of the good administrator (or the good politician or technocrat). Both the dictator and the administrator create and support a non-market environment. In other words, they live by making non-market decisions. In so doing, they involve themselves in autarchic exchange: they decline to recognize the humanness of other people.

A non-market environment requires individuals who are able to create and support non-market patterns of redistribution. In order to become such an individual, one has to have certain moral traits, the first of which is the ability to treat other human beings as resources, not as resource owners. The more such traits one has, the more chances there are to successfully rule the non-market environment. We live in a world full of kings, presidents, and prime ministers. Irrespective of their political creeds and the number of their supporters, in order to become a king, president, or prime minister, one has to have a strong complement of those moral traits that we usually deplore, but that are necessary prerequisites of

---

[8]   To better understand why Hobbes took such a view, see Oakeshot (1991).

success within a non-market environment. In other words, 'honest Statesman,' 'honest politician,' 'honest technocrat,' and the like are but contradictions in terms.[9]

A free market can survive only when embedded within a tradition of individual human worth. More precisely, a free market generates such a tradition – because free exchanges are possible when we have a double inequality, *and, at the same time, when both parties recognize the humanness of the other* – and is supported only by such a tradition.[10]

3.2 A Critical Inquiry into the Ethical Ambiguity of Firms

The weak point of contemporary free-market theory (the theory of the partially aggressive free market) is the theory of the firm. According to this theory, firms are economic entities emerging on the market, but organized by completely or partially abnegating the market laws. Such entities are useful – because they reduce transaction and information costs – but, nevertheless, they are somehow external to the market. Firms are built vertically, and, to develop themselves, they need a bureaucratic (managerial) level able to harmonize the decisions of the leader (i.e. the firm's owner) with the actions of the workers. In other words, a firm is a market bureaucracy (see also Coase, 1937).

More than this, a company's employees consume for their own benefit the employer's goods: his capital. As a consequence, they are tempted to become wasteful and neglectful. On the other hand, an employer consumes for his own benefit the employees' good: their working capacity. He is thus tempted to consume this good in excess. Therefore, a firm is an unstable equilibrium between two aggressive processes (or movements) directed against one another.

This suggests that the firm is an ambiguous entity in ethical terms. On the one hand, it emerges within a free market out of economic reasons – and from this point of view it seems to be a part of the trans-finite order. On the other hand, the order *within* a firm is hardly a market order.

The order within a firm is grounded in a common goal between the employer and the employee. On the simplest level of analysis, both the employer and the employee share the same goal of producing a certain good or service (or, more precisely, a certain *brand* of a specific good or service). This is why many contemporary companies develop programs like 'team building', for instance. However, the very fact of building a team demonstrates that all the members of a firm are supposed to share common values and common goals.

Yet this sharing of a common goal is the key feature of a finite order. And it is interesting to notice that within a firm the idiom of finite order reemerges. One is described as 'altruistic' (and altruism itself becomes a valued virtue) if he or she behaves in such a way as to put the company's interests and wellbeing above his or her own interests and wellbeing. Conversely, one is considered 'selfish' when he or

---

[9] This is an extension of Hayek's argument on 'why the worst get on top' (Hayek, 1993, p. 154-173).

[10] The argument provided in this subsection is further developed in Cucerai, (2003).

she fails to behave in the way prescribed by the common values and goals which are presumed to be held by all the members of the firm. And, as in any other finite order, altruism is at least notionally rewarded, while selfishness is punished (often by exclusion).

More than this, within a firm, redistributive patterns similar to the statist ones emerge and develop. Individual agents usually have to answer practical questions like who has access to bonuses and in what amount, what the criteria for promotion are, and so on. In other words, a firm is a society whose features are specific to a finite order. Within a firm debates take place among employees, and these debates are held in terms of 'meritocracy', 'equivalence', and so on – that is to say, in terms of identifying the rational principles according to which the redistribution is to be made. The similarities between such debates and the more sophisticated ones held by moral and political philosophers are too striking to be ignored.

On the other hand, within a firm, strategies to reshape the current patterns of redistribution are developed. Sycophancy, cultivation of personal relations with superiors ('face time'), the emergence of a 'court' with specific manners, with 'favorites', 'allies' and 'enemies' are as frequent within a private firm as in every other expression of finite order.

And this system of alliances suggests that the other strategy – namely, the strategy of threat – is also practiced when, for instance, current power is threatened with a counter-power. When formalized, this counter-power usually is expressed by labor unions, for instance; however, this is not to suggest that only formalized versions are to emerge and to be recognized as effective. Any employee learns quickly that he or she has to integrate within a finite order with (often unwritten) rules. And failure to identify these rules may have (and often has) as a consequence the ostracization of the 'rebel', in spite of his or her economic value for the firm.

Therefore, a firm confronts us with a fundamental ethical incongruity, insofar as an 'ocean' of trans-finite order seems to generate with necessity such 'islands' of finite order.[11] This is not to suggest that such an incongruity doesn't have a

---

[11] Although versions of the practices herein described do exist in various degrees and shapes within various industries, it is important to note that the analysis herein provided was meant to show how, in practical terms, the free market as expression of trans-finite order has to deal with the problem of aggression as it occurs in those market bureaucracies known as firms. Since ethics is not a quest for life as such, but a quest for *good* life, there is a strong connection between ethical reasoning and practical reasoning. On this issue, see also MacIntyre, (1988). It is equally important to notice that an ethical vision is connected not only with practical reasoning, but also with ontological assumptions. We have seen that concepts like *altruism*, *selfishness*, or *conspiracy* make sense only when combined with a vision of finite order. (And perhaps the same is also true for the concept of *power*. If one defines power as the capacity to control – that is, to shape or reshape – the patterns of redistribution, then both *power* and *powerlessness* are meaningless concepts outside a finite order). On closer scrutiny, one will discover that all the ethical theories developed so far (including the modern ones like Kantianism or utilitarianism and their derivatives) are grounded in one version or another of finite order. Hence the underlying thesis of this chapter, that ethics is to be reinvented.

resolution, or that market hierarchies are perfectly similar to non-market ones.[12] However, in the quest for such a resolution we should, first of all, provide an accurate description of the incongruity. It seems plausible that the resolution we are looking for is to be found in the transformation of the firm from an entity which occurs on the market into an entity able to generate a market by its simple existence. In other words, we are to ground our practical and ethical description of the firm upon an ontological vision of trans-finite order.

The analysis worked out in this Section may enable us to develop a new version of the ethics of virtue. In this I will elaborate on Vlastos' analysis of Socratic ethics (Vlastos, 2002). Vlastos interprets Socrates as adhering to what he calls 'the Principle of the Sovereignty of Virtue', according to which virtue is happiness (that is, only the virtuous is happy), and therefore the supreme *telos* of every human being. However, although virtue is constitutive to happiness, non-moral goods are also relevant – for instance, when an individual has to choose between two actions, both of them equally virtuous. In this case, the individual will choose that action which will allow him to obtain more (or better) non-moral goods.

In a similar way, we may conceive the individual within a trans-finite order as virtuous (in the sense of applying the principle of non-aggression). This virtuous individual will make an ethical decision to consider those with whom he engages in exchanges as fellow humans. In so doing, he practices virtue in the Socratic sense (or at least in the sense in which Vlastos interpreted Socrates). Yet, if he or she understands virtue as happiness, and therefore as the supreme *telos*, he or she would also necessarily prefer more (or better) non-moral goods, as a means for a fuller and richer happiness. And because of such an ethical scheme, he or she will engage in developing a free-market order. This is not to say that a Socratic ethics necessarily emerges from a market order, but that an ethical vision has to derive from, and be compatible with, the ontological vision of a trans-finite order.

On the other hand, it is important to emphasize that the analysis developed in this Section was not only meant to refine our understanding of some economic practices. It was also intended to provide us with an answer to the following question: How are the individuals living within a trans-finite order able to deal with the ethical problem of aggression? From this point of view, this Section suggests that an expansion of such a trans-finite order is also a means to overcome ethical impasses. In so doing, one has to deal with the ethical incongruity posed by the existence of firms.

However, such a demonstration may not seem sufficient. Therefore, in the following section of this chapter I will turn to a somewhat different approach – a

---

[12] On the difference between market bureaucracies and non-market ones, see, for instance, Mises, (1983). However, although almost all contemporary literature avoids facing the problem of the ethical ambiguity of the firm, this shouldn't obscure from us the fact that in the 19th century many thinkers, especially the American individualist anarchists, elaborated on this topic, and they often did so with much insight. On this, the reader may also consult Martin, (1953). For such individualist anarchists there was a strong connection between individual freedom and self-employment.

discussion of the practical rationality implied in the emergence of trans-finite orders.

4 The Actual Emergence of Trans-finite Orders: Real-Life Examples

So far, we have seen how trans-finite orders provide means and manners to dispense with aggression. What remains uninvestigated is the emergence of non-aggressive institutions. To do so, in this section we analyze two case studies featuring real-life agents in a developing country (Romania, in the 1990s). The first sub-section deals with an economic institution – money –, while the second gives apt attention to the spontaneous emergence of arbitration rules and practices. The case for the intrinsic ethic of trans-finite orders is thus completed.

4.1 Real People with Real Money

Laura is a 27-year-old woman living in Bucharest, Romania. She has a seven-year-old daughter who just entered a public school. Parents naturally want their children to be well taken care of – and they typically pay what in the West might be viewed as bribes for this, despite the fact that teachers' salaries are paid by the state. It's as if parents are trying to outbid one another for favored educational services for their children. So they give the teacher coffee, cigarettes, or even spirits (if the teacher is a male). (Actually they give him or her good quality coffee, cigarettes or spirits; the same goods, but of lower quality, are considered an offense). In return, they expect their children to be more carefully educated; if not, the payment ceases. In other words, parents pay the teachers an amount of certain consumer goods of a certain quality, aiming to obtain educational services of a certain quality for their children.

The same thing is customary when Laura or her daughter gets sick. She pays the (state-employed and paid) doctor one or two packs of good quality coffee, or good quality cigarettes, to get better medical services. But what do teachers and doctors do with all this coffee, cigarettes, or spirits? Apparently they don't turn into heavy smokers, heavy coffee drinkers, or alcoholics. Doctors may need better educational services for their children; and teachers may need better medical services. And both teachers and doctors may need better services from plumbers, from auto mechanics, from people who repair personal computers or TV sets, and so on. So they keep at least a part of these goods as capital to be used when extra payments are required.

To put it differently, all these goods are partially consumed, and partially used in exchanges. This system gives everyone an incentive to improve himself or herself as a supplier of services. A better doctor gets more coffee, cigarettes, or spirits, and therefore he or she can afford to pay for more services of a better quality. The same thing goes for the teacher, for the plumber, or for the auto mechanic. At this juncture, allow me to quote Murray Rothbard:

> Now just as in nature there is a great variety of skills and resources, so there is a variety
> in the marketability of goods. Some goods are more widely demanded than others, some

are more divisible into smaller parts without loss of value, some more durable over long periods of time, some more transportable over large distances. All of these advantages make for greater marketability. It is clear that in every society, the most marketable goods will be gradually selected as media for exchange. As they are more and more selected as media, the demand of them increases because of this use, and so they become even more *marketable*. The result is a reinforcing spiral: more marketability causes wider use as a medium which causes more marketability, etc. Eventually, one or two commodities are used as general *media* – in almost all exchanges – and these are called money (Rothbard, 1990, p. 18).

In contemporary Romania, coffee, cigarettes or spirits are used, first of all, as consumer goods. These goods are bought and sold on the market in relatively small packages – which means they are easily divisible. They are also easily transportable, and they can maintain their quality for at least one or two years (or for even longer periods, in the case of spirits). Certain brands of coffee, cigarettes or spirits increased their marketability because of their better quality. People became more and more aware that they could more easily obtain things in return for these specific goods. Therefore, they began using them more and more widely in exchange, until certain brands of coffee, cigarettes or spirits emerged as quasi-universal media of exchange. That is to say, certain brands of coffee, cigarettes or spirits became *money* (at least on the Romanian market).

This natural process of money emergence on the market has nothing to do with the political regimes. Certain brands of coffee, cigarettes, or spirits functioned as market money during the totalitarian communist regime, and they are still functioning as market money today, when Romania looks like a democracy and her market is rather free.

On the other hand, this process has little to do with the relative rarity of the market chosen money. The brands of coffee, cigarettes, or spirits that functioned as market money during the communist regime were available to common people only from the black market. Today, they are openly available to everyone in larger quantities; yet they still function as market money. The only thing that changed is their purchasing power: if, during the communist regime, one could obtain a certain service for one pack of cigarettes, today he must pay two packs for the same service.

So it happens that we simultaneously live under two monetary systems: a system of market money, where money naturally emerges from consumer goods in a non-aggressive manner; and a system of governmental money, where banknotes issued by the National Bank of Romania (or by any other central bank, for that matter) are imposed by force as money.[13]

Some may object that governmental money is not imposed by force. Governmental money operates as a quasi-universal medium of exchange, and because of this it is freely accepted. Yet in what currency does your government 'ask' you to pay your taxes? Does it accept market money? No; it requires from you to pay your taxes in governmental money. And, since taxes are always paid

---

[13] See also Hoppe, Huelsmann and Block, (1998).

under the threat of force, governmental money is always imposed under the threat of force.

On the other hand, if governmental money is freely accepted, why does market money still emerge? If gold and silver were forbidden, and the entire so-called civilized world 'accepted' the governmental fiat money, how come that other commodities still emerge as market money – commodities like coffee, cigarettes, or spirits in Romania, for instance?

The persistence of market money proves that real money is not a conventional entity. Market money is not the result of the arbitrary will of an individual, or of a group of individuals. In other words, market money is one institution that emerges within a trans-finite order, and this is precisely why its existence is so precarious within the finite statist order.

4.2 The Case of Private Justice

In general, gypsies are reluctant to have recourse to the state judicial system. Therefore, in disputes among them, they often rely on their customary law, and they hire private judges. Nanu Frederica is a 60-year-old gypsy, living somewhere on the periphery of Bucharest, Romania. He is a private judge called on to arbitrate disputes arising between the members of his own gypsy community.[14]

How does the system work? Let's suppose that a gypsy stole from another gypsy. The victim must, first of all, find a judge. The judge, as I said, is a private person, noted for his moral integrity. To avoid any doubts as to the quality of the judgment, one can hire a judge from a different community.

Once the judge is found, the plaintiff must pay him a fee. The fee is relative to the personal wealth of the plaintiff, and to the nature of the alleged crime. Depending upon the complexity of the trial, one to three judges are required. If the plaintiff or the offender considers necessary, the judge (or the judges) must take an oath to give a just verdict. I will explain a little later why the oath is an extremely powerful means to induce such a just verdict. After considering the case and receiving the fee, the judge fixes the time and the place of the trial. Trials usually begin at noon, and last until sunset – at the most. If this period of time is not enough to conclude the trial, it continues the next day. However, this happens very rarely. Trials are public: any member of the community is free to attend.

During a trial, the plaintiff speaks first, then the plaintiff's witness(es), then the alleged offender, and finally the alleged offender's witness(es). Because many gypsies were illiterate until recently, nothing is written down. Therefore, apart from reputation for moral integrity, a judge must also have a good memory.

If the plaintiff or the alleged offender is prepared to take a solemn oath that he or she will speak the truth, the witnesses become unnecessary, and the trial stops right there if the offender is so sworn. However, such cases are extremely rare, because if any misfortunes happen afterwards to the person who took the oath, the community will interpret them as a curse caused by perjury, and that person will

---

[14] The factual information provided in this sub-section is based upon Golea, (2001). See also Wlislocki, (2000).

instantly lose his or her reputation. Such public oaths are therefore seen as ultimate tests of good faith and veracity. And this is why I noted earlier that an oath taken by the judge to give a just verdict is an extremely powerful means to induce such a right verdict.

On the other hand, the institution of public oath interpreted in the manner herein described, combined with the possibility to hire a judge from a different community, places effective barriers against those who would otherwise be tempted to bribe the judge, and consequently to corrupt the system. In other words, the legal system developed within the gypsy communities is stable and able to replicate itself over many generations.

After listening to all the parts, the judge chooses a few persons from those who attended the trial to help him. He consults them, asks for their opinion, and then makes his own decision. As in all the other customary law systems, crimes are defined as torts, and punishments take the form of fines payable by the offender to the victim.[15] Just like the fees paid by the victim to the judge, the fine is relative to the nature of the crime, and to the personal wealth of the offender. This is a discretionary device meant to provide equal justice to equal individuals, leaving no incentive for the wealthy and powerful gypsies to engage themselves in criminal activities only because they can afford to pay the price. The decision of the judge is usually final. However, in special cases like when one of the parties is believed to have committed perjury, the person who considers the verdict unjust may appeal for a different judge – and his verdict is taken as the final one.

I should note here that the legal system developed within the gypsy communities is not completely autonomous. Murder cases, for instance, are automatically taken over by the State police and State courts. This doesn't happen because the gypsies are willing to leave such cases in the hands of State police and State courts, but because, like any other Romanian citizen, they are compelled to accept the statist legal system operating in Romania.

There are several reasons that led me to cite the example of Nanu Ferdica and of his legal system. First of all, the legal system herein described is not a hypothetical one, but an existing one. To theoreticians of the free market as a trans-finite order, the system herein described offers solid grounds for a refutation of the legal positivist claim that legal systems are necessarily creations of the States, and that they can survive only within a statist framework.

In the second place, the legal system herein described is fully compatible (or at least it can be interpreted as being fully compatible) with a strong version of natural law and natural rights theory. The relativity of fines, for instance, is a device that could not have been imagined unless all the members of the community were considered equally distinct and equally free individuals. And if natural rights are universal, the legal model offered by such gypsy communities is, *in practical terms*, capable of being expanded to wider groups of human beings. In other words,

---

[15] On this topic, see also Benson, (1989).

this system is not intrinsically dependent upon some peculiar local traditions and happenstance.[16]

In the third place, the legal system herein described does not belong to an ancient community, or to a contemporary *primitive* community. It is a system accepted and replicated by individuals who are fully capable of understanding modernity and of coping with it. I focused on a community whose members live in a modern city and are fully able, in practical terms, to understand and to use modern concepts and modern technology. Gypsies may be said to live within closed communities only in the sense that they adhere strictly to their customary law, and not in the sense that they are unwilling or unable to interact with other human beings within a complex modern world. That is to say, this legal system successfully avoids the objection of being unfit for modern individuals.[17]

5 Conclusions

The classical liberal tradition was unproblematic in the sense that it perceived the coexistence between the finite and the trans-finite order either as possible, or as even desirable. It was the task of this chapter to argue that this coexistence is far from being desirable. Finite orders are prone to aggression, being bound to ontological solipsism and to a logical fallacy that compels us to think of human interactions in conspiratorial terms. Trans-finite orders, on the other hand, successfully developed means and manners to neutralize aggression, while allowing for the emergence of institutions (like language, money, or justice) that rely upon – and promote – the fundamental ethical decision to offer human status to all human beings. However, one should be aware that the apparent tendency of trans-finite orders to spawn (finite) firms still confronts us with an incongruity in need of a resolution.

---

[16] We should not misinterpret trans-finite orders as traditions. Both trans-finite orders and traditions belong to the same wider sphere of emerging orders. However, unlike traditions, trans-finite orders allow for, and perhaps require, external standards of explanation, evaluation, or justification. For instance, the emergence of market money may be explained either historically, as an account on how, given certain circumstances, a specific commodity emerged as money, or theoretically (i.e. by developing a monetary theory able to explain not specific occurences, but the rules of emergence). In other words, trans-finite orders allow for, and perhaps require, something distinct from themselves, something which transcends them. On the other hand, these external standards of explanation, evaluation or justification are themselves open to debate and inquiry. Nothing like this is possible within a tradition, where all explanation, evaluation and justification is to be made according to means provided *only from within* that particular tradition. That is to say, an external explanation, evaluation or justification of a tradition is a contradiction in terms. It is equally true, however, that traditions may turn themselves into trans-finite orders and vice versa, but this is an argument to be developed elsewhere.

[17] For an analytical model of a modern customary law model, see Benson, (1990).

From my point of view, the coexistence between the finite and the trans-finite order is not only undesirable; it is also impossible. And while the usual way of looking at things is to interpret the statist finite order as the paradigm of order itself, perhaps the time has come to appreciate it as what it really is: aggressive disorder.

References

Augustine (1995), *The City of God*, English translation by H. Bettenson, Penguin Books, London.

Benson, B. (1989), Enforcement of Private Property Rights in Primitive Societies: Law without Government, *Journal of Libertarian Studies*, 9, 1, pp. 1-26.

Benson, B. (1990), Customary Law with Private Means of Resolving Disputes and Dispensing Justice: A Description of a Modern System of Law and Order without State Coercion, *Journal of Libertarian Studies*, 9, 2, pp. 25-42.

Coase, R. (1937), The ature of the Firm, *Economica*, 4, pp. 386-405.

Cucerai, S. (1999), Aggression and Anarchy, *Polis*, 6, 4, pp. 102-113.

Cucerai, S. (2003), Free Exchange and Ethical Decisions, *Journal of Libertarian Studies*, 17, 2, pp. 1-10.

Friedman, M. and Friedman, R. (1980), *Free To Choose: A Personal Statement*, Secker & Warburg, London.

Golea, S. (2001), The Secrets of a Stabor, *Libertatea*, October 15.

Hayek, F. A. von, (1993, [1944]), *The Road to Serfdom*, Romanian translation by Eugen B. Marian, Humanitas, Bucharest.

Hayek, F. A. von, (2000), *The Fatal Conceit – The Errors of Socialism*, Romanian translation by Mihnea Columbeanu, Antet, Bucharest.

Hobbes, T. (1996), *Leviathan*, edited by J. C. A. Gaskin, Oxford University Press, Oxford.

Hoppe, H-H. (1993), *The Economics and Ethics of Private Property*, Kluwer Academic Publishers, Boston, Dordrecht, London.

Hoppe, H-H., Huelsmann, J. G., and Block, W. (1998), Against Fiduciary Media, *Quarterly Journal of Austrian Economics*, 1, 1, pp. 19-50.

MacIntyre, A. (1988), *Whose Justice? Which Rationality?*, University of Notre Dame Press, Notre Dame, Indiana.

Martin, J. J. (1953), *Men Against the State: The Expositors of Individualist Anarchism in America, 1827-1908*, Adrian Allen, Dekalb, Illinois.

Mises, L. von, (1983), *Bureaucracy*, Center for Futures Education, Cedar Falls, Indiana.

Nozick, R. (1997), *Anarchy, State, and Utopia*, Romanian translation by Mircea Dumitru, Humanitas, Bucharest.

Oakeshot, M. (1991), *Rationalism in politics and other essays*, new and expanded edition, Liberty Press, Indianapolis.

Popper, K. R. (2001), *Conjectures and Refutations: The Growth of Scientific Knowledge*, Romanian translation by C. Stoenescu, D. Stoianovici, F. Lobont, Trei, Bucharest.

Rand, A. (1964), *The Virtue of Selfishness: a New Concept of Egoism*, New American Library, New York.

Rothbard, M. (1990), *What Has Government Done to Our Money?*, Ludwig von Mises Institute, Auburn University Press, Auburn, Alabama.

Vlastos, G. (2002), *Socrates: Ironist and moral philosopher*, Romanian translation by M. Van Schaik Radulescu, Humanitas, 2002.

Wlislocki, H. von (2000), *On the Nomad Rroma People*, Romanian translation by Octavian Rogojanu, Atlas, Bucharest.

Chapter 8

The Spirit of Free Enterprise: Ethics and Responsibility

Arnaud Pellissier-Tanon

1 Introduction[1]

In the conclusion to his article 'The Moral Element in Free Enterprise', Friedrich Hayek upholds the idea that free enterprise is no more than a means at the service of whatever ends people choose to aim for. He goes on to argue that we must distinguish between the value of the products men exchange among themselves and the esteem which these men accord to one another.

> When we defend the free enterprise system, we must always remember that it deals only with means. What we make of our freedom is up to us. We must not confuse efficiency in providing means with the purposes which they serve. A society which has no other standard than efficiency will indeed waste that efficiency. If men are to be free to use their talents to provide us with the means we want, we must remunerate them in accordance with the value these means have to us. Nevertheless, we ought to esteem them only in accordance with the use they make of the means at their disposal.

> Let us encourage usefulness to one's fellow by all means, but let us not confuse it with the importance of the ends which men ultimately serve. It is the glory of the free enterprise system that it makes it at least possible that each individual, while serving his fellows, can do so for his own ends. But the system is itself only a means, and its infinite possibilities must be used in the service of ends which exist apart (Hayek, 1967, pp. 235 and 236).

The relevance of Hayek's distinction between ends and means may be questionable – after all, one end is often simply a means to a further end – but this is not the important point here. What is important is the distinction between the payment obtained for a service provided and the esteem which men accord to the use of this payment. A man's self-esteem cannot be measured in terms of the value others place on the services he provides. There is room for a moral valuation, over and above the market estimation of value, and this valuation bears on the use that

---

[1] The author would like to thank Laurent Bibard, Norbert Col, Jean-Philippe Dalbin and Radu Vranceanu for their helpful criticism and advice.

each person makes of the products they have received in the exchange. Some may contend that Hayek evades the question of the intrinsic morality of the products exchanged, and the resulting argument that products that can only serve an immoral end are themselves immoral. We believe, rather, that his position lies implicitly within the classic liberal tradition, according to which the morality of a product is founded on the use made of it by the consumer and, in terms of *foro interno*, on his intentions. This tradition, championed notably by Frédéric Bastiat (1841/1996), adopts the view that ultimate power lies, not in the hands of the authorities who could ban the use of a given product for a given purpose, but in the hands of the consumers who buy these products and make their own specific use of them, as exemplified by the black market. Consequently, enterprise is no more than an efficient means of ensuring the prosperity of men. Its morality is extrinsic, and depends on the use to which men put it.

This does not resolve the question of the ends to which exchange and enterprise are used. Are these ends really good? Do they really contribute to men's happiness? This raises the question of the ethics underlying corporate practices, and this question must be addressed primarily by entrepreneurs. This chapter will therefore be devoted to the way in which entrepreneurs can shape the ethics of their business. Having expressed the question in philosophical terms and, at the same time, analyzed the attitudes adopted by many in response, we shall argue that the source of ethics lies in responsibility. Responsibility encourages those on whom it is laid to control their desires in such a way as to refrain from any action that could be prejudicial to themselves or others. They examine their conceptions of happiness in the light of their experience and judge them at their rightful value. Consequently, they construct an experienced conception of happiness and learn how to control their behavior in accordance with this conception. Their behavior thus becomes more intelligent: they are not prevented from attaining their goal of happiness by a lack of self-discipline. In short, accepting one's responsibilities means disciplining one's desires, and attributing responsibility to someone means encouraging them to exercise better and better discipline over themselves. Let us start by considering the practices which, in the first instance, concern entrepreneurs.

2 Moving beyond the Consensus of the Day

It is tempting for entrepreneurs to proclaim adherence to values that fit in with the expectations of society, and to breathe this 'corporate ethics' into their business. The morality of their employees can be heightened either by the drafting of a participative charter or, if their responsibility is of the nature of a legal liability, by the promulgation of a code which they can enforce by means of their disciplinary powers. It then remains for these company leaders to conduct themselves in an exemplary fashion, so that the moral values do not become a dead letter, and so that their proclamation does not give rise to hypocritical behavior that would detract from their communication. As Jean-Gustave Padioleau (1989) affirmed, for 'corporate ethics' in general, such an approach, if it is truly participative, has the advantage of 'making explicit the contractual social form of the company' (p. 89, our translation). As a result of a reciprocal agreement between the players, the company and its ethics are founded on the undertaking made, after negotiation and deliberation, to respect the values that will legitimize their decisions. The same author defines corporate ethics as all the 'rules defining the relations judged to be efficient and legitimate between the immediate and more distant partners in a trade or management interaction' (Jean-Gustave Padioleau, 1989, p. 86, our translation).

At this purely sociological level of analysis, corporate ethics is no different from the consensus determining the relations, held to be legitimate and efficient, which the company maintains with its stakeholders. It provides directors with a rule by which the members of their companies can adapt the strength of their desires to satisfy the requirements of their collective action. However, this rule, by nature consensual, is neither stable nor definitive. Moral standards, which until only a generation ago held the fabric of our society together, are clearly eroding, and the culture shock provoked by globalization is further restricting its range of influence. Yet the militarization of emotions has sharpened the pressure of public opinion, and companies are finding themselves increasingly answerable for their behavior. More than ever before, they are caught between the inadequacies of their principals and the demands of their stakeholders.

As with all constraints, however, the imperative of social responsibility provides companies with new opportunities for action. In truth, this moral value is not so much an imposition on companies as a useful tool, in that it legitimizes the relations they maintain with their stakeholders. In other words, it authorizes them to maintain these relations, to such an extent that it is by establishing legitimate actions that a company acts efficiently. Today, in concrete terms, showing compassion in the face of the world's misfortunes is a good way of doing business. This is demonstrated by the mediatization of fair trade and the development of profit-sharing funds. After all, in a competitive environment, a company must satisfy its customers. Consequently, it will seek to ensure not only that its product meets the quality requirements of its customers, but also that the act of purchase is in harmony with the ideals of these consumers, who can thus enhance the value of this act, or at least heighten their self-esteem.

This is not to discredit the good that companies do when they adopt a socially responsible approach, but simply to point out that they can well afford to do so when their customers give them the means. This is a new phenomenon. Up until recently, it would have been unimaginable for a company to claim to contribute, in whatever way, to the good of the political community to which it belonged – at least within the social democracies of Europe. All actions of this kind were the rightful domain of the State, and the only contribution expected from companies was their taxes. This fact deserves to be emphasized: by adopting a socially responsible attitude companies have transformed, from within, a movement which had originally developed against them. One may wonder what truly legitimizes the extension of companies' activities beyond their corporate purpose. Advocates of a contractualist vision of politics may adopt a critical attitude, as Milton Friedman did, when he asked: 'Can self-selected private individuals decide what the social interest is?' (Friedman, 1962, p. 133).

3 Understanding the Requirements of Ethics

We should not interpret the adoption by companies of a socially responsible attitude as a cynical exercise, even if certain businessmen are motivated more by the thirst for profit or power than by the desire for self-fulfilment or the pleasure of helping others. Nor should we treat it as sheer hypocrisy, gratifying society's expectations simply in order to paint a veneer of legitimacy over the search for efficiency – the latter taken to be the sole valid criterion in business – even if this is true for some entrepreneurs. Asking whether it is possible to conduct one's professional affairs in harmony with one's conscience or with the moral values of our society demonstrates a fundamental misunderstanding of the issue. Why place moral values, taken to be self-evident, in opposition to desires, taken to be sources of violence? On the contrary, moral philosophers have always upheld that moral values do not oppose desires, but that each person places a certain value on the happiness he obtains from the satisfaction of his desires. By organizing the different possible sources of happiness into a hierarchy, different ethics help people to avoid mistaking the value of their desires. Even better, they invite each person to examine his conduct: to verify, notably, that he really does obtain the happiness he expected from the satisfaction of his desires. In short, they teach people only to engage in activities in proportion to the real concerns of their lives. Entrepreneurs seek to bring to light the hierarchy of happiness by which each person determines the value of the desires they satisfy, in their companies, when they conduct trade or management relations. This is no doubt a way of providing the morals prevailing in their companies with a more solid foundation than the simple consensus of the day.

To do so, they must go beyond the sociological observation of the values of efficiency and legitimacy which predominate in our society, and seek philosophical foundations for these values. This is what Jean Moussé (1992, p. 66, our translation) proposed to entrepreneurs when, in reply to Jean-Gustave Padioleau, he defined corporate ethics as a 'path': as man is free to choose his reasons for acting, 'it becomes necessary, on the basis of business experience, to elaborate conceptions that can explain [his] decisions.' It remains to be seen how such conceptions can be elaborated from experience. The author notes that 'an entrepreneur is obviously responsible for the effects of his decisions on his own business, but he is also responsible for the remote consequences of his acts.' He observes that 'such a requirement is not foreign to sociology, in that we can understand its significance by studying the functioning of business. However, there is little chance of this requirement being clearly evinced through surveys and polls.' He concludes that philosophy in general, and corporate ethics in particular, 'consist in a critical reflection (...) based on experience' (p. 63, our translation). It remains to be seen what form this critical reflection takes and how the entrepreneur can participate in it.

Any body of values or hierarchy of happiness can become a morals when a consensus in its favor forms within one or another group of people. But this morals can been experienced as an ethic, by each member of the group, to the extent that the legitimacy of the values it promulgates is derived, not from the consensus itself, but from the validity of the hierarchy of happiness of which it is composed. It is this hierarchy which founds the primacy of one value over another, consecrated by the morals, and which consequently founds the legitimacy of a given trade or management interaction, in which one value is set over and above another by consensus. In other words, when we regulate our desires according to the values of happiness indicated by a given ethic, we do so not because we wish to follow the consensus, but because we are convinced of the validity of this ethic. The ethical rule thus differs from the sociological requirement to respect the moral values embodied in the consensus. It consists in the self-discipline of satisfying one's desires only in proportion to the happiness one expects from life. It is therefore with sincerity and intelligence that each person within the firm adapts his professional activity to match the value of the happiness that he and his stakeholders obtain from his activity.

4 Referring each Person to His/Her Own Conception of Happiness

If each ethics consists in a hierarchy of happiness, an ethical approach can be summed up as the self-discipline by which we measure the satisfaction of each desire according to this hierarchy, to such an extent that the hierarchy of happiness each person adopts is the ethical rule they practice. Employers who wish to prevent their companies from foundering in hypocrisy should be wary of promulgating the respect of a given set of values, even the most consensual. More specifically, they will be careful not to impose a hierarchy of happiness on their members of staff, but, for the sake of sincerity, they will refer each person to their own values, to their own hierarchies of happiness. Referring each person to their own values or hierarchy of happiness does not mean foundering in a moral subjectivism, where the only solution lies in a consensus that shifts with each change in circumstances. It means going beyond the consensuses that prevail in our society, and putting the convictions of our contemporaries to the test. It means adopting the reality of happiness and its hierarchy as a foundation, without which any ethics stiffens into an ideological discourse and any sociological requirement turns into 'ethical' totalitarianism.

Employers seeking an ethics for their companies will therefore ask their employees about their respect for certain values, ultimately about the rule by which their hierarchies of happiness govern the satisfaction of their desires – does this respect, or this rule, provide the happiness that each of them, and their stakeholders, expect from their involvement in the firm? This task is not made easier by the fact that the very terms of the question are losing their meaning.

The word happiness appears to have become outmoded. How many people still use it to signify the feeling of fulfillment accompanying the achievement or perfection of an action, both the fulfillment of the senses – nowadays we use the word pleasure – and of the action itself – referring precisely to happiness? Aristotle made this point explicit in the *Nicomachean Ethics* when, discussing the origin of sensual pleasure, he observed that 'the best activity is that of the best-conditioned organ in relation to the finest of its objects. And this activity will be the most complete and pleasant.' He then expanded on this analysis by noting that 'there is a particular pleasure corresponding to each sense, and the same is true for discursive thought and contemplation' (1174 b 20). He went on to state that 'pleasure completes an activity, as a sort of additional end' (1174 b 35). Pleasure, or happiness, thus covers the feeling of fulfillment which marks the achievement of an action.

In parallel, moral values are perceived less and less in terms of self-fulfillment and more and more in terms of the right to enjoy life. Take the motto of the French Republic as an example: 'liberty, equality and fraternity' no longer means the immunity from constraint, absence of privilege and unity of the political body so highly cherished in the eighteenth century; it now signifies the means of living, the leveling of possessions and the sharing of resources to which our contemporaries aspire. This evolution in moral values appears to sanction a decline in law, but not in legislation, to use a phrase dear to Friedrich Hayek (1959 and 1976). Obligations are perceived less as precautions that must be taken to avoid harming others, as drawn by judicial practice from the experience of social life, and more as contributions or services to be rendered to those eligible to them, imposed by an authority capable of penalizing their non-fulfillment.

5 Re-examining the Institutions of the Market Economy

However difficult this task may be, the company head in search of an ethic must question his employees about their respect of moral values, hence their hierarchy of happiness. This means clearing away the commonplaces which obscure personal conscience, asking staff to look into their own conceptions of happiness and encouraging them to judge their behavior in relation to these conceptions. However, inner convictions must pass through the filter of customs, and the institutions which embody them, before they can be expressed in practice. It is unthinkable not to behave in the way expected by one's trading partners: they would find our attitude incomprehensible and lose their trust in us. The customs of the market economy may not concern every aspect of our lives, but trade and business play such an important role in daily life that they leave their mark on our behavior. So we shall now examine the institutions of the market economy and the behavior they induce.

According to Friedrich Hayek (1976), the market economy is characterized by the existence of 'rules of good conduct', what David Hume called 'the three fundamental laws of nature: the stability of possession', the transfer of possession by consent, and the performance of promises. As Friedrich Hayek pointed out (1976), these rules determine 'the essential contents of all contemporary systems of private law.' Léon Duguit spoke in terms of 'the liberty of contract, the inviolability of private property and our obligation to compensate others for the wrongs we do them.' Bastiat used the more abstract vocabulary of property, freedom and responsibility. Voluntary exchange would be impossible without private property, contractual freedom and the exercise of responsibility. There would be no free enterprise. There would, quite simply, be no market economy. Evidently, lying and stealing are prohibited – inasmuch as legislation avoids the consecration of false rights – and irresponsibility is forbidden, inasmuch as, as Bastiat proposed (1841/1996), legislation imposes the consequences of an act on its author and strengthens their effects.

What shocks our contemporaries is not freedom and property, but their abuse – in other words, irresponsibility. Of course, cheats of all kinds do their best to cover their traces, in order to evade the consequences of their actions, and right-thinking people demand that companies manifest their solidarity towards the worst-off or make some kind of contribution to worthy causes, on pain of excommunication. This becomes worrying when legislation, through its imperfections or distortions, encourages the vices of cheats or consecrates the demands of right-thinking people. In a market economy, the large majority of people do not possess these shortcomings, either because they have a genuine desire to do the right thing or because they are afraid of legal retribution. What contribution does legal practice make to this question? When he examines a plaintiff's case, the judge must ascertain whether the defendant has committed an offence for which he can be held responsible, or, more specifically, whether he has failed to respect one of his obligations. Here, 'offence' should not be interpreted in a moral sense, as a weakness of the will, stigmatized, for example, by remorse. As Michel Villey (1977) explained, basing his argument on the etymology of the word responsibility, (in Roman law, it meant being answerable for the debts of others), the concept of offence is a fiction adopted by jurists through misunderstanding of the true meaning of the word, and the origin of this misunderstanding lies in the influence that the morals of conscientious rectitude has had on the law.

This 'offence' comes within the scope of *foro externo*. Human justice cannot apprehend the sincerity of moral conscience, nor can it always grasp the voluntary character of the offensive act. It considers whether the person who caused the damage could have avoided doing so. As Georges Ripert (1949) pointed out, man acts, and 'action comports risks both for oneself and for others; no matter since action is the law of man. But man should not act badly, and he acts badly when he causes harm to others that he could have foreseen, prevented or reduced' (p. 219, our translation). This is the case even when the harm is involuntary, because justice does not apprehend *foro interno*. Ripert thus appears to found law on morality, but this morality is not concerned so much with the rectitude of the conscience as with the intelligence which governs the action. More precisely, it involves that intelligence which foresees the consequences of the action and rejects actions that would cause harm either to the author or to others. Each time he has to make a ruling, the judge forms an opinion of the damages that could have been foreseen and avoided. To do so, he refers to a model of responsible action and of the understanding of the consequences governing this action.

6 The Reasonable Limits of Individual Responsibility

Our conception of responsible action is slowly changing. If we talk so much about 'corporate social responsibility' nowadays, this is, of course, to encourage companies to take into account the social and environmental stakes which have recently evolved. But the aim is also to invite them to change their frame of mind. This frame of mind is probably what really distinguishes the modern West from other civilizations. Laurent Bibard has explored its genesis in the first chapter of this book. As Max Weber (1919/1959/1963/1997) observed, we Westerners 'know or believe that at any moment we *could*, provided *simply that we wanted to*, prove to ourselves that, in principle, there exists no mysterious and unpredictable power to interfere in the course of our lives; in short, we can *control* everything through *foresight*' (p. 90, our translation). We therefore find it unacceptable that a product should present any kind of risk or that the provision of a service should not come up to our expectations. Our society consequently encourages customers to become ever more exacting in their requirement of risk-free products and faultless service from their suppliers. We should not be surprised, therefore, to observe the legal manifestation of this trend, in the more and more frequent recourse to professional civil liability suits.

Over less than a century, as a reaction to this line of thought, the opinion has grown that our contemporaries do not realize that they are destroying, through their desire for power, the very conditions necessary for their survival. Some say that the ecological balance has been broken, others that our development is anything but sustainable. Hans Jonas (1979/1984) argues for this point of view, and gives it an ethical expression in *The Imperative of Responsibility*: the disproportionate power which man has acquired to control 'destiny and nature', in all its fragility and vulnerability, 'entails the obligation to safeguard, the integrity of man's world and essence.' Such is man's responsibility. This opinion is on its way to becoming unanimous: the failure of utopias has discredited the figure of the social engineer who, with absolute faith in his science, claimed to have the solution to the organization of society. And multinational corporations, the multiform incarnation of the 'capitalist' world, are accused of trying to impose their will on governments. Companies, large companies, find themselves called upon to safeguard the integrity of the human ecosystem.

It appears to us that protecting the integrity of the human ecosystem is not a responsibility that we can expect the courts to enforce. Of course, a polluter, caught in the act, can be sentenced to pay a fine, but more generally, cause and effect are entangled in such a complex web that it is impossible to blame any specific person for a given deterioration in the ecosystem. This does not call into question the need to protect the human ecosystem. This protection covers, in our modern jargon, the very purpose attributed to politics by the ancient Greeks and the theme of corporate social responsibility sanctions its denationalization and defends implicitly that the administrations have a subsidiary function. The impossibility of designating a given deterioration in the human ecosystem as the 'fault' of any specific person can help us to understand the spirit of the institution of responsibility. As Friedrich Hayek (1959) pointed out, if we wish to encourage provident behavior, the ascribing of responsibility must concern perceptible 'damage' which the 'responsible' person really could have avoided, in other words the foreseeable consequences of his own actions which cause evident harm to a clearly identified person:

> Since we assign responsibility to the individual in order to influence his action, it should refer only to such effects of its conduct as it is humanly possible for him to account for in ordinary circumstances. To be effective, responsibility must be both definite and limited, adapted both emotionally and intellectually to human abilities. It is quite as destructive of any sense of responsibility to be taught that one is responsible for everything as to be taught that one cannot be held responsible for anything. Freedom demands that the responsibility of the individual extend only to what he can be presumed to judge, that his actions take into account effects which are within his range of foresight, and particularly that he be responsible only for his own actions (or those of persons under his care), not for those of others who are equally free (Hayek, 1959, p. 83).

7 Acting with Intelligence

The distinction between *foro interno* and *foro externo* provides a clearer understanding of the scope of the attribution of responsibility. As the domain of the conscience eludes human justice, ascribing responsibility does not mean designating a sinner who should be brought to penitence, but forcing someone to answer for their behavior, whether voluntary or involuntary, and to make good any harmful consequences this behavior may have had. Consequently, it means encouraging them to adopt more provident behavior in the future and so to develop their capacity to foresee and control the consequences of their actions. As Friedrich Hayek put it (1959, p. 76), 'The assigning of responsibility thus presupposes the capacity on men's part for rational action, and it aims at making them act more rationally than they would otherwise. It presupposes a certain minimum capacity in them for learning and foresight, for being guided by a knowledge of the consequences of their action.' Thus, accepting our responsibilities means examining our behavior, and ultimately verifying whether we obtain the happiness we expected from the satisfaction of our desires.

As the reader will have realized, our analysis of responsibility is based on the Aristotelian conception of prudence. Prudence is a virtue of action, containing a fair share of foresight, by means of which 'the prudent man is capable of making the correct decisions about what is good and right for himself' (*Nicomachean Ethics* 1140 a 26), and which is a characteristic trait of men of experience (see 1141 b 18). We would simply emphasize the point that if no one bore the consequences of their actions, in other words if there were no ascribed or accepted responsibility, no one would be motivated to learn the lessons of experience or to develop prudence. This idea has always been present in the classical liberal tradition. One of its advocates was Frédéric Bastiat, who contended that responsibility, provided that it is delimited and strengthened by legislation, encourages the identification of evil and is thus at the origin of experience, which is the source of progress for individual free will: 'the only way to eradicate the cause [of evil], is to enlighten free will, to improve choices, to suppress bad actions or habits; and all this can only be done through the law of Responsibility' (Bastiat, 1841, p. 605, our translation).

In short, for firms, their managers and their employees, accepting their responsibilities means adapting their professional commitments to match the value of the happiness they and their stakeholders obtain from their activity. Thus, although it is not an ethic in itself, responsibility is an ethical lever: it is the means by which entrepreneurs can question the members of their staff about the moral values they respect and their hierarchies of happiness. And they know the mechanism by which this functions: ascribing responsibility to someone is only useful insofar as the person incriminated could have refrained from an action which he knew to have harmful consequences. It is already difficult to accept that others hold us responsible for damage for which, in all conscience, we do not hold ourselves to blame. It is even more intolerable to have to take the blame for a superior who has failed to verify our abilities or experience, who has not given us the necessary resources to carry out our task or, worse still, who passes the buck on to us to evade his own responsibility.

Here we clearly see the lasting influence in our minds of the ideal of the Enlightenment: the producer, faced with his customer, or the employer, faced with his staff, are not held to be responsible because they are supposed to possess a certain knowledge which enables them to predict and control the world, or at least their world. It is because they undertake to supply the customer with a product of the agreed quality or to provide their employees with work suited to their abilities. Of course, given the persuasive tone of modern advertising, the producer undertakes, at least morally, to ensure that the consumer obtains from his product the degree of satisfaction it is claimed to provide, on condition that the product is used appropriately. Likewise, the employer undertakes to maintain employment, or at least the employability of his staff, on condition, of course, that they adopt an attitude of real collaboration. But these 'social responsibilities' are reciprocal undertakings to behave reasonably. They are not obligations attributed unilaterally by possession of knowledge, clearness of foresight and control over the surrounding world.

8 A Concluding Comment

We have implicitly drawn the portrait of the responsible man. He knows and understands his ethics and succeeds in living it daily, to the happiness of himself and his stakeholders. He disciplines his desires so as not to permit himself any action that would cause harm either to himself or to others. We have also described the socially responsible man, who does whatever is in his power to avoid harming others or, even better, does whatever he can for their good. These men have closely examined their conceptions of happiness in the light of their experience, and judged them at their true worth. They have formed an experienced conception of happiness and can now guide their behavior to match this conception. Their behavior is thus intelligent: they do not fail, through lack of discipline, to achieve the happiness they aim for. We see clearly how the attribution of responsibility influences such intelligence: accepting one's responsibilities means disciplining one's desires, and ascribing responsibilities to people encourages them to discipline their own desires.

However, one point must be made clear. We have just said that the responsible man does not permit himself any action that could harm himself or others. We should specify that this is to the best of his knowledge. More specifically, he is limited by the forecasts he can reasonably make. Our world is a tangled web of contingencies, and the forecasts we make are far from certain: they depend on a multitude of factors which are themselves contingent. It is through being vigilant that each person adapts their behavior to suit the circumstances. Experience helps us to refine on our forecasts and makes it easier for us to adapt. Nevertheless, the fact remains that action contains an irreducible element of uncertainty; it can turn out to have more damaging or more profitable consequences than we expected. Consequently, being responsible does not mean refraining from taking any action that might possibly provoke harm – for we would cease to act altogether – but accepting responsibility for the harm that results from our actions and, in concrete terms, being as careful as possible to avoid such harm. Being responsible thus means only allowing oneself to act on the condition that one has enough foresight and vigilance to avoid possible harm.

Nothing could be more obvious. Driving licenses, for example, are only issued to people who have proved they can drive safely. And nothing could be more full of implicit meaning. Throughout its hierarchy, the running of a company requires experience, not to mention maturity and professionalism. Besides the decision-maker, more and more figures involved in the company define themselves as professionals (Dégot, 1990): project managers of all kinds, in-house and outside consultants, salaried managers and executives of all levels possessing wide freedom of action, with high potentials and wishing to leave a positive image behind them, etc. Entrusted with a mission, which he carries out in full independence, the professional achieves his aim without disrupting the organization. He has control over the people working for him and over the circumstances of his own intervention, just as he has control over himself. He constantly reflects on his experience and, on the look-out for the signs which inform him of the specificities of the company, he anticipates the circumstances in which he will be called on to act and he adapts his attitude accordingly.

The professional maintains a particular relation with the company. He could be said to be opportunist, for although he loyally serves the company he works for, his career horizons extend much further. What he actualizes is his potential. What he cherishes is his reputation for being the master of his world, as he is the master of himself. He lays claim to this mastery and is prepared to answer for the use he makes of it to all those who may question him: his principal, of course, to whom he is accountable for his mission, but also the different stakeholders who may ask him for an explanation. He is profoundly independent, because it is in his interest to be so: his sense of responsibilities is his greatest potential. But he is also independent because of his desire for integrity: he will not compromise over the responsibilities that he assumes in all conscience. For the professional, self-interest and duty go together. Given this, employers concerned with ethical practice could make good use of the modern aspiration for professional independence: they could thus endow the attribution of responsibility with its full significance as the foundation of autonomy matched to capability, and contribute to the spread of the spirit of free enterprise.

References

Aristotle (1990), *Ethique à Nicomaque*, trad. franç. par J. Tricot, Vrin, Paris, 7ème tirage.
Bastiat, F. (1841), *Harmonie économique*, Guillaumin, Paris, trans. by W. Hayden Boyers, ed. by George B. de Huszar: *Economic Harmonies*, Irvington on Hudson: FEE, 1996.
Dégo,t V. (1990), Le professionnel, nouvel acteur dans l'entreprise, *Revue française de gestion*, n° 78, pp. 77-87.
Friedman, M. (1962), *Capitalism and Freedom*, Chicago University Press, Chicago.
Hayek, F. (1959), *The Constitution of the Liberty*, Routledge & Kegan Paul, London and Henley.
Hayek, F. (1967), The Moral Element in Free Enterprise, *Studies in Philosophy, Politics and Economics*, Routledge and Kegan Paul, London and Henley, pp. 229-236.
Hayek, F. (1973, 1976, 1979), *Law, Legislation and liberty*, tome 1: *Rules and Order*, tome 2: *The Mirage of Social Justice*, tome 3: *Political Order of a Free People*, Routledge & Kegan Paul, London and Henley.
Jonas, H. (1979), *Das Prinzip Verantwortung*, Francfort a. M.: Insel Verlag, 1979, trans. by H. Jonas and D. Herr: *The Imperative of Responsability. In Search of an Ethics for the Technological Age*, The University of Chicago Press, Chicago, 1984.
Moussé, J. (1992), Le Chemin de l'Ethique, *Revue française de gestion*, n° 88, mars-avril-mai, pp. 60-66.
Padioleau, J.-G. (1989), L'Ethique est-elle un outil de gestion?, *Revue française de Gestion*, n° 74, Juin-Juillet-Août, pp. 82-91.
Ripert, G. (1949), *La Règle morale dans les obligations civiles*, LGDJ, Paris.
Villey, M. (1977), Esquisse historique sur le mot responsabilité, *Archives de philosophie du droit*, tome 22, *La Responsabilité*, Paris: Sirey, pp. 45-58.
Weber, M. (1919), *Wissenschaft als Beruf, Politik als Beruf*, trad. franç. de J. Freud: *Le savant et le politique*, Plon, coll. Recherches en sciences sociales, Paris, 1959, reéd. Union générale d'édition, Paris, 1963, Plon, coll. 10/18, Paris, 1997.

Chapter 9

On Ethical, Social and Environmental Management Systems

Antonio Argandoña

1 Introduction[1]

Recent debate on the reform of corporate governance has highlighted the fact that there are basically two approaches to reform: one that places the emphasis on laws and regulations, and one that prefers to rely on voluntary undertakings by organizations themselves. Advocates of the former point of view seem very sure of what is right and wrong, and so are confident that legal standards and regulations will achieve the desired results. Those who take the latter view are not so sure that what is right for one company will necessarily be right for another, or that what works in one set of circumstances will necessarily hold true in different circumstances. They are naturally reluctant, therefore, to establish rules and regulations, preferring to leave it to corporate initiative to find the best approach in each case.

The former model will therefore rely primarily on compulsory rules that all companies must obey – rules that say whether or not a company's CEO may also serve as chairman of the board of directors, for example, or how many or what proportion of outside directors it should have, or exactly who shall count as an outside or independent director. The latter model, in contrast, will lay down a small number of legal requirements and then leave the companies themselves to regulate

[1] This text was published in the *Journal of Business Ethics*, 53, 1, 2004, pp. 191-201 (© 2004 Kluwer Academic Publishers; republished with kind permission form Springer Science and Business Media). It is part of the activities of the Chair of Economics and Ethics. It was presented at the 11th Annual Conference of *Etica, Economía y Dirección* – EBEN Spain (Barcelona, June 2003), at the EBEN Research Conference (Oslo, June 2003) and at the Society for Business Ethics Annual Meeting (Seattle, August 2003). I would like to thank the referees and participants at these meetings, and in particular Prof. Joan Enric Ricart, for their comments, and the Fundación José y Ana Royo for financial assistance. I would also like to thank the members of the AEN/CTN 165 Working Group on 'Ethics' at Aenor (Asociación Española de Normalización y Certificación – Spanish Standards and Certification Association) for the ideas they have contributed to the development of the experimental project for a Spanish draft standard entitled 'Ethics. A Management System for Corporate Social Responsibility', which I have drawn upon in writing this study.

everything else. Of course, as such regulation is vital to the soundness of companies and the efficiency of the financial markets, and indeed of the market economy as a whole, they will demand that companies take definite measures in this respect and disclose information about their rules of operation and how those rules are applied, subjecting them to internal and external audit as necessary.

The same tension between compulsory regulation and self-regulation exists in other fields. For example, the complex world of environmental protection, food quality or health and safety at work. In all of them, market failures (incomplete and asymmetrical information, externalities or public goods, lack of competition, etc.) need to be corrected, and this often takes the form of regulations laid down by an authority, be it political (a government department) or administrative (a regulatory agency).[2]

However, regulation of this kind is so costly that people have looked for other ways to achieve the same results. Thus, alongside command and control regulatory approaches, we find market-based approaches and management-based approaches. The goal of market-based approaches is to design and put in place incentive systems that will lead the regulated parties to produce the desired results of their own accord. Management-based approaches, in contrast, shift the locus of decision making from the regulator to the company being regulated, requiring it to plan and decide for itself how best to achieve the outcomes that have been identified as desirable (Coglianese and Lazer, 2001).

The purpose of this article is twofold. On the one hand, it explains how implementing voluntary ethical, social and environmental management systems or programs may help to develop and sustain ethical behavior in organizations, overcoming the conflict between compulsory regulation and occasional ethical practices. On the other, it shows what conditions must be met for an ethical management program to be effective. It is not intended to give a detailed account of the whys and wherefores and the different forms of self-regulation, which have been thoroughly dealt with in the literature, but merely to point out its importance within the field of ethics applied to business.

In the following section we discuss the advantages and disadvantages of leaving companies to voluntarily develop their own ethical, social and environmental management systems as opposed to having a system of rules laid down by authority. After that, we explain what an ethical management system or program consists of, its possible strengths and weaknesses, and what it can be expected to achieve. We then consider how a company may go about preparing and implementing a program of this kind, ending with some conclusions.

2 Legal Regulation and Ethical Management

Society has an undeniable interest in ensuring that the results of corporate activity

---

[2] For a detailed specification of when market failures occur, see Winch (1971). For a modern treatment of the subject, see Viscusi et al. (2000).

are compatible with ethics.[3] Even from a purely economic point of view, ethical behavior in business helps to reduce transaction costs and internalize negative externalities, thus improving efficiency. Yet there are other, deeper reasons why organizations and the people who belong to them should always behave in a consistently ethical manner.

When society decides that certain outcomes obtained by ethical behavior are desirable, it may resort basically to any of three different procedures to achieve them (or to any combination of the three): 1) allow the authorities to dictate compulsory regulations (*command and control*); 2) establish market incentives that favor ethical behavior (*market-based*); or 3) seek voluntary undertakings by the agents involved (*management-based*). If we distinguish between the *planning*, the *process* and the *outcome* of business activities, we find that:[4]

1. The command and control approach tends to stipulate a desired outcome, leaving the organization free to organize the planning and the process as it sees fit. An example would be when the law prohibits discrimination between job applicants on the grounds of race, gender, political or religious beliefs. Alternatively, the law may stipulate a process which is expected to lead to the desired outcome. An example of this would be when the regulatory body obliges companies to use certain technologies and adopt certain measures to ensure the safety of employees in the workplace.

2. The market-based approach also fixes certain desired outcomes and sets conditions under which companies may achieve those results, giving them considerable freedom in the planning and process stages. An example of this would be when the authorities create a market for pollution, such that the 'dirtiest' factories may purchase pollution rights from other, more modern and more efficient factories that have not used up their full pollution allowance.[5]

3. The management-based approach, in contrast, leaves the company free, right from the planning stage, to choose whatever processes it likes to obtain the outcomes it has previously identified as a desirable goal, taking into account not only the internal interests of the company itself but also those of society (which also is to some extent involved in setting the goals and monitoring the entire process).

Let us take a closer look at the advantages and disadvantages of each of these three procedures:

---

[3] Society cannot demand that people or organizations be ethical, but only that certain outcomes of their decisions be compatible with ethical principles. However, it is unquestionably in society's interest that people and companies should always behave ethically, because then it can be sure, at least in most cases, that the outcomes will be ethical. It is also clearly in society's interest that organizations should constantly improve as centres of ethical and economic decision making.

[4] See Coglianese and Lazer (2001).

[5] In practice, one rarely finds a purely market-based system; it tends always to be combined with coercive standards and rules.

1. The authority-driven approach gives rise to a complex body of laws, rules and regulations on a wide range of subjects, including the recognition and exercise of property rights, freedom of enterprise, protection against fraud, disclosure of accounting information and protection of the environment, which, at least in theory, are capable of producing the desired economic, social and ethical outcomes.

However, legal or governmental regulation of ethical behavior has certain obvious limitations. First, because the relationship between ethics and the law is ambiguous. On the one hand, many aspects of human behavior have to do with ethics and yet cannot be dealt with by legal means – everything to do with intentions and motivations,[6] for example. On the other hand, not everything required by law has an immediate ethical dimension.[7] Also, laws must be formulated, enacted and brought into force according to established procedures and so cannot be continuously updated or swiftly adapted to advances in knowledge, technology and practice.

What's more, there are laws that are immoral because of what they require or prohibit – and the legality of the process is not a proof of their morality. There are also 'government failures' which can result in sub-optimal legislation – through the 'capture' of the regulator, for example, or the abuse of power by a majority. Lastly, laws change the agents' behavior, so that the results tend not to be exactly as the legislator originally intended.

2. In the market-based approach the authorities specify certain outcomes that are considered desirable and allow the private agents considerable freedom to choose the most suitable mechanisms for achieving them. In the case of a particular company, for example, the regulator may stipulate a maximum level of exposure of workers to toxic particles in the production process, leaving each individual plant to find the most appropriate means to achieve this outcome, depending on the peculiarities of its technology. On the one hand, this clearly gives companies an incentive to meet the desired standard as efficiently as possible, but not to aim for even higher standards, even though they may be well within the companies' reach. On the other hand, although each company may comply with the established standards, the outcome will not be optimal for society as a whole, as the marginal costs and benefits of the different plants or companies will not be balanced to achieve the sought-after social outcomes.

The market incentive-based approach is capable of overcoming these problems, at least in theory (Hahn and Hester, 1989; Stavins, 1998). Measures such as taxes on toxic emissions or the creation of a market for pollution rights can be used to shift production towards companies that use less highly polluting technologies,

---

[6] Ethics cannot be reduced to a set of consequences, because what shapes people's and companies' behaviour and learning are precisely those same intentions and motivations (Pérez López, 1993).

[7] Whether traffic drives on the left or on the right is not, in itself, an ethical issue, merely a practical issue. The fact that once the direction of the traffic has been established by law, obeying that law is an ethical act, is a different matter.

while at the same time creating incentives to keep pollution to a minimum in the long term at the lowest possible cost.

And yet this approach, too, has its limitations (Coglianese and Lazer, 2001). First, continuing with the example of the pollution caused by a factory, the authorities will have to define the social value of private companies' product, which is no easy task – and much less so if we turn instead to ethical problems such as accounting disclosure or non-discrimination of employees. Second, this approach has proved liable to run into serious political difficulties. And lastly, measuring compliance with the established standards can be very difficult – for example, determining when a food product is sufficiently free from the risk of bacterial contamination.

3. The assumption behind the management-based approach is that when it comes to ordering the relationships between planning, process and outcomes, companies have lower transaction costs than governments. In a slaughterhouse, for example, the company's own technicians will know better than outside experts where the real risks of contamination lie, whether in the transport of the animals for slaughter, in the cutting rooms or in the refrigerated rooms. Therefore, it would seem logical to let them decide what procedures should be adopted to prevent contamination. And this means that the procedures will be different for each slaughterhouse, depending on the technology it uses, the way it is organized, its location, its working practices, etc.

In the case of ethics, the arguments in favor of a management-based approach are even stronger:

1. Companies can be forced to adopt certain practices and attain certain outcomes, but they cannot be forced to behave ethically. Therefore, in a truly ethical management system the agents involved need to be given scope for free initiative.[8]

2. Except in certain extreme cases, ethics is never black or white, but a choice between more or less ethical behaviors. Therefore, what is ethically desirable for a company at any given moment will be subject to different interpretations, not because there is any difference in the basic principles underlying the interpretation but because the way those principles are applied to the particular circumstances, and people's perception of those circumstances, are liable to differ.[9] Therefore, the government may insist on certain outcomes or processes that it considers desirable, but any truly ethical, social and environmental management system must leave a wide margin for the interested parties to decide of their own free accord.

3. Often, a company that has introduced an ethical management system will try to go beyond an ethics of minimums and aspires to excellence (Solomon, 1992). Therefore, given that there are degrees of excellence

---

[8] This is not to say that laws or regulations imposed from outside cannot also be accepted willingly and therefore obeyed ethically.

[9] On the permanence of the higher-order principles or values, despite differences in their application, see Argandoña (2001).

and excellence can be achieved in different areas, it is only just that the company should be given scope to define its own action program.

4.   The regulator is most unlikely to be able to predict or assess the outcomes of a command and control program once the program enters the field of ethics, as many of those outcomes will materialize in the attitudes, values and virtues of the people in and around the organization and so will not be observable. An exclusively command and control-based ethical regulation system is therefore likely to be suboptimal.

5.   Legal regulation cannot take account of the variety of circumstances of different companies. A program that is right for a large chemicals firm may not be right for a small travel agency. And the same is true of the socioeconomic environment: in a country in which corruption is rife, a program focused on fighting extortion and bribery may be more important than an environmental protection program, while in another country the priorities may be reversed.

6.   Similarly, a command and control program cannot take into account all the changes that take place over time, because these changes affect the learning that people undergo in terms of knowledge, abilities, attitudes and values. Consequently, a program that is optimal at one point in time may not be optimal some time later, not only because outer circumstances (market, technology, etc.) will have changed but also because the company's culture and the values on which it is built will have changed.

7.   For the same reason, a clearly defined and relatively rigid public program may thwart any attempt to adapt the ethical measures to future developments of the program.

8.   A program established on a voluntary basis may be more motivating and represent more of an obligation for the company's management and those of the employees who have had a say in preparing it than one imposed coercively by a regulatory body.

However, the management-based approach will not be optimal, nor even workable, unless the company and its personnel have the right training and, above all, the right incentives to put the necessary monitoring procedures into practice. Herein lies the first difficulty of the management-based approach.

The second difficulty derives from the play of interests, information and pressures between the company, the regulatory authorities, the auditors and civil society when it comes to setting demanding but achievable goals, and updating them frequently and efficiently.[10]

---

[10] If only the company knows what is best, it may choose to conceal this information from the regulator, so that the resulting plans will not be optimal: it is precisely when it most important that the company should use its knowledge of the process and the circumstances to detect ethical failures that it is most likely to have least incentive to do so. There is an 'agency problem' here between the regulator and the company that draws

And thirdly, management-based programs are liable to run into political difficulties when they are first introduced. They may be rejected by society or by policy makers because they seem to leave regulation in the hands of precisely the people who are to be regulated, or to reduce regulation to an undemanding minimum, etc. Therefore, before any program of this kind is implemented certain conditions must be met.

3 Ethical Management Systems

All of the above argues in favor of adopting ethical management systems or programs similar to those already in use in fields such as environmental protection or health and safety, etc., which obviously also have major ethical implications.[11]

Management systems have a long history in the world of business, particularly applied or specific ones, such as systems for quality, information, environmental management, or health and safety at work. The chief characteristic of any management system is its rational focus, the fact that it is designed mainly to monitor, standardize and, if necessary, certify and audit processes (Zwetsloot, 2003). An ethical management system or program is, then, a set of internal rules that a company's management uses to standardize and mould behaviors and to monitor and supervise processes with a view to achieving within the organization certain goals of an ethical nature.[12]

To make an ethical management system work a company needs to have at its disposal tools such as rules of conduct, lines of communication (ethical helplines for queries, reports or complaints, for example), ethics committees (to develop ethics policies, review performance, conduct research and impose sanctions), ethical officers and ombudspersons, ethical training programs, ethical reporting, disciplinary procedures, and so on. However, an ethical management program must go beyond this. Even assuming these tools are in place and are effective, it must include, as we shall see later, specific management actions aimed at formulating ethical goals, defining formal processes, ensuring that ethics is present in all aspects of the company's management, implementing clear (internal or external) auditing and review processes, and designing continuous improvement mechanisms.[13] Instituting an ethical management system does not, therefore, imply

---

up the rules by which it will be judged (a problem that will be further complicated if external auditors, who are also agents of the regulator, are involved).

[11] We shall use the terms ethical, social and environmental programme and ethical, social and environmental system interchangeably, even though the former has more specific and operational connotations while the latter tends to be more abstract (Meidinger, 2001). Other commonly used terms are ethics programmes, shared values programmes, compliance programmes, responsible conduct programmes, etc. (Weaver and Treviño, 1999).

[12] This definition is based on one given in Coglianese and Nash (2001).

[13] Some authors seem to adopt this less ambitious viewpoint when defining ethics programmes; see, for example, Cohen (1993), Hoffman (1995), Jackson (1997), while

any criticism of efforts to draw up and implement a code of conduct, as to a large extent the two processes coincide (Sethi, 2003). In any case, the ethical management system will add the elements of rationality, standardization, strict stage definition, monitoring and auditing, continuous improvement and innovation that the task of designing an ethical management system entails.[14]

An ethical management system may be introduced in the following circumstances:

1. When the goal is to achieve certain outcomes that the authorities consider desirable, but it does not seem appropriate to lay down strict rules as to exactly how they are to be achieved. For example, the law forbids extortion and bribery, but companies and private citizens are free to decide what should be done to ensure that they do not occur. Thus, there may be a wide range of possible means to the desired end, and the means will vary from one geographical region or industry to another, and from one company to another.[15] In any case, when the authorities take the initiative, they tend to lay down certain rules, demand compliance with certain formal requirements, set certain conditions concerning the content and scope of the program, or make it subject to regulatory approval, etc.[16]

2. When the companies in a particular industry decide, in concert with one another, to set themselves the target of achieving certain ethical, social or environmental results[17] – a reduction in industrial accidents, for example, or the eradication of bribery and extortion in public sector procurement.

3. When the management of an individual company wishes to demonstrate or enhance its social legitimacy, change the corporate culture, guard against illegal or immoral behavior on the part of its employees, or obtain certain ethical, social or environmental outcomes.[18]

---

others espouse the more demanding conception proposed here; for example, Berenbeim (1992), Brenner (1992), Weaver et al. (1999a,b).

[14] Zwetsloot (2003) also points out the inadequacies of a management system when it comes to implementing ethics in a company.

[15] On the role of regulation in the preparation of ethical management systems, see U.S. Sentencing Commission (1994); also Dalton et al. (1994), Rafalko (1994).

[16] Sometimes regulators turn the undertakings freely assumed by companies and approved by the authorities into legal obligations. Or they demand that companies have such programmes in place in order to be eligible for government contracts, or make them a point in companies' favour. Or they allow companies that have such programmes to benefit from less stringent government controls. Or they authorize companies to use special logos that mark them out as ethically, socially or environmentally responsible, etc. Intervention by regulators in private ethical management programmes should not be confused with what is known as negotiated rule making (Coglianese, 2001).

[17] There is no such thing as 'social, ethical or environmental results': all results are to a greater or lesser extent ethical, social and environmental. What we are referring to here are results or outcomes that are desirable not only from an economic and socio-political point of view, but also and above all on account of their ethical dimension, insofar as they contribute to improving people and organizations.

[18] Companies may have all sorts of reasons for starting an ethical management programme: the demands of a regulatory agency; pressure from the media, NGOs or the general

In a nutshell, an ethical management system is a set of internal efforts to formulate, plan and implement policies to achieve certain outcomes that will result in the company performing its ethical duties more satisfactorily and the people who work for the company improving ethically. The following are some guidelines that may inspire such programs:[19]

1. A systematic approach adopting specially designed measures will yield better results than a sporadic and haphazard approach.
2. Ethical management is a process, not an outcome. Accordingly, the focus must be on the process.
3. The goal is to achieve the desired behavior; values and intentions are not enough. Values must be projected into policies, procedures and training plans, which in turn will influence behavior and outcomes.
4. Ethical management must be integrated with other management practices. Strategic planning and all the company's actions must be driven by the organization's values and measured in terms of their economic, socio-political and ethical effects.
5. The fact of having an ethical, social and environmental management system will encourage a company to search for solutions that would not otherwise have been considered.
6. The program will also motivate managers and employees to achieve the results they are aiming for.
7. The program will establish valuable links between the company and other stakeholders, such as the local community, the unions, customers and suppliers, and NGOs.

If the program is not a success, its results will be limited to fulfilling the letter of the program. If it is a success, however, it may bring about a change of culture, thanks to the emphasis placed on meeting program objectives and creating new working routines, new information and communication patterns, and new incentive systems. Putting an ethical management program in place may create a new awareness of the relationship between the company's culture and the ethical outcomes of its actions, and so provide a framework for identifying possible changes that may improve the company's ethical and business performance.

Obviously, there is no guarantee that these possible benefits of adopting an ethical management system will actually be obtained. Success is never guaranteed, certainly not unless a company's top management is seriously and deeply involved and commits the necessary means and resources. On the other hand, success may be due not to the program itself but to other factors such as top management's commitment to ethical excellence and the spirit in which the organization as a whole is managed. And there are always bound to be those within the organization who will see the program as nothing more than pointless red tape.

---

public; the recommendations or requirements of industry associations; imitation; the influence of consultants; internal initiative (values and commitments of managers or owners), and so on.

[19] See McNamara (1999), among other sources.

And yet there is good reason to believe that a combination of determination and vision on the part of top management, enthusiasm in preparing and implementing the ethical management system, prudence in administering it and perseverance in correcting, updating and continuously improving it will lead to change of culture in the company, which we earlier identified as the key to success from the ethical point of view.[20]

4 How to Draw up and Implement an Ethical, Social and Environmental Management System

Very generally speaking, an ethical, social and environmental management system or program is based on four pillars:
1. Design an ethical, social and environmental management program.
2. Put it into practice, assigning responsibilities, allocating resources and training employees.
3. Monitor progress by means of systematic audits.
4. Act to correct any problems that may be detected, constantly updating the system.

In practice, an ethical, social and environmental management system will tend to include the following stages:[21]
1. Define the company's activities.
2. Identify the stakeholders and their representatives, as well as any ethical issues deriving from their relations with the company and the impacts the company's activities may have on them. The ethical scope of the program will depend to a large extent on how complete this list of stakeholders and impacts is.
3. Define publicly and in writing the organization's ethical commitments and policies towards itself, towards relevant stakeholder groups and towards society. In this as in subsequent stages, the fact of making the

---

[20] Also, a continuous and ongoing programme has obvious advantages over occasional measures taken to put things right or improve the ethical quality of management decisions: organizational roles are created for ethical management; the programme is monitored continuously; efforts are made to bring behaviour into line with values; management and employees develop an awareness of and interest in ethical issues; ethics becomes an integral part of decision making; mechanisms are devised to deal with any problems that may occur; the programme is regularly evaluated and reviewed, and so on.

[21] Here we are drawing on the Experimental Standards Project carried out in Spain by Aenor, under the title of 'Ética. Sistema de gestión de la responsabilidad social corporativa' ('Ethics. A Management System for Corporate Social Responsibility') (draft, December 2002). It is important to point out that it is not a collection of juxtaposed components, but a combination of values, policies, procedures and activities that make up an organization's morality (Brenner, 1992).

program public is important, as it represents an undertaking towards the company's stakeholders and towards society.[22]

4. Draw up an ethical code of conduct and management manual (in consultation with the interested parties).[23]

5. Select, within the company's top management, an individual or body with sufficient power and independence to ensure that the policy is complied with and the program works as it should.

6. Identify the processes affected by the ethical management system and the organization's ethical undertaking.

7. State the specific objectives and actions that must be performed to ensure that the different processes adopted satisfy the requirements of the ethical, social and environmental management program. This is the core of the program.

8. Plan these specific objectives and actions in good time and in the appropriate way so that they can be performed effectively.

9. Make sure that the necessary resources and information to support the operation and monitor the actions are available. The resources required include employee and management training in ethical, social and environmental matters.

10. Perform the necessary actions to achieve the planned objectives.

11. Determine the necessary criteria and methods to ensure that the solutions adopted are maintained and remain effective.

12. Define a system to verify and, wherever possible, measure the objectives, activities and results. Not all the parts of the program will be measurable, but it is important that those that *are* measurable be formulated in those terms, and that the results also be presented in that way.[24]

13. Define and implement internal and external audits to provide independent verification that the ethical, social and environmental management system has been fully implemented, is effective, and is fit for its purpose. Independent verification of the program's results is vital for its credibility and also for its improvement over time.[25]

---

[22] Although the programme is voluntary, it may end up becoming a de facto requirement, as a way to improve stakeholder relations and the company's reputation, avoid compulsory regulation, improve organizational efficiency, respond to customer and supplier demands, inspire confidence in shareholders, and so on. (Meidinger, 2001).

[23] The ethical management manual specifies the organization's ethical management system. Obviously, it will have to take account of the size and nature of the company.

[24] This may make the programme too rigid and will need to be considered. Having clearly defined, measurable goals removes ambiguity and makes it easier to meet requirements, but it also lends itself to a purely formal, top-down control system that is liable to elicit hostile reactions to what may be seen as coercion or even indoctrination (Nijhof et al., 2000).

[25] Treviño and Weaver (2001) stress the importance of monitoring to ensure the programme remains effective, give employees a sense of justice, discourage immoral behaviour and continually identify problems as they appear.

14. Review the system at regular intervals to check that it fulfills its purpose and is effective.

15. Put in place the necessary improvement processes and measures to achieve the planned results and ensure the continuous improvement of the program. This is another crucial aspect of management systems, as it entails a commitment to continuous improvement, which is the key to ethics in companies.

16. Establish methods to inform stakeholders of the commitments acquired and the extent to which they are being met, giving them access to internal information that is relevant to them.

17. Foster personal commitment and, if necessary, demand that the requirements of the ethical, social and environmental management system be met.

18. If the organization chooses to outsource some of the processes that may be affected by the ethical, social and environmental management system, steps must be taken to ensure that these processes are carried out in accordance with the requirements of the program.

As we said earlier, an ethical, social and environmental management program should not be simply the brainchild of a company's top management, but should involve all of the company's stakeholders, each according to its particular interests and abilities. This is especially important at certain stages, such as the drafting of the code of conduct, the identification of the processes affected by the ethical management system, the training of personnel, the implementation of the continuous improvement processes, and the nurturing of employee and managerial commitment.[26]

An ethical management system centered on compliance, control and discipline may be very useful, but it may also generate perverse behavior. Therefore, it is best if it is accompanied by a system that strengthens people's values, which implies showing confidence in employees and other stakeholders and allowing them to have a say in the process and take a share of responsibility for its results.[27] This means that there are two parts to an ethics program: an explicit part made up of the codes, manuals, programs, training seminars, decisions, etc., and an implicit part made up of the company's culture, incentive systems, personnel policies, performance measurement systems, etc.[28]

---

[26] The dialogue must never stop with the drafting of the code of conduct but must continue throughout the entire process (Jackson, 1997).

[27] The distinction between compliance-based and values-based systems of ethical management comes from Weaver and Treviño (1999); see also Paine (1994). Values-based systems place the emphasis on developing shared values and supporting the aspirations of all employees, on identification and commitment; they are, in theory, more effective, particularly when it comes to changing an organization's culture, but they are more open to manipulation and uncertainty of behaviour. Compliance-based systems place the emphasis on rules, control, and sanction of unethical behaviour; in appearance they are more effective, but they tend to be minimalist, insisting on outward compliance, and are less effective in changing culture and building active and creative commitment.

[28] On these two components of the programme, see Brenner (1992).

It is also common to try to get other parties involved, such as:

1. The authorities and regulators, at least insofar as they are the ones who draw up and enact the laws and rules to which the company's ethical system must conform.[29]

2. External auditors, who may help to monitor and certify the processes and results. They tend to be professional auditors or non-governmental organizations specifically qualified for this purpose.[30]

3. Standards bodies, which may be public or private, national or international, including NGOs and industry associations.[31]

4. It is also common to use outside consultants, either to help design the ethical management system or to help get it certified. Their role must always be auxiliary, so as not to detract from the involvement and responsibility of the company's managers and employees.

5. If appropriate, public or private certification agencies may also be involved.

6. In one way or another, all of the company's stakeholders should be involved in preparing and implementing the ethical management program. This means that the company will need to open up channels of communication to allow a fruitful dialogue to take place between management, employees and other stakeholders (Nijhof et al., 2000).

5 Conclusions

Whether they know it or not, all companies have an ethical management system which conditions the ethical outcomes of their decisions, moulds the behavior of their managers and employees, and creates their distinctive culture (Brenner, 1992). There is no denying, however, that it is best for the company if it deliberately designs and implements a coherent ethical system based on the values that it specifically wishes to foster and that are most likely to lead to the goals it wishes to achieve on an ethical, social and environmental level. Nevertheless, it is true that certain small companies that have a sound ethical culture will not need the highly varied and complex provisions of the type of ethical programs proposed here (Weaver et al., 1999a).

Designing a good ethical program and persevering in the effort to put it into practice is something of an art. It is important to make sure that the program matches the peculiarities of the company, industry and geographical area (Weaver,

---

[29] We already explained earlier some other ways in which regulators may become involved in private ethical management systems.

[30] There are reasons why this should be done by professional, outside auditors, as they bring to the job their experience and knowledge, a thorough justification of each of their decisions, and their independence (if they are, in fact, independent). See Meidinger (2001).

[31] For example, the ISO (International Organization for Standardization) standards, those developed by the Forest Stewardship Council (FSC) for the forestry industry, and those of the American Responsible Care (ARC) program for the chemicals industry.

2001). It is important to anticipate any cultural changes that are likely to occur as a result of the implementation of the program, and the learning that will take place in managers, employees and other stakeholders. It is important to meticulously pinpoint the areas where ethical problems are most likely to arise, in order to prepare measures to prevent them, or to resolve them if they do arise. It is important to stimulate a process of ethical dialogue within the company, a process that will start with the drafting of the ethics code but will continue throughout the following stages. An ethical management program is an open, ongoing process that should grow continuously, because, as we said earlier, the commitment to continuous improvement is an important part of any such program.

In this chapter we have shown that there are sound reasons for companies to establish ethical management systems, whether on their own initiative or in response to the demands of society, their stakeholders, the regulators or industry itself. Beyond introducing useful tools, such as ethical codes, ethical ombudsmen, ethics hotlines, ethical training and ethical reporting, companies would be well advised to develop an integrated system that combines declarations of principles, commitments and codes with specific measures to give them practical effect and the means to evaluate, correct and update them. This is no substitute for individual ethical behavior, nor for a corporate culture and strategy that allows ethical behavior. But it may be a good means to achieve these objectives by orienting them towards corporate excellence, including ethical excellence.

References

Argandoña, A. (2001), Algunas Tesis sobre los Valores, *Revista Empresa y Humanismo*, III, 1/01, pp. 45-74.

Berenbeim, R. (1992), *Corporate Ethics Practices*. New York: Conference Board.

Brenner, S. N. (1992), Ethics Programs and Their Dimensions, *Journal of Business Ethics*, 11, pp. 391-399.

Coglianese, C. (2001), Assessing the Advocacy of Negotiated Rulemaking: A Response to Philip Harter, *New York University Environmental Law Journal*, 9, 2.

Coglianese, C. and Lazer D. (2001), Management-based Regulation: Using private-Sector Management to Achieve Public Goals, John F. Kennedy School of Government, Harvard University, *Faculty Research Working Paper Series*, RWP01-047, December.

Coglianese, C. and Nash J. (2001), Bolstering Private Environmental Management, John F. Kennedy School of Government, Harvard University, *Faculty Research Working Paper Series*, RWP01-011, April.

Cohen, D. V. (1993), Creating and Maintaining Ethical Work Climates, *Business Ethics Quarterly*, 3, 343-358.

Dalton, D. R., Metzger M. B. and Hill J. W. (1994), The 'New' U.S. Sentencing Commission Guidelines: A Wake-up for Corporate America, *Academy of Management Executive*, 8, pp. 7-13.

Hahn, R. W. and Hester G. (1989), Marketable Permits: Lessons for Theory and Practice, *Ecology Law Journal*, 16.

Hoffman, W. M. (1995), A Blueprint for Corporate Ethical Development, in: W. M. Hoffman and W. Frederick, (eds), *Business Ethics*. New York: McGraw-Hill, 3rd ed.

Jackson, K. T. (1997), Globalizing Corporate Ethics Programs: Perils and Prospects, *Journal of Business Ethics*, 16, pp. 1227-1235.

McNamara, C. (1999), *Complete Guide to Ethics Management: An Ethics Toolkit for Managers*, www.mapnp.org/library/ethics/ethxgde.htm.

Meidinger, E. E. (2001), Environmental Certification Programs and the U.S. Environmental Law: Closer than you May Think, *Environmental Law Reporter*, 31, pp. 10162-10179.

Nijhof, A., O. Fisscher and Looise J. K. (2000), Coercion, Guidance and Mercifulness: The Different Influences of Ethics Programs on Decision-making, *Journal of Business Ethics*, 27, pp. 33-42.

Paine, L. S. (1994), Managing for Organizational Integrity, *Harvard Business Review*, 72, 2, March-April, pp. 106-117.

Pérez López, J. A. (1993), *Fundamentos de la Dirección de Empresas*. Madrid: Rialp.

Rafalko, R. J. (1994), Remaking the Corporation: The 1991 U.S. Sentencing Guidelines, *Journal of Business Ethics*, 13, 625-636.

Sethi, S. P. (2003), *Setting Global Standards: Guidelines for Creating Codes of Conduct in Multinational Corporations*. Hoboken: Wiley.

Solomon, R. C. (1992), *Ethics and Excellence: Cooperation and Integrity in Business*, New York: Oxford University Press.

Stavins, R. N. (1988), What Can We Learn From the Grand Policy Experiment? Lessons from SO2 Allowance Trading, *Journal of Economic Perspectives*, 12.

Treviño, L. K. and Weaver G. R. (2001), Organizational Justice and Ethics Program 'Follow-through': Influences on Employees' Harmful and Helpful Behavior, *Business Ethics Quarterly*, 11, pp. 651-671.

U.S. Sentencing Commission (1994), *Federal Sentencing Guidelines Manual*. Washington D.C., U.S. Sentencing Commission.

Viscusi, K. W., J. M. Vernon and Harrington J. E. (2000), *Economics of Regulation and Antitrust*. Cambridge: MIT Press.

Weaver, G. R. (2001), Ethics Programs in Global Businesses: Culture's Role in Managing Ethics, *Journal of Business Ethics*, 30, 1, pp. 3-15.

Weaver, G. R. and Treviño L. K., (1999), Compliance and Values Oriented Ethics Programs: Influences on Employees' Attitudes and Behavior, *Business Ethics Quarterly*, 9, April, pp. 315-336.

Weaver, G. R., L. K. Treviño and Cochran P. L. (1999a), Corporate Ethics Programs as Control Systems: Influences on Executive Commitment and Environmental Factors, *Academy of Management Journal*, 42, pp. 41-57.

Weaver, G. R., L. K. Treviño and Cochran P. L. (1999b), Integrated and Decoupled Corporate Social Performance: Management Commitments, External Pressures, and Corporate Ethics Practices, *Academy of Management Journal*, 42, 5, pp. 539-552.

Winch, D. M. (1971), *Analytical Welfare Economics*. Harmondsworth: Penguin Books.

Zwetsloot, G. I. J. M. (2003), From Management Systems to Corporate Social Responsibility, *Journal of Business Ethics*, 44, pp. 201-207.

PART THREE

ETHICAL ISSUES IN PRACTICE

Chapter 10

Is Ethical Marketing a Myth?

1 Introduction

The general public and the critics of marketing have often accused marketers of unethical practices and behaviors. Some even see marketing as a business function that has inherent adverse effects on individuals and/or society that should be of moral concern to any marketer. These critics are not deprived from facts for backing up such accusations. In the recent past, a number of situations have fueled the critics' arguments. From 1996 on, the meat industry has been under close ethical scrutiny as the result of the bovine spongiform encephalopathy crisis (Smith and Young, 1999). Recently, the Buffalo Grill steak house chain has been formally charged of illegally importing beef that was deemed improper for consumption. In the late nineties, the Chrysler Corporation had to recall an unprecedented number of 900,000 cars as a result of several motor defects (Smith, Thomas and Quelch, 1996). In addition, dissatisfied consumers are finding increased support from the courts. More frequently than ever, marketers are sued in the courts. In the US, Dow Corning was found guilty of manufacturing defective products and of fraudulently concealing evidence of safety problems (Lawrence, 1993). McDonald's was recently condemned for not informing customers that they were selling 'very hot' coffee that could eventually burn unwary consumers. In the US again, tobacco companies have had to pay some 413 billion euros in 1997 as compensation to smoking victims (Buckley, 2000). This list could be expanded...

In the mean time, consumers in developed countries are increasingly expecting good conduct from marketers. After the consumerist movements of the seventies, consumers are exerting increasing pressures for more environmentally and socially responsible marketing. They advocate sustainable economic development, equitable trade, and ethical marketing conducts.

As a result, academics have been devoting more attention to ethical issues in marketing (Bellizzi and Hite, 1989; Chonko and Hunt, 1985; Dunfee, Smith and Ross, 1999; Duke et al., 1993; Ferrell and Gresham, 1985; Hunt and Vasquez-Parraga, 1993; Hunt and Vitell, 1986; Robin and Reidenbach, 1987; Thompson, 1995; Tsalikis and Fritzsche, 1989; Wotruba, 1990). In spite of ethical issues receiving broader coverage, greater visibility, and stronger theoretical and empirical foundations (Ferrell, Gresham and Fraedrich, 1989; Williams and Murphy, 1990; Laczniak and Murphy, 1993; Laczniak, 1993), marketing ethics has remained until recently an area of relative neglect by theorists and researchers. As Robin and Reidenbach (1993) point out:

> Without a consistent and coherent ethical philosophy, the marketing discipline suffers both theoretically and practically. The effort to develop such a philosophy is hindered by a lack of single moral philosophy that is sufficient to accommodate the realities faced by the marketing discipline.

This chapter examines the question of whether marketing (and marketers) can ever behave ethically, based on an analysis of the marketing function's objectives and current practices. Starting with generally accepted definitions of such concepts as ethical behavior, marketing's role, consumers' rights and duties, the various accusations voiced at many marketers' practices and marketing's effects on individuals and society are examined. After this first introductory section, Section 2 sets the boundaries of what should be considered as ethical marketing behavior. Section 3 investigates the ethical responsibilities that marketers should bear collectively by the mere fact of performing their functions. Section 4 discusses the individual responsibilities of marketers. Finally, a few concluding comments are provided in the last section.

2 The Boundaries of 'Ethical' Marketing Behavior

Marketing ethics cannot be properly analyzed without a good grasp of marketing's role and functions in our society. Marketing may be viewed both as an economic exchange process and as the management of information asymmetry between producers and consumers.

2.1 Marketing as an Economic Exchange Process

The American Marketing Association (2004) defines marketing as 'an organizational function and a set of processes for creating, communicating, and delivering value to customers and for managing customer relationships in ways that benefit the organization and its stakeholders.' This definition clearly delineates a marketer's role in society. Marketers are responsible for taking actions that will induce consumers and buyers from various market segments to exchange against a price, products and services that satisfactorily answer their needs and wants, taking into account the business constraints to make a profit and to account for environmental constraints (i.e., economic, behavioral, institutional, legal, and competitive constraints).

As an institution of the free enterprise economy, marketing relies on market competition. In this type of economy, individual entrepreneurs, and marketers in particular, have no vested interest in enhancing competition. One reason is that a lack of competition increases consumer prices and profits. In order to reduce competition and improve profits, marketers may sometimes (Abratt and Sacks, 1988) find it easier to engage in such anticompetitive behaviors as price fixing agreements with competitors, resale price maintenance, price discrimination, reciprocal dealings, tying arrangements, or exclusive dealing (Boatright, 2003). This is the reason why maintaining competition must be enforced by laws and regulations (McMurtry, 1997). The sets of antitrust regulations in the United States and in Europe, as well as various laws prohibiting such anticompetitive practices, are necessary for ensuring the efficient workings of the economic system. Such legislation sets the boundaries marketers' permissible actions.

2.2 Marketing as an Information Asymmetry Management Process

To fulfill their functions, marketers must entertain two-way communications with individuals (consumers, buyers), organizations (other firms, etc.), and markets in general. Establishing strong and lasting relationships with customers has become the basis of the current marketing philosophy (Gundlach and Murphy, 1993). One communication stream stems from the marketer's responsibility to learn and understand the various consumer needs, wants, preferences, likes, and dislikes. Letting aside relationships within distribution channels that relate more specifically to general business ethics (Vermillion, Lassar and Winsor, 2002), these communications are necessary to design products and services that will be acceptable to consumers once they are on the market, and that consumers will be willing to acquire at the set price, in the selected outlets. Another communication stream is necessary for marketers to inform and convince consumers that the product and services (that have been designed according to their own specifications) are now available, with certain features, prices, availability, etc.

One important part of the marketing function may be viewed as managing the information asymmetry that takes place between manufacturers and consumers or buyers. Consumers have information about themselves, their needs and wants, their likes and dislikes, their purchase intentions, etc. This information is not readily available to marketers, and consumers have no incentive to provide it to marketers. As a result, in order to acquire it, marketers must establish processes especially designed to that effect, such as consumer and market research or market information systems.

In turn, marketers have information about product features and characteristics. They know all the technical details (among others) about production, quality levels, or costs of raw materials. Typically, this information that is not fully available to consumers. Consumers and buyers, however, need at least some of this information, because they will engage in a transaction only if they perceive that they can obtain value through the exchange. In order to assess the value they can expect from a contemplated transaction, consumers need sufficient relevant information. This is why marketers use such communication devices as advertising, personal selling, or promotional tools to provide them with the needed information. Managing this information asymmetry between producers and consumers is an essential marketing function.

2.3 Where Ethics Fits into the Picture

Addressing the question of whether certain marketing activities are 'ethical,' one should define what constitutes 'ethical marketers' behavior. If, following the Encyclopedia Britannica (2004), ethics is 'the discipline dealing with what is good and bad and with moral duty and obligation,' and morals, the '...principles of conduct governing an individual or a group,' these definitions leave the analyst with the difficult and subjective task of deciding what are right (and wrong) marketing practices (Singhapakdi et al., 1999). Note that it is easier to point at unethical behavior, and to consider ethical any conduct that does not qualify as unethical.

Resulting from the above definitions, to be judged unethical, a marketer's action must have been taken deliberately, with knowledge of its potential harmful effects on one individual's and/or group's welfare or values. Note that does not necessarily exonerate marketers from their responsibility. In addition, there is no such thing as 'universal ethics.' Judgments about ethical behavior may depend on such variables as situation (Lund, 2000), culture (Singhapakdi et al., 2001), organizational ethical climate (Honeycutt et al., 2001; Brinkmann, 2002; Singhapakdi and Vitell, 1991), demographic characteristics (Hartman and Beck-Dudley, 1999; Ricks and Fraedrich, 1999), or personality variables such as ethical sensitivity (Sparks and Hunt, 1998).

In addition to their individual responsibilities for their specific actions, marketers may also incur collective responsibilities by the mere fact of fulfilling marketing functions. If such collective responsibilities do exist, then individual marketers cannot be individually accountable for fulfilling an important economic function in society. It becomes society's responsibility to provide marketers with the laws, regulations, and guidelines, including industry self-regulations and codes of ethics that minimize any adverse effects of the marketing function. In this case, a marketer's individual responsibility and ethical behavior consists is to abide to such regulations. This collective responsibility of marketers will be discussed in the next section.

Much more latitude is given to marketers when they manage their information asymmetry with customers. Consumers and buyers are entitled to expect truthful relationships with suppliers. This entails obtaining from suppliers *accurate* and, as far as possible, *complete* information concerning the transaction, in order for them to minimize the risks of the transaction.

On their side, marketers must provide customers with only part of the information they have. One major difficulty faced by marketers is to decide how much and which information to provide to consumers. Not only consumers do not need perfect information in order to make sound purchase decisions, but too much information may prove to be as unproductive for them as too little information. Providing too much information involves the risk of consumers overwhelmed with data that are irrelevant to their decision. For instance, giving all the technical details on computers to consumers who are not technically oriented is, at best, a waste of time, energy, and manufacturers' resources. At worst, it can mislead consumers who misinterpret the information and/or it pollutes the communication through overloading consumers with irrelevant (even if accurate) information. Then, what information level should a marketer provide to consumers? The decision is not easy to make for the simple reason that all consumers in the marketplace do not need the same information level to make their purchase decision; they do not have the same initial information levels or the same tolerance for risk; they do not use the same information or have the same abilities to process information. As a result, whatever the information decisions marketers make, they can be sure to be beyond optimality for a number of consumers in their target market segments.

From an ethical point of view, given that marketers are users and the major providers of market information, and given that they control the communication processes, it is clear that they can take advantage of such a privileged position. No doubt, marketers have an incentive to in take advantage of the information asymmetry and give consumers the information that is most beneficial to themselves. When this goes against the consumers' interests, such behaviors may sometimes be labeled unethical. Such actions are discussed in the following section.

3 Marketers' Collective Responsibilities

One important question is whether marketers are induced to collectively behave unethically as a result of the very nature of the marketing function. For instance, marketers have been frequently accused of marketing harmful or poor quality products in order to meet competition. Marketers may be induced to match any advantage offered by competitors to consumers, even though this competitive advantage has been gained through unethical practices. Marketers have also been accused of unduly charging higher prices than they should (and consequently depriving poor consumers from part of their purchasing power) because of the high advertising and promotion costs that consumers must bear. According to critics, advertising expenditures decided by marketers are a waste of economic resources because such expenses constitute a substantial part of the price of the goods sold.

Other critics argue that marketing, as an institution, has a strong negative impact on society. To them, marketers are collectively responsible for adversely affecting various aspects of our social and cultural lives. For instance, marketers may unethically manipulate consumers against their own will. These points deserve careful consideration.

3.1 Marketers' Responsibility for Adverse Economic Effects

Marketers have often been given the responsibility of causing higher distribution costs and consumer prices (Farris and Albion, 1980; Farris and Reibstein, 1979). The argument that promotion expenditures are a waste of economic resources that often constitute a substantial part of the price of the good sold, may seem to carry some weight. It must be, however, seriously qualified. It relies on two underlying assumptions that do not always hold. The first assumption is that marketers always use a cost-oriented pricing strategy (such as cost-plus pricing), which is not always the case. If a demand-oriented pricing strategy is followed – and assuming that marketing expenses could be suppressed without decreasing the demand for a product – then any cost reduction would not be passed on to consumers but would increase the firm's profits.

The second assumption is that promotional activities have no definite impact on sales and that marketers could do without it at no extra cost. Obviously, this assertion is at variance with the unanimous belief that promotional activities play a key communication role in any marketing program. Even more, there are strong arguments and empirical evidence to suggest the contrary, i.e., that promotional expenses often decrease a product unit distribution cost. This is the result of economies of scales (and their resulting decreased unit cost) that promotional expenses have on demand (unless marketers are – unwillingly – inefficient), and that allow for larger production runs.

That marketing leads to higher consumer prices and higher profits through market concentration is a more subtle argument (Telser, 1964; Backman, 1967; Mann, Henning and Meeham, 1967; Preston, 1968). Economists have studied this problem theoretically and empirically, and although there is no clear evidence in either direction, this argument can be substantiated more than the preceding one. The process would be an endless loop: marketing leads to market concentration, which leads to more marketing expenses, and so on. Marketing expenditures may lead to market concentration if they constitute a barrier to market entry. Such barriers prevent a new firm from entering a market and competing with well-entrenched firms.

There are three ways in which marketing can give firms differential advantages that may constitute a barrier to entry. First, marketers build brand loyalty by establishing strong brand names and developing close relationships between the brand name and consumers' expectations of a certain quality level. Although this relationship has not always been strongly supported by empirical data (Telser, 1964), economists argue that new competitors may find it very difficult to break the loyalty that consumers have developed to well-established brands. Loyal customers are essentially satisfied consumers, and breaking loyalty patterns is a difficult endeavor. A second way is that marketers can get preferential treatments from the advertising media that could not be obtained by a smaller newcomer. A third way is that there is a threshold effect for marketing expenditures before they can be effective. Thus, the large resources required to overcome this handicap may discourage new competitors from entering a market.

Barrier to entry eventually leads to market concentration, which means that a small number of competitors share a substantial part of the market. Market concentration leads to lower competition, especially price competition. The rationale of this assertion is that in markets that are characterized by a small number of large competitors, a price decrease initiated by any manufacturer is likely to be immediately matched by competitors. Consequently, there is no incentive to compete on prices. Lack of price competition usually means higher prices for consumers and larger profits for the manufacturer (Comanor and Wilson, 1967).

Feedback loops tend to perpetuate and even accelerate this process. Market concentration can lead to product differentiation. Because in concentrated industries firms do not compete on prices, they differentiate products that are essentially similar in their primary function. They artificially alter some secondary product attributes. From an economic point of view, product differentiation is not a bad strategy when it better serves the differentiated needs of consumers. However, if this process is pursued to an extreme, it can result in an artificial proliferation of brands.

To sum up, marketers play an essential role in our economy. They provide consumers with relevant information on a variety of goods and services that are desired by various consumer groups, at a price they can afford, and available at the place they wish to find them. Whether marketing expenses put an upward pressure on consumer prices as the result of increased distribution costs or lessened competition is still a matter of debate. Very likely, marketing does have desirable and undesirable economic effects. The real problem is to assess whether the benefits brought by marketing activities are worth the economic costs. If, as an institution, marketing wastes some economic resources, and if this can be avoided, it is up to the legislator to provide the common guidelines that will regulate marketers' activities. A large number of laws regulate markets in most countries and are designed to enhance competition. As discussed above, they set the boundaries of marketers' behavior.

3.2 Marketers' Responsibility for Adverse Social Effects

There is a high degree of subjectivity in the assessment of marketers' social responsibility, because it is related to values, lifestyles, tastes, and to preferences for social economic systems. Contradictory points of view can be quite legitimately held about the role and effects of social marketing (Andreasen, 1994), depending on one's values and views about what society should be. Some critics see marketing as a force that negatively affects values and lifestyles. Without necessarily granting such power to marketing, others deplore its polluting effects and argue that it undermines aesthetic and intellectual values.

3.2.1 Marketers' Responsibility for Selling Harmful Products

Generally, marketers have an interest to sell any product for which there is sufficient market demand and which they can supply so as to earn a profit. Because in most cases there is the economic necessity to satisfy consumers (a necessary – if not sufficient – condition to build consumer loyalty and repeat purchases), designing and selling quality products is a marketer's best interest. In this respect, the societal marketing concept is nothing but an extension of the consumer-oriented marketing concept (Crane and Desmond, 2002; Gaski, 1999).

There are some notable exceptions to the general principle. The marketing of goods like tobacco products is a case in point. It is by now well established that smoking cigarettes constitutes a health hazard. In spite of this negative impact on public health, of the warnings that manufacturers are obliged to write on cigarette packs, of the ban on cigarette advertising, of the condemnations they face in court, tobacco companies continue to satisfy consumers' demand for cigarettes. This example clearly shows that the economic system does not induce marketers to behave 'ethically.' Marketers are motivated to fulfill their economic function, be it moral or not.

This view may not be shared by everybody. Some advocates of *altruistic* marketing (Petty and Cacioppo, 1996) assert that marketers should be responsible for changing consumer attitudes toward such health hazardous behaviors like compliance to antihypertensive drugs, diet, smoking, lack of exercise, alcohol and drug abuse. No matter how socially desirable such attitude changes may be, and although marketing techniques can be effective for achieving such goals, they cannot be left to the sole marketers' responsibility. Like for ensuring market competition, it is up to the legislators to set the boundaries to permissible marketing actions. Does that mean that marketing tobacco products or drugs should be prohibited? This is a question that society, not manufacturers or marketers should answer. One should keep in mind, however, the even worse situation that prohibition had created in the US when selling alcoholic beverages was outlawed in the thirties! A blend of regulations and public authority sponsored communication campaigns have been effective at inducing drivers to wear seat belts and to avoid driving after drinking alcoholic beverages. This responsibility seems to go well beyond that of manufacturers and should be borne by political or moral authorities.

3.2.2 Marketers' Responsibility for Manipulating Consumers

Are marketers guilty of manipulating consumers? This question can be addressed from different angles. One is that marketing seeks to create needs. Another is that marketers manipulate consumers through questionable tools and techniques like motivation research or subliminal advertising. This second aspect is discussed in a latter part of this chapter.

An important ethical question is whether marketers and advertisers can create needs and induce consumers to buy products that they do not really want. Are marketers unscrupulous individuals who persuade consumers to buy, unwillingly, products and services that cannot bring them satisfaction? Fortunately, this view of marketers creating irresistible desires and changing otherwise intelligent consumers into easily manipulated robots is far removed from reality. More than eighty per cent of new products introduced into the marketplace are rejected by consumers (Bolding, Morgan and Staelin, 1997). Recent notable examples are the failures of Motorola's Iridium portable telephone system (Olson, Slater and Czaplewski, 2000) or Xerox personal computers. Analyses of these cases point to one fundamental fact: these companies tried to sell products that did not answer consumers' needs or desires at the time. If consumer needs could have been created, why would companies ever experience product failures?

The view that marketers create needs negates the very foundations of marketing. Although some critics see manufacturers as developing products and then creating a need for those products, the process works the other way around: marketers first recognize, identify, and discover unsatisfied consumer needs in order to design products and services that are wanted by and acceptable to consumers. If marketers do exert a powerful influence on consumer behavior, rather than creating needs, they stimulate existing needs or arouse needs that consumers do not feel strongly or consciously.

3.2.3 Marketers' Responsibility for Adversely Effecting Values and Lifestyles

Marketers are often accused of unduly raising the expectations of economically deprived segments of our society and of promoting materialistic values. By making consumers aware of products and services and by inducing them to buy, they encourage consumers to desire products that they would not even dream of if they were not marketed. If a consumer cannot financially afford certain products, marketers may be a cause of consumer frustration and discontent. When consumers are not affluent and must cope with many marketing stimuli, this problem is more acute. If they can afford to buy the products, critics argue that marketers foster materialism, i.e., the excessive importance given to material welfare as compared to such non material values as love, freedom, and intellectual development.

Following this line of thought, then, marketers may generate negative social effects by the mere fact of answering or stimulating 'unwarranted' consumer needs and wants. Need is an encompassing concept that covers physical as well as even more important psychological needs. In addition, needs vary in importance across individuals and cultures. What is considered a necessity by one individual may be trivia to another. A necessity in a developed economy may be luxury in a developing country. Under such circumstances, what needs are 'warranted'? As Dicksen, Kroeger and Nicosia (1983) point out, 'much of the criticism that advertising sells people things they do not need is directed more to the fact that people buy things the critic does not think they should want.' Thus, if consumers are responsible adults who should enjoy freedom of choice, this argument does not hold unless ones believes that wants are legitimate only when they originate from the individual and are not influenced by external marketing forces. In addition, one should note that people also buy products to pursue non-materialistic goals. For instance, one may purchase products as gifts to express love or esteem, or books and records for intellectual development. In our society, consumption has become one of the most natural ways by which people achieve even nonmaterial goals.

Although the argument of consumer discontent and materialism may be valid, it cannot be attributed to marketers alone. The criticism should rather be addressed to society and the economic system, which favor and rely on mass consumption. Marketing is part of the system because it is an institution designed to serve this society and this economic system. If the value system on which society is built is responsible for fostering discontent or materialism, it is useless or misleading to attack an institution that is only one of its logical consequences. The debate should focus instead on the roots of the problem rather than on its symptoms.

3.2.4 Marketers' Responsibility for Favoring Stereotypes

Advertising messages sometimes feature 'slice of life.' They picture customers in various roles and situations, as they are – or supposedly are – in their daily lives. Inasmuch as advertisers assign definite roles to various types of individuals, such as minority groups or women, it can promote or perpetuate certain stereotypes. Over the years, such minority groups (Green, 1993) as the blacks in the United States, or women have been vocal in making such accusations.

It is in the best advertisers' and marketers' interests to take those concerns into account. One might question whether advertising should promote new ideas and/or fight undesirable social stereotypes or should communicate effectively with markets. As society evolves, it is normal and probably more efficient for advertisers to picture society as it is rather than as it was, or what it should or will be. As a result, if marketers properly understand their function as serving the market, their vested interest lies in addressing consumers within their current actual contexts. Perpetuating stereotyping constitutes, not so much an ethical issue as a poor marketing practice.

3.2.5 Marketers' Responsibility for Fostering Bad Taste

Another criticism toward marketers is that they contribute to the creation and spread of bad taste in society. Obviously, not all advertising to which the public is exposed is conceived and created by responsible professionals. Some advertising is the work of individuals who have the questionable philosophy of selling at any cost. These people usually have little concern about the aesthetic value of their advertisements. A certain percentage of advertising (hopefully, a small one) falls into the latter category, but this can be sufficient to give the entire advertising industry and marketing a poor image.

Taste is relative; it varies within societies, regions, age groups, and individuals. Consequently, it may be inevitable that advertising messages are evaluated and judged differently by various segments of the market. This may be a result of imperfect segmentation (Nairn and Berthon, 2003). Because advertisers cannot perfectly match the desired target market and the media audiences, consumers may see or hear messages that are not intended for them. They may object to messages directed at market segments that would not find the message offensive.

Here again, should marketers be concerned with and try to promote good taste, or should they essentially focus on the long-run efficiency of their actions? Their task is to give consumers what they want in the most efficient and effective manner, and not to judge the quality of their tastes. Given that marketing's final objective is to satisfy consumers, marketing practices simply reflect the values and tastes of the society that it serves. Responsible marketers should try to avoid offending potential buyers, knowing that offended consumers will develop a poor image of their products and brands.

3.2.6 Marketers' Responsibility for Unduly Increasing Pollution

Marketing is omni present. The large amounts of wastes caused by used product packages certainly make a substantial contribution to environmental pollution (Hackley and Kitchen, 1999). The trend toward ecologically oriented marketing should curb this tendency in the future. In the same way, if all or part of what consumers see or hear in commercials and advertisements offend their feelings or aesthetic values, then, advertising can be considered as a polluting agent. Commercials are often criticized for being too loud, repetitive, or boring, for overusing sex or fear appeals, or emphasizing sensitive product classes, such as products that some consumers would not like to see advertised, or even talked about, for example, personal hygiene or contraceptive products.

Another form of marketing pollution happens when marketers aggressively solicit consumers for selling their products and services. They are often accused of invading consumers' privacy, a problem substantially increased with the general usage of recent electronic technologies for selling (Foxman and Kilcoyne, 1993) or carrying market research (Kozinets, 2002).

To sum up, marketers have some adverse social effects on consumer and market behaviors. These effects, however, have often been overestimated. Marketers cannot create consumer needs. At best, they can stimulate latent needs, perhaps unconsciously felt by the consumers, but they do not manipulate consumers. Whether marketing has undesirable effects on value systems, lifestyles, on social discontent, whether it is deceptive or in bad taste, or perpetuates undesirable stereotypes, are more complex issues to assess. If one excludes some individual undesirable unethical practices that are reviewed in the following section) of a small minority of marketers, marketing, as an institution, reflects, more than changes, our values, lifestyles, and cultures.

If fulfilling marketing functions of providing individuals, families, and organizational consumers and buyers with the goods and services they need and want, is 'right,' then a marketer's behavior is ethical as long as they fulfill their societal function in the most efficient manner possible, within the constraints of the laws, industry rules and regulations. It should be up to the society to provide the guidelines within which marketers should operate.

4 Marketers' Individual Responsibilities

As already mentioned, marketers may take advantage of information asymmetry to provide consumers with selective information. Such practices include deliberately providing customers with false information, inducing consumers to infer false information, retaining part or all relevant information and capitalizing on the possibility that at least some consumers will bear the risks of the transaction, providing 'irrelevant' information that may influence the consumers to purchase the supplier's products and services, take advantage of the influence process on some weaker audiences, or any combination of these activities.

4.1 Deliberately Providing Customers with False Information

The charge that marketers are dishonest and tell lies or only half-truths is often heard. Although the critics tend to put all marketing practices in the same category, several situations may be recognized. There are unfortunately cases in which some marketers are guilty of deliberately making outright lies in order to protect their own interests at the expense of those of their clients. When the Dow Corning Corporation continued to assert that their silicone gel-filled breast implants could not cause health problems, in spite of evidence they tried to conceal (Lawrence, 1993; Mascarenhas, 1995), they deliberately lied to consumers. Some unscrupulous marketers may claim that their product does things that it cannot do, or has characteristics it does not possess. In other cases, marketers may lie and pretend to carry market research in order to identify prospects with the sole objective to sell their products to the respondents (Malhotra and Miller, 1998). In such cases, there is an obvious and deliberate intent to deceive and mislead consumers to get them into buying the manufacturer's product, whether or not the product can deliver the promised satisfaction. These are clear cases of unethical marketing behavior that all professional marketers would condemn and that are also forbidden in all the ethics code to which they subscribe, in particular, the prevalent Codes of ethics of the American Marketing Association (2004) and of the Academy of Marketing Science (Ferrell, 1999; O'Boyle and Dawson, 1992).

All cases of marketers providing customers with 'half-truths' or 'false' information, however, may not always call for such a definite moral condemnation. For instance, marketers often use grossly exaggerated claims in their advertisement, which, at first glance, may be considered as outright lies. Is it unethical for marketers, for instance, to promise greater attractiveness or to hint at irresistible success with the opposite sex if their products and services are purchased and used? Marketers are often guilty of such puffery. Some critics view these as outright deceptive claims, and *stricto sensu*, they are right. It is true that marketers cannot believe in good faith that their brand of detergent can fulfill a consumer's life. The real question though, is whether people can be deceived by such claims.

Language is full of exaggeration, even if one ignores marketers' claims. Who has not been 'terribly sorry' for some cigarette ashes falling on a carpet? Or who has not expressed 'profound sympathy' for a neighbor who is experiencing some painful event? From the cards that people send to their families and friends to celebrate the main events of their lives, one can draw a good sample of dramatized overstatements and could conclude that this type of language has become part of our culture. In the same way, people have become accustomed to marketing's inflated language and have learned to somewhat discount the hyperbole that is part of advertising. Such advertisements are effective not because they slightly exaggerate, but because they appeal to the right consumers' motivation.

More questionable is the conduct of salespersons that provide customers with false information for obtaining orders, often against the will of their hierarchy. Such practices are generally not encouraged by marketers, because they run against their own interests and generally result in disenchanted and lost customers

(Chonko, Wotruba and Loe, 2002; Lagace, Dahlstrom and Gassenheimer, 1991). Interestingly, sales managers' moral philosophies do not differ significantly from other marketers (Bass, Barnett and Brown, 1998; Singhapakdi and Vitell, 1992). Ethical conflict between management and salespeople is less likely to occur when salespersons are committed to their organization, but more likely to happen when salespersons express an intention to quit (Hunt, Wood and Chonko, 1989; Schwepker, 1999). Marketers should and frequently do enforce strict policy guidelines to make sure that salespersons behave ethically with their customers as well as with their supervisors (Bellizzi and Hasty, 2001).

4.2 Deliberately Inducing Consumers to Infer False Information

Some marketers may deliberately take actions that may mislead consumers into inferring false information (Preston, 1976). Here again, there is a complete range of practices, from the most clearly dishonest to some prevalent and accepted marketing practices. A typical example falling in the former category is when oversized packages may induce consumers to believe that the package contains more product than it actually does. Another typical example of outright dishonest marketing conduct is given by marketing promotions that tend to make believe that consumers have gained an important prize, when the fine prints actually indicate that the prize will be won only after a very improbable lottery draw. Such (unfortunately too frequent) practices are unethical and are prohibited by any marketing ethics code.

Other practices, however, are well accepted and do not seem to raise ethical issues in the general public. For instance, the use of odd pricing (also called psychological pricing) is frequent and may not seem to be singled out by the critics. The idea is to price, for instance a box of cereals at 4.99 euros instead of 5.00 euros, because the consumer may (wrongly) infer that the price is 'somewhat over 4.00 euros' and consequently much cheaper than a 5.00 euros cereal box.

4.3 Deliberately Retaining Part or All Relevant Information

In this case again, there is a whole range of situations in which marketers may decide to retain part or all relevant information. This runs the gamut from the most obviously unethical marketing practice of lies by omission to the least condemnable situations, and the borderline between acceptable and unacceptable marketing practices is not always easy to draw.

At one extreme, deliberately hiding to consumers that a drug may have some serious negative side effects is a case of obvious unethical marketing practice. Unless forced to do so by the Law, no cigarette manufacturer will volunteer to tell consumers that smoking can result in lung cancer. Some may take advantage of consumers' ignorance to involve them into pyramid or multi-level schemes (Koehn, 2001). These types of business practice have been extensively used in the past. They are associated with a business philosophy known as *caveat emptor*, which means that it is up to the consumers to beware of the claims and unethical marketing practices. Needless to say that with the recent advent of market-orientation, this business philosophy may have become a practice of the past.

At the other extreme, marketers of two competitive products might both claim that that their respective products are the best or the first. Besides exaggeration, which dramatize the product and would not deceive most consumers, marketers could claim the superiority of their product by refereeing to specific functions or characteristics, or to a specific usage occasion or they could use a different product category than that used by a competitor making a similar claim. Sometimes there are subtle and very technical arguments in these claims that are impossible to explain in a short advertisement. In such cases consumers receive imperfect information, but it is impossible for advertisers in a 30-second commercial or in a half-page ad to give all the facts. Consequently, advertisers must exercise judgment as to what should be said to consumers. It is only logical that the facts or aspects of the product that give a differential advantage over competitive products will be emphasized.

In the same way, a watch manufacturer might claim that his watches are, for instance, 'unbreakable.' Such a claim seems at best an outright exaggeration. There is no such thing as an unbreakable product, provided the proper destructive means are employed. An unbreakable watch would not resist a steamroller. What the advertiser's claim generally means is that the product is unbreakable under typical and normal usage conditions. Here again, because of time and space constraints and because of the need to sustain consumers' attention and interest for extended periods, advertisers are obliged to use short-cuts that may seem to be, if not pure lies, at least overstatements or part-truths. But do consumers really need to be told that an unbreakable watch could not actually resist a steamroller?

Note that some marketers have made the 'ethical' move of telling consumers 'the whole truth.' In one of its recent advertising campaign, IKEA humorously warns consumers that they can expect long queues and lack of assistance in their stores, and makes fun of the hassle of self-assembly. Similar policies have been followed by Guinness and Skoda with some success (Halls, 2000).

4.4 Deliberately Collecting and Using 'Intimate' or 'Irrelevant' Information

Marketers may collect and use 'too intimate', or provide consumers with 'irrelevant' information, in order to better influence consumers to purchase their products and services. A moot point over which has evolved much of the controversy is what constitutes 'relevant' information.

4.4.1 Taking Advantage of 'Intimate' Consumer Knowledge

Some critics object to the fact that marketers collect and use quite intimate knowledge of consumers and consumer behavior in order to be in a position to better influence them, sometimes against their 'true' will. During the fifties, under the lead of Ernest Dichter (1962), motivation research was used to reveal motives buried in consumers' subconscious minds. This was the time when such authors as John Galbraith (1969) or Vance Packard (1957) vigorously attacked marketers for manipulating consumers though identification and usage of 'their points of vulnerability':

> People's surface desires, needs, and drives were probed in order to find their points of vulnerability. Among the surface motivating factors found in the emotional profile of most of us, for example, were the drive to conformity, need for oral stimulation, yearning for security. Once these points of vulnerability were isolated, the psychological hooks were fashioned and baited and placed deep in the merchandising sea for unwary prospective customers (Packard, 1957).

More recently, Ziems (2004) advocates the use of morphological psychology to understand the underlying motivating forces behind brand and product purchase decisions. According to this author, the basic idea consists of revealing the hidden symbolic meaning of products. As a result, marketers should advertise one single proposition that conveys one 'core feeling' of 'emotional value' that accounts for the complex psychological mechanisms that create such emotional values.

In order to achieve such intimate consumer knowledge, the tools and techniques at the disposal of marketers are far from perfect. Even if properly used, they have only a limited effect. Assuming that marketers could arrive at such intimate knowledge of consumers, they still lack the ability to translate this knowledge into effective and manipulative advertisements and promotions. As discussed above, manipulating consumers should not be part of the moral objectives of marketers. But would they wish to do so through motivation analyses, their power remains extremely limited.

4.4.2 Appealing to Emotions

Those who contend that marketers manipulate often point at the extensive use advertisers make of emotional appeals (Hyman, 1990), especially for household or beauty care products. They imply that advertising should use only rational appeals, such as economy, or provide consumers with objective information about the physical characteristics of the product. The problem, however, is not as clear cut as it may appear at first glance. A marketer faced with the problem of advertising a beauty care or grooming product, could advertise the product's price, its chemical ingredients, or any other objective characteristic of the product. But how would that relate to the real motives of most people when they make such purchase decisions? Most buyers use beauty care or grooming products in order to look attractive, to feel better, or for other emotional reasons.

When marketers promise people that they will look more attractive if they use the advertised brand, they attempt to use the same language the consumers probably use when they contemplate making such purchases. Consumers are known to make choices and purchase choices (and the more so for products and services that have strong psychological and social meanings), by using a large number of criteria and dimensions, emotional as well as economic and objective. What economists and social critics label 'emotional appeal' is what marketers view as making sales presentations that use the consumers' logic and language. For marketers, even highly emotional motives are considered rational, because buyer behavior is rational behavior: it always result from consumers' logic. Is the position of such critics, who deny consumers' rationality to anyone who does not use their own value judgments and behavior standards, more ethical than that of marketers, who abide to consumers' logic?

Fear appeals, however, a special case of emotional appeals, raise specific ethical concerns (Duke *et al.*, 1993). Fear appeals for changing attitudes and behaviors rely on the theory of cognitive dissonance (Festinger, 1957). The rationale is to dramatize the negative consequences that will result from not using a product or from using a brand different from the manufacturer's one. In so doing, consumers are plunged into a state of cognitive dissonance by more or less artificially creating a gap between the current situation and the envisioned situation. The objective is to induce the consumer to reduce this gap by avoiding the worst situation by buying the product. Messages that arouse the highest level of anxiety seem to be the most effective, provided that the communicator can suggest a convincing and plausible solution to reduce their anxiety (Hovland, Janis, and Kelly, 1953).

Note that according to the theory, consumers may also react by rejecting the information. This may also explain why the effects produced by a message based on fear and anxiety related inversely to the intensity of the fear aroused in the subjects (Janis and Fishback, 1953).

4.5 Deliberately Abusing of Influence Processes

4.5.1 Unduly Influencing Disadvantaged Markets

Other important ethical questions relate to the deliberate abuse by marketers of influence processes at their advantage (Truly Sauter and Oretskin, 1997). In certain occasions, marketers might address more gullible target audiences such as children. Marketers might induce children to desire objects that parents cannot afford or may not wish to give them. This has been an increasing concern with the large penetration of television and cable TV in homes throughout Europe, and with the higher number of viewing hours by children. The same phenomenon in North America has led countries like the United States and Canada (province of Quebec) to pass laws forbidding advertising directed to children.

The underlying ethical issue is whether it is appropriate to advertise to children if it is proved that they are audiences overly susceptible to persuasion. One cannot doubt of the effectiveness of advertising to children. It has been showed that toy advertising influenced children's choices, especially during the Christmas season (Tannenbaum, 1956; Rigaux-Bricmont, 1982). These effects, however, are relatively limited. Advertising increased by only five per cent the quantity of toys and games chosen by children as Christmas presents (only for those items that were heavily advertised during the Christmas season). Interestingly, the increase was not related to the children's age. Empirical evidence suggests that the effects of advertising on children may have been overestimated because children develop skeptical attitudes and defense mechanisms against advertising messages at an early age.

A related question is whether children exert pressure on parents, and whether parents do give in. One study found only slight correlation between five to ten year olds' attempts at exerting influence and the actual instances in which parents have given in to such pressure, when the age factor was not considered (Katz and Lazarfeld, 1955). However, when age is considered, it was found that children's attempts to pressure parents decrease with age, and the instances in which parents give in increase with age. This phenomenon seems quite normal since parents lend more judgment to their children as they grow older (Katz, 1957). Parents often give in to their child's preferences when they lack other criteria on which to base their decision.

Most studies in this area tend to show that children are generally not gullible agents working unknowingly for the marketer, who are used by marketers to influence parents. Children usually have more judgment than some people think. They show interest in advertisements directed at adults when they are concerned about the advertised product, and they can remember the product brands much better than their parents can (Carlson, 1956).

4.5.2 Using Questionable Methods

Marketers have been charged to use more or less questionable techniques such as motivation research (see above), subliminal advertising, or high-pressure selling techniques.

Subliminal Advertising. An important debate is to what extent advertisers can influence subjects without their being consciously aware that they have been exposed to information. Can a communication be effective when it is received by subjects at such a high speed that it falls below their perceptual threshold? Psychologists call this phenomenon subliminal perception. For advertisers, the problem is to assess whether subliminal advertising, which delivers advertisements so quickly that subjects cannot consciously perceive them, is effective in influencing consumers. Although early experiments suggested a strong effectiveness of subliminal advertisements (Dember, 1961), subsequent studies failed to confirm these results. Experiments in psychology have shown that subjects' perceptual defenses are still operative, even at levels lower than their perceptual threshold (McGuinnies, 1949). At the extreme, when no perception is possible, the message has no effects whatsoever (Voor, 1956). Irrespective of the ethical issues involved, the power of subliminal advertising for triggering purchases from consumers is at least doubtful (Moore, 1982). In any case, needless to say that subliminal advertising is banned by all codes of advertising ethics.

High-Pressure Selling. Sometimes, salespersons are trained and induced to engage in high-pressure selling, especially when they sell directly to the general public such products as encyclopedias, life insurances, or properties. As discussed before, salespersons behave sometimes unethically (Abratt and Penman, 2002) and pressure people into buying products or services that they had not planned before, without leaving consumers the time to think over the opportunity of making such purchases. For some time, marketing ethics researchers have studied salespeople's ethical behavior (Chonko, Tanner, and Weeks, 1996), and how sales managers cope with unethical practices (Bellizzi, 1995; Bellizzi and Hasty, 2001). They have found that salespeople's ethical behavior leads to higher customer satisfaction, trust, and loyalty to the firm (Romàn, 2003). In addition, salespersons are generally eager to receive more guidance from management than they are currently receiving concerning their ethical situations they face in the field (Dubinsky *et al.*, 1992). Here again is an area of intervention for legislators for protecting consumers against high pressure selling from unethical marketers. In many countries like France, consumers are left a few days' period after the order has been signed during which they can cancel their purchase.

5 Conclusion

To this chapter's title question (i.e., is ethical marketing a myth?), the preceding analyses suggest that there may not be a clear cut answer. Marketers fulfill an essential and important economic function in our society. To do so, they are essentially motivated by their own interests, which, especially in the short-run, do not necessarily match those of the consumers or those of a free market economy. They have at their disposal tools and techniques the power of which is usually more limited than the general public believes. In many cases, there is no built-in mechanism that ensures that marketers should behave ethically. As a result, it is up to society itself to ensure moral marketers' conduct by providing the legal boundaries within which they should operate. Some authors notice that ethical marketing guidelines are limited to obey the law and to act in the marketers' best self-interest (Gaski, 1999). Others state that this may not be sufficient (Hodgson, 2001) and point at cases where ethics, the law, and self-interest are inconsistent (Smith, 2001).

Even if many of their tools and techniques are limited, marketers still have the means to engage in unethical behaviors through managing information asymmetry with customers in their own interest. Tools and techniques (marketing or otherwise) have no moral or ethical connotation *per se* because they are not actions, conducts, or behaviors. Only human beings can make ethical or unethical usage of the techniques and tools at their disposal. A hammer has no ethical value *per se*. It can be involved into quite ethical or unethical behaviors depending upon whether it is used to build a house for the poor or smash the head of a passer-by in order to steal him. The same applies to marketers and their tool kits.

Although the laws, regulations, or professional codes of ethics provide useful guidelines for marketers to follow, this is by no means sufficient. Many actions that marketers must take have ethical aspects that sometimes are clearly covered by professional standards, but sometimes not. Only a high sense of moral values and personal ethical standards can guide marketing actions in the latter cases. Depending on how one sees such ethical conscience as becoming prevalent in the marketing profession, one can answer the question of whether ethical marketing will remain a myth or become a reality.

References

Abratt, R. and Penman, N. (2002), Understanding Factors Affecting Salespeople's Perceptions of Ethical Behavior in South Africa, *Journal of Business Ethics*, 35, pp. 269-280.

Abratt, R. and Sacks, D. (1988), The Marketing Challenge: Towards Being Profitable and Socially Responsible, *Journal of Business Ethics*, 7, pp. 497-507.

American Marketing Association (2004), www.marketingpower.com/mg-dictionary-view1862.php?

Andreasen, A. R. (1994), Social Marketing: Its Definition and Domain, *Journal of Public Policy and Marketing*, 13, pp. 108-114.

Backman, J. (1967), Advertising and Competition, New York University Press.

Bass, K., Barnett, T. and Brown, G. (1998), The Moral Philosophy of Sales Managers and Its Influence on Ethical Decision Making, *Journal of Personal Selling and Sales Management*, 18, pp. 1-17.

Bellizzi, J. A. (1995), Committing and Supervising Unethical Sales Force Behavior: The Effects of Victim Gender, Victim Status, and Sales Force Motivational Techniques, *Journal of Personal Selling and Sales Management*, 15, pp. 1-15.

Bellizzi, J. A. and Hasty, R. W. (2001), The Effects of a Stated Organizational Policy on Inconsistent Disciplinary Action Based on salesperson Gender and Weight, *Journal of Personal Selling and Sales Management*, 21, pp. 189-198.

Bellizzi, J. A. and Hite, R. E. (1989), Supervising Unethical Salesforce Behavior, *Journal of Marketing*, 53, pp. 36-47.

Boatright, John R. (2003), Ethics and the Conduct of Business, 4th ed., New Jersey: Prentice-Hall.

Bolding, W., Morgan, R. and Staelin, R. (1997), Pulling the Plug to Stop the New Product Drain, *Journal of Marketing Research*, 34, pp. 164-176.

Brinkmann, J. (2002), Business and Marketing Ethics as Professional Ethics: Concepts, Approaches and Typologies, *Journal of Business Ethics*, 41, pp. 159-177.

Buckley, N. (2000), New Tobacco Regulations on Heath Supported, *Financial Times*, June 15, p. 10.

Carlson, E. R. (1956), Attitude Change Through Modification of Attitude Structure, *Journal of Abnormal and Social Psychology*, 52, 256-261.

Chonko, L. B. and Hunt, S. C. (1985), Ethics and Marketing Management: An Empirical Investigation, *Journal of Business Research*, 13, pp. 339-359.

Chonko, L. B., Tanner, J. F. and Weeks, W.A. (1996), Ethics in Salesperson Decision Making: A Synthesis of Research Approaches and an Extension of the Scenario Method, *Journal of Personal Selling and Sales Management*, 16, pp. 35-52.

Chonko, L. B., Wotruba, T. R. and Loe T. W. (2002), Direct Selling Ethics at the Top: An Industry Audit and Status Report, *Journal of Personal Selling and Sales Management*, 22, pp. 87-95.

Comanor, W. S. and Wilson T.A. (1967), Advertising, Market Structure, and Performance, *Review of Economics and Statistics*, 49, pp. 423-440.

Crane, A. and Desmond, J. (2002), Societal Marketing and Morality, *European Journal of Marketing*, 36, pp. 548-570.

Dember, W. N. (1961), *The Psychology of Perfection*, New York: Holt, Rinehart and Winston.

Dichter, E. (1962), The World Customer, *Harvard Business Review*, 40, pp. 87-98.

Dirksen, C. J., Kroeger, A. and Nicosia, F. M. (1983), *Advertising Management*, Homewood, Ill., Richard Irwin.

Dubinsky, A. J., Jolson, M. A., Michaels, R. E., Kotabe, M. and Lim, C. U. (1992), Ethical Perceptions of Field Sales Personnel: An Empirical Assessment, *Journal of Personal Selling and Sales Management*, 12, pp. 9-21.

Duke, C. R., Pickett, G. M., Carlson, L. and Grove, S. J. (1993), A Method for Evaluating the Ethics of Fear Appeals, *Journal of Public Policy and Marketing*, 12, pp. 120-129.

Dunfee, T. W., Smith, N. C. and Ross, W.T. (1999), Social Contract and Marketing Ethics, *Journal of Marketing*, 63, pp. 14-32.

Encyclopedia Britannica (2004), www.britannica.com/dictionary?book=Dictionary&va= ethics&vao.

Farris, P. W. and Albion P. A. (1980), The Impact of Advertising on the Price of Consumer Products, *Journal of Marketing*, 44, pp. 17-35.

Farris, P. W. and Reibstein, D.J. (1979), How Prices, Ad Expenditures, and Profits Are Linked, *Harvard Business Review*, 57, pp. 173-184.

Ferrell, O. C. (1999), An Assessment of the Proposed Academy of Marketing Science Code of Ethics for Marketing Educators, *Journal of Business Ethics*, 19, pp. 225-228.

Ferrell, O. C. and Gresham, L. G. (1985), A Contingency Framework for Understanding Ethical Decision Making in Marketing, *Journal of Marketing*, 49, pp. 87-96.

Ferrell, O. C., Gresham, L. G. and Fraedrich, J. (1989), A Synthesis of Ethical Decision Models for Marketing, *Journal of Macromarketing*, 9, pp. 55-64.

Festinger, L. (1957), *A Theory of Cognitive Dissonance*, Stanford, CA, Stanford University Press.

Foxman, E. R. and Kilcoyne, P. (1993), Information Technology, Marketing Practice, and Consumer Privacy: Ethical Issues, *Journal of Public Policy and Marketing*, 12, pp. 106-119.

Galbraith, J. K. (1969), *The Affluent Society*, Boston, Houghton-Mifflin.

Gaski, J. F. (1999), Does Marketing Ethics Really Have Anything to Say? – A Critical Inventory of the Literature, *Journal of Business Ethics*, 18, pp. 315-334.

Green, M. K. (1993), Images of Native Americans in Advertising: Some Moral Issues, *Journal of Business Ethics*, 12, pp. 323-330.

Gundlach, G. T. and Murthy, P. E. (1993), Ethical and Legal Foundations of Relational Marketing Exchanges, *Journal of Marketing*, 57, pp. 35-46.

Hackley, C. E. and Kitchen, P. J. (1999), Ethical Perspectives on the Postmodern Communications Leviathan, *Journal of Business Ethics*, 20, pp. 15-26.

Halls, E. (2000), Roll Up to the Truth Zone, *The Times*, July 7, p. 30.

Hartman, C. L. and Beck-Dudley, C. L. (1999), Marketing Strategies and the Search for Virtue: A Case Analysis of the Body Shop, International, *Journal of Business Ethics*, 20, pp. 249-263.

Hodgson, B. J. (2001), Can the Beast be Tamed?: Reflections on John McMurty's Unequal Freedoms: The Global Market as an Ethical System, *Journal of Business Ethics*, 33, pp. 71-78.

Honeycutt, E. D., Glassman, M., Zugelder, M. T. and Karande, K. (2001), Determinants of Ethical Behavior: A Study of Autosalespeople, *Journal of Business Ethics*, 32, pp. 69-79.

Hovland, C. I., Janis, I. L. and Kelly, H. H. (1953), *Communication and Persuasion*, New Haven, Yale University Press.

Hunt, S. D. and Vasquez-Parraga, A. (1993), Organizational Consequences, Marketing Ethics, and Salesforce Supervision, *Journal of Marketing Research*, 30, pp. 78-90.

Hunt, S. D. and Vitell, S. (1986), A General Theory of Marketing Ethics, *Journal of Macromarketing*, 6, pp. 5-16.

Hunt, S. D., Wood, V. R. and Chonko, L. B. (1989), Corporate Ethical Values and Organizational Commitment in Marketing, *Journal of Marketing*, 53, pp. 79-90.

Hyman, M. R. (1990), The Ethics of Psychoactive Ads, *Journal of Business Ethics*, 9, pp. 105-114.

Janis, I. L. and Fishback, S. (1953), Effects of Fear-Arousing Communication, *Journal of Abnormal and Social Psychology*, 48, pp. 78-92.

Katz, E. (1957), The Two-Step Flow of Communication: An Up-to-Date Report on an Hypothesis, *Public Opinion Quarterly*, 21, pp. 61-78.

Katz, E. and Lazarfeld, P. E. (1955), *Personal Influence: The Part Played by People in the Flow of Mass Communication*, Glencoe, Ill., Free Press.

Koehn, D. (2001), Ethical Issues Connected with Multi-Level Marketing Schemes, *Journal of Business Ethics*, 29, pp. 153-160.

Kozinets, R. V. (2002), The Field Behind the Screen: Using Netnography for Marketing Research in Online Communities, *Journal of Marketing Research*, 39, pp. 61-72.

Laczniak, G. R. (1993), Marketing Ethics: Onward Toward Greater Expectations, *Journal of Public Policy and Marketing*, 12, pp. 91-96.

Laczniak, G. R. and Murphy, P. E. (1993), *Ethical Marketing Decisions: The Higher Road*, Needham Heights, MA, Allyn and Bacon.

Lagace, R. R., Dahlstrom, R. and Gassenheimer, J. B. (1991), The Relevance of Ethical Salesperson Behavior on Relationship Quality: The Pharmaceutical Industry, *Journal of Personal Selling and Sales Management*, 11, pp. 39-47.

Lawrence, A. T. (1993), Dow Corning and the Silicone Brest Implant Controversy, *Case Research Journal*, 13, pp. 87-112.

Lund, D. B. (2000), An Empirical Examination of Marketing Professionals' Ethical Behavior in Differing Situations, *Journal of Business Ethics*, 24, pp. 331-342.

Malhotra, N. K. and Miller, G.L. (1998), An Integrated Model for Ethical Decisions in Marketing Research, *Journal of Business Ethics*, 17, pp. 263-280.

Mann, H. M., Henning, J. A. and Meeham, J. W. (1967), Advertising and Concentration: An Empirical Investigation, *Journal of Industrial Economics*, 16, pp. 34-45.

Mascarenhas, O. A. J. (1995), Exonerating Unethical Marketing Executive Behavior: A Diagnostic Framework, *Journal of Marketing*, 59, pp. 43-57.

McGuinnies, E. (1949), Emotionality and Perceptual Defense, *Psychological Review*, 56, pp. 244-251.

McMurtry, J. (1997), The Contradictions of Free Market Doctrine: Is There a Solution? *Journal of Business Ethics*, 16, pp. 645-662.

Moore, T. E. (1982), Subliminal Advertising: What You See Is What You Get, *Journal of Advertising*, 46. pp. 27-47.

Nairn, A. and Berthon, P. (2003), Creating the Customer: The Influence of Advertising on Consumer Market Segments – Evidence and Ethics, *Journal of Business Ethics*, 42, pp. 83-100.

O'Boyle, E. J. and Dawson, L. E. (1992), The American Marketing Association Code of Ethics: Instructions for Marketers, *Journal of Business Ethics*, 11, pp. 921-932.

Olson, E., Slater, S. and Czaplewski, A. (2000), The Iridium Story: A Marketing Disconnect? *Marketing Management*, 9, pp. 54-57.

Packard, V. (1957), *The Hidden Persuaders*, New York, Pocket Books.

Petty, R. E. and Cacioppo, J. T. (1996), Guest Editorial: Addressing Disturbing and Disturbed Consumer Behavior: Is it Necessary to Change the Way We Conduct Behavioral Science? *Journal of Marketing Research*, 33, pp. 1-8.

Preston, I. L. (1976), A Comment on 'Defining Misleading Advertising' and Deception in Advertising, *Journal of Marketing*, 40, pp. 54-60.

Preston, L. E. (1968), Advertising Effect and Public Policy, *Proceedings of the AMA 1968 Fall Conference*, Chicago, American Marketing Association, pp. 563-564.

Ricks, J. and Fraedrich, J. (1999), The Paradox of Machiavellianism May Make for Productive Sales but Poor Management Reviews, *Journal of Business Ethics*, 20, pp. 197-205.

Rigaux-Bricmont, B. (1982), Structure des Attitudes du Consommateur à l'Égard des Sources d'Information qui l'Entourent, Laroche, M. (ed.), *Marketing*, Administrative Sciences Association of Canada, 3, pp. 263-275.

Robin, D. P. and Reidenbach, R. E. (1987), Social Responsibility, Ethics, and Marketing Strategy: Closing the Gap Between Concept and Application, *Journal of Marketing*, 51, pp. 44-58.

Robin, D. P. and Reidenbach, R. E. (1993), Searching for a Place to Stand: Toward a Workable Ethical Philosophy for Marketing, *Journal of Public Policy and Marketing*, 12, pp. 97-105.

Romàn, S. (2003), The Impact of Ethical Sales Behavior on Customer Satisfaction, Trust and Loyalty to the Company: An Empirical Study in the Financial Services Industry, *Journal of Marketing Management*, 19, pp. 915-940.

Schwepker, C. H. (1999), The Relationship Between Etical Conflict, Organizational Commitment and Turnover Intentions in the Salesforce, *Journal of Personal Selling and Sales Management*, 19, pp. 43-49.

Singhapakdi, A., Karande, K., Rao, C. P. and Vitell, S. J. (2001), How Important Are Ethics and Social Responsibility? A Multinational Study of Marketing Professionals, *European Journal of Marketing*, 35, pp. 133-154.

Singhapakdi, A. and Vitell, S. J. (1991), Analyzing the Ethical Decision Making of Sales Professionals, *Journal of Personal Selling and Sales Management*, 11, pp. 1-12.

Singhapakdi, A. and Vitell, S. J. (1992), Marketing Ethics: Sales Professionals Versus Other Marketing Professionals, *Journal of Personal Selling and Sales Management*, 12, pp. 27-38.

Singhapakdi, A., Vitell, S. J., Rao, C. P. and Kurtz, D. L. (1999), Ethics Gap: Comparing Marketers with Consumers on Important Determinants of Ethical Decision-Making, *Journal of Business Ethics*, 21, pp. 317-328.

Smith, A. P. and Young, J. A. (1999), How Now, Mad-Cow? Consumer Confidence and Source Credibility during the 1996 BSE Scare, *European Journal of Marketing*, 33, pp. 1107-1123.

Smith, N. C. (2001), Ethical Guidelines for Marketing Practice: A Reply to Gaski and Some Observations on the Role of Normative Marketing Ethics, *Journal of Business Ethics*, 32, pp. 3-18.

Smith, N. C., Thomas, R. J. and Quelch, J. A. (1996), A Strategic Approach to Managing Product Recalls, *Harvard Business Review*, 74, pp. 102-112.

Sparks, J. R. and Hunt, S. D. (1998), Marketing Researcher Ethical Sensitivity: Conceptualization, Measurement, and Exploratory Investigation, *Journal of Marketing*, 62, pp. 92-109.

Tannenbaum, P. H. (1956), Initial Attitude Toward Source and Concept as Factors in Attitude Change Through Communication, *Public Opinion Quarterly*, 20, pp. 413-425.

Telser, L. G. (1964), Advertising and Competition, *Journal of Political Economy*, 72, pp. 537-562.

Thompson, C. J. (1995), A Contextualist Proposal for the Conceptualization and Study of Marketing Ethics, *Journal of Public Policy and Marketing*, 14, pp. 177-191.

Truly Sauter, E. and Oretskin, N. A. (1997), Tobacco Targeting: The Ethical Complexity of Marketing to Minorities, *Journal of Business Ethics*, 16, pp. 1011-1017.

Tsalikis, J. and Fritzsche, D. J. (1989), Business Ethics: A Literature Review with a Focus on Marketing Ethics, *Journal of Business Ethics*, 8, pp. 695-743.

Vermillion, L. J., Lassar, W. M. and Winsor, R. D. (2002), The Hunt-Vitell General Theory of Marketing Ethics: Can it Enhance our Understanding of Principal-Agent Relationships in Channels of Distribution? *Journal of Business Ethics*, 41, pp. 267-285.

Voor, H. (1956), Subliminal Perception and Subception, *Journal of Psychology*, 41, pp. 437-458.

Williams, O. F. and Murphy, P.E. (1990), The Ethics of Virtue: A Moral Theory for Marketing, *Journal of Macromarketing*, 10, pp. 19-29.

Wotruba, T. R. (1990), A Comprehensive Framework for the Analysis of Ethical Behavior, With a Focus on Sales Organizations, *Journal of Personal Selling and Sales Management*, 10, pp. 29-42.

Ziems, D. (2004), The Morphological Approach for Unconscious Consumer Motivation Research, *Journal of Advertising Research*, 44, pp. 210-215.

Chapter 11

Firms and the Environment: Ethics or Incentives?

André Fourçans

1 Introduction[1]

In a capitalist system, can we expect firms to take into consideration the social environment in which they operate, and the environment *per se*, in their decision making process? If not, should we appeal to the moral values of managers to satisfy social and environmental needs? Or should we set up the right institutional structure so as for firms and managers to strive also for the satisfaction of these needs? In other words, should we rely on 'ethics' or 'incentives' to reach desired social goals, and, more specifically, not to pollute or to clean the environment?

Needless to say, the answers given to these questions are of paramount importance not only for society as a whole, but also to define the proper role of individuals, firms and the government in order to satisfy both economic and environmental (social) objectives.

The view of this chapter is that in general incentives dominate ethics as a means of economic and social organization. After studying the meaning of the so-called social responsibility of the firm, and the on-going debate between economists and moral philosophers that follows, we show that their respective perception of man is at the heart of the dispute (Section 2). This conceptual background being established, we analyze the misunderstandings occurring between economists and environmentalists with respect to cost-benefit analyses and, more generally, with respect to the role of the market and government in dealing with the subject matter (Section 3). Based on this analysis it is possible to investigate and evaluate the main types of environmental policies, be they market-based or not, and their impact on firms' behavior (Section 4). Finally, our conclusion recaptures the main arguments of our thesis (Section 5).

---

[1] This chapter benefited from helpful comments, especially from M. Fratianni, E. Izsak-Niimura and R. Vranceanu.

2 Is there such a Thing as the 'Social Responsibility' of the Firm?

2.1 The Economist and the Moral Philosopher

'Is there such a thing as the "social responsibility" of the firm?' Asking such a question, in such a manner, can be seen as provocative. 'Of course, corporations have a wide ranging set of social responsibilities' would be the answer of the vast majority of the population, except may be for some greedy and heartless executives or no less heartless economists. Yet the 'right' answer is not as obvious as it would appear at first sight.

No one, be they workers, customers, suppliers, shareholders or citizens, would contend that firms do not have an impact on the environment in the widest meaning of the word, *via* the pollution created by such firms. No one would deny that. But that is not the real issue. The real issue is whether firms should take into consideration *explicitly* and *purposely* these factors in the conduct of their activities. In other words, the question is whether the role of corporations is to simply maximize profits (or wealth value), thereby serve shareholders direct interests, or take a broader more proactive role in dealing with major social problems, the environment being one, and not the least important.

This debate is not new. For several decades now corporate social responsibility has been advocated for by many, demanding that corporations recognize their responsibility to society and deal with social problems such as poverty or unemployment, and more recently the environment. Nowadays it is safe to assume that the importance of firms' influence vis-a-vis these problems is almost unanimously accepted. But should firms, and more precisely their managers, take such objectives as a behavioral background in their decision-making process? If the answer to this question were 'yes', the managers and their firms would behave 'ethically.' Otherwise they would not.

The moral philosopher, essentially concerned with ethical behavior *per se*, would give an affirmative answer to the above question. The economist is more hesitant and careful in his answer. He does not want to engage in an endless philosophical debate about what is or what is not ethical (which does not mean he is not concerned with ethics, but, as such consideration barely belongs to his scientific tool box he prefers, as a professional, to remain on the sidelines of such debate), but seeks to define the proper role of the firm in a market system. He knows that *under certain conditions* – the 'rules of the game' –, by having its self-interest as an objective, as narrow as it may appear to other social scientists or to the population at large, a firm may behave in a 'social way.' And more, self-interest would be the *best* way to reach the desired social results. To paraphrase Adam Smith's famous sentence about the butcher, brewer and baker providing our dinner, if we want social results such as a clean environment, let us address ourselves not to the ethics of the managers, 'but to their self-love and never talk to them about our necessity but of their advantages.'

To be more explicit, contrary to what many seem to believe, it is wrong to consider that economists do not take into consideration the social responsibility of the firm when they contend, as in the Classical view of the firm (see for example

Friedman, 1962), that the latter must only strive for economic objectives such as profits. They are not 'heartless' or 'socially irresponsible' or 'unethical', they just consider that the best way for firms to help solve the more general social problems is, always under certain conditions (we will come back to these later), to focus on economic targets.[2] The favorable consequences for the environment will emerge as a collateral benefit. Hence, managers and the firms they manage would not be explicitly ethical in the moral meaning of the word, and one would not have to appeal to their moral sentiments to solve social problems such as pollution; yet their actions would be ethical as far as they *lead* to ethical outcomes. Without elaborating on the respective moral value of intentions *versus* deeds, suffice to say that we face what seems to be a thick wall of bricks between the views of the economist and those of the moral philosopher as to the social responsibility of the firm. For the economist the socially responsible firm is not judged in function of the 'good sentiments', the preannounced explicitly ethical behavior of its managers, but with respect to its social *results* regardless of the moral judgment one could draw as to its managers' behavior. If good sentiments lead to the worsening of pollution, for example, could one judge the managers' behavior as ethical? 'The road to hell is paved with good intentions' said the philosopher... Which does not necessarily mean that bad intentions or explicit unethical behavior would automatically pave the road to heaven on earth either!

Another issue must be raised: how to entangle 'ethical' behavior from 'self-interested' behavior? When firms make contributions to community organizations, or cultural groups, or compensate citizens for the inconvenience of the pollution they generate, or spend money to decrease such pollution, do they do that in order to behave ethically or to maximize their long-run profits, i.e., their self-interest, as far as they receive over time more benefits from this behavior? Difficult indeed to give an answer to this type of question. But is such an answer relevant? 'Not at all' says the economist, since the 'ethical' *result* is satisfied, that is all that counts as far as society's welfare is concerned. In other words, since the days of Mandeville and Smith the economist is cautious of 'private virtues' – such as ethics – as a means to reach 'social virtues', because he knows how complex social problems are. And how the exercise of private virtues may lead to 'public vices' and to perverse side effects. And how the announced use of these private virtues can be a disguised way of maximizing one's self-interest (see for example on the subject of altruism and social efficiency: Barro, 1974; Becker, 1976, 1981; Phelps, 1975; Cahuc and Kempf, 2000).

2.2 The Economic versus the Sociological Man

The above considerations boil down to the view of man and of the 'good' social

---

[2]   Adam Smith, himself a professor of moral philosophy, argued that selfish interest such as profits yield good (ethical?) outcome. The zero excess profits of perfect competition constitutes good (ethical?) outcome. As we will see, market failures pose problems, but ethics, just like markets and governments, may also fail. This is part of the historical background of economics.

order, i.e., the incentive structure that can be derived so as to maximize human and social welfare.

Seeking to solve environmental problems by appealing to the ethical behavior of firms is based upon a sociological model of man (Brunner and Mekling, 1977). First, it considers that a firm exists in itself like a single body rather than as an organization which is the result of individuals' behaviors interacting within a set of constraints and incentives created within and outside the organization. Second, with such a view the behavior of man 'is a product of his cultural environment ... and is determined by acculturation' (Meckling, 1975). Said otherwise, with this model of man, there is no room, or very little, for adaptive creativity, or for evaluating responses to incentives. This model attributes a crucial significance to the exogenous existence of social values and social norms such as ethics. These values and norms establish the social order independently of individuals.

The economist has a different perception of man, the basic outline going back to the Scottish philosophers (Mandeville, Ferguson and Smith). Man is viewed as a resourcefully groping, coping and evaluating maximizer. He is foremost an evaluator, his evaluation taking into consideration the context of his actions, that is the set of constraints, incentives and social norms to which he is subjected. But contrary to the sociological man he evaluates these various factors according to *his own* objectives and interests rather than just reacting passively to social norms (among them, ethics). In the R.E.M.M (Resourceful, Evaluating, Maximizing Man) model, man appears as responding to incentives and stimuli, some of these being associated with institutional arrangements surrounding him. This man's behavior is thus the consequence of interaction between the individual's value system and constraints or opportunities. And the role of these constraints and opportunities (the incentive system) in his behavioral changes dominate the role of the value system (the so-called 'preferences' for the economist). To induce a change in man's behavior one must alter the incentive structure (constraints and opportunities) rather than the value structure.

To avoid any misunderstanding one must emphasize the fact that the REMM view does *not* consider that preferences (values, ethics) do not have an impact on individual behavior. This view merely contends that *changes* in behavior depend more on *changes* in the costs and benefits, in the wide meaning of these words, associated with one's behavior than on *changes* in the value system. And that changes in the costs and benefits are easier and quicker to implement than changes in values. In other words, this view of man does not deny the role of values, here the role of ethics, in striving for the solution to society's problems, but maintains that changing the incentive structure is a more operational and more efficient route to get desired results.[3] The economist, the main proponent of this view, does not

---

[3]   Some, such as Jenkins (1998, p. 154), go as far as proposing a rejection of the Cultural Western heritage with its 'environmentally destructive tendencies in sciences, economics and public policy', in favor of traditional Chinese culture supposedly more in harmony with contemporary environmental ideals. Without entering an analysis of this question, and even by admitting the value of this cultural change, if one must wait for such a

believe that changing the nature of man, i.e., having a more ethical man, is the most efficient way to solve social problems such as pollution. Again, that does not mean that ethical considerations should be outright discarded but that they are superseded, in terms of social efficiency, by the incentive system.[4] Waiting for the 'new man' to solve problems is a very inefficient and lengthy process, indeed may be an infinitely long route to bring about desired social results. Not to mention other perverse and unexpected effects that may be the outcome of such strategy. History speaks for itself on this matter...

This approach can be frustrating for the moral philosopher seeking correlation between consequences of human behavior and intentions, and looking for an explicit ethical behavior of managers aimed at social (environmental) responsibility. From the economic point of view (the REMM model), it is not the 'good' intentions, the 'ethical' intentions, the 'moral quality' that count but the 'good' desired results and the efficiency through which these results are achieved. Hence different analyses of the market system and, more generally, of the institutional structure best capable of leading to socially defendable results. And more specifically to a good quality of the environment.

Said differently, the economist considers the achievements of the desired social (environmental) results in an efficient way, whatever the explicit intentions behind businessmen's behavior, of a higher ethical value than getting a lower level of social results (or even none) by having a so-called 'ethical' background of behavior. He prefers the ethics of results to the ethics of intentions.

These differences explain a great deal the difficulties economists face being understood by, and communicating with, even well-meaning moral philosophers and environmentalists.

3 Misunderstandings between Economists and Environmentalists

3.1 Cost-benefit Analysis and Ethics

Proponents of the economic approach to environmental problems also insist on the need for cost-benefit analyses as a decision-making tool necessary to evaluate in a systematic way the consequences of different courses of actions, with the trade-offs and constraints involved. With all the misunderstandings so created between economists and traditional environmentalists.

---

revolution to happen in order to solve our environmental problems, can one be really sure that in between now and then the earth will still exist?!

[4] This view is in the same vein as in Norcia and Tigner (2000, p. 3) who argue that 'business practices involve multiple motives and, like other social practices, normally involve ethical values.' Our position does not conflict with Norcia and Tigner's, yet it considers that even if there are mixed motives in business decisions, changes in the incentive structure offers the most efficient and fastest way to alter these decisions in the direction of the desired social (environmental) objectives.

Cost-benefit analyses imply that an action should be undertaken to the extent that the benefits it generates are greater than its costs. And between different courses of actions must be chosen the action with the highest profit (benefits minus costs).

Many environmentalists consider that a decision resulting from such an analysis may not be morally right and should not therefore be undertaken (for example, Kelman, 1981). Why? Because there are situations 'where certain duties – duties not to lie, break promises, or kill, for example – make an act wrong, even if it would result in an excess of benefits over costs' (Kelman, 1981, p. 359). Hence, only ethical considerations should enter the picture when deciding on a certain course of action. Decisions about our natural environment would enter that category of situations. For supporters of this view, when decision makers (government officials, elected or not, managers) determine a legal level of pollution for example, they should consider in particular the harm inflicted upon certain vulnerable individuals (such as the elderly or asthmatics) even if it does not harm others, that is, even if *total* benefits for society are higher than *total* costs. In other words, even if such a level of pollution leads to an increase in living standards for the rest of us, it would be morally wrong to accept such a level. More generally, for these environmentalists, cost-benefit analyses do not consider the fact that there exists 'specially valued' things that should outweigh the pure economic analysis.

The answer of the economist to such views is several fold. Cost-benefit analysis is not only about the (traditional) economic costs and benefits *per se*, it also encompasses *all* the aspects of what people want, those being in a way or another valued in monetary terms. And 'specially valued' things can be dealt with in such a way, even if it is not always easy and errors can be made. Valuing costs and benefits with such a perspective renders environmental problems specially prone to this type of economic analysis, complemented by an analysis of trade-offs between competing ends, subject to the constraint that people cannot have everything they want, a means of analysis often judged morally deplorable by many environmentalists! But is the moral argument so convincing?

Let us come back to this special value issue such as 'the right' of vulnerable groups such as the elderly or the asthmatics 'not to be sacrificed on the altar of somewhat higher living standards for the rest of us'. This view assumes that the costs involved in such a social choice are trivial. But what if the price to be paid is not 'somewhat higher living standards' but the jobs of a number of workers.[5] How to decide whether the health of asthmatics or the elderly has more 'moral importance' than for example the jobs and the livelihood of workers? More: is the moral issue the same if one asthmatic is harmed at the cost of the jobs of 1000 workers, or 1000 asthmatics harmed at the cost of the job of one worker? Of course the two situations are not equivalent. And the abstract and subjective ethical argument does not differentiate between both situations, whereas the economic argument does and clarifies the choice.

---

[5]   As mentioned by Delong (1981) in a reply to Kelman (1981).

As a whole, replacing cost-benefit analyses, and more generally economic analyses, by ethical considerations would be a poor way of treating environmental issues. Which does not mean that ethical, moral, esthetical, or other general values (such as duties and rights) considerations should be dismissed; rather they should to the extent possible be incorporated into the analysis by assigning monetary values to them. Obviously it is difficult to place objective monetary values to such intangibles, but economists have tools to do that in a reasonable if not perfect way. Anyway, in spite of its shortcomings and limitations economic analysis is essential for decision makers to consciously evaluate the trade-offs, to minimize the waste of scarce resources, and to improve their decisions over time when more information about costs and benefits is available.

The economist is also aware that cost-benefit analysis is not always possible in precise terms because there is great uncertainty in the estimates of costs and benefits – the greenhouse effect and the increase in world temperature that seems to go along with it is a good example of such difficulty (Nordhaus and Boyer, 2000; Fourçans, 2002, 2003). In that case 'precautionary' considerations (ethical issues may be part of such precautionary motive) may also enter the analysis and the decision-making process. But that does not negate the possibility of economic analysis. It can be conducted, even if imprecisely and with results not absolutely reliable. Such analysis introduces some rationality into the decision making process, sets up a methodology to deal with the problem and establishes a rational background to improve decisions over time as new information and knowledge emerge (Fourçans, 2004).

3.2 The Market and the Environment

Other sources of misunderstandings between economists and environmentalists are related to several myths as to the way our profession thinks about the environment. Particularly about the role of markets in solving environmental problems.

Economists are portrayed as asserting that markets can solve all environmental problems (not to say anything about the whole array of economic and social problems). Of course, this caricature is nothing but a caricature. What the economist says is that, *under certain conditions*, markets lead to the most efficient economic results. Production and trade in the market between self-interested producers and consumers achieve the greatest good for the greatest number, through the famous 'invisible hand' of Adam Smith (1776). This market process leads to the economic optimum without interference from the government.

Yet economists are well aware that the conditions for markets to reach this economic optimum are not necessarily met. And they have analyzed these conditions and their consequences almost from the beginning of the development of the economic paradigm. The literature on the subject is voluminous, with hundreds of books and papers. Since the famous contribution of A. C. Pigou (1920) and especially over the last 30 years, great theoretical as well as empirical progress has been made in environmental economics. 'In short, the intellectual structure of environmental economics has been both broadened and strengthened since... 1976' (Cropper and Oates, 1992, p. 728).

Welfare economics clarifies the conditions under which markets do not deal efficiently with some situations, and therefore do not lead to an optimal allocation of our scarce resources. This is especially true with respect to so-called public goods and when there are externalities. Public goods concern goods that can be 'consumed' by market participants even though they do not pay for it – the light from a lighthouse is a typical example, or missiles to defend a country. In that case, nobody would want to incur the cost of production of this good, the free market would 'fail' or lead to an underproduction of the good. Externalities are related to more traditional environmental problems. Externalities exist whenever the production of goods or services entails consequences 'external' to the market, that is when some costs (sometimes benefits), of pollution for example, associated with the production of these goods and services are not taken into consideration by the producer. To say it with the economic jargon, there exists negative externalities such that the total social cost of production exceeds the private cost of production. Let to its own devices, the market produces too many pollution-generating goods and services. This is used as an argument for government 'to enter the game' in an attempt to correct these types of market failures and thus to improve welfare and lead to greater efficiency.

But this argument does not mean that government intervention cannot have failures in itself. The 'political man' or the 'regulatory man' has also objectives of his own, he does not obligatorily maximize the public interest. There can also exist 'political failures' and 'regulatory failures' in dealing with the externalities, as analyzed by the wide Public Choice literature.

As paradoxical as it may seem, the existence of externalities does not necessarily imply that market solutions cannot be used to deal with market failures. For example, pollution can be dealt with by the market through a system of taxes on firms' emissions, taxes reflecting the external social costs. Or by rights being exchanged on a market for tradable emission permits. Through these methods pollution can be 'internalized' and the market outcome be efficient. In addition, there may be private alternatives to public intervention such as transactions in property rights (Coase, 1960) or the organization of Clubs (Buchanan, 1965).

As can be seen, contrary to what many environmentalists believe, economists do not hold that the market alone always leads to the desired environmental outcome. Their position is subtler. And they accept that, under certain circumstances, government may intervene to create incentives – or constraints, a form of 'strong' incentives – so as to have some chances of getting the desired outcome. And different types of incentives are possible.

4 Incentives, the Market and the Government

4.1 The Main Types of Environmental Policies

The role of incentives is to ensure that producers and consumers face the true costs of their actions, i.e., the full social costs and consequences of these actions. As far as firms' behavior is concerned these incentives, or constraints, fall within one of five major categories: command and control regulatory approaches, pollution charges, market barriers reduction, subsidies elimination;[6] and possible changes in property rights.

Command and control regulatory approaches are the traditional and more widely used methods of fighting pollution. Through regulations, governments set uniform standards, mostly technological or performance-based, for all firms. All businesses must then adopt the same measures and practices for pollution control. For example, firms in an industry can be required to use the 'best available technology' to control water or air pollution. Performance standards set uniform control target for each firm (such as the maximum amount of pollutant permitted) but also allow some latitude as to the way to meet such target. Obviously, command and control approaches are not the economist's favorite tool of creating 'incentives' to deter pollution – in their constraining nature, as noted above, command and control measures are more 'forced-incentives' or 'compulsory incentives' than typical incentives. The economist, in general, prefers more market-oriented incentives such as pollution charges.

Pollution charges consist of imposing a fee or a tax on the amount of pollution a firm creates. Theoretically, the applied tax must lead to an amount of pollution such that its marginal cost equals the tax rate. In that case firms have incentives to control their pollution as long as the costs of controlling it are sufficiently low, therefore having incentives to develop new and less expensive pollution-control technologies. This approach is used often enough in water pollution and smoke pollution controls. And it works. In 1991, Sweden, for example, introduced a sulfur tax: the sulfur content of fuels dropped to 50% below legal requirements and stimulated power plants to invest in abatement technology. Norway's carbon tax, also levied in 1991, lowered emissions from power plants by 21%. This method is now proposed by some economists to help control global warming through a carbon tax.

Though this type of method can be efficient, it is not easy to evaluate precisely the level of pollution it would lead to. Tradable permit systems eliminate, at least in theory, this problem.

Under a *tradable permit system* the global overall level of pollution is determined by the organizers of the market (the government, or private operators), but the repartition between firms is made through the allocation of tradable permits. Firms keeping their emissions below their allocated level can sell their surplus permits, *via* a market for these permits, to firms that would emit beyond their allotted level. Hence, firms with low costs of pollution abatement have an incentive to reduce their pollution beyond the pre-established target level, whereas firms with high costs of pollution abatement will reduce their pollution less than the pre-established target level. The authorized *total* level of pollution is respected but its allocation between firms is determined by a market trading in these pollution rights. The total cost for society as a whole of cleaning the air is minimized.

---

[6] This part is based on Stavins (1990, 1992).

This market procedure has been used in the US with great success for sulfur dioxide emissions control. It could be established at the international level to reduce greenhouse gas pollution, as proposed by the *Kyoto Protocol*.

Removal of market barriers resulting from governmental rules and regulations can also lead to great gains in environmental protection, through for example disclosure of information on the greenness of companies. This method has been used with success to promote more efficient allocation and use of scarce water supplies. It can also be used *via* a least-cost bidding process for electricity utilities, thus entailing a more rational energy transformation.

In this category of measures we can also incorporate the removal of barriers to *international trade*. As surprising as it can be to environmentalists, trade liberalization appears to lead to a cleaner environment, notably in the less developed countries. Many studies have shown that environmental degradation and income have an inverted U-shaped relationship, with pollution increasing with income at low levels of income and decreasing with income at higher levels of income (for example, World Bank, 1992; Grossman and Krueger, 1995). The reason of such improvement? As countries develop, firms substitute cleaner technologies for the more polluting ones and citizens demand that more attention be paid to their environmental conditions (Grossman and Krueger, 1995; Antweiler, Copeland and Taylor, 2001; Dean, 2002). Again, incentives, and not direct ethical considerations, together with increase in income that is brought about by international trade help the global environment, at least after a certain level of income is reached and a minimum level of political certainty is insured (Fredriksson and Mani, 2004; Copeland and Taylor, 2004).

Finally, *eliminating some government subsidies* can also promote a more efficient and more environmentally friendly use of resources. Suppressing the enormous subsidies given to coal producers in various countries, for example, would help decrease CO_2 pollution. The same would be true with respect to timber subsidies that lead to excessive timber cutting and damage not only forests but also habitat and various watershed values. One could add subsidies for pesticides (to make them more affordable to farmers), for water (often free, or very cheap, both for farmers and city dwellers), or for electricity (often underpriced for everybody).

More radical solutions are proposed by 'market purists' through a shift to a policy grounded in private *property rights* (Coase, 1960). The proponents of this approach argue that the incentives and markets created by such rights would protect the environment better than any government action. Inappropriately assigned property rights, or the lack thereof, may lead to a 'tragedy of commons' whereby users over exploit a resource, such as over-fishing. In the long-run all fishermen would benefit from a thriving fishery, but in the short-run each catches as many fish as he can, thus cutting the branch the industry is sitting on. If fishermen had rights with an assigned quota, and could freely trade such quota, they would behave in a more 'sustainable' way and stocks would be revived – as has been the case with such schemes in New Zealand, Iceland and parts of America. Though this approach can be very powerful in dealing with specific environmental situations, it is problematic to use more broadly as a solution to the wide array of environmental issues.

4.2 An Evaluation of Market-based versus Command and Control Policies

Holding all businesses under the same target, command and control regulatory approaches can be expensive and even counterproductive. Although uniform standards can sometime be effective in limiting emissions of pollutants, they do so at relatively high costs to society. The same standards can force some firms to use unduly expensive means of controlling pollution whereas the cost of doing so can vary between firms; also, the right technology in a given corporation may be the wrong one in another.

Furthermore, since little or no financial incentive exists for firms to go beyond their control targets, command and control approaches may hinder the development of technologies that could provide greater level of pollution abatement.

Finally, command and control regulatory approaches may be the final outcome resulting from firms lobbying to eliminate competition. For example, lobbying by big firms as a method of eliminating small competitors, hence increasing the cost of regulation and decreasing social welfare.[7]

Market-based approaches achieve the same aggregate level of pollution control as a command and control approach, but they allocate the burden of this pollution control more efficiently among firms. By providing monetary incentives for the maximum reductions in pollution by the firms that can do so most cost effectively, market approaches allow pollution control at a lower cost, thus more efficiently, for society as a whole. Not only do they drive firms toward cost-efficient solutions but also toward more R&D in search of cheaper and better pollution-abatement techniques, and toward the development of new pollution-control technologies, as far as such technologies lead to positive effect on profits.

The costs of market-based instruments can be *much* lower than command and control ones. For example, it has been estimated that abatement costs of sulfur dioxide (SO_2) emissions in the United States through a tradable permits system has saved about one billion dollars a year in compliance costs (Stavins, 2003). And the phase down of leaded gasoline, accomplished through a tradable permits system among refineries, was associated with savings of about 250 millions dollars per year to consumers. The cost of reducing greenhouse gas via a world market for permits could decrease the cost by a factor of four compared to specific measures applied without a market procedure by each country independently of the others (Nordhaus and Boyer, 2000).

Economists, of course, also stress the necessity to use cost-benefit analyses in the evaluation of the different programs (as discussed above). As resources are limited, such analysis makes the trade-offs involved in different social investments more explicit. It informs decision-makers as to how can scarce resources be put to the greatest social good. As can be seen from Table 4.1 the estimated costs of regulations per life saved, in the United States, vary widely (by a factor of more

---

[7] As shown in Table 4.1 below, the very high cost per life saved through regulation in solid waste disposal facility is highly correlated to this type of anti-competitive measure.

than a million!) (Stavins, 2003). One can deduct from these cost figures the extent to which, for a given cost, some measures can save more lives than others – certainly not too light a consideration...

It spite of all their advantages, market-based policies are not widely used as pollution-control methods. For at least three reasons.

First, they do not fit every problem. They are tailor-made for problems where concern focuses on *aggregate* pollution levels such as the fight against acid-rain or greenhouse gas. But when concerns are with respect to *local* environmental problems it is the level emitted by individual firms that must be controlled. In this case, a conventional command and control approach, such as uniform standards, may be the preferred policy.

Second, environmentalists (except, in general, environmental economists) view the pollution problem more as a moral failing of corporations and political leaders than as a by-product of our societies that can be reduced in an efficient way by economic techniques. 'Ethics' comes then at the forefront of the debate rather than 'incentives.' In addition, environmentalists and social philosophers have a tendency to reject market-based approaches as being 'unethical', as establishing 'rights to pollute'. They worry that increased flexibility in pollution control would lower the level of environmental protection.

We find again the misunderstanding between environmentalists and economists, even if, over the years, the gap between the two views seems to narrow, except may be for the hard core militants.

Third, environmental professionals and government officials do not like to see their experience and skills, in other words their power in dealing with command and control programs, dissipate. Businesses are also hesitant to pursue market-based instruments such as taxes or tradable permits because of their lack of experience with these instruments and the limitations in their internal structures as to such approaches. There is also a concern that these new fees or taxes would not be compensated by lowering other fees or taxes. Hence one reason, among others, that many environmentally sensitive industries argue in favor of voluntary approaches to environmental policy.

4.3 The Limitations of Business Structures in dealing with Market-based Instruments

'Economic-incentive instruments require a very different set of decisions than do traditional command and control approaches, and most firms are simply not equipped internally to make the decisions necessary to take full advantage of these instruments' (Stavins, 1998). Indeed, firms are not familiar with the use of these tools, are not sure whether they would remain a lasting component of government intervention in the realm of environmental control, and, as a result, are hesitant to incorporate this new approach in their organization. They fear that rules may be modified over time and hesitate to incur the investment costs associated with market-based instruments. A more predictable set of 'rules of the game' and a higher sense of stability over time would improve the rate at which such tools would be used. Corporations are also concerned that the availability of economically efficient tools of environmental cleaning may lead to more stringent limits imposed on the amount of pollution permitted.

The fear of being considered 'unethical' by environmentalists and the public at large may also be a concern. Would not 'buying the right to pollute', as some environmentalists present tradable permits programs, for example, give the firm a bad image and therefore have an adverse impact on the corporation and its management? These considerations, as well as the lack of public understanding of market tools, should not be neglected as disincentives in the use of market-based instruments (Hockenstein, Stavins and Whitehead, 1997, also for the end of this section).

Furthermore, being accustomed to minimizing the costs of complying with command and control techniques, firms do not have extensive enough experience in evaluating costs of dealing with market instruments and do not make the necessary strategic decisions towards implementation thereof. So long as the functions of managers responsible for pollution control in their respective corporations are not clearly integrated with those of the business units, the latter have no incentive to introduce such pollution control objectives into their decision-making process. As a consequence, the relevant and necessary strategic and production decisions are not made.

Also, managers in charge of these issues have a tendency to strive for risk reduction and problem avoidance rather than to concentrate on the opportunities of the market-based incentive system. In general, these are engineers or law-related professionals, possessing technical and legal skills rather than the economic and managerial skills required to deal with market-based instruments.

One can expect that more certainty derived from public policy in the application of market instruments should over time increase the impact of the incentives so created on the structure of the firm. And as a result raise the efficiency of these incentives in cleaning the environment.

4.4 Voluntary Approaches

Voluntary approaches for environmental policy have been developed in OECD countries since the 1960s and 1970s, with a significant increase in the 1990s, especially in Japan, the European Union and the United States. These approaches consist in firms making commitments to improve their environmental performance beyond what is legally required. Three main types can be identified. First, public voluntary programs whereby governments invite corporations to participate if they so desire. Second, negotiated agreements that lead to environmental commitments through a bargaining process between an industrial sector and the public authority. Third, unilateral commitments whereby firms act independently without any public authority involvement (Börkey, Glachant and Lévêque, 1998; Argandoña, 2004). A fourth type could be added through direct agreements between polluters and pollutees for example.

Within the terminology of this chapter, should these voluntary approaches be classified as being based on 'ethics' or 'incentives'? Whereas the moral and social philosopher would tend to consider them as ethically rooted, the economist views such approaches as primarily based on some 'materialistic' background, i.e., on some economic incentives. The main incentive being an effort to avoid the costs of public regulation. When governments plan to introduce new environmental regulations or a new tax to fight pollution, firms may attempt to pre-empt such public regulation by opting to reduce their emissions and demonstrating that they are 'good environmental citizens.' Clearly, in that case, the reason for so doing does not stem from the 'ethics of intentions' of the managers but from their desire to avoid the costs of the governmental regulation or the tax. It can also be a means, for corporations, of signaling to consumers (and stockholders) their responsibility to the environment in order to increase the market share of their products and improve stock performances. Other incentives may be working towards an improved partnership with the surrounding communities, be they local public authorities or employees. In any event the goal is to improve the firm's reputation, and consequently its long-run profits.

With that view in mind, economic incentives make up the basic background of voluntary approaches rather than explanations based on vague moral arguments.[8] Yet, in our view, these behaviors are ethical as far as the 'ethics of results' is satisfied, that is as far as the environment is cleaned in an economically efficient way.

But what is the real efficacy of these approaches in reducing pollution?

There is a debate among policy-makers, scholars, environmental groups and corporations about the proper answer to this question. It is suspected that by giving corporations a prominent role in setting and implementing these instruments, corporations would 'capture' environmental policy and make it too 'business friendly.' Hence voluntary approaches would result only in cosmetic effects on the environment.

The evidence is not clear-cut and covers only a limited number of cases. Whatever little evidence is available, it suggests that voluntary approaches seem to provide 'soft effects', in other words they help raise the level of information and of awareness of different groups on environmental issues (Börkey, Glachant and Lévêque, 1998). But they seem to provide only meager incentives to innovate, and are not really understood by environmentalist groups and by public opinion at large. Yet they may be a useful first step in new policy areas that are not covered by existing rules, such as waste recycling problems or, most importantly, climate change policies. Many big corporations have committed themselves to reducing their production of greenhouse gas in line with the principles of the Kyoto Protocol (chemical, concrete, housing and road construction, utilities, etc.). Some also accept to be more transparent and even work with green NGOs in their dealing with pollution. Finally, over the last couple of years, in London as well as Chicago (the Chicago Climate Exchange), markets for trading pollution allowances have been established by major companies. These initiatives can be seen as a first step

---

[8] Again, as was discussed earlier in the chapter, the economic analysis of these problems does not eliminate the role of ethics. As Argandoña (2004) explains, these approaches can help develop and sustain ethical behavior in firms, and make corporate activity compatible with ethics.

toward the European Union market for rights that should commence in 2005 and, perhaps, toward a worldwide market for these rights that could (should) be created in order for society to be efficiently dealing, with the most cost effective means, with climate change (Nordhaus and Boyer, 2000; Fourçans, 2002).

5 Conclusion

The question of the social responsibility of the firm in a market economy, especially in terms of environmental protection, has been debated for several decades. And no doubt the debate will be on-going for many years to come. Though no one would deny the concept of corporations having an important role to play in the cleaning of the environment, the question remaining is whether one should rely on the 'ethics' of managers to strive for a clean environment or on the set of 'incentives' that can be created to make them behave in such a social manner. The moral philosopher relies on moral values, another terminology for ethics, of the managers whereas the economist, cautious of private virtues as means to obtain social virtues, prefers to rely as much as possible on incentives and the right institutional structure associated therewith. The economist considers that at least on these matters deeds must be judged based on results rather than on intentions. The ethical behavior is the behavior leading to a clean environment (more generally, the desired social results), without judging the underlying intentions (within certain limits, of course).

This view is based on a different perception of man than that of the moral philosopher's. For the economist, man is resourceful, evaluating and maximizing. For the moral philosopher, man's behavior is determined by exogenous social values and social norms such as ethics, independently of individuals. The economic man responds to incentives and stimuli. Efficient and swift changes in the social order are better brought about by changes in the incentive structure than by changes in the value system (ethics). Though the REMM model does not deny the role of ethics, it considers that changes in the incentive system dominate changes in ethics as far as efficient social change is concerned.

This different perception of man may explain several misunderstandings between economists and environmentalists, notably with respect to the use of cost-benefit analyses in evaluating environmental policies. The moral philosopher-environmentalist considers that this decision-making tool is badly suited to incorporate 'specially values' things, i.e., ethical considerations such as 'rights' of vulnerable persons or groups, into the picture. The economist is not indifferent to these considerations but considers that they can more often than not be incorporated into the analysis by assigning monetary values thereto. At any rate, these values do not eliminate the need for evaluating the trade-offs involved in social choices so as to minimize the waste of scarce resources and improve decisions over time as more knowledge and information about costs and benefits emerges.

Yet contrary to what many an environmentalist may say, economists do not contend that the market can solve all environmental problems. They just demonstrate that under certain conditions, markets lead to the most efficient result. Even more: economists have widely analyzed these conditions and in so doing established the role that government may play in dealing with questions such as public goods or externalities – the latter being at the heart of environmental economics. But if there can exist 'market failures', there can also exist 'political' and 'regulatory failures.' The solution to environmental problems requires therefore not forgetting the trade-off between market and government failures.

That perspective in mind, the economist prefers market-based environmental policies to command-and-control ones. Incorporating pollution charges or establishing a tradable permit system is preferred to uniform standards for all firms. And a cleaner environment can be achieved through the removing of market barriers, among them international trade barriers, or of some government subsidies, or by changing the structure of property rights. These market-based approaches, by creating the 'right' incentives lead to favorable environmental results at least cost for society. But these approaches cannot fit every problem. In those cases where they do not, command-and-control policies should not be discarded.

Finally, especially since the early 1990s, voluntary approaches whereby firms make commitments to promote their environmental performance beyond what is legally required have been developed. If their efficiency is not clearly established they seem to at least raise the level of information and awareness of different groups on environmental issues, the fight against greenhouse gas being at the forefront on that matter.

At any rate, whatever the method used, the incentive structure (constraints included as a kind of compulsory incentives when there is no other solution) dominates ethics as a way of solving the problem of pollution generated by businesses.

TABLE 4.1 COSTS OF SELECTED ENVIRONMENTAL, HEALTH, AND SAFETY REGULATIONS THAT REDUCE MORTALITY RISKS*

(United States)

Regulation	Year Issued	Cost per Statistical Life Saved (Millions of 2002 Dollars)
Logging operations	1994	0.1
Unvented space haters	1980	0.2
Trihalomethane drinking water standards	1979	0.3
Food Labeling	1993	0.4
Passive restraints/belts	1984	0.5
Alcohol and drug control	1985	0.9
Seat cushion flammability	1984	1.0
Side-impact standards for autos	1990	1.1
Low-altitude windshear equipment and training standards	1988	1.8
Children's sleepwear flammability ban	1973	2.2
Benzene/fugitive emissions	1984	3.7
Ethylene dibromide drinking water standard	1991	6.0
NO_x SIP Call	1998	6.0
Radionuclides/uranium mines	1984	6.9
Grain dust	1988	11
Methylene chloride	1997	13
Arsenic emissions standards for glass plants	1986	19
Arsenic emissions standards for copper smelters	1986	27
Hazardous waste listing for petroleum refining sludge	1990	29
Coke ovens	1976	51
Uranium mill tailings (active sites)	1983	53
Asbestos/construction	1994	71
Asbestos ban	1989	78
Hazardous waste management/wood products	1990	140
Sewage sludge disposal	1993	530
Land disposal restrictions/phase II	1994	2.600
Drinking water/phase II	1992	19.000
Formaldehyde occupational exposure limit	1987	78.000
Solid waste disposal facility criteria	1991	100.000

* From Stavins (2003), whose source is Morral (2003). Estimates are from respective agencies. Non-mortality and non-health benefits were subtracted from the annual cost (numerator) to generate *net cost*. For each entry, the denominator is the estimated number of statistical lives saved by the regulation annually.

References

Antweiler, W., Copeland, B. R. and Taylor, M. S. (2001), Is Free Trade Good for the Environment?, *The American Economic Review*, 91, 4, pp. 877-908.

Argandoña, A. (2004), On Ethical, Social and Environmental Management Systems, *Journal of Business Ethics*, 51, April, pp. 41-52. Also available as a chapter of this book.

Barro, R. J. (1974), Are Government Bonds Net Wealth?, *Journal of Political Economy*, 81, pp. 1095-1117.

Becker, G. S. (1976), *The Economic Approach to Human Behavior*, Chicago, University of Chicago Press.

Becker, G. S. (1981), Altruism in the Family and Selfishness in the Market Place, *Economica*, 48, pp. 1-15.

Börkey, P., Glachant, M. and Lévêque, F. (1998), *Voluntary Approaches for Environmental Policy in OECD Countries: An Assessment*, Mimeo, C.E.R.N.A., Paris.

Brunner, K. and Meckling, W. (1977), The Perception of Man and the Conception of Government, *Journal of Money, Credit and Banking*, February, 9, 1, pp. 70-85.

Buchanan, J. M. (1965), An Economic Theory of Clubs, *Economica*, 32, 125, pp. 1-14.

Cahuc, P. and Kempf, H. (2000), L'Altruisme Est-il Socialement Efficace?, *Revue du MAUSS*, First Semester, 15, pp. 223-246.

Coase, R. H. (1960), The Problem of Social Cost, *Journal of Law and Economics*, 3, pp. 1-44.

Copeland, B. R. and Taylor, M. C. (2004), Trade, Growth, and the Environment, *Journal of Economic Literature*, 42, pp. 7-71.

Cropper, L. and Oates, W. E. (1992), Environmental Economics: A survey, *Journal of Economic Literature*, 30, pp. 675-740.

Dean, J. M. (2002), Does Trade Liberalization Harm the Environment?, *Canadian Journal of Economics*, 35, 4, pp. 819-842.

Delong, J. V. (1981), Reply to S. Kelman, *AEI Journal of Government and Society Regulation*, March/April, in Stavins R., 2001, *Environmental Economics and Public Policy*, Northampton, US, Edward Elgar, pp. 365-367.

Di Norcia, V. and Tigner, J. (2000), Mixed Motives and Ethical Decisions in Business, *Journal of Business Ethics*, 25, pp. 1-13.

Fourçans, A. (2002), *Effet de Serre: le Grand Mensonge?*, Edition du Seuil, Paris.

Fourçans, A. (2003), Le Protocole de Kyoto, Relance ou Enlisement?, *Revue d'Economie Politique*, 4, pp. 477-484.

Fourçans, A. (2004), Le Principe de Précaution: un Principe à Manier avec Précaution, *Risques*, 57, pp. 93-97.

Fredriksson, P. G. and Mani, M. (2004), Trade Integration and Political Turbulence: Environmental policy consequences, *Advances in Economic Analysis and Policy*, 4, 2, pp. 1-27.

Friedman, M. (1962), *Capitalism and Freedom*, University of Chicago Press, Chicago.

Grossman, G. M. and Krueger, A. B. (1995), Economic Growth and the Environment, *The Quarterly Journal of Economics*, 110, 2, pp. 353-377.

Hockenstein, J. B., Stavins, R. and Whitehead, B. W. (1997), Crafting the Next Generation of Market-based Environmental Tools, *Environment*, 39, 4, pp. 13-33.

Jenkins, T. N. (1998), Economics and the Environment: A Case of Ethical Neglect, *Ecological Economics*, 26, pp. 151-163.

Kelman, S. (1981), Cost-benefit analysis: An Ethical Critique, *AEI Journal on Government and Society Regulation*, January/February, pp. 33-40.

Meckling, W. (1975), Values and the Choice of the Model of the Individual in the Social Sciences, *Second Interlaken Seminar on Analysis and Ideology*, Fall.

Morrall, J. F. (2003), Saving Lives: A Review of the Record, *Journal of Risk and Uncertainty*, 27, 3, pp. 221-237.

Nordhaus, W. and Boyer, J. (2000), *Warming the World: Economic Models of Global Warming*, The MIT Press, Mass.

Phelps, E. S. (ed.) (1975), *Altruism, Morality and Economic Theory*, New York, Sage.

Pigou, A. C. (1920/1978), *The Economics of Welfare*, AMS Press, New York.

Smith, A. (1776 1976), *An Inquiry into the Nature and Causes of the Wealth of Nations*, Whitestone, Dublin.

Stavins, R. N. (1990), Innovative Policies for Sustainable Development: The Role of Economic Incentives for Environmental Protection, *Harvard Public Policy Review*, 7, 1, pp. 13-25.

Stavins, R. N. and Whitehead, W. (1992), Dealing with Pollution, *Environment*, 34, 7, pp. 7-43.

Stavins, R. N. (1998), Economic Incentives for Environmental Regulation, in: Newman, P.K. (ed.), *The New Palgrave Dictionary of Economic and the Law*, Palgrave Macmillan, London, pp. 6-13.

Stavins, R. N. (2003), Environmental Protection and Economic Well-being: How Does (and How Should) Government Balance these Two Important Values?, *Resources for the Future*, August.

Chapter 12

Deregulating Dishonesty: Lessons from the US Corporate Scandals

Radu Vranceanu

1 Introduction:[1] The US Corporate Scandals of the Nineties

All scholars in social sciences would agree that what can be called 'ethical behavior' plays an important role in the well-functioning of capitalist economies: given that their resource allocation system builds on voluntary exchange between individuals, positive social externalities such as trust, loyalty and truth-telling are needed to oil the economic machinery (inter alia: Arrow, 1974; McKean, 1975; Becker, 1976; Hirshleifer, 1977; Noreen, 1988; Brickley et al., 2002). The wave of corporate scandals that marked the turn of the century, mostly in the US but also in Western Europe, were a forceful reminder that in the realm of trust and honesty, capitalism comes with its own limits.

After ten years of continuous growth, in 2001 the American economy ran into a period of deep trouble. GDP growth almost vanished and unemployment rose by almost two percentage points in one year. Over the same period, shareholders lost some 7000 billion dollars, in what appears to have been the worst stock market decline since the *Great Depression*. Everybody now agrees that a speculative bubble took off in the late nineties, when abnormal growth was supported by overconfident expectations about the long-lasting high returns to be generated by the new information technologies. This 'Internet bubble' burst in March 2001.

The situation would have not been so critical if the collapse of so many stock prices had simply reflected normal readjustment to their fundamental value; but then the US economic outlook become really bleak when a wave of corporate scandals surfaced, filling newspaper front pages with several cases of outrageous misconduct by chief executive officers (CEOs) and/or chief financial officers

---

[1] This chapter is an extended version of a research first published in *Acta Oeconomica*, 55, 1, 2005 with the title 'Financial Architecture and Manager Dishonesty: Lessons from the US Corporate Scandals.' It is reprinted here with the kind permission of the publisher, *Academiai Kiado*, Budapest. The author would like to thank Laurent Bibard, Daniel Daianu, Marie-Laure Djelic, André Fourçans, two anonymous referees of the journal, and participants to the workshop on 'Economy and Ethics' organized by the New Europe College and the Romanian Economic Society in Bucharest, 12-13 December, 2003 for their useful suggestions and comments on an early draft.

(CFOs) at leading US companies. William H. Donaldson, Chairman of the US Securities and Exchange Commission, describes the problem in concise terms: 'Starting with the unfolding of the *Enron* story in October 2001, it became apparent that the boom years had been accompanied by fraud, other misconduct and serious erosion in business principles' (Donaldson, 2003a).

It subsequently emerged from the legal investigations into typical cases such as *Enron, WorldCom, Global Crossing, Tyco, Qwest, Adelphia*, etc., that on the eve of the crisis, several large companies' CEOs had produced false financial statements with the complicity of corrupt auditors, and reaped personal gains from the resulting short-term overvaluation of their companies by massively selling their shares just before the firm's collapse.[2] Sometimes, the motives for information manipulation were more subtle: either to 'win time' for a distressed company, or to use overvalued shares to pay for the target company in a takeover. In all cases, once revealed, these frauds entailed major costs in terms of reputation, that have ultimately been passed on to shareholders and the other stakeholders. 'Creative accounting' and 'earnings manipulation' were basic ingredients of all the corporate scandals (Carson, 2003; Lev, 2003). This variety of manager misconduct can be interpreted as an extreme development of the basic conflict of interest between an agent and the principal, as put forward by traditional corporate governance literature (Alchian and Demsetz, 1972; Jensen and Meckling, 1976). Conflicts of interest may take place whenever an economic agent in charge of a public mission derives a private benefit from his job; in many cases, his private interest may conflict with the public interest at large. While conflicts of interest between managers and shareholders are nothing new, the Internet bubble period proved to be a fertile ground for fraud, which is an extreme development of such conflicts (Demski, 2003; Donaldson 2003a; 2003b; Healy and Palepu, 2003).

Some broad figures give a better idea of the scale of the problem. To fight corporate crime, the United States set up a *Corporate Fraud Task Force* in July 2002 within the Department of Justice. In the course of one year, this public body charged 354 defendants with some type of corporate fraud in connection with 169 cases; it has already obtained over 250 corporate fraud convictions or guilty pleas, including guilty pleas or convictions concerning at least 25 former CEOs. From October 1st through June 30th 2003, the Securities and Exchange Commission (SEC) filed 443 enforcement actions, 137 of which involved financial fraud on reporting. Eleven companies were suspended from trading, and the assets of 30 companies were frozen. The SEC filed almost 50% more financial fraud and reporting cases in 2003 than in the previous fiscal year.[3] Of course, while these absolute numbers are alarming, they seem less so when weighed against the total 15000 US public companies under the SEC's supervision. The most important

---

[2] All these companies were related one way or another to the telecommunications and Internet sector.

[3] *Press Release* by SEC Chairman, William Donaldson, and Deputy Attorney General, Larry Thompson, July 22nd, 2003, www.usdoj.gov/dag/cftf/press/072203whitehousecftfbriefing.htm.

stylized fact was not the total number of cases, which is relatively small, but the unusual surge in wrongdoings.

The US economy was deeply affected by these corporate scandals. Managerial abuses brought about a wave of public distrust and criticism, directed at everything from CEOs' individual behavior to shareholder capitalism as a whole. An opinion poll in July 2002 by the *Harvard Business School* and the *Pew Research Center* showed that only 23% of Americans would trust bosses of large companies (yet 75% trusted people who run small businesses).[4] The loss of trust in the main institutions of capitalism such as publicly traded companies and the financial market exacerbated the economic crisis by adversely affecting investment, since it increased the cost of raising capital. As a signal of distrust, for more than three years following the stock market collapse, the market for initial public offerings has been almost inexistent.

In his celebrated work, Arrow (1974) pointed out that nothing guarantees that contemporary capitalist economies can produce sufficient amounts of trust and the other positive social externalities. If the notorious cases of managerial abuses are interpreted as a shortage of honesty and loyalty, the recent US experience seems to validate his viewpoint.

The main aim of this chapter is to emphasize the economic and institutional factors that supported development of dishonest managerial behavior in the US during the Internet bubble years (1995-2001). It will be argued that more managers crossed the honesty border because incentives to behave well had, for some reason, been attenuated. Somehow, the US had deregulated dishonesty. Our policy recommendations build on the reverse argument: to prevent managers from following further dishonest strategies, new regulations should make those strategies impossible, ineffective or much more expensive.

Changes in regulation and the economic environment only partially explain managerial misconduct. At the corporate level, the company-specific culture probably played an important role in encouraging or blocking unethical behavior. As noted by Sims and Brinkmann (2003, p. 246) who analyzed the *Enron* case in depth, 'the company culture of individualism, innovation, and aggressive cleverness left Enron without compassionate, responsible leadership.' It may also be surmised that every individual has his own stance on ethical behavior; while many managers are concerned about ethics, some are not. Many would agree with Watley and May, (2003) and Sims and Brinkmann, (2003) that dishonest behavior is a characteristic of bad management. But while bad regulations can be changed without delay, changing a corporate culture or an individual ethical stance can take many years. In order to focus on elements that are under the control of policymakers, this chapter will leave the major cultural or individual dimensions out of the picture.[5]

---

[4] See: 'Tough at the top. A survey of corporate leadership', *The Economist*, October 25th 2003.

[5] Other chapters of this book – for instance those written by Antonio Argandoña and Nicoletta Ferro – cover these important topics.

The chapter is organized as follows. The next section analyses changes in the US economic and financial structure that paved the way for dishonest in depth managerial behavior during the Internet bubble. Section 3 comments on the US policy response to this phenomenon and draws some recommendations for further reform. The final section presents the conclusion.

2 What caused the Surge in Dishonest Managerial Behavior?

2.1 A Broad Picture of the US Economic Environment

The US economy features both a mature financial market and a powerful sector of publicly traded companies. These two major institutions are not independent: publicly traded companies need an efficient capital market for financing, and financing instruments issued by publicly traded companies (corporate bonds and shares) are essential 'commodities' in the financial market. The quality of the financial instruments traded on the market, and the quality of the transactions themselves depends on the existing corporate governance structures. Last but not least, the information disclosure rules and the financial information system have an impact on the allocative efficiency of the financial market.

Since the focus here is on conflicts of interest between managers and shareholders, the relevant field of analysis is the publicly traded companies sector. Most of them are large companies. While large companies contribute only about half of the total US economy in terms of GDP, their influence on the rest of the economy cannot be underestimated given their coverage of the essential sectors (water and energy distribution, transportation, telecommunications, electronics and engineering, etc), their leading role in innovation, and their position as client for many small companies. According to the *US Census Bureau*, in 2000, the 17000 companies with 500 employees and more (0.3% of the total number of companies) accounted for about 55% of the annual payroll and 50% of total employment. Large companies finance themselves by reinvesting profits, through bank loans and issuing shares and bonds. A distinctive feature of the US economic system is the prevalence of this third financing channel. More precisely, contrary to the Continental European model, where many large companies are still private (non-listed) and where bank loans represent the main external source of funding, in the Anglo-Saxon model, the capital market (where companies sell bonds and shares) provides the bulk of new business finance resources. This leads to major differences between the incentive systems at work in the two zones, and calls for a specific form of regulation.

On the savings side, in the nineties, one American out of two held shares, either directly or through various types of investment funds. The development of a dispersed shareholder base was backed by several structural changes. The population aging problem increased the amount of savings and pension funds emerged as major players in the capital market. Mutual funds, those important vehicles for 'popular' capitalism, made share ownership accessible to many small investors.

The emergence of new financial instruments such as derivative products brought further momentum to the development of the capital market. New markets have emerged, now connected to economic risks that a few years ago were beyond the realm of the financial sphere, for instance natural catastrophes or climate change. The creation of hedge funds, those lightly regulated investment vehicles, allows (wealthy) private investors to participate in financial transactions reserved in the past for expert institutional traders (leverage investments, short-selling of assets and so on).

This widening and deepening of the financial market occurred against a background of additional deregulation in the goods markets: the state was pulling out of many traditional sectors, for instance transportation, energy and telecommunications. Even in sectors traditionally controlled by the state (e.g. the defense industry), the government increasingly resorted to managed competition.

Technical progress, mainly in the information technologies, is changing the way people communicate, organize business and trade. In the goods markets, price information can easily reach buyers in this Internet era; since search costs are lowered, spatial differentiation attenuates and local market power declines: as a result, many goods markets are tending to move closer to a situation of perfect competition, to the benefit of consumers. In the financial sphere, trade orders travel at the speed of light, and many financial markets quote prices in real time. Yet all practitioners will agree that information in financial markets is far from perfect; this happens because the traded 'commodity' is a claim on future resources. But future resources can only be contingent on the state of affairs at the time the claim is due, making them random variables. When trading future claims, people have to form expectations about their value, but these expectations involve a high degree of subjectivity in the choice of the relevant probabilities. In this specific context, many economists have pointed out that rumors, herding behavior, inside trading and expectation bubbles may all explain why at some given time the transaction price of an asset can drift away from its fundamental value.[6]

In particular, privileged traders have the ability to influence prices, either because they are big (i.e. they trade large volumes) and/or because they have a high reputation. In recent years, managers have discovered that the way they communicate about their company's performances also has considerable influence on share prices. Since they have significant control over the outgoing information flow, they may be tempted to use their 'market power' in the corporate information market in order to achieve self-interested objectives (Besancenot and Vranceanu, 2004).

Against this background of deregulation in the financial and goods markets, a mix of institutional and economic factors joined forces to set off a proliferation of dishonest managerial behavior during the late nineties. The first factor can be termed *cyclical*, as it is closely connected to the economic boom; it provided the ground layer for the others factors to become active. The other factors may be

---

[6] See Stiglitz and Greenwald (1991) for an analysis of the economic functions of contemporary financial institutions with special emphasis on the imperfect information issue.

called *structural*, to emphasize their relative independence of the macroeconomic outlook.

2.2 The Cyclical Factor

Economic history shows that many 'affairs' have come to light at the end of every period of exuberant growth driven by overoptimistic expectations, to mention only the railroads or the electricity episodes (Malkiel, 1973; Kindelberger, 1978). In a 'bubblish' environment, the gap between the market value and the fundamental value of selected commodities and financial assets widens sharply, so that prices no longer convey relevant information. Borrowing the physicist's vocabulary, we say that the 'noise' of the system increases. In such an environment, decision-makers have more difficulties in extracting the relevant signals. Periods where economic agents believe that large profits can be obtained in a short period of time, and behave accordingly, are supportive for unethical managerial behavior for at least three reasons.

Firstly, in a 'bubblish' environment shareholders must process a large amount of information; in particular, they may be blinded by the ongoing rise in the share price (becoming victims of a kind of price illusion). This makes it easier for dishonest managers to hide their actions. As the probability of being caught decreases, the expected cost of fraud declines and more managers may be tempted to increase their own wealth by fraudulent means.

Secondly, 'good conduct' is a relative concept: in general, people believe they are behaving well when they are doing what their peers do. To take a basic example, if in a given country all drivers drive slowly, within the legal speed limit, individuals internalize this norm and derive some satisfaction from driving like everybody else, i.e. slowly. If everybody drives fast, the individual will be satisfied if driving fast too. Both situations are stable Nash equilibria, but the second is socially dominated, since it comes with an increased number of lethal road accidents. In the business world, if all managers were concerned with sustainable corporate development, a 'ruthless' outlier would never get enough support for his action; conversely, in a world where all managers are obsessed with heuristically-given, excessive targets (like a yearly 15% profit rate), anyone who speaks seriously about environmental protection or corporate social responsibility will only be marginalized.

Thirdly, and this relates to the above point, the task of the external authorities in charge of policing deviant behavior is much more difficult in a 'noisy' environment. These public bodies use comparisons (benchmarking) as their main method of controlling managerial performances and actions. In a favorable equilibrium, if someone deviates, the authorities can easily detect and correct the deviation. In the unfavorable equilibrium where all drivers drive fast, how can the police helicopter observe all those exceeding the speed limit? Detection technology exists, but can be expensive.

The risk with economic bubbles such as the Internet bubble is that they replace social norms assigning a significant role to 'hard work' and responsibility with norms where easy short-term gains seem both possible and consistent with the common good. In general, people come to realize the absurdity of such a situation only after the bubble has burst. Unfortunately, once a social norm has collapsed, the costs of reinstating it can be quite considerable.

We turn now our attention to those structural factors that contributed to the increase in unethical managerial behavior. Emphasis is set on information manipulation, whither internal control, perverse incentives related to option-based compensation, and corruption of auditors and financial analysts.

2.3 Information Manipulation and 'Creative Accounting'

Most of the CEOs' frauds during the Internet bubble period consisted of information manipulation causing abnormal stock prices. Many managers carried out such actions with total disregard for shareholders and/or stakeholders' goals, pursuing a short-term objective of large personal gain, for instance by selling shares just before the company collapsed. Sometimes motives were subtler than straightforward personal gain. Some financial misstatements were intended to keep share prices up during a take-over (generally by way of exchange of shares). While incumbent shareholders (and the CEO) may have gained from such action, the target company's shareholders were robbed. In one notorious example from early 1997, the management team of *Boeing*, the US airplane maker, deliberately omitted to report abnormal costs due to late delivery and other production difficulties, in order to shore up the share price before the take-over of a rival, *McDonnell-Douglas*; they then reported losses of 2.6 billion dollars three months after the share exchange.[7] In other cases, fraudulent behavior by the CEO aimed at 'winning time' for a distressed company facing difficulties in its relations with clients and suppliers. Even though personal gain was not necessarily the main goal of this manipulation, clearly such unethical behavior can only penalize shareholders and stakeholders in the long run, since nobody would wish to deal with a company whose management has a reputation as liars.

How can managers push up share prices? Managers are better informed about the company status than anyone else, be they employees, investment bankers or auditing firms. Sometimes, top executives lie by describing the company's outlook in excessively rosy terms; at other times, all they have to do to keep prices up is to hide a relevant piece of information. Of all the various techniques for manipulating investors' expectations, one was particularly extensively used during the last crisis. Managers understood that the easiest way to keep the company share price up is to report high earnings. As shown by theoretical and empirical analyses, for various reasons, investors tend to highly rate companies reporting high earnings, and vice-

---

[7] In November 2003, *Boeing* fired its CFO, Mike Sears, for communicating with a US Air Force acquisition official about her future employment with the company while she was in charge of purchases of tanker aircraft for the Pentagon and was processing *Boeing* and *Airbus'* offers. The CEO, Phil Condit, had to resign soon afterwards. See *Business Week*, Mai 20, 2002; *The Economist*, November 29th, 2003; *WSJ*, December 2nd, 2003 and November 14th, 2004.

versa.[8] Based on a survey of 31 countries, Leutz, Nanda and Wysoki (2003) argued that earnings manipulation is positively correlated with managers' benefits.

How can managers manipulate earnings? Under the US accounting standards – Generally Accepted Accounting Principles, or GAAP – companies use *accrual accounting*, that is: 'attempts to record financial effects on an entity of transactions … in the periods in which those transactions … occur rather than only in the period when the cash is received or paid by the entity' (FASB 1985, SFAC 6, para. 139). As emphasized by Xie et. al. (2003), the principle of accrual accounting gives managers great discretion in reporting earnings over a given period. The scope for 'creative accounting', that is the capacity of dishonest managers to push the existing accounting standard to its limit, increased with the emergence of new financial instruments: derivatives, offshore markets, new debt instruments, and so on.

During the boom period, many companies systematically understated liabilities and/or inflated assets. For instance, *WorldCom* management deliberately reported ordinary expenses of seven billion dollars as an investment. *Enron* set up 'special vehicles' – read outside units working as affiliates in all respects except in their name – and sold them gas against a promise to buy it back one year later; it then reported the revenues but not the liabilities. *Qwest Communications* improperly counted more than one billion dollars as revenues in the 1999-2001 period; in particular, the company booked the revenues on fiber optic sales before delivering the product to customers. *Computer Associates* also booked more than two billion dollars in revenues through accounting sleight-of-hand that involved backdating of contracts. Some companies had recourse to 'swap' trades that both parties recorded as revenue (e.g. *Dynegy, Qwest, Global Crossing*). Many other manipulations took the form of mis-estimating reserves and provisions (see Lev, 2003; Stiglitz, 2003; Healy and Palepu, 2003; Sims and Brinkmann, 2003).

Boards of directors clearly failed in their mission of monitoring the financial statements provided by the CEOs and CFOs. While no empirical relationship between earnings manipulation and the overall structure of boards has been put forward, Xie et al. (2003) point to the essential monitoring rule played by the audit committee. In an empirical study covering 110 US companies over three years, they show that earnings manipulation (what they call 'earnings management') is less likely to occur in companies whose audit committees include more independent outside directors, and directors with corporate experience.

When a manager succeeds in manipulating investors' expectations by issuing a false signal and thus pushes up the share price for a limited period, the result is not a zero sum game where some shareholders lose (those who keep their shares) and some win (those who sell the shares before the truth comes out). One of the capital market's main roles is to provide information about the economic position of a given company; evolutions in its share price provide early signals for investors and boards, which must implement corrections in the company's strategy and management. If these corrections are timely, adjustments are smooth; otherwise,

---

[8]   As pointed out by Zhang (2000), the relationship between share value and earnings may not be linear.

adjustments happen in jumps, which are always costly (especially if the firm is filling for bankruptcy).

2.4 Whither Internal Control

In general, publicly traded companies are governed by a board of directors; in the US this is a legal requirement for incorporation. The board must oversee top management's actions on behalf of the shareholders. According to the Conference Board's annual survey, boards have on average nine members, meet about six times per year and each member receives basic compensation within the range of 10000 to 70000 dollars (Demski, 2003). Some of the members come from within the company, while others are outsiders.

The conflict of interest between directors and the CEO is nothing new: while directors aim at building and maintaining a reputation as honest experts, CEOs have incentives to 'capture' them, so as to protect their positions and extract greater benefits (Hermalin and Weisbach, 2003). The situation is clearly described by William H. Donaldson, the SEC Chairman (since December 2002):

> Over the past decade or more, at too many companies, the chief executive position has steadily increased in power and influence. In some cases the CEO had become more of a monarch than a manager. Many boards have become gradually more deferential to the opinions, judgements and decisions of the CEO and senior management team. This deference has been an obstacle to directors' ability to satisfy the responsibility that the owners – the shareholders – have delegated and entrusted to them (Donaldson, 2003b, p. 17).

That managers are taking control over boards is obvious to anyone who observes CEOs' compensation over a long period. A first spectacular jump occurred in the period 1980-1985; over those few years, the CEO compensation per dollar of profit doubled. In the nineties, this tendency was even more pronounced. The average real compensation for the 500 S&P CEOs leapt from 3.5 million dollars in 1992 to 14.7 million in 2000. The fall in average incomes was fairly limited during the crisis, since it was still as high as 9.4 million dollars in 2002.[9] Bebchuck et al. (2002) were among the first to suggest that in the Internet years, entrenched CEOs set out to 'capture' boards of directors and grant themselves large pay increases at the expense of shareholders. Arthur Levitt, a former and influential Chairman of the Securities and Exchange Commission, wrote that 'unseemly excessive compensation and separation packages are a consequence of boards falling victim to a seduction by the CEO' (Levitt, 2004, p. A7). Perel (2003, p. 384) points out that many directors are 'ill-qualified to proffer opinions on executive compensation; hence, many boards will decide on top executive compensation based on the advice of external consultants, most often

---

[9] See Hall and Murphy (2003). Similar data can be found in: 'Tough at the top. A survey of corporate leadership', *The Economist*, October 25th, 2003.

hired by ... the same top executives.' In an empirical analysis, Core at al. (1999) found that companies with weaker governance tend to pay their CEOs more.[10]

In a notorious example of lack of transparency and weak board control, the former *NYSE* chairman Richard Grasso obtained from the board, whose members were in general appointed by him, secret compensation of 48 million dollars on top of his declared 140 million dollars. When in September 2003 the authorities uncovered this hidden amount, the chairman was forced to resign and the board began a restructuring process.[11]

2.5 The Problem with Stock-option Based Compensation

As emphasized by Carson (2003, p. 392), 'terms of employment and compensation schemes can create incentives for unethical conduct' and 'rules, decision procedures and schemes for reward and compensation all need to be scrutinized for the incentive they create'. Let us follow his advice and take a closer look at the US executive compensation system.

In 1994, the US enacted Section 162(m) of the *Internal Revenue Code*, which capped corporate tax deductibility of compensations awarded to the five highest-paid executives at one million dollars per executive, *unless the additional income qualified as performance-based pay*. Unsurprisingly, after this regulatory change was implemented, many large companies set their managers' salary right at the upper limit, and then awarded them more in performance-related compensation. There are many ways to relate pay to performance, the traditional methods being bonuses based on profits or other quantitative targets (market share, customer satisfaction, innovation, etc.), and shares that can be sold at a later time. In practice, stock options became the preferred form of incentive pay.

In general, a *call* option gives the holder the right to buy a share prior to an 'expiration time' at an 'exercise price' fixed at the time the option is issued.[12] In most compensation schemes, the exercise price is equal to the market price at the issue date, and managers may convert a quarter of the total stock option grant at the end of every year over a five-year period. In many cases, when the manager decides to exercise his options, the company will issue new shares. This means the value of each individual share is diluted, since the company's market value is distributed between a higher number of shares.

Is this option worth anything? It certainly is for the executive concerned. He does not know what the exact price of the share will be at the time of exercise, but

---

[10] A caveat is put forward by Hermalin and Weisbach (2003): highly successful CEOs may command both high compensation and low monitoring by the board. Murphy and Zabojnik (2004) suggest that, to some extent, the increase in wages may be explained by increased competition between firms to attract good managers.

[11] None of the new board members will belong to institutions regulated by the NYSE, as was the case with the former board. See: 'John Reeds modest proposal', *The Economist*, November 22nd, 2003. See also the next chapter.

[12] Holders of 'American options' may exercise the option at any time prior to expiration, whereas 'European options' can be exercised only at the pre-determined expiration time.

he has an idea of the statistical distribution of the future price. He knows that if the share price goes up, he will benefit from the spread between the exercise price and the market price, while in the worst of cases, if the share price goes down, he will lose nothing. As a consequence, his expectations about the future gain can only be positive. For the company on the other hand, any compensation scheme including the value of a stock-option grant is a cost with manager labor input that affects corporate profit.

From a US tax standpoint, the spread between the market and exercise prices is considered as an expense and can be deducted from the company's taxable earnings. But strange as it may seem, US accounting rules in force in the late nineties did not require that stock option grants to managers and employees should be recorded as an expense; if stock-option pay expenses had been recorded as such, US companies' earnings per share would have been 14% lower than reported in the nineties (Botosan and Plumlee, 2001). The US accounting rules merely required the estimated market value (or 'fair' value) of the stock-option grant to be reported in a footnote to the annual financial statement! So, paradoxical though it may be, the massive recourse to stock option grants enabled companies to pay lower corporate taxes, while simultaneously declaring higher accounting earnings.

The main thrust of the argument against expensing stock option grants emphasizes that the traditional Black and Scholes (1973) option pricing model, which is extensively utilized for valuing publicly traded options, cannot apply to option-based compensation, since it takes no account of vesting periods (the option cannot be exercised immediately), non-transferability, the possibility of early exercise, shifts in earnings distribution that the option grant itself may entail, variable stock volatility, and so on. This argument remains unconvincing: theoretical research in the field is well-developed and more powerful models, able to take these specificities into account, can and have been designed (e.g. Huddart, 1994; Hemmer et al., 1994; Cuny and Jorion, 1995). The US regulatory board in charge of accounting standard-setting, the *Financial Accounting Standards Board* (FASB), has long acknowledged that satisfactory methods exist; FASB Statement No.123 (December 1995) *recommended* that companies should utilize fair value methods for assessing the cost of stock-based compensation. The general idea was that although no perfect evaluation method was available, a rough estimate was better than no estimate at all. But companies did not follow this sensible advice.

The only group of people that could benefit from this obvious shortage of transparency was the executives (Carson, 2003; Hall and Murphy, 2003; Levitt, 2004; Stiglitz, 2003). As pointed out by Guay et al. (2003, p. 408) the lack of transparency specific to un-expensed options helped top managers 'to justify awarding themselves excessively lucrative pay packages.' It does appear to be easier to convince boards to grant a manager a million-dollar pay increase in the form of an option plan (since no expense is recorded, and annual earnings are not affected) than in a million-dollar cash bonus.

For all these reasons, the volume of option-based revenues kept on increasing. In the nineties, nearly 80% of the rise in CEO pay took the form of stock options; given this dynamic, in the bubble years the share of option-based compensation represented as much as 60% to 70% of CEOs' total compensation (Perel, 2003).

Proponents claim that they provide an efficient mechanism for aligning manager and shareholder interests, and retaining good managers and staff in young companies that face cash shortages. Do massive stock option grants entail any risks? The answer to that question must bring both the compensation structure and the manager's decision horizon into the picture.

Let us consider the case of the manager of a company whose fundamentals are weak, and whose market value is being driven upwards by the bubble. Of course, the CEO knows that at some time in the future the game will be up. If most of its compensation consists of pending shares or options to become exercisable in the near future, the rational strategy for the manager will be to push up the share price as high as possible, cash the options, and watch the company collapse. This may have been the case at *Enron*, whose 'Old Economy' background (gas distribution) was shrinking, while the bulk of its earnings came from its risky dotcom branch, trading gas end energy. Kenneth Lay, the *Enron* CEO, cashed 120 million dollars in options a few weeks before the company went bankrupt, while employees were prevented from selling *Enron* shares (mostly components of their retirement plans). In the same vein, Gary Winnick, the CEO of *Global Crossing*, also made more than 130 million dollars by selling shares during the few weeks immediately before the company's bankruptcy. Studying a poll of 600 companies listed with the SEC, Rosner (2003) shows that fragile firms with no obvious signs of distress prior to bankruptcy were more likely to succeed in reporting overstated earnings in their financial statements than firms considered as fragile ex ante.

This logic may also explain why the majority of 'Old Economy' firms were not affected by this type of opportunistic behavior. If the manager knows that his company is robust, and that once the bubble bursts its value will realign with fundamentals, will he behave in the same way? Probably not. If he has to choose between a large one-off gain followed by job termination and the discounted value of future benefits on the job, the incentives to cheat are less powerful.

2.6 Corrupt Auditors and Financial Analysts

Accounting information would not have been so easy to manipulate without the complicity of corrupt *auditors*. Accounting firms were also greedy. They all carried out auditing and consulting activities, and most of them provided both services to the same client. In November 2000, alerted by the increasing signals that conflicts of interest were probably under way, the SEC made every endeavor to pass a rule that would have prohibited accounting firms from providing consulting services to their audit clients; but in the face of strong opposition from both audit firms and their clients, the SEC had to scale back its proposal (Palmrose and Saul, 2001). This failed regulation is an indicator of the global mood in the 'bubblish' US environment at the time, where common sense was completely overtaken by almost generalized opportunistic behavior. After the crises, the SEC's worst fears were validated.

The case of *Andersen*, one of what were five audit firms with a global network, is probably the most significant example of dishonest accounting firms. The name of this now defunct company was linked with almost all the notorious corporate scandals. In June 2002, after five weeks of evidence and ten days of deliberation, a jury found *Andersen* guilty of obstructing the course of justice in the *Enron* case. David Duncan, the leading *Andersen* partner in charge of auditing *Enron*, pleaded guilty to the charge of shredding thousands of documents. How could *Andersen* have been 'independent in fact and appearance' as required by the law, when more than half of its billion-dollar-a-week bills to Enron concerned non-audit services? (Demski, 2003).

Many other audit firms, including the other four major firms, allowed varying degrees of significant scope for abusive interpretation of the accounting rules, or even outright fraud. For instance, on September 25th, 2003, Thomas Trauger, a former auditor with *Ernst and Young*, was arrested for his alleged participation in the destruction of audit working documents during the audit of *NextCard*. Then, memorably, in early 2002 *Deloitte&Touche* reviewed the auditing practices of *Andersen* and concluded that the firm complied with the best standards. The accounting profession's reputation is likely to remain tarnished for a long time.

Beside boards and accounting firms, the financial status of public companies comes under close scrutiny from *security analysts* at banks, investment funds and rating agencies such as *Moody's*, *Standard & Poor's* or *Fitch*. Company management put tremendous pressure on these people too. Traditionally, analysts who advised their clients to buy the shares of a given company used to benefit from all the firm's favors, while those who advised to 'sell' were persecuted quite openly (for instance, being prevented from attending general shareholders' meetings, among other tactics). Rating agencies only downgraded *Enron's* bonds on November 28th, 2001, when the company was nearly bankrupt.

Companies obtained new means of putting the pressure on bank security analysts in 1999, when the *Gramm-Leach-Bliley Act on Brokers Rules* put an end to the *Glass-Steagall Act* of 1933. This had been introduced in the aftermath of the Great Depression, when 11000 of the US' 40000 banks went out of business, causing major disruption to the financial system and huge social pain for those who had seen their lifetime savings vanish. It set out a clear separation of financial intermediaries' investment activities and commercial activities. The generally accepted rationale for this law was well expressed in the brief filed by the *First National City Bank* (1970) in support of the Comptroller of the Currency:

...three well-defined evils were found to flow from the combination of investment and commercial banking: (i) banks were investing their own assets in securities with consequent risk to commercial and savings deposits; (ii) unsound loans were made in order to shore up the price of securities or the financial position of companies in which a bank had invested its own assets; (iii) a commercial bank's financial interest in the ownership, price, or distribution of securities inevitably tempted bank officials to press their banking customers into investing in securities which the bank itself was under pressure to sell because of its own pecuniary stake in the transaction (FNCB, 1970, pp. 40-42).[13]

---

[13] See: www.cftech.com/BrainBank/specialreports/GlassSteagall.html.

All these evils came back to haunt the economy of the late nineties, once the *Glass-Steagall Act* was on the verge of being abrogated. Banks rushed to underwrite bonds issued by star companies, while also having to advise the public whether or not to buy shares in these firms. The conflict of interest was more than obvious. In a typical example, *WorldCom* issued five billion bonds with *Citibank* as the legal underwriter. The same bank also granted Bernie Ebbers, *WorldCom's* CEO, a 400 million-dollar loan with *WorldCom* shares as collateral. Let us assume that the bank got hold of some information about the company's true financial position. Would it disclose it? Jack B. Grumman, financial analyst at *Salmon Smith Barney*, a *Citibank* partner, maintained his recommendation to buy *WorldCom* shares and even issued a forecast of a 100% increase in the share price, only three months before the company's bankruptcy (Stiglitz, 2003). In 2002, investigations by New York Attorney General Eliot Spitzer showed that Merrill Lynch analysts were doctoring their reports to win business for their banks' investment arms.[14]

To sum up, many factors contributed to the surge in dishonest managerial behavior during the Internet bubble years. At that time, increased 'noise' in the economy lowered the probability of the existing supervision system detecting deviant action. There are also many signs suggesting that the detection system itself, where boards of directors play the central role, was gradually 'captured' by the managers. CEOs succeeded in granting themselves ever increasing compensation packages, mostly in the form of stock options. This reinforced incentives for short-term planning, which proved to be an extremely dangerous practice in the context of the most fragile companies. Finally, by blocking the early signals that a slide in share prices might have conveyed, managers prevented timely error correction (any adjustment would probably have involved the loss of their jobs) and made bankruptcy inevitable.

3 Fighting Dishonesty

To restore trust after the crisis, the US administration threw itself energetically into developing business regulations, with the aim of strengthening corporate surveillance, fighting fraudulent accounting practices and enhancing the effectiveness of the legal system in this field.

On July 9th, 2002, a *Corporate Fraud Task Force* including US Attorneys, the FBI and the SEC was set up to oversee the investigation and prosecution of financial fraud, accounting fraud and other corporate criminal activity, and to provide enhanced inter-agency coordination of regulatory and criminal investigations. The *Sarbanes-Oxley Act*, signed in July 2002, was designed to tighten up supervision of the practices of the accounting profession, strengthen auditor independence rules, increase the accountability of executive officers and board directors, enhance the timeliness and quality of financial reports of public

---

[14] See: 'Wall Street's Top Cop', *Time*, December 22nd, 2002.

companies, and protect employees' retirement plans from insider trading.[15] Both the SEC and the new law require the CEOs and CFOs of large public companies to personally certify the accuracy and fairness of their companies' public filings.

The increased effectiveness of the US anti-fraud agencies helped them address more complex and insidious cases than the more trivial early frauds; notorious examples are the mutual funds scandal, where over fifteen large US mutual funds came under scrutiny for illegal practices, and the foreign exchange rate fraud. The list of top executives indicted for fraud grew longer every day (see the Corporate Task Fraud website).[16] Some of them have already been convicted and sentenced to jail terms and fines. Changes in the federal sentencing guidelines in 2001 and 2003 significantly raised the penalties for fraud; economically damaging frauds are now on the same level as armed robberies, and prison sentences of over 20 years are not unusual.[17]

All in all, the legal system has significantly stepped up both its effectiveness and toughness in dealing with corporate crime. But when it comes to dealing with the economic factors that contributed to the proliferation of dishonest manager behavior in the Internet bubble years, the US Administration has taken a comparatively soft stance on post-bubble reform.

The valuation of stock-based compensation became one of the most controversial issues in recent accounting history (Guay et al. 2003). Although many US companies unilaterally decided after the 2001 troubles to adopt fair value methods of expensing stock-option pay, the FASB did not make it mandatory. In December 2002, the FASB issued Statement No. 148, *Accounting for Stock-Based Compensation – Transition and Disclosure*, as an amendment to Statement No. 123 of December 1995. The document made only minor changes to existing regulations, mainly improving the quality of information available in the footnote to the yearly financial statements referred to earlier, and asking that this information should also be disclosed in the quarterly statements. But the FASB is pushing the reform further, and the chances of seeing it implemented improved in 2004; the Exposure Draft *Share-Based Payment* (March 31st, 2004) advocates the mandatory expensing of stock-option grants; companies may choose one of several accepted evaluation methods. It remains to be seen whether the industrial lobby from the west coast high-tech companies will manage to block this reform too.[18]

During the Internet bubble years, many boards of directors were actually 'captured' by the CEO and failed in their chief mission of monitoring the manager. After 2001, many companies spontaneously undertook a process of reviewing and 'cleaning up' their governance systems. While everybody agrees that directors

---

[15] The text of the *Sarbanes-Oxley Act* is available at www.pcaobus.org/rules/Sarbanes_Oxley _Act_of_2002.pdf.

[16] See www.usdoj.gov/dag/cftf/.

[17] 'Bosses behind bars', *The Economist*, June 12th, 2004.

[18] See: 'FASB Project Update Equity-Based Compensation', www.fasb.org/project/equity-based_comp.shtml, and 'US warned over options reform', *Financial Times*, July 1st, 2004. In Europe, companies using the International Accounting Standards will have to start expensing stock options from January 2005.

should not fall under the manager's influence, the question of how independence can be enforced is still open to debate. It is generally assumed that outsiders are more impervious than insiders to managers' charms. This is not necessarily true; for instance, if the manager has a say in recruiting a new board member, that board member may want to support the manager in troubled times (the 'gift exchange' principle, where one good turn deserves another). This uncertainty would explain why no new regulation addressed this important issue. In a notable exception, Section 301 of the *Sarbanes-Oxley Act* marks a singular step in the right direction: it stipulates that all boards of directors' audit committees should be made up of independent members of the board. The audit committee is important since it supervises the relationship between the company and the auditing firm.

As required by the *Sarbanes-Oxley Act*, a *Public Company Accounting Oversight Board* was set up in January 2003, to 'oversee the audit of public companies subject to the securities law...' (Section 101). This Board, an independent non-profit organization financed by compulsory contributions from all listed companies and security issuers, has wide-ranging inspection and rule-making authority over all auditing firms.[19] In an economic context where more than half of the American people hold shares and trade in shares is highly decentralized, providing accurate information about the financial position of listed companies should be seen as a *public good*. This information is needed by a myriad of shareholders; they should be considered the legitimate clients of the accounting firms. So far such a market for information – with direct trade in information between shareholders and accounting firms – has not emerged spontaneously. Mancur Olson's (1971) theory on collective action perhaps provides an answer to this coordination failure: the market cannot emerge, since no single small consumer would pay for the production of information, and all consumers have an incentive to free-ride on the collective production of information. One possible solution would be to let the government organize the production of high quality financial information. If, on behalf of shareholders, a government agency became the main client of auditing firms, it could then set up some form of managed competition between auditors (as has happened in the US defence sector).

Section 201 of the *Sarbanes-Oxley Act* prohibits auditing firms from providing a wide range of consulting services to their clients for at least 180 days after the end of the audit process. However, that implies that only six months after an audit, any auditor could be hired on a consulting contract by the same client. It will be interesting to see how frequently such dubious situations emerge in the future. Conflicts of interest can be ruled out only if the law imposes strict separation of audit and consulting firms. To comply with the law, in 2003, the 'big four' auditing firms split from their legal advisory arms and terminated their partnerships with major law firms.

The 2001 crisis differed from the *Great Depression* with respect to the relatively good financial position of the banking sector (the amount of bad loans was moderate). With some cynicism, it can be surmised that the US were lucky that the

---

[19] See 'Testimony before the United States Senate', by William J. McDonough, Chairman of the PCAOB at: www.pcaobus.org/transcripts/McDonough_11-20-03.asp.

bubble burst no later than 2001, only two years after the abrogation of the *Glass-Steagall Act*. By allowing banks to carry out brokerage activities, the *Gramm-Leach-Bliley Act* of 1999 left the door wide open for conflicts of interest between same-bank commercial and investment activities, and an increasing number of abuses have been recorded since. By strengthening the independence of research analysts relative to officials involved in investment activities, the Section 501 of the *Sarbanes-Oxley Act* makes a timid step in the right direction. In the same vein, on July 29, 2003 the Securities and Exchange Commission approved rules proposed by the New York Stock Exchange to specify the period over which a member firm engaged in a public offering of a security or as an underwriter or a dealer cannot publish research on this security. The rules also require analysts and members to disclose any conflicts of interest; in particular, they must provide information on whether in the past they had received any compensation from the issuer that is the subject of the research report.[20]

However, the current system of regulations is so complex it is hardly surprising that 'innovative' bankers find ways to circumvent it. The only sensible policy choice would be to reinstate a modern version of the *Glass-Steagall Act* imposing a clear separation of commercial and investment activities. Some may criticize this recommendation, pointing to the experience of Germany, where such conflicts of interest do not occur systematically and despite the lack of separation between investment and commercial/savings activities; but it must be borne in mind that the capital market is much less developed in Germany than in the United States. Relying more on banks to finance the corporate sector may provide a workable alternative to a highly regulated capital market.

4 Conclusion

The US corporate scandals of the early 2000s have provided a forceful reminder of a basic principle of economic analysis: when weak internal corporate control allows managers to set up policies that diverge significantly from shareholders' interests, corrections are ultimately brought about by external forces in the financial and goods markets. While these market-driven adjustments are necessary, they may be extremely brutal and may come with heavy social costs: firms go bust, growth is hampered and millions of employees may lose their jobs.

Most abuses were carried out by managers in companies with weak fundamentals, and most of them were related one way or another to speculation on the Internet and telecommunications markets. Managerial misconduct consisted essentially of manipulating investors' expectations, through artificially inflated earnings by means of false financial statements or other forms of fraudulent accounting. They successfully avoided early detection with the complicity of corrupt accounting firms and excessively tolerant financial analysts, and by taking

---

[20] In 2003, ten major US security firms agreed to pay 1.4 billion dollars to settle regulators' accusation that their analysts wrote too favorable reports in order to win underwriting assignments (*Wall Street Journal*, November 23, 2004).

advantage of the wave of naïve public faith in the New Economy saga. As shown by the US experience, the economic cost of reneging on ethical principles can be extremely high. Managers come to focus on short-term performances, and recourse to unethical actions – even those not motivated by hopes of personal gain – can only damage a firm's reputation and precipitate corporate collapse.

The best policymakers can do to avoid future corporate scandals is to make dishonest behavior a very expensive or ineffective strategy for managers. Of course, this presupposes the existence of an efficient legal system able to detect and sanction abuses. This system cannot work properly without clear economic rules. Those rules cannot be minimalist; it would be a mistake to believe that in the absence of external constraints, the resulting equilibrium will necessarily be optimal. The recent corporate scandals in the US provide support for Arrow's (1974) claim that without proper regulation, the capitalist economy would produce an insufficient amount of positive social externalities such as trust, loyalty and honesty.

References

Alchian, A. and Demsetz H. (1972), Production, Information Costs and Economic Organization, *American Economic Review*, 52, 5, pp. 777-795.

Arrow, K. J. (1974), *The Limits of Organization*, Norton, New York.

Bebchuck, L., Fried J. and Walker, D. (2002), Managerial Power and Rent Extraction in the Design of Executive Compensation, *University of Chicago Law Review*, 69, 3, pp. 751-61.

Becker, G. S. (1976), Altruism, Egoism, and Genetic Fitness: Economics and Sociobiology, *Journal of Economic Literature*, 14, 3, pp. 817-826.

Besancenot, D. and Vranceanu, R. (2004), The Information Limit to Managerial Honest Behavior, *Essec Working Paper* 04008, www.essec.fr.

Black, F. and Scholes, M. (1973), The Pricing of Options and Corporate Liabilities, *Journal of Political Economy*, 81, 3, pp. 637-654.

Botosan, C. and Plumlee, M. (2001), Stock Options Expense: the Sword of Damocles Revealed, *Accounting Horizons*, December 2001, 15, 4, pp. 311-327.

Brickley, J. A., Smith, Jr. C. W. and Zimmerman, J. L. (2002), Business Ethics and Organizational Architecture, *Journal of Banking and Finance*, 26, pp. 1821-1835.

Carson, T. L. (2003), Self-interest and Business Ethics: some Lessons of the Recent Corporate Scandals, *Journal of Business Ethics*, 43, pp. 398-394.

Core, J., Holthausen, R. and Larcker, D. (1999), Corporate Governance, Chief Executive Compensation and Firm Performance, *Journal of Financial Economics*, 51, pp. 371-406.

Cuny, C. J. and Jorion, P. (1995), Valuing Executive Stock Options with Endogenous Departure, *Journal of Accounting and Economics*, 20, pp. 193-205.

Demski, J. S. (2003), Corporate Conflicts of Interest, *Journal of Economic Perspectives*, 17, 2, pp. 51-72.

Donaldson, W. H. (2003a), *Testimony Concerning the Implementation of the Sarabanes Oxely Act of 2002*, Before the Senate Committee on Banking, Housing and Urban Affairs, September 9. www.sec.gov/news/testimony/090903tswhd.htm.

Donaldson, W. H. (2003b), Corporate Governance: What Has Happened and Where We Need to Go?, *Business Economics*, July, pp. 16-20.

Guay, W., Kothari S. P. and Sloan, R. (2003), Accounting for Employee Stock Options, *American Economic Review*, 93, 2, pp. 405-409.

Hall, B. J. and Murphy, K. J. (2003), The Trouble with Stock Options, *Journal of Economic Perspectives*, 17, 3, pp. 49-70.

Healy, P. M. and Palepu, K. G. (2003), The Fall of Enron, *Journal of Economic Perspectives*, 17, 2, pp. 3-26.

Hemmer, T., Matsunaga S. and Shelvin, T. (1995), Estimating the 'Fair Value' of Employee Stock Options with Expected Early Exercise, *Accounting Horizons*, 8, 4, pp. 23-42.

Hermalin, B. E. and Weisbach, M. S. (2003), Boards of Directors as an Endogenously Determined Institution: a Survey of the Economic Literature, *FRBNY Economic Policy Review*, April 2003, pp. 7-26.

Hirschleifer, J. (1977), Economics from a Biological Viewpoint, *Journal of Law and Economics*, 20, 1, pp. 1-52.

Huddart, S. (1994), Employee Stock Options, *Journal of Accounting and Economics*, pp. 207-231.

Jensen M. C. and Meckling, W. H. (1976), Theory of the Firm: Managerial Behavior, Agency Costs and Ownership Structure, *Journal of Financial Economics*, 3, 4, pp. 305-360.

Kaler, J. (2003), Differentiating Stakeholder Theories, *Journal of Business Ethics*, 46, pp. 71-83.

Kindelberger, C. P. (1978), *Manias, Panics, and Crashes: a History of Financial Crises*, Basic Books, New York.

Lev, B. (2003), Corporate Earnings: Facts and Fiction, *Journal of Economic Perspectives*, 17, 2, pp. 27-50.

Leutz, C., Nanda D. and Wysocki, P. (2003), Investor Protection and Earnings Management: an International Comparison, *Journal of Financial Economics*, 63, 9, pp. 507-527.

Levitt, A. (2004), Money, Money, Money, *The Wall Street Journal Europe*, November 23.

Malkiel, B. G. (1973), *A Random Walk Down Wall Street*, W.W. Norton, New York.

McKean, R. N., (1975), Economics of Trust, Altruism and Corporate Responsibility, In Phelps, E. S. (ed.), *Altruism, Morality and Economic Theory*, Russel Sage Foundation, New York, pp. 29-44.

Murphy, K. J. and Zabojnik, J. (2004), CEO Pay and Appointments: a Market Based Explanation for Recent Trends, *American Economic Review*, 94, 2, pp. 192-196.

Noreen, E. (1988), The Economics of Ethics: A New Perspective on Agency Theory, *Accounting, Organizations and Society*, 13, 4, pp. 359-369.

Olson, M. (1971), *Logic of Collective Action: Public Goods and the Theory of Groups*, Harvard University Press.

Palmrose, Z-V. and Saul, R. S. (2001), The Push for Auditor Independence, *Regulation*, Winter, pp. 18-23.

Perel, M. (2003), An Ethical Perspective on CEO Compensation, *Journal of Business Ethics*, 48, pp. 381-391.

Rosner, R. L. (2003), Earnings Manipulation in Failing Firms, *Contemporary Accounting Research*, 20, 2, pp. 361-408.

Sims, R. R. and Brinkmann, J. (2003), Enron Ethics (or Culture Matters more than Codes), *Journal of Business Ethics*, 45, 3, pp. 243-256.

Stiglitz, J. E. (2003), *The Roaring Nineties*, W.W. Norton.

Stiglitz, J. E. and Greenwald, B. C. (1991), Information, Finance, and Markets; the Architecture of Allocative Mechanisms, *NBER Working Paper*, No. 3652.

Watley, L. D. and May, D. R. (2003), Enhancing Moral Intensity: the Role of Personal and Consequential Information in Ethical Decision Making, *Journal of Business Ethics*, 50, 2, pp. 105-126.

Xie, Biao, Davidson, W. N. and DaDalt, P. J. (2003), Earnings Management and Corporate Governance: the Role of the Board and Audit Committee, *Journal of Corporate Finance*, 9, pp. 295-316.

Zhang, G. (2000), Accounting Information, Capital Investment Decisions, and Equity Valuation: Theory and Empirical Implications, *Journal of Accounting Research*, 38, 2, pp. 271-295.

Chapter 13

An Exchange of Values:
The NYSE's Governance Crisis

Andrei Postelnicu

1 Introduction[1]

The *New York Stock Exchange* is more of an icon of Western capitalism than any other institution. Without it, corporations such as *General Electric, IBM* or *Boeing* would not exist as we know them today, because the NYSE helps the vital process of capital formation that fuels the growth of such corporations. Central to the NYSE's standing at the core of Western capitalism is its credibility, the perception that corporations coming to raise capital and investors investing their capital through the exchange are getting a fair chance at doing so in a transparent and equitable manner.

The credibility of the NYSE and the validity of its governance structure were under close scrutiny by the summer of 2003, when an apparent attempt to improve the governance of the exchange grew into a scandal. For the first time in its history, the NYSE disclosed the compensation of its chairman and chief executive, Richard Grasso. The amount involved – a lump-sum payment of $1395m, and other benefits – spurred a public furor and led to Mr Grasso's resignation. In addition, the compensation crisis compounded already existing credibility shortcomings of the NYSE and sharpened criticism of its governance.[2]

However, the crisis at the NYSE not only reflects – yet again – Arrow's (1974) assertion that capitalist organizations fail to produce a sufficient amount of trust and other such positive social externalities when left to their own devices. It also presents numerous lessons about the importance of ethical behavior in an organization, and about the importance of solid institutions, lessons that warrant careful examination over time. It is not yet clear how Dick Grasso broke the norms of conduct at the NYSE. While Mr Grasso, since he was dismissed, has argued he is the victim of a witch-hunt aimed at sullying his reputation, his former employer

[1] Revised and updated version of the paper presented to the international seminar on 'Economy and Ethics' organized by the New Europe College, the Romanian Economic Society and the Konrad Adenauer Foundation, Bucharest, 12-13 December, 2003.

[2] 'NYSE Announces New Contract For Dick Grasso Through 2007', NYSE Website, August 27, 2003 http://www.nyse.com/Frameset.html?displayPage=/press/2_2004.html; Andrei Postelnicu, 'NYSE pays chief $139m lump sum', *Financial Times*, August 28, 2003.

contends he must give back a large portion of his compensation, because the NYSE board broke the law when it calculated it and approved it. A legal battle between him and the exchange seeks to clarify the legality of his pay package and has long until it will conclude.[3]

The next section of this chapter sets the background against which the Grasso compensation crisis erupted, describing Mr Grasso's ascent into the higher echelons of Wall Street leadership. Section 3 chronicles the investigation into trading practices on the NYSE floor and the questions arising about Mr Grasso's leadership of the exchange. The forth section recounts the debacle over Mr Grasso's compensation and the furor that ensued, leading to his dismissal by the NYSE board. Section 5 looks at the reforms drawn up by John Reed, Mr Grasso's successor, in a bid to address the most pressing issues revealed by the Grasso scandal; Section 6 describes the early measures taken by John Thain, the new NYSE chief executive officer, as he tries to set a new direction for the NYSE and address criticism of its trading system by radically reforming it. The seventh section consists of Mr Reed's own assessment of these measures and his view on the importance of ethics at the NYSE, as described in a specific interview for this project. The eighth section analyzes the early outcome of this crisis and the effectiveness of the NYSE's attempts to reform itself, contrasting the findings with the need for government intervention when the capitalist system proves ineffective in fostering ethical behavior. In the end the chapter argues that the Grasso controversy has showed that government intervention to reform institutions following crises is not required provided the institutions in question are strong enough to reform themselves in a culture of accountability. However, such institutions and such a culture are the exception and not the rule, leaving government the task of at least overseeing resolutions to crises similar to the NYSE's and raising the possibility of inadequate response to such crises for a variety of reasons.

2 From Rags to Riches – A Wall Street Hero Makes his Name

On September 11th, 2001 and in the aftermath of the terrorist attacks on New York's World Trade Center, two strong personalities emerged as the city's leaders, leading it through turmoil with steely resolve. They were both of Italian descent, both came from poor upbringing and had come to embody the American dream. One was Rudy Giuliani, the mayor of the Big Apple, as New York is known.

The other was Richard Grasso, the chairman of the New York Stock Exchange. He took the attacks as an attack on capitalism, for which he fancied himself to be

---

[3] See Vincent Boland and John Labate, 'SEC asks markets to review governance', *Financial Times*, March 27, 2003; Vincent Boland, 'NYSE chairman slips up on governance', *Financial Times*, March 28, 2003; Mary Chung and Andrei Postelnicu, '"Specialists" at NYSE face probes of abuses', *Financial Times*, April 21, 2003; Vincent Boland, 'NYSE chief's pay under scrutiny', *Financial Times*, May 8, 2003 and Andrei Postelnicu, 'NYSE in push to improve governance', *Financial Times*, June 6, 2003.

the meta-CEO. Born in the immigrant neighborhood of Jackson Heights in Queens, a long train journey and worlds away from Wall Street's lure, Mr Grasso joined the NYSE 37 years ago after stint in the army and having decided college wasn't for him. He then earned little over $80 per week, and worked his way through every nook and cranny of the exchange, learning it by heart over the years.[4]

By the time Dick Grasso became chairman of the NYSE he had to put up with being sidelined for four years for the post he had readied himself for his entire life. He took the world's leading stock market on a roller coaster ride of technology-driven reform in a bid to make it the choice venue for the world's top companies to list shares. Out went paper trading tickets, in came thousands of screens and dozens of television camera, and the NYSE trading floor became one of the world's largest TV studios, broadcasting the daily spectacle of stock trading to an audience of millions around the globe. By building an unprecedented media outreach operation, Dick Grasso built the NYSE into a worldwide brand with which he wanted to persuade other companies that they needed to be associated.

And the companies did come. The number of NYSE-listed companies grew spectacularly in the mid- to late-1990s, as the fever of the economic expansion cheapened capital and made the US an even more attractive place to tap the markets than it already was by virtue of its size, depth and liquidity. Under Dick Grasso's tenure the NYSE had indeed become a world-recognized brand, synonymous is success in global business at the peak of the most spectacular market rally in recent memory. Mr Grasso had managed to best critics of the NYSE who had predicted its demise once again in favor of the computer servers of the electronic NASDAQ stock market and others like it.

But by September 11th it was evident the NYSE was in battered shape from the post-bubble shocks, yet still fit enough to survive, while its electronic competitors were a lot worse for the wear.

So after the two jetliners flew into the Twin Towers that fateful Tuesday morning in September, Dick Grasso made it a life-and-death goal to show the world that American capitalism would not be bowed into submission. Working day and night with members of the NYSE, telephone companies, IT engineers, and co-coordinating their efforts, Mr Grasso tested the systems of the NYSE to ensure proper functionality and the markets opened the Monday following the attacks, September 17th. It later emerged that they could have opened earlier. In that first trading session after the attacks, about 2bn shares were traded, and every trade was executed, true to the form Mr Grasso had built into the NYSE culture.

He became Wall Street's hero at a time when Wall Street needed heroes more than anything. It was the finest hour of a career that had long been on a vertiginous upward path. But careers fall on Wall Street as quickly as they rise. A mere two years after the attacks, to the day, Mr Grasso was finding himself at the centre of a public furor over his compensation. On September 11th, 2003, the *Financial Times* ran a front-page story saying Mr Grasso's leadership of the NYSE in the aftermath of the attacks had earned him a $5m bonus, one of many he received to amount to a $187.5m pay package, of which he received $139.5m in late August in a lump sum.

---

[4]   See Andrei Postelnicu, 'The bull market hero at bay', *Financial Times*, August 30, 2003.

The $5m bonus story was one of dozens about Mr Grasso's salary and about the NYSE's ongoing series of embarrassments dating from the beginning of this year, in a storm that gathered pace at alarming speed.[5]

3 The Gathering Storm

The early signs of trouble at the Big Board came in early 2003, when Martha Stewart, a board member and one of America's most prominent business icons, resigned from her directorship amid mounting scrutiny of insider trading allegations. Further trouble emerged when Mr Grasso's decision to appoint Sandy Weill, the chief executive of Citigroup, to the board, triggered angry responses from Eliot Spitzer, the New York state attorney general. Mr Spitzer had just concluded a $1.4bn settlement with Wall Street firms that included Citi over allegations of improper behavior among analysts. He felt that appointing Mr Weill to the NYSE board as a representative of the public amounted to a shameful decision, and said so loudly and frequently enough, joining others, until Mr Weill's nomination was withdrawn.

Then during Easter week in April, it emerged that a floor trader responsible for making markets in *General Electric* had been suspended from his job amid allegations of violations of trading rules. The media, including the FT, wrote this was in the context of a broader investigation of so-called 'front running', or trading ahead of customer orders, by the specialists at the heart of the NYSE's trading model. The exchange later said it was in effect another offence, which was not a federal crime but only a breach of its own rules.

The investigation wreaked havoc in the close-knit community of the NYSE trading floor, the last remaining market model in which humans have a central role of all the leading stock exchanges in the world. Allegations started to mount that the NYSE was not enforcing the rules properly on its own member firms, that its trading system was outdated and prone to human error, and that it should be scrapped. Through it all, Mr Grasso defended his investigators vigorously and promised a swift resolution of the matter. But behind the scenes, there was increased acrimony between exchange regulators and floor traders, many of whom were contending they had done nothing wrong, and the problems were not as widespread as they were portrayed.

To top it all off, the regulators at the *Securities and Exchange Commission* stepped up scrutiny of corporate governance at the US exchanges, in May 2003 asking them to obey the same rules they are enforcing on their listed companies. In an interview with the FT a few months before, Mr Grasso scoffed at the idea that the NYSE should obey the same rules it imposes on the companies that list shares on it. Among other things, these rules include disclosing the compensation of top executives. The SEC's move to step up scrutiny of the US stock exchanges was largely seen as a reaction to a *Wall Street Journal* story in early May 2003

---

[5] See Andrei Postelnicu and Vincent Boland, 'Grasso got $5m bonus for "9/11 leadership"', *Financial Times*, September 11, 2003.

reporting that Mr Grasso had taken home at least $10m in 2002, in the midst of a bear market that had significantly diminished the profits of the NYSE's member firms and the financial-services industry in general. Responding to the SEC request, the NYSE said it was drawing up reforms of its governance and would take action soon.

After a board meeting in June, when it elected several new directors including Madeleine Albright, former state secretary, to the board, the NYSE said that it would adopt a broad agenda of governance reforms that included measures meant to resolve conflict of interest in its board, disclosing executive pay, and so on. Meanwhile, it was struggling to resolve the specialist investigation, with firms refusing to settle charges they felt were not clear, much less just. The largest of the floor trading firms, *LaBranche*, was challenging the regulatory authority of the NYSE by refusing to hand over some 8,000 emails, saying it needed to protect its employees' privacy.[6]

By the time the summer lull of late August came to Wall Street, resentment reigned supreme on the trading floor of the NYSE. There was talk of gathering signatures to replace the board and remove the one that was seen as too subservient to Mr Grasso. Traders who had not gone on holiday were increasingly vocal in their criticism of the exchange and its chairman. Senior members of the NYSE were frequently saying that its legacy was at stake.

4 Payday at the NYSE

It was in this context that in the last week of August the New York Stock Exchange announced it decided to extend Dick Grasso's contract until 2007, even though it had not been due for renegotiation until the following year. The exchange board, in a press release gushing with praise for Mr Grasso, said that it would disburse a total of $139.5m to him, the sum representing deferred compensation, incentive awards and savings accounts balances.

> Under Dick's leadership, the NYSE has experienced tremendous growth and success. It has added 1549 of its 2800 listed companies, including most of our 500 non-US companies. During this period the market capitalization of the companies listed on the NYSE has more than doubled to $14.8 trillion. In the process, Dick revolutionized the Exchange's technological platform, making it the most efficient and sophisticated in the industry. The value of a seat on the exchange has nearly tripled during his tenure. And throughout his term, Dick has shown an unwavering commitment to regulation and the interests of America's 85 million investors...Dick's leadership has been outstanding. (Source: NYSE.)

Traders who were reading the press released could not believe their eyes, they spliced it in every direction and were keen to point out everything wrong with it.

---

[6] See Andrei Postelnicu and Adrian Michaels, 'LaBranche defies NYSE over e-mails' Financial Times, August 9, 2003; Andrei Postelnicu, 'NYSE regulatory role challenged', Financial Times, August 22, 2003, Andrei Postelnicu and John Labate, 'LaBranche hearing set to turn focus on governance at NYSE', *Financial Times*, August 26, 2003.

One senior exchange member said to me: 'He's taking credit for the market going up...next thing you know he'll take credit for the sun coming up.' The former chairman of ITT, Rand Araskog, whose own compensation package had been questioned, said the sum was an outrage. With every day that went by, the chorus of critics grew larger.

Elsewhere on Wall Street, where such sums did not raise eyebrows, other executives were puzzled that Mr Grasso was guaranteed an 8 per cent return on his retirement savings, thus reducing the risk element that other executive packages included.

Less that a week later William Donaldson, chairman of the *Securities and Exchange Commission*, sent a stern and exasperated letter to the NYSE board asking for full disclosure of the process through which the sum awarded to Mr Grasso was decided. He wanted minutes of compensation committee meetings, briefings by outside compensation consultants, minutes of board meetings at which compensation was discussed, copies of Mr Grasso's contracts going back several years. And he wanted it all in a week.

Gathered at the briefing in which the NYSE announced it sent the requested documentation, the journalists were wondering what that day's surprise would be. The NYSE didn't disappoint. Dick Grasso started off by saying that he never asked for any of the money awarded to him. He wanted to put the matter behind him so that the NYSE can focus on the future and running the world's best stock exchange. He said that his only words to the board were: 'I feel blessed, thank you.'

In order to put the controversy behind him, Mr Grasso announced that he would renounce an additional $48m in bonuses and awards to which he was also entitled. Consternation in the room was palpable.[7]

Journalists gathered at the briefing asked Mr Grasso how much he estimated his job was of a regulatory nature, and how much was of an entrepreneurial nature. He said that only a third of his time was spent on regulatory issues. In addition, Mr McCall repeatedly said how the entire board of the NYSE was fully behind Mr Grasso.

Neither this fact, nor anything else Mr Grasso and Mr McCall said in the briefing could stem the vituperative flows from the public and trading floor community following the news conference. Whereas before many traders at the NYSE were reluctant to go on the record with their criticism, every day that went by in early September added new names to the list of those disapproving of Mr Grasso's and the NYSE board's behavior. And this included increasingly more people calling on Mr Grasso and the board to resign. James Needham, former chairman of both the SEC and the NYSE, James Maguire, James Rutledge, both senior members of the NYSE, alongside other members were but a few of those asking the board to resign along with Mr Grasso.

In the meantime divisions emerged among board members in their position towards Mr Grasso's package. While never on the record, powerful NYSE

---

[7] See Andrei Postelnicu, 'NYSE chairman forgoes $48m package to stem pay criticism', *Financial Times*, September 10, 2003.

directors were signaling their concern for the damage being inflicted on the NYSE by the crisis.

The critical mass to calls for resignation came when the heads of two public pension funds from California, *Calpers* and *CalSTRS*, representing more than $240bn in capital, called on Mr Grasso to resign on September 16th, 2003. This move, from two of the NYSE's biggest clients, gave the board the impetus it was lacking and at an emergency meeting called the following day, Richard Grasso's 36-year career at the NYSE ended. The press release said he had offered to resign 'with the deepest reluctance' if the board asked him to do it, which the board did, with a convincing majority of votes.[8]

What ensued next was a flurry of speculation about Mr Grasso's successor, while the board appointed Mr McCall as lead director to represent it and the exchange to the public. Names such as Paul Volcker, the former chairman of the Federal Reserve Board, or Robert Rubin, the former Treasury secretary, and William McDonough, the former head of the New York Fed, were all thrown out in the press but systematically the persons in charge denied any interest in leading the New York Stock Exchange through its worst crisis in decades.

5 Fixing the NYSE – A Statesman Returns to Wall Street

Three days after Mr Grasso's resignation, Hank Paulson, chairman of Goldman Sachs and a NYSE board member, picked up the phone and called an old friend in France, to try to lure him from a very happy retirement in Ile de Ré.

'Hi John, this is Hank. We have a little problem,' began Mr Paulson. At the other end of the phone was John Reed, the former chief executive of Citigroup and a legend of the banking industry. Having turned banking on its head by heavy use of technology and having engineered the merger that created the world's biggest financial services group, Mr Reed did not stand for re-election as chairman in 1996, letting Sandy Weill run the merged Citigroup. Seven years later, he agreed to come and start work at healing the NYSE the day before Mr Weill was to retire from Citi. Aside from that irony, Mr Reed made a poignant statement about the compensation issue at the NYSE by asking for $1 as salary. Upon taking the job, Mr Reed described the NYSE as too important to be left alone, adding that this was one of those requests he couldn't possibly shirk from.[9]

Mr Reed started his new job with a narrow and focused agenda that highlighted the ethical dimension of his mandate: first, he would implement a new architecture

---

[8] See Andrei Postelnicu and Vincent Boland, 'Pension funds tell Grasso to go', Financial Times, September 17, 2003; Vincent Boland and Andrei Postelnicu, 'Grasso forced out as chief of NYSE', Financial Times, September 18, 2003; 'Press Release announcing Grasso resignation' New York Stock Exchange Sept. 17th 2003 http://nyse.com/Frameset.html? displayPage=/press/2_2004.html.

[9] Vincent Boland, Andrei Postelnicu and Lionel Barber, 'There has to be a careful, deliberative process, there is only one New York Stock Exchange', *Financial Times*, November 13, 2003.

of the exchange in order to solve its governance problems and address potential conflicts of interest; second, he would find a permanent successor for himself; third, he would get back to retirement.

He systematically refused to broaden this agenda on grounds that only a full-time chairman of the NYSE should implement any more radical reforms than what he proposed. By the end of November 2003, Mr Reed had fired the former board of 27, and replaced it with one of eight directors, only two of whom were on the former body: Madeleine Albright, the former state secretary, and Herbert Allison, the head of the public sector teachers' retirement fund, TIAA-CREF. According to the changes voted by NYSE member to the exchange constitution, no executive of a Wall Street firm would be allowed to be on the board.

The centerpiece of Mr Reed's reform plan was to put the NYSE's regulatory arm directly under the board's supervision, while the stock trading arm was left to be overseen by a Board of Executives, which would be made of executives from NYSE member firms, floor traders, investors, and exchange members renting out their seats, or right to trade.

The reforms drew immediate fire from some constituencies arguing that investors did not get sufficient representation on the new board. Additionally, Mr Reed's early tenure was marred by the leaking of a confidential report in which the SEC was slamming the NYSE for dragging its feet in investigating its member firms.[10]

However, the overall verdict on Mr Reed's tenure as interim chairman and chief executive of the New York Stock Exchange seems to be that it has been a qualified success, in that Mr Reed has achieved most of this agenda, albeit with some delays. In early January 2004, the NYSE board appointed John Thain, a former executive at Goldman Sachs, as chief executive officer of the NYSE, with a salary that is substantially lower than Mr Grasso's – $4m per annum.[11]

6 John Thain and The New Era

Within three weeks of taking up his post as chief executive of the NYSE, Mr Thain announced a broad set of changes to the way the exchange trades stocks, aimed at silencing criticism that the world's largest stock exchange is rigged in favor of a small set of insiders. Shortly thereafter, the SEC settled charges of trading violations with the NYSE traders for $241.5m and the firms have made efforts to

---

[10] See Vincent Boland and Andrei Postelnicu, 'John Reed returns to Wall Street's limelight', *Financial Times*, September 22, 2003; Vincent Boland, 'Calpers says NYSE reforms "doomed"', *Financial Times*, November 7, 2003.

[11] See Andrei Postelnicu, Lionel Barber and David Wighton, '"A great part of America": John Thain sets out to restore trust in the New York Stock Exchange', *Financial Times*, April 2, 2004; Andrei Postelnicu, 'Ketchum aims "to build culture of compliance"', *Financial Times*, June 29, 2004 Tuesday.

put the scandal behind them, focusing on how the proposed reforms of the market will affect their business.[12]

The NYSE also appointed a new Chief Regulatory Officer in Richard Ketchum, a respected former regulator at the National Association of Securities Dealers, who has worked on increasing the staff of his division and in an interview has said he wanted to 'create a culture of compliance' at the NYSE. Under the new structure of the NYSE, Mr Ketchum reports directly to the board of directors, which is still chaired by Mr Reed, who agreed to stay as chairman of the NYSE.

Both the appointment of Mr Ketchum and Mr Thain's proposed reforms of the NYSE market structure attempt to address head-on what critics have called structural shortcomings of the NYSE that invited breaches of ethical conduct that appear separate from the controversy of Mr Grasso's compensation but are closely linked to it.

The main reason why Mr Grasso's compensation was contentious had to do with the regulatory function of the New York Stock Exchange. Under a system of self-regulation designed in the 1930s, the exchange also polices the market it runs, ensuring trading is done according to complex rules. Under this system, Mr Grasso was the first-line regulator for most of Wall Street's biggest firms. The chief executives were sitting on his board and also deciding his compensation.

Furthermore, as the *Financial Times* and other media pointed out, Mr Grasso had been deciding the composition of the board committees, including the compensation committee. Therefore, Mr Grasso decided who would set his salary, and many of those in that position were heads of firms he was responsible for regulating. In repeated public interviews, Mr Reed characterized this system as inherently riddled with conflicts of interest, of which the compensation issue is the most blatant. While on the surface the regulation of the NYSE itself appeared sufficient, it was a fitting example of Arrow's view on the failures of an unregulated organization, showing that to be effective, regulation must exist in practice and not just on paper.

The reforms to the NYSE market trading systems attempt to eliminate opportunities for illegal/unethical behavior at the heart of the NYSE's market. By using human traders to conduct auctions in which buyers and sellers of shares are matched, the NYSE differs from competing markets where computers do the matching of orders. The exchange argues its system ensures 'fair and orderly' markets, which offer better prices to both buyers and sellers, and reduces volatility in stock prices, something companies issuing shares have said they appreciate – in general volatile markets are seen as prone to manipulation, so the NYSE is perceived as more stable.

---

[12] See Vincent Boland and Demetri Sevastopulo, 'NYSE to seek big fines from specialists', *Financial Times*, October 17, 2003; Andrei Postelnicu and Gary Silverman, 'Thain to tackle NYSE reforms', *Financial Times*, December 19, 2003; Andrei Postelnicu, 'NYSE ready to back more automation', *Financial Times*, February 5, 2004; Andrei Postelnicu and Adrian Michaels, 'NYSE specialists agree $240m settlement', *Financial Times*, February 18, 2004.

However, critics use the most recent investigation of trading violations, as well as others in the past as evidence that this system invites traders to take advantage of information they see before the rest of the market in order to make profits for themselves. While rules attempt to restrict the traders' opportunities for abuse and enforce punishments on those who are caught, the chaos of the trading floor provides ample opportunity to skirt these rules, critics contend.

Consequently, the reforms proposed by Mr Thain aim to expand electronic trading where computers handle many of the orders sent to the NYSE. In addition, Mr Ketchum's regulation division has implemented monitoring systems that put all the steps involved in trading a stock under close scrutiny and provide a back-up.

While these measures can be seen as necessary from a business standpoint, they have an ethical component to them that targets opportunities for misconduct and aims to eliminate them. And while the expansion of automatic trading can be seen as a use of technology to encourage ethical behavior, Mr Reed noted, alongside numerous other securities industry insiders, that computers can be programmed to act unethically and their use does not guarantee proper behavior. To this extent, the failure of organizations to produce trust is not related to how much technology they use.

7 View from Within – John Reed's Assessment[13]

Little over a year after taking the job of chairman of the NYSE, John Reed gave an overall assessment of the impact of the measures undertaken on the ethical blueprint of the organization. In assessing the debacle surrounding Mr Grasso's compensation, Mr Reed characterizes it as a failure of governance, rather than ethics per se, but later on he equated the two notions. By failing to adopt sound compensation practices and awarding an oversized package to Mr Grasso, the former NYSE board failed to meet both a 'standard of care – they pay attention – and a standard of loyalty – ensuring there are no conflicts', Mr Reed said. He added that as chairman, Mr Grasso also failed in his duties to run a board that functioned properly. The NYSE chairman pointed out that sound ethical practices are a 'necessary but not sufficient' component of the exchange. 'When you run a trading floor ... you have to make it clear that it is an environment where ethical lapses will not be tolerated,' he said.

The NYSE did fail from an ethical standpoint, Mr Reed said, when traders on the floor of the exchange were proven to be taking advantage of their position for personal gain, breaking their fiduciary trust to their customers. The specialist investigation in 2003 is the most recent example of that, with a similar one having taken place in the late 1990s. Mr Reed said the exchange had to work with the trading firms to ensure the compensation policies of those firms are re-designed in order to eliminate de facto incentives to engage in unethical behavior. However, he

---

[13] John Reed, chairman of the NYSE, agreed to a telephone interview for this chapter, interview which was conducted on October 31st, 2004. All quotes attributed to Mr Reed in the subsequent section are excerpts from that interview.

said the exchange itself had to re-organize in order to reduce incentives for unethical behavior. During the investigation, many specialists complained the NYSE's regulatory arm was being abused by Mr Grasso to carry out vendettas. LaBranche refused to let NYSE regulators see its email but offered to make them available to the SEC, in a statement of lack of confidence in the NYSE regulators.

To avoid such occurrences, or others in which unethical behavior is tolerated because it is beneficial for the business of the NYSE, Mr Reed separated the regulatory arm of the exchange from its operational division, and Mr Ketchum is reporting directly to the board, not to the chief executive, Mr Thain. The ultimate goal, Mr Reed said, is 'not to create a regulatory structure to catch them [violators], I'm sure we could create that but that's not the issue, the issue is that there shouldn't be anything to catch.'

According to Mr Reed, the NYSE remains vulnerable if any other lapses are unveiled. A trading organization such as the NYSE has to be presumed as ethical if it is to function at all. 'If you don't have ethical behavior, it doesn't make any difference what else you do, you're finished, because an exchange has to be trusted.'

Mr Reed said that 'a tremendous amount of mail' from ordinary people he never met suggests the exchange is headed on the right path and appears to be generally perceived as more ethical a year after its crisis.

8 Concluding Remarks

The dimension of the NYSE crisis that involves Mr Grasso's compensation illustrates a breach of the most fundamental tenet of the capitalist system as an ethical one – to each according to his/her contribution (Keren, 2003). The NYSE – through retroactive investigation – has arrived at the conclusion that Mr Grasso's compensation was outsized relative to his contributions to the exchange and is seeking some of its back. Using a law governing not-for-profit corporations in New York State, the attorney-general of New York is litigating the case to get those sums restituted to the NYSE.

There is evidence that several NYSE boards wrestled with how to measure Mr Grasso's economic contribution to the exchange. As a not-for-profit corporation, the NYSE had no share price to gauge its success in the public market, and also could not offer its chief executive options that might have caused him to manipulate the share price. In this respect, Mr Grasso's compensation and his behavior, as well as that of the NYSE boards at the time, do not fit well into the analytical framework outlined by Shleifer (2004).[14]

The NYSE boards that set Mr Grasso's pay appeared to have adopted a strategy derided by William Donaldson, the chairman of the SEC. 'The conventional wisdom of many corporate boards these days has become that In order to remain

---

[14] Shleifer (2004, p. 414) asserts that 'shareholders during the [internet] bubble were happy to compensate these executives for promoting the bubbles in their shares'. He studies the link between share prices and executive compensation.

competitive, executive compensation must be in the top quarter of companies in their industry' (NABE, 2003, 19). However, the NYSE is unlike any other company, it does not have a group of companies like it from where the board could gather information on executive compensation. As a consequence, the boards that set Mr Grasso's pay used a group of financial-services firms to assess benchmarks for Mr Grasso's compensation, and paid him above those benchmarks. A further twist to this comes from the fact that the NYSE is also a regulatory authority, much like the Securities and Exchange Commission or partially, the Federal Reserve. The chairmen of those two bodies, however, have a yearly salary of less than $200,000 per year, without the bonuses and the incentive awards in Mr Grasso's compensation. Even after accepting Mr Grasso's own description of his job duties as being only one-third regulation-related, his pay package appeared outsized. The furor about Mr Grasso's compensation, however, had less to do with the amount of money in question than with the way in which it had been arrived at. Throughout the crisis, I heard frequent references to the legacy and symbolism of the NYSE, the values for which it stands, namely giving everyone an equal opportunity at being successful. Grey-haired traders would reverently refer to the NYSE as a jewel of the American and world economy, and were more furious at Dick Grasso for desecrating those values than for the actual sums he had been awarded. They were all in that business to make money, but Mr Grasso's lapses were seen as egregious departure from the rules that ensured that money was made fairly, because the people who awarded him his pay package had an incentive to keep Mr Grasso well-rewarded, as he was their regulator. To some traders at the NYSE, the procedure through which Mr Grasso's pay had been arrived at corrupted the very essence of what made Wall Street what it is, the capital of world capitalism.[15]

It is noteworthy that Mr Grasso's dismissal did not come as a result of intervention from government, but rather after public outcry. This highlights the unique role of the NYSE as a private institution with a very clear public mandate – while government regulators did not feel compelled to intervene in the crisis, the general public and stakeholders from the public acted to influence the NYSE.

The reluctance of US government authorities to intervene in the Grasso debacle at the NYSE, and indeed the limited manner in which the SEC did intervene – by asking the NYSE to provide ample documentation about Mr Grasso's pay and the rationale behind it – have to do with the NYSE's status as a self-regulatory organization (SRO). As one of a handful of SROs, the NYSE is responsible for setting and enforcing its own set of policies and measures that ensure the stock market it operates functions properly. As a member organization, it can enforce those rules on the firms that elect to become its members, which they are required to do if they want to participate in the stock market operated by the NYSE. At the same time, however, the NYSE competes with other stock exchanges both in the US and elsewhere for new stock listings and flow of stock trading orders, which are vital to maintain its liquidity. To that end, the NYSE must create and implement measures that ensure its continued efficiency in trading stocks. This

---

[15] See Vincent Boland, Andrei Postelnicu and Adrian Michaels, 'NYSE members "appalled" at Grasso pay', *Financial Times*, September 13, 2003.

makes the NYSE very similar to any other for-profit corporation and Mr Grasso felt he deserved to be paid for maintaining the NYSE as a leading market for stocks, competitive globally with others.

The furor over Mr Grasso's compensation, coming shortly after the investigation of the specialist trading firms and its related dispute between LaBranche – the biggest of these firms – and the NYSE, cast a very bright light in the potential for conflicts of interest resulting from the NYSE's regulatory and operational roles. While no public evidence of this emerged from the NYSE itself, media organizations such as the *Financial Times, The Wall Street Journal* and the *New York Times* wrote about Mr Grasso's use of his regulatory clout to rule over the NYSE with an iron fist. Brickley et al. (2002, p. 1821) point out that 'business ethics and the internal structure of the organization are inextricably linked.' Therefore, Mr Grasso's use of his regulatory authorities illustrated that link and the failure of the NYSE's organizational architecture at the time to promote ethical behavior. The proof that the revelations of Mr Grasso abusing his regulatory powers had substance came when Mr Reed devised the NYSE's new organizational architecture that took supervision and control of the NYSE's regulatory division away from the chief executive officer and directly under the oversight of a now independent board of directors. The recognition for a need for those reforms came when they were approved by an overwhelming proportion of the NYSE's members and by the SEC. In order to promote ethical behavior, the NYSE removed the link between the chief executive and the regulatory division of the NYSE. As Brickley et al. (2002, p. 1822) note, 'to increase the likelihood that individuals will behave in desired ways in their roles … the firm's organizational structure can be structured to encourage those behaviors.'

Further recognition of the justification of the NYSE reforms came in early November 2004 when the SEC proposed a rule that would mandate other SROs such as the NYSE to also separate their regulatory divisions from their market operations and business interests, in addition to imposing other changes on SROs that mirror closely the steps taken by the NYSE. (SEC Rules 6a-5 and 15Aa-3, 2004).[16]

A discussion of the ethical implications of the Grasso scandal and the broader crisis at the NYSE would not be complete without looking at the effect of that crisis on the operations of the exchange. The NYSE, the world's largest stock market, continued to function as it the institution running it were not facing any difficulty, much less its worst crisis in decades. While leadership, governance and the very structure and way of trading stocks at the NYSE were being questioned, order flow continued to pour in, and trades were executed, the problems of the institution have not transpired into actual market activity. There is no evidence that the Grasso debacle had an impact on the levels of the indices measuring the NYSE stock market, or on the prices of shares of companies listed on the NYSE. Indeed, these prices and indices continued to respond to corporate earnings, world events

---

[16] Securities and Exchange Commission, 'Fair Administration and Governance of Self-Regulatory Organizations: Open Meeting agenda', Nov. 9th 2004. www.sec.gov/news/openmeetings/agenda110904.htm.

and other factors in very much the same way as they would have otherwise. It could be argued that a better reflection of the impact of the crisis on the operations of the exchange would be decisions by non-listed companies to list shares at the NYSE or by already listed companies to take those listings elsewhere. Officials of the NYSE have acknowledged that the Grasso debacle had caused some companies to temporarily halt plans to list shares on the NYSE.[17] However, those decisions came in a broader context of an inauspicious time in the market for initial public offerings, further clouded by the implementation of new securities legislation in the US. On the other hand, while noting that no companies de-listed their shares from the NYSE, it is worth noting that that process is time-consuming and complex, thereby thwarting the clarity needed to link a de-listing and the Grasso debacle, should such a de-listing have occurred to begin with. Overall therefore, a more direct impact of the Grasso crisis on the business operations of the NYSE cannot be established by looking at the price levels in the stock market operated by the NYSE.

However, this does not offer an exception to the contention by Brickley et al. (2002, p. 1822) that 'a firm's reputation is part of the firm's brand-name capital; as such it is reflected in the value of its securities.' While the NYSE is not a publicly-held company and does not have securities in the form of equities or bonds, the closest proxy to them, and arguably the best instrument for assessing the impact of the Grasso crisis on the welfare of the exchange as a business, is the market for the NYSE's 1,366 seats, or licenses allowing NYSE members to operate in the stock market operated by the exchange. The price of such a seat reflects the prospects for its owner to make a profit by using his/her right to trade at the NYSE. While it cane be argued that this has more to do with conditions in the global capital markets, the NYSE itself says seat prices 'reflect the profitability of the brokerage business, the level of trading volume on the Exchange, general economic conditions, and other factors.'[18]

Amid a general decline in the profitability of the equities-trading business on Wall Street, the value of the NYSE seat prices has fallen dramatically in the last year. By mid-October 2004, a seat sale fetched $1.1m, or 59 per cent less than the all-time highest prices reached in August 1999 and 40 per cent less than a sale shortly after Mr Grasso's resignation. Since Mr Grasso's departure, 33 seats have exchanges hands and even thought the price of the transactions has fallen, the number of seat sales has risen, reflecting increased willingness by seat owners to willingly give up their stake in the NYSE. Just as sales of a company's stock, this can be seen as a sign of lower confidence in the future of the NYSE. An important caveat to this conclusion is the fact that confidence in the NYSE could also have been undermined by proposed regulatory changes in the structure of the US stock market that might threaten the NYSE's dominant market share in trading of stocks listed on it. There is no evidence that the relationship between such regulatory changes and the NYSE's crisis in the last year is might be causal, or that the SEC

---

[17] Andrei Postelnicu, 'Listing chief sets sights abroad', *Financial Times*, August 23, 2004.

[18] New York Stock Exchange, 'Seat Price Information', November 2004, www.nyse.com/ Frameset.html?displayPage=/press/1022834145706.html.

has proposed these changes as a direct result of the NYSE's difficulties after the Grasso debacle. At best, the climate following Mr Grasso's departure created an opportunity for change in US stock markets and created public support for such structural reform. But it is by no means evident that the ethical lapses at the NYSE in and of themselves led to the proposal of Regulation NMS, together with its potentially adverse effects on the NYSE.

The crisis that has engulfed the New York Stock Exchange in 2003 illustrates the wide-reaching consequences of a series of ethical lapses within an organization previously held in the highest of regards by much of the participants in the modern capitalist system. These lapses took place when a board of directors somehow failed to set appropriate benchmarks for rewarding the contribution of one individual to the organization. In turn, this highlighted questionable ethical practices in the use of the NYSE's regulatory powers; while these practices emerged after the Grasso crisis, they became possible due to the architecture of the NYSE, which it later emerged invited such unethical behavior and conflicts of interest, some of which arguably influenced NYSE directors when they set Mr Grasso's pay.

That the NYSE has been able to function flawlessly as a stockmarket and that it has been able to reform itself without the direct intervention of government regulators speaks to the strength of the NYSE as an institution and to the faith of US authorities in it to give it time to change from within. We cannot know whether US authorities would have continued to be benevolent observers if the debacle had worsened and continued over a longer period of time.

The NYSE's crisis and the measures it took to get out of it gained credibility when they were found in industry-wide proposals set forth by the SEC in early November 2004.

As its chairman, Mr Reed, acknowledged, the NYSE remains vulnerable to the aftermath of another scandal. It is undeniable that the Grasso debacle severely dented its reputation, but the exchange was left standing in its wake, with a chance to emerge stronger from it. Should another incident occur before it does so, it is likely to strike a lethal blow in the heart of the capital of capital and shatter the Big Board to a pathetic shade of its former, once glorious, self.

References

Arrow, K. J. (1974), *The Limits of Organisation*, W.W. Norton, New York.

Brickley, J. A., Smith C. and Zimmerman, J. (2002), Business Ethics and Organizational Architecture, *Journal of Banking and Finance*, 26, pp. 1821-1835.

Donaldson, W. H. (2003), Corporate Governance – What Has Happened and Where We Need to Go, *Business Economics*, July issue, pp. 16-20.

Keren, M. (2003), Capitalism as an Ethical System: The Ideal and its Feasibility, Presented to the *Conference on Ethics and the Economy*, Bucharest, 12-13 December 2003; also available as the Chapter 2 of this book.

Shleifer, A. (2004), Does Competition Destroy Ethical Behavior?, *American Economic Review, AEA Papers and Proceedings*, 94, 2, pp. 414-418.

Chapter 14

A Concluding Comment

Daniel Daianu and Radu Vranceanu

At the turn of the century, capitalism succeeded in becoming the dominant economic model worldwide. Its major features are: private ownership of resources, significant specialization in production and coordination of economic agents through markets. Private property gives individuals enough incentive to behave responsibly, specialization enhances productivity in the workplace and the free market is a highly efficient way of coordinating the actions of a multitude of individuals. This system of organizing economic activity involves a huge amount of human interaction. Since in this context one person's economic choices have a bearing on the well-being of others, economic actions have an essential ethical dimension. In a nutshell, ethics aims at defining good conduct for life in society; it also tries to provide a set of guiding principles for everyday human action.

Several authors have joined forces in this book to provide a broad picture of a range of essential ethical dilemmas closely related to the economic foundations of capitalist societies. Does capitalism support the emergence of ethical behavior between market participants, or does it on the contrary provide a prolific breeding ground for greed and aggressive rivalry? Can society support the development of ethical behavior by appropriate regulations and institutions? Should corporations be concerned with broad social objectives or should they focus only on wealth maximization?

As is generally the case with ethical issues, there is no simple answer to these questions. Going through the chapters of this book, the reader might even reach the conclusion that there is no single answer, but a constellation of answers. Depending on the author, the analysis has focused on either the consequences of economic action, or its goals, or the character of the individual, or various combinations of these. Some researchers argue that human beings are born with an innate sense of moral justice, while others surmise that morals are always a matter of culture, which itself is subject to change. In some chapters, ethics has been examined in relation to fairness in the distribution of goods. Some authors have emphasized the prevalence of incentives over ethics in guiding human choices, while others have supported the opposite point of view.

Should it be concluded that Ethics is nothing but a bundle of controversial speculations? The answer is a resounding 'No.' All the contributors to this book agree with Kenneth Arrow that positive social externalities like trustfulness, truth-telling, integrity, justice in future dealings, and honesty are instrumental to the good functioning of a decentralized economy. The opposite implication is also true: reneging on these values would bring about major economic costs for a free economy.

It was the Editors' deliberate aim to bring together specialists from various fields – economists, sociologists, management scientists, philosophers – with varying personal experience (some of them live in Western countries, others live in emerging economies). The idea behind this editorial strategy was that in encountering all these points of view in a single book, the reader would get a sharper picture of the contemporary ethical challenges facing capitalism. This is a moral lesson in itself: no matter how different scientists may be ideologically, the desire to contribute to a better understanding of complex social reality prompts them to collaborate.

The question of whether the capitalist system is able to deliver a sufficient amount of ethical behavior did not find such a clear-cut answer. In the past, critics have denounced the individualistic foundations of the capitalist economic model: since individuals had every incentive to pursue self-interested goals, was there not a risk that selfishness, greed and aggressive competition would become overwhelming social norms? Experience did not validate these fears. True, in the developed world, corporate fraud, corruption and abuses of market power can still be observed, but they are exceptions rather than the rule. Why is this so? As pointed out long ago by Adam Smith in the *Theory of Moral Sentiments* (1759), human beings may be born with a sense of moral justice. The virtuous person – prudent, responsible and just – will not become a slave to wealth accumulation; he will dismiss greedy and excessively selfish behavior in order to achieve higher ends. Some contributors to this book have argued that even if individuals pursued self-interested objectives, the free market principle would support the emergence of norms favorable to ongoing moral development, since the impersonal nature of the exchange itself in the capitalist system is the guarantor of human dignity. Other authors have claimed, however, that suitably-tailored regulation is needed to contain abuses of power and support ethical behavior in the capitalist economy, even if this regulation has to bring about its effects through market-based mechanisms and incentives for internalizing ethical constraints.

The capitalism model is characterized by significant economic dynamism, a capacity for rapid responses to external shocks, and an outstanding flow of innovation leading to economic growth. It still faces difficulties in fighting corporate fraud, corruption and rent-seeking by large players in the marketplace. Attenuating the effects of these drawbacks is an important challenge for the developed and the developing world. This book suggests that a decentralized economy can only function better if society becomes more aware of the importance of the ethical dimension of economic choice. Ethical conflicts can and must be anticipated, both at individual and corporate level. In particular, as pointed out by several authors, the business sector would perform better if the ethical dimension were to become a fully-fledged component of corporate management systems; and the overall quality of social analyses would undoubtedly improve if more attention was paid to ethical considerations.

Index

accounting firms, 230
a-ethical system, 61
aggression, 128
altruism, 120
American capitalism, 53
    the six pillars of, 58
antitrust, 58
Austrian school of economics, 114

board of directors, 33, 157, 227, 246
bounded rationality, 5

Calvinism, 50
capitalism, 44, 80, 255
    allocation system, 219
    soul, 55
    violence, 56
capture, 25, 36
CEO compensation, 33, 247
Christianism, 18
code of conduct, 97
competition, 177
conflict
    of cultural tradition, 90
    of interest, 227
    of relative development, 90
conspiracy theory, 130
control, 12
cooperation, 119, 120
corporate capitalism, 57
corporate culture, 169, 242
corporate ethics, 146, 159
Corporate Fraud Task Force, 220
corporate scandals, 33, 220
corporate social responsibility, 66,
    86, 89, 200
corruption, 25, 34
cost of behaving ethically, 107
cost-benefit analysis, 203
creative accounting, 225

crime, 25
criminality, 34
cross-cultural ethical dilemma, 89
culture, 12

Darwinism, 54
desire, 19, 111
development, 66

earnings manipulation, 226
economic model of man, 46, 202
economic system, 26, 28
ends vs. means, 145
entrepreneur, 148
environmentalists vs. economists, 199
ethical behavior, 107, 159
    creativity, 117
    decision, 134
    environmental issues, 201
    excellence, 170
    lapses, 253
    relativism, 65, 93
    universalism, 93
ethics
    capitalism, 4, 26, 43
    defined, 4, 17, 107, 149
    free market, 47, 135
    of reward, 107
    management system, 163
    marketing, 178
    within the firm, 135
ethology, 3
evolutionary history, 121
evolutionary theory, 54
exploitation, 44

fairness, 10
fellow feeling, 49
finite order, 128
firms and ethics, 135

free enterprise, 145
fuzziness, 76

Glass-Steagall Act, 81
globalization, 79, 85
God, 12, 51
golden rule, 94
governance, 32, 38
Gramm-Leach-Bliley Act, 231
greed, 44
guilt, 66

hierarchy, 149
humanism, 14

ideology, 67, 106, 121
illegals, 30
imperfect information, 177
incentives, 38, 108, 158, 199
    economic system, 29
individual responsibility, 152
information
    as a public good, 234
    imperfect, 177, 223
information manipulation, 179
international standards, 96
Internet bubble, 33, 68, 219
Invisible Hand, 46
iron cage, 55
irresponsible business practices,
    90

Judaism, 18

Kyoto Protocol, 208

law and ethics, 160
law and morality, 151
legality, 70

management, 7
management system, 163
managment programme, 168
market concentration, 180
marketers
    good conduct, 175

individual responsibilities, 185
    social responsibilities, 181
marketing
    ethics, 178
    social role, 176
marketing ethics, 176
media rule, 247
moral capital, 67
moral divide, 85
moral stance, 88
moral values, 150
motivation, 165

NYSE crisis, 239, 243
NYSE reforms, 247

oligarch, 34
ontological realism, 132
order, 127
organizational culture, 87
organizational theory, 7

path dependency, 68
perfect rationality, 5
polical liberalism, 45
pollution, 207
preferences, 114
pride, 13
private interest, 47
profit, 110
Protestant ethics, 49, 106
prudence, 153
public goods, 130
Puritanism, 50

regulation, 36, 44, 72, 158
relativism, 178
reputation, 74, 77
responsible man, 154
results vs. intentions, 203
reward, 108
Robber Barrons, 60

Sarbanes-Oxley Act, 81, 232
scarcity, 19
science, 4

self-interest, 47, 48, 60, 105, 156, 201
shame, 66
Sherman Antitrust Act, 58
shock therapy, 34
social contract, 19
social custom, 93
socialism, 36
socialist principle of distribution, 27
sociological model of man, 202
stakeholders, 147, 169
State, 25, 30
stock-option based compensation, 228

team building, 135
technology and ethics, 248
teleonomy, 114

terrorist attacks, 5
theory of the firm, 135
transition, 81
transnational corporation, 85, 90
tyranny, 112

underground economy, 71
unethical behavior, 70, 211, 224

virtue ethics, 70

welfare economics, 206
Western
    capitalism, 4, 239
    corporation, 88
    ethics, 22